NEW CONCEPTS IN DEPRESSION

Pierre Fabre Monograph Series

Series Editors:

D. BIGG, M. BRILEY, J. P. COUZINIER, P. HATINGUAIS,
P. LENOBLE, J. TISNE-VERSAILLES
Centre de Recherche Pierre Fabre
Avenue Jean Moulin 17
81100 Castres Cédex
France

PIERRE FABRE MONOGRAPH SERIES

VOLUME 2

NEW CONCEPTS IN DEPRESSION

Edited by

M. BRILEY

Centre de Recherche Pierre Fabre
17 Avenue Jean Moulin
81100 Castres
France

G. FILLION

Unité de Pharmacologie Neuroimmunoendocrinienne
UA CNRS 1113, Institut Pasteur
75015 Paris
France

MACMILLAN
PRESS

First published 1988

Published by
THE MACMILLAN PRESS LTD
Houndmills, Basingstoke, Hampshire RG21 2XS
and London
Companies and representatives
throughout the world

Distributed in North America by
SHERIDAN HOUSE PUBLISHERS
145 Palisade St, Dobbs Ferry, NY 10522

Printed in Great Britain by
Camelot Press Ltd, Southampton

British Library Cataloguing in Publication Data
New concepts in depression. – (Pierre Fabre
monograph series; v. 2).
1. Depression, Mental – Chemotherapy
2. Psychotropic drugs
I. Briley, M. II. Fillion, G. III. Series
616.85′27061   RC537
ISBN 0-333-44133-8

Contents

The Contributors

Agnati, L. F.
Department of Human Physiology
University of Modena
Modena
Italy

Ansseau, M.
Biological Psychiatry and
Psychopharmacology Unit
Centre Hospitalier Universitaire (B33)
B-4000 Liège Sart Tilman
Belgium

Asnis, G. M.
Department of Psychiatry
Albert Einstein College of Medicine
Montefiore Medical Center
New York
USA

Assie, M.-B.
Biochemical Pharmacology Department
Centre de Recherche Pierre Fabre
17 Avenue Jean Moulin
81100 Castres
France

Barbaccia, M. L.
Fidia-Georgetown Institute for the
Neurosciences
Georgetown University Medical School
3900 Reservoir Road
Washington, DC 20007
USA

Barone, P.
Institut Pasteur
28 rue du Dr Roux
75724 Paris
France

Bauer, M.
Pharmaceutical Research and
Development
Centre de Recherche Pierre Fabre
17 Avenue Jean Moulin
81100 Castres
France

Bennett, G. W.
Department of Physiology and
Pharmacology
Medical School
Queen's Medical Centre
Nottingham NG7 2UH
UK

Biziere, K.
Department of Neurobiology
Sanofi Recherche
34082 Montpellier
France

Bleich, A.
Department of Psychiatry
Albert Einstein College of Medicine
Montefiore Medical Center
New York
USA

Blier, P.
  Department of Psychiatry
  McGill University
  1033 Pine Avenue West
  Montréal, Québec H3A 1A1
  Canada

Briley, M.
  Department of Biochemical
    Pharmacology
  Centre de Recherche Pierre Fabre
  17 Avenue Jean Moulin
  81100 Castres
  France

Broadhurst, A.
  Biochemical Pharmacology Department
  Centre de Recherche Pierre Fabre
  17 Avenue Jean Moulin
  81100 Castres
  France

Brown, S. L.
  Department of Psychiatry
  Albert Einstein College of Medicine
  Montefiore Medical Center
  New York
  USA

Buckett, W. R.
  Research Department
  The Boots Company plc
  Nottingham NG2 3AA
  UK

Cerfontaine, J.-L.
  Biological Psychiatry and
    Psychopharmacology Unit
  Centre Hospitalier Universitaire (B33)
  B-4000 Liège Sart Tilman
  Belgium

Chaput, Y.
  Department of Psychiatry
  McGill University
  1033 Pine Avenue West
  Montréal, Québec H3A 1A1
  Canada

Cintra, A.
  Department of Histology
  Karolinska Institutet
  Box 60400
  S-104 01 Stockholm
  Sweden

Coppen, A.
  MRC Neuropsychiatry Research
    Laboratory
  West Park Hospital
  Epsom KT19 8PB
  UK

Costa, E.
  Fidia-Georgetown Institute for the
    Neurosciences
  Georgetown University Medical School
  3900 Reservoir Road
  Washington, DC 20007
  USA

Costentin, J.
  Laboratoire de Pharmacodynamie et
    Physiologie
  UER de Médecine et Pharmacie
  Avenue de l'Université
  76800 St Etienne Rouvray
  France

Coutou, N.
  Department of Neurobiology
  Sanofi Recherche
  34082 Montpellier
  France

Crawley, J. N.
  Clinical Neuroscience Branch, NIMH
  9000 Rockville Pike
  Bethesda, MD 20892
  USA

Crespi, F.
  Istituto Mario Negri
  62 Via Eritrea
  20157 Milano
  Italy

Crocq, M. A.
  CHS Rouffach
  68250 Rouffach
  France

Dam, T. V.
  Douglas Hospital Research Centre
  McGill University
  6875 Lasalle Boulevard
  Verdun, Québec H4H 1R3
  Canada

de Montigny, C.
  Department of Psychiatry,
  McGill University
  1033 Pine Avenue West
  Montréal, Québec H3A 1A1
  Canada

DeFlores, S.
  Douglas Hospital Research Centre
  McGill University
  6875 Lasalle Boulevard
  Verdun, Québec H4H 1R3
  Canada

Deutsch, S. I.
  Clinical Neuroscience Branch, NIMH
  9000 Rockville Pike
  Bethesda, MD 20892
  USA

Dose, M.
  Max Planck Institute for Psychiatry
  Kraepelinstr 10
  D-8000 Munich
  FRG

Drian, M.-J.
  Laboratoire Neurobiologie
      Développement
  Institut de Biologie
  Boulevard Henri IV
  34060 Montpellier
  France

Drugan, R. C.
  Clinical Neuroscience Branch, NIMH
  9000 Rockville Pike
  Bethesda, MD 20892
  USA

Dufois, S.
  Institut Pasteur
  28 rue du Dr Roux
  75724 Paris
  France

Duval, F.
  CHS Rouffach
  68250 Rouffach
  France

Edwards, R. M.
  Department of Physiology and
      Pharmacology
  Medical School
  Queen's Medical Centre
  Nottingham NG7 2UH
  UK

Emrich, H. M.
  Max Planck Institute for Psychiatry
  Kraepelinstr 10
  D-8000 Munich
  FRG

Eneroth, P.
  Research & Development Laboratory
  Department of Obstetrics and
      Gynaecology
  Karolinska Hospital
  Stockholm
  Sweden

Fayolle, C.
  Institut Pasteur
  28 rue du Dr Roux
  75724 Paris
  France

Fillion, G.
  Institut Pasteur
  28 rue du Dr Roux
  75724 Paris
  France

Fillion, M. P.
  Institut Pasteur
  28 rue du Dr Roux
  75724 Paris
  France

Finberg, J. P. M.
  Faculty of Medicine
  Rappaport Institute for Medical Research
  The Technion-Israel Institute of
      Technology
  Haifa
  Israel

Finiels-Marlier, F.
  Laboratoire Neurobiologie
      Développement
  Institut de Biologie
  Boulevard Henri IV
  34060 Montpellier
  France

Fleck, F.
  Laboratoire de Radioimmunologie
  CH Colmar
  68000 Colmar
  France

Fone, K.
  Department of Physiology and
      Pharmacology
  Medical School
  Queen's Medical Centre
  Nottingham NG7 2UH
  UK

Franck, G.
    Psychoneuroendocrinology Unit
    Centre Hospitalier Universitaire (B33)
    B-4000 Liège Sart Tilman
    Belgium

Fuxe, K.
    Department of Histology
    Karolinska Institutet
    Box 60400
    S-104 01 Stockholm
    Sweden

Gauthier, S.
    Douglas Hospital Research Centre
    McGill University
    6875 Lasalle Boulevard
    Verdun, Québec H4H 1R3
    Canada

Grahame-Smith, D. G.
    MRC Unit and University
        Department of Clinical Pharmacology
    Radcliffe Infirmary
    Oxford OX2 6HE
    UK

Guidotti, A.
    Fidia-Georgetown Institute for the
        Neurosciences
    Georgetown University Medical School
    3900 Reservoir Road
    Washington, DC 20007
    USA

Gustafsson, J. Å.
    Department of Medical Nutrition
    Huddinge Hospital
    Huddinge
    Sweden

Härfstrand, A.
    Department of Histology
    Karolinska Institutet
    Box 60400
    S-104 01 Stockholm
    Sweden

Harsing, L. G., Jr.
    Hungarian Academy of Sciences
    Institute of Experimental Medicine
    H-1450 Budapest
    Hungary

Hovevy-Sion, D.
    National Institute for Neurological
        Disorders and Stroke
    NIH
    Bethesda, MD
    USA

Janson, A. M.
    Department of Histology
    Karolinska Institutet
    Box 60400
    S-104 01 Stockholm
    Sweden

Kahn, R. S.
    Department of Psychiatry
    Albert Einstein College of Medicine
    Montefiore Medical Center
    New York
    USA

Keane, P. E.
    Sanofi Recherche
    195 Avenue d'Espagne
    31036 Toulouse
    France

Kitayama, I.
    Department of Histology
    Karolinska Institutet
    Box 60400
    S-104 01 Stockholm
    Sweden

Koenig, N.
    Laboratoire Neurobiologie
        Développement
    Institut de Biologie
    Boulevard Henri IV
    34060 Montpellier
    France

Kopin, I. J.
    National Institute for Neurological
        Disorders and Stroke
    NIH
    Bethesda, MD

Kordon, C.
    U. 159 INSERM
    Unité de Neuroendocrinologie
    Centre Paul Broca
    2 ter, rue d'Alésia
    75014 Paris
    France

Korn, M. L.
Department of Psychiatry
Albert Einstein College of Medicine
Montefiore Medical Center
New York
USA

Lacabanne, C.
Solid State Physics Laboratory
UA 74, University Paul Sabatier
118 route de Narbonne
31062 Toulouse
France

Lacroze, S.
Département de Pharmacie
Hôpital du Vinatier
95 Boulevard Pinel
69677 Lyon Bron
France

Lafaille, F.
Douglas Hospital Research Centre
McGill University
6875 Lasalle Boulevard
Verdun, Québec H4H 1R3
Canada

Lamure, A.
Solid State Physics Laboratory
UA 74 University Paul Sabatier
118 route de Narbonne
31062 Toulouse
France

Laval, J.
Biochemical Pharmacology Department
Centre de Recherche Pierre Fabre
17 Avenue Jean Moulin
81100 Castres
France

Legros, J.-J.
Psychoneuroendocrinology Unit
Centre Hospitalier Universitaire (B33)
B-4000 Liège Sart Tilman
Belgium

Lemoine, P.
Unité Clinique de Psychiatrie Biologique
Hôpital du Vinatier
95 Boulevard Pinel
69677 Lyon Bron
France

Lieberman, H. R.
Massachusetts Institute of Technology
Brain and Cognitive Sciences
02139 Cambridge
Massachusetts
USA

Lighton, C.
Neuroscience Research Centre
Merck, Sharpe and Dohme
Terlings Park
Harlow, Essex
UK

Llorens-Cortes, C.
U. 109 de Neurobiologie et
Pharmacologie
Centre Paul Broca de l'INSERM
2 ter, rue d'Alésia
75014 Paris
France

Lonati-Galligani, M.
Max Planck Institute for Psychiatry
Kraepelinstr. 10
D-8000 Munich
FRG

Luscombe, G. P.
Research Department
The Boots Company Plc
Nottingham NG2 3AA
UK

Maassen, D.
Biological Psychiatry and
Psychopharmacology Unit
Centre Hospitalier Universitaire (B33)
B-4000 Liège Sart Tilman
Belgium

Macher, J. P.
CHS Rouffach
68250 Rouffach
France

Marlier, L.
Laboratoire de Neurobiologie du
Développement
Institut de Biologie
Boulevard Henri IV
34060 Montpellier
France

Marsden, C. A.
    Department of Physiology and
        Pharmacology
    Medical School
    Queen's Medical Centre
    Nottingham NG7 2UH
    UK

Martin, K. F.
    Department of Physiology and
        Pharmacology
    Medical School
    Queen's Medical Centre
    Nottingham NG7 2UH
    UK

Mašek, K.
    Institute of Pharmacology
    Czechoslovak Academy of Sciences
    Albertov 4
    128 00 Prague 2
    Czechoslovakia

Megret, C.
    Solid State Physics Laboratory
    UA 74, University Paul Sabatier
    118 route de Narbonne
    31062 Toulouse
    France

Minot, R.
    CHS Rouffach
    68250 Rouffach
    France

Minuit, M.-P.
    Unité Clinique de Psychiatrie Biologique
    Hôpital du Vinatier
    95 Boulevard Pinel
    69677 Lyon Bron
    France

Moret, C.
    Biochemical Pharmacology Department
    Centre de Recherche Pierre Fabre
    17 Avenue Jean Moulin
    81100 Castres
    France

Mouret, J.
    Unité Clinique de Psychiatrie Biologique
    Hôpital du Vinatier
    95 Boulevard Pinel
    69677 Lyon Bron
    France

Nair, N. P. V.
    Douglas Hospital Research Centre
    McGill University
    6875 Lasalle Boulevard
    Verdun, Québec H4H 1R3
    Canada

Ögren, S. O.
    Astra Research Laboratory
    Astra
    Södertälje
    Sweden

Oudar, P.
    Institut Pasteur
    28 rue du Dr Roux
    75724 Paris
    France

O'Rourke, D.
    Department of Brain and Cognitive
        Sciences
    Massachusetts Institute of Technology
    Cambridge, MA 021939
    USA

Palmier, C.
    Department of Biochemical
        Pharmacology
    Centre de Recherche Pierre Fabre
    17 Avenue Jean Moulin
    81100 Castres
    France

Papart, P
    Biological Psychiatry and
        Psychopharmacology Unit
    Centre Hospitalier Universitaire (B33)
    B-4000 Liège Sart Tilman
    Belgium

Paul, S. M.
    Clinical Neuroscience Branch, NIMH
    9000 Rockville Pike
    Bethesda, MD 20892
    USA

Pawłowski, L.
    Institute of Pharmacology
    Polish Academy of Sciences
    12 Smętna Street
    31-343 Kroków
    Poland

Pirke, K. M.
    Max Planck Institute for Psychiatry
    Kraepelinstr. 10
    D-8000 München
    FRG

Poulat, P.
  Laboratoire Neurobiologie
    Developpement
  Institut de Biologie
  Boulevard Henri IV
  34060 Montpellier
  France

Privat, A.
  Laboratoire de Neurobiologie du
    Développement
  Institut de Biologie
  Boulevard Henri IV
  34060 Montpellier
  France

Quirion, R.
  Douglas Hospital Research Centre
  McGill University
  6875 Lasalle Boulevard
  Verdun, Québec H4H 1R3
  Canada

Rogue, P.
  CHS Rouffach
  68250 Rouffach
  France

Schmauss, C.
  Max Planck Institute for Psychiatry
  Kraepelinstr 10
  D-8000 München
  FRG

Schwartz, J.-C.
  U. 109 de Neurobiologie et
    Pharmacologie
  Centre Paul Broca de l'INSERM
  2 ter, rue d'Alésia
  75014 Paris
  France

Skolnick, P.
  Section on Neurobiology
  Laboratory of Bioorganic Chemistry
  NIDDK
  Bethesda
  USA

Somogyi, G. T.
  Institute of Experimental Medicine
  Hungarian Academy of Sciences
  H-1450 Budapest
  Hungary

Stenger, A.
  Biochemical Pharmacology Department
  Centre de Recherche Pierre Fabre
  17 Avenue Jean Moulin
  81100 Castres
  France

Suranyi-Cadotte, B.
  Douglas Hospital Research Centre
  McGill University
  6875 Lasalle Boulevard
  Verdun, Québec H4H 1R3
  Canada

Swade, C.
  MRC Neuropsychiatry Research
    Laboratory
  West Park Hospital
  Epsom KT19 8PB
  UK

Thomas, P. C.
  Research Department
  The Boots Company plc
  Nottingham NG2 3AA
  UK

Timsit-Berthier, M.
  Department of Clinical Neurophysiology
    and Psychopathology
  University of Liège
  B-4000 Liège Sart Tilman
  Belgium

van Amsterdam, J.
  U. 109 de Neurobiologie et
    Pharmacologie
  Centre Paul Broca de l'INSERM
  2 ter, rue d'Alésia
  75014 Paris
  France

van Praag, H. M.
  Department of Psychiatry
  Albert Einstein College of Medicine
  Montefiore Medical Center
  New York
  USA

Vizi, E. S.
  Institute of Experimental Medicine
  Hungarian Academy of Sciences
  H-1450 Budapest
  Hungary

Vocci, F. J.
  Clinical Neuroscience Branch, NIMH
  9000 Rockville Pike
  Bethesda, MD 20892
  USA

von Frenckell, R.
    Biological Psychiatry and
        Psychopharmacology Unit
    Centre Hospitalier Universitaire (B33)
    B-4000 Liège Sart Tilman
    Belgium

Wachtel, H.
    Department of
        Neuropsychopharmacology
    Schering AG
    Müllerstr. 170–8
    D-1000 Berlin 65
    FRG

Weber, M.
    Max Planck Institute for Psychiatry
    Kraepelinstr. 10
    D-8000 München
    FRG

Weizman, A.
    Clinical Neuroscience Branch, NIMH
    9000 Rockville Pike
    Bethesda, MD 20892
    USA

Weizman, R.
    Clinical Neuroscience Branch, NIMH
    9000 Rockville Pike
    Bethesda, MD 20892
    USA

Wetzler, S.
    Department of Psychiatry
    Albert Einstein College of Medicine
    Montefiore Medical Center
    New York
    USA

Worms, P.
    Neurobiology Department
    Sanofi Recherche
    34082 Montpellier
    France

Wurtman, J. J.
    Department of Brain and Cognitive
        Sciences
    Massachusetts Institute of Technology
    Cambridge, MA 021939
    USA

Wurtman, R. J.
    Department of Brain and Cognitive
        Sciences
    Massachusetts Institute of Technology
    Cambridge, MA 021939
    USA

Preface to the series

Created in 1961, the Pierre Fabre Group is one of Europe's youngest research-based ethical pharmaceutical and beauty-care groups. From its base in Castres in south-west France, the group has expanded in the last 27 years to become one of the major privately owned French companies in its field.

The Pierre Fabre Research Centre, which has existed in its present form for about 10 years, had adopted a basic strategy of encouraging collaboration between its own research centre in Castres and academic research scientists throughout the world. The creation of the Pierre Fabre Monograph Series is a further development of this strategy. Certain monographs in this series will be based on international symposia organised or sponsored by the Pierre Fabre Research Centre. Others will group together chapters from acknowledged international experts and dynamic young scientists destined to become tomorrow's experts. In all cases, the subjects of these monographs will be those presenting a major challenge to therapeutic medicine.

The Editorial Board;
D. Bigg
M. Briley
J. P. Couzinier
P. Hatinguais
P. Lenoble
J. Tisne-Versailles

Preface

The pharmacotherapy of depression has advanced in irregular steps since the first introduction of monoamine oxidase inhibitors and tricyclic antidepressants in the 1950s. The latest surge has come from the series of new selective antidepressants which have been recently introduced or are in the final stages of development. Since our fundamental understanding of a disease is often limited by the availability of specific drugs, it is not surprising that there has also been a recent acceleration in fundamental research in depression. The discovery of new receptor subtypes, neurotransmitter and cotransmitter interregulations and a deeper understanding of adaptive processes in pharmacology have also opened new horizons.

This second volume in the Pierre Fabre Monograph Series brings together chapters describing these new events and especially the new concepts that are emerging. The underlying themes of interaction, regulation and adaptive responses of the major neurotransmitter systems, especially serotonin and noradrenaline, are found in many of the chapters and are at the basis of a new consensus. This consensus of opinion may not lead immediately to new antidepressant therapies, but, by concentrating basic research effort in new promising areas, it should lead to a new major therapeutic advances in the not-too-distant future.

The symposium on which this book is based took place in Castres in South-West France in March 1987. It was sponsored by the Pierre Fabre Research Centre with generous contributions from the Conseil Général de Midi-Pyrénées, the Centre National de la Recherche Scientifique and the Macmillan Press.

We would like to thank everyone from the Pierre Fabre Research Centre who helped with this symposium, especially the members of the Biochemical Pharmacology Department who undertook the local organisation. Special thanks are due to the symposium secretary, Martine Dehaye, who so charmingly and efficiently organised the secretarial affairs of the sumposium and of this book. Our thanks are also due to Andy Broadhurst and Elisabeth Carilla for their invaluable help as editorial assistants.

Castres and Paris, 1987   M.B.
                                                            G. F.

1

Neuropharmacological Adaptive Effects in the Actions of Antidepressant Drugs, ECT and Lithium

D. G. Grahame-Smith

1.1 Introduction

It has long been assumed that there is a latent period of one to two weeks between beginning treatment with antidepressant drugs and evidence of clinical improvement (Oswald *et al.*, 1972). However, there is an increasing feeling that this may be an over-simplification. Depression is a complex illness with many facets of which mood is only one. Overall rating scales may be a blunt instrument for detecting improvements in a multi-symptomatic state. There are hints in the literature that the response of certain symptoms to antidepressants may occur within a few days. There are also confounding factors: for example, some antidepressants, e.g. amitriptyline, are sedative and may improve sleep early, so altering responses as judged by rating scales.

No one would deny, however, that generally it takes about two weeks to see an appreciable global clinical response and indeed it may take several weeks for that response to reach its steady state.

In the case of electroconvulsive therapy (ECT) the view is that when treatments are given twice or three times a week, improvement in mood, sleep and appetite are usually noted after the third or fourth seizure and a stable state of efficacy achieved after six to eight treatments, although more treatments may be necessary in severely ill patients (Fink, 1979).

It would appear then that something happens (presumably in the brain) with one electroconvulsive treatment, which somehow mounts with each convulsive treatment to relieve the depressive illness.

Although the straightforward treatment of acute mania with lithium is not frequently applied, when it is then the manic state takes a week or so to come under control. I have found it very difficult to assess from the literature how long it takes for lithium to be effective in the prophylaxis of manic-depressive disorder. Studies to find out the answers to such a question would be extremely difficult to design, considering the nature of the illness.

So in the cases of antidepressant drugs, ECT and lithium, there are grounds for believing that it takes some time for treatment to exert its therapeutic effect. Plainly, for antidepressant drugs and lithium, this could be related to the pharmacokinetic properties of the drug, i.e. that it takes time to achieve an appropriate level of the drug in the brain. This is a question which cannot be decisively answered. We do know that, within hours, levels of antidepressant drugs are reached in the periphery which inhibit platelet 5-hydroxytryptamine (5-HT) uptake and inhibit the tyramine-induced hypertensive response. Lithium dosage can be arranged to reach therapeutic plasma levels quite quickly and one doubts whether this would lead to a quicker therapeutic response.

If one accepts that it truly takes some time for these treatments to act then the question arises whether this is because the pharmacological action responsible for the therapeutic effect takes some time to occur, or whether the illness gets better slowly. Unfortunately, distinguishing between these two is not easy, particularly as we do not know precisely what is wrong with the brain in depressive illness.

Taking the medical model, consider the time it takes for thyrotoxicosis to improve even with adequate treatment with an anti-thyroid drug which acts almost immediately on thyroid hormone synthesis. It may take weeks to observe the clinical response, presumably because it takes time for the thyroid hormone that is present initially to disappear and then for the metabolic changes to reverse. One might thus speculate that there is a minimum time for the brain changes underlying the depressive illness to revert to normal. Against that idea, however, are the occasional cases of quick reversal of depressive illness to normal mood. One does not know whether all cases of depressive illness are due to the same abnormalities in brain function, but, presuming they are, then the fact that some cases of depression can revert to normal mood spontaneously in twenty-four to forty-eight hours is against the proposal that gradual reversal of brain function must be an essential factor in the recovery from depression.

It is nevertheless reasonable to propose that the time that antidepressant drug therapy, ECT and lithium (in the case of mania) take to exert their full clinical effects is dependent upon neuropharmacological adaptive responses to the acute effects of these treatments.

When an antidepressant drug reaches its receptor, or lithium reaches a neurone, or an electroconvulsive shock produces a seizure, acute actions occur. In the case of tricyclic antidepressant drugs, it seems likely that the important acute effect is central blockade of noradrenaline or 5-HT reuptake. There are many possibilities for electroconvulsive shock (ECS), as a number of neurotransmitters are likely to be released acutely by a shock and seizure. One change that does occur early and provides a plausible adaptive sequence is the inhibition of GABA release which occurs after an ECS (Green, 1986a,b). These changes in GABA function will be considered later.

Although many adaptive changes take place with lithium, the 'acute' mechanisms by which these are triggered are still a mystery. In the last few years the effects of lithium upon the second messenger system mediated by phosphatidylinositol breakdown have been invoked (Berridge et al., 1982). So far it has not been easy to relate this effect to the effects seen in monoamine neuronal system function.

One envisages, therefore, various steps in the adaptive response. First there is the acute point-to-point molecular pharmacological action of the agent. This is then envisaged as having an effect upon one or more neurotransmitter functions which then may ripple throughout the brain to produce changes in many neurotransmitter functions. The more investigations are done on these matters, the more adaptive responses are discovered.

One of our problems is that in studying these adaptive responses we are hampered by not having pharmacologically 'clean' agents to work with. Several of the monoamine uptake blockers are non-specific and have other actions, for instance receptor blocking activity. It then becomes difficult to be sure that the adaptive changes detected are due to an initial specific pharmacological action.

What follows is a discussion of some of the more important features of these adaptive responses.

1.2 Tricyclic and Atypical Antidepressant Drugs

It is necessary to consider these two types of antidepressant drugs separately because of their presumed different acute modes of action. The general view would be that the monoamine reuptake blockers exert their acute action through raising the synaptic concentration of monoamines, but this cannot be the case with atypical antidepressants, for instance mianserin, which does not block monoamine reuptake and yet produces many of the adaptive responses which the monoamine reuptake blockers produce.

Raisman et al. (1979) reported specific Na^+-dependent, high-affinity binding sites for [^{3}H]-imipramine in rat brain. Rehavi et al. (1980) confirmed this for human brain. It is thought that this imipramine binding site modulates 5-HT uptake at the 5-HT nerve terminal (Green and Nutt, 1983; 1985). Binding sites for [^{3}H]-desipramine, which are distinct from imipramine binding sites, have been described in relationship to blockade of noradrenaline reuptake. Barbaccia et al. (1983) have evidence for modulation of 5-HT uptake by an endogenous ligand of the imipramine binding site.

It is assumed, therefore, that the initial effect of the monoamine reuptake blocking antidepressant drugs is to bind to sites modulating 5-HT or noradrenaline uptake at the 5-HT or noradrenergic nerve terminal and to inhibit reuptake of the monoamine, and raise the concentration of the monoamine in the synaptic cleft.

Many of the reuptake blocking antidepressants have variable affinities for other binding sites and receptors, including α_1- and α_2-adrenoceptors, muscarinic receptors, histamine receptors and opiate receptors, but it is not thought at present that these pharmacological actions are linked with their therapeutic effect.

The presumed increase in synaptic cleft concentration of the monoamine is thought to lead to alterations in monoamine synthesis and metabolism and pre- and post-synaptic receptor binding and function. The effects in one system are thought to 'ripple' throughout other neurotransmitter/neuronal systems to produce a complex network of adaptive change. The details of some of these changes are dealt with in reviews by Green and Nutt (1983; 1985), Sugrue (1983) and in a recent CIBA Foundation Symposium (Porter *et al.*, 1986). Table 1.1 summarises some of the more important of these adaptive changes and indicates some of their functional implications.

Table 1.1   Adaptive responses of brain to monoamine uptake blockers

Receptor	Change in receptor number	Functional correlate
α_2-Adrenoceptor (pre-synaptic)	?Decreased	Yes (behavioural and biochemical)
α_1-Adrenoceptor (post-synaptic)	Unchanged (conflicting)	?Increased α_1-mediated functions (behavioural/electrophysiological)
β-Adrenoceptor (post-synaptic)	Decreased	Yes (biochemical)
5-HT$_2$-Receptor (post-synaptic)	Decreased	Yes
5-HT$_{1A}$ (somatodendritic)	?	Reduced 5-HT$_{1A}$ somato-dendritic autoreceptor function
GABA$_B$ receptors	Increased	Yes (biochemical and behavioural)
Dopamine autoreceptor	No change	Decreased function (behavioural and electrophysiological)
postsynaptic	No change	No change

1.3 Neuropharmacological Adaptive Responses to Repeated Electroconvulsive Shock (ECS) as a Paradigm for Electroconvulsive Therapy (ECT)

The neuropharmacological changes brought about in rodent brain by a single or repeated ECS have been studied by several groups (Grahame-Smith *et al.*, 1978; Lerer *et al.*, 1984). The protocol of ECS administration in many of the studies reported has tried to mimic the way ECT is administered in man in respect to frequency of administration, placement of electrodes, severity of seizure and duration of electric shock, and has involved controlled experiments with anaesthesia and muscle relaxants. Plainly, because of the different shape of the head, resistance of tissues, anatomy of the brain, etc., it is not possible to precisely mimic ECT in man in experiments in rodents, but it is likely that the neuropharmacological changes seen are, in principle, those that would occur in the human brain under similar circumstances.

One common criticism of experiments in normal rodents to investigate the mechanism of action of antidepressant drugs, or indeed psychotropic drugs of any sort, is that the animals are not mentally ill, and some workers try to overcome this problem by studying animal models of depression. There are problems with this approach. The question is whether the animals are really depressed in the same way that man is depressed. There is no way out of this problem at the moment.

Studies on repeated electroconvulsive shock have shown some neuropharmacological adaptive responses identical to those produced by chronic antidepressant drug treatment (see Table 1.2) but with some important differences.

Table 1.2 Adaptive responses of brain to repeated electroconvulsive shock

Receptor	Change in receptor number	Functional correlate
α_2-Adrenoceptor (pre-synaptic)	Decreased	Yes (behavioural and biochemical)
α_1-Adrenoceptor (post-synaptic)	Unchanged	?
β-Adrenoceptor (post-synaptic)	Decreased	Yes (biochemical)
5-HT$_2$ Receptor (post-synaptic)	Increased	Yes (behavioural)
5-HT$_{1A}$ (somatodendritic)	?	Reduced 5-HT$_{1A}$ somato-denditic autoreceptor function
GABA$_B$	Increased	Yes
Dopamine		
autoreceptor	No change	Decreased function
post-synaptic	No change	Increased function

The most striking of these differences is the effect of ECS on 'post-synaptic' dopamine function, i.e. the hyperactivity and stereotyped movements in normal intact rats and the circling syndromes in nigro-striatal lesioned rats, produced by agents increasing dopamine function by pre- or post-synaptic actions, e.g. L-DOPA and monoamine oxidase inhibitors, amphetamine or apomorphine. All these dopamine functions are markedly enhanced by repeated ECS but not by antidepressant drugs. We have been unable to find any upregulation of dopamine receptors associated with these changes in dopamine function. At the moment the mechanism of their production is unknown.

Another difference is that ECS produces upregulation of $5\text{-}HT_2$ binding sites in cortex, with good evidence of enhance $5\text{-}HT_2$ mediated behavioural functions (e.g. 5-HTP-induced mouse head-twitch). This is quite different from long-term antidepressant drug administration in which $5\text{-}HT_2$ receptor number is decreased and is accompanied by a decrease in the $5\text{-}HT_2$ mediated head-twitch in the mouse (Tables 1.2 and 1.3).

The changes in α_2-adrenoceptor, β-adrenoceptor and $5\text{-}HT_{1A}$ receptor functions are very similar between the two treatments.

More recently, changes in GABA function have been found in response to antidepressant drug and ECS administration. Lloyd et al. (1985) showed that $GABA_B$ receptor number in rat frontal cortex was increased by repeated antidepressant drug and ECS administration. Gray and Green (1986a) have shown increased sensitivity of the inhibition of K^+-evoked release of 5-HT from brain slices by baclofen, a $GABA_B$ agonist, and this has a behavioural correlate (Gray and Green, 1986b).

1.4 Other Antidepressant Drug Therapies

The adaptive responses to the atypical antidepressants and monoamine oxidase inhibitors have many features in common with those following the administration of the monoamine uptake blockers and ECS. Such similarities are the down regulation of β-adrenoceptor function and the reduction of $5\text{-}HT_{1A}$-mediated behavioural functions. (See Table 1.3 for effects on 5-HT functions.)

1.5 Lithium

There are a number of factors which make lithium of interest in this context. There is clear evidence of efficacy of lithium in the prevention of manic and depressive episodes in manic-depressive disease. There is probable efficacy of lithium in the prevention of episodes of unipolar depression. There are also glimpses of its efficacy in combination with other therapies in the treatment of the depressive state itself.

Table 1.3 Effects of repeated long-term administration of antidepressant drugs, monoamine oxidase inhibitors, electroconvulsive shock and lithium upon 5-HT-mediated behavioural functions in rat and mouse

	8-OH-DPAT, rat 5-HT behavioural syndrome (5-HT$_1$)	8-OH-DPAT hypothermia rat (5-HT$_1$)	8-OH-DPAT hypothermia mouse (5-HT$_1$)	Head twitch mouse (5-HT$_2$)
Antidepressants	All aspects decreased	Attenuated	Attenuated	Decreased
MAO Inhibitors	All aspects decreased	Attenuated	Attenuated	Decreased
ECS	Stereotypes decreased Locomotor activity ?increased	Attenuated	Attenuated	Increased
Lithium	All aspects increased	No change	Attenuated	Decreased

De Montigny and Blier (1984) have shown that in patients with depression that is resistant to antidepressant drug therapy, the addition of lithium may bring about relief of the depression.

Lithium has effects on neurotransmitter systems in several experimental protocols designed to study neuropharmacological adaptation. Perhaps the best known of these is the effect of chronic lithium administration in the rat to decrease the behavioural dopamine-mediated supersensitivity produced by the denervation of dopaminergic pathways (Swerdlow et al., 1985).

However, it is the effects of lithium upon 5-HT function which are particularly relevant to depression and its treatment. Grahame-Smith and Green (1974) showed that when rats are chronically treated with lithium then the administration of a monoamine oxidase inhibitor results in the 5-HT behavioural hyperactivity syndrome. Prior treatment with parachlorophenalanine prevented this 5-HT-mediated behaviour. On the basis of behavioural, pharmacological and biochemical findings, it was suggested that lithium acted in some way to increase the amount of 5-HT released as a proportion of the amount synthesised. Atterwill and Tordoff (1982) followed this up and found that when the 5-HT pool size in the nerve terminal was increased by *in vivo* treatment of the rat with tranylcypromine, then pre-treatment with lithium twice daily for three days caused: (a) a further increase in 5-HT pool size; (b) a change in intra-neuronal compartmentation such that more 5-HT was apparently unbound in the cytoplasm. Exactly how these changes are brought about is unclear. Changes in synthesis and vesicular binding have been proposed.

Trieser et al. (1981) found evidence for an increase in K^+-stimulated release of 5-HT in hippocampal slices from animals treated long-term with lithium.

Biier and De Montigny (1985) have provided electrophysiological evidence that short-term lithium treatment, producing plasma levels similar to those obtained in patients, enhances the effect of the electrical activation of the ascending 5-HT pathway on the firing activity of hippocampal neurones. The responsiveness of these post-synaptic neurones to directly applied 5-HT was not modified by lithium treatment and so it was concluded that lithium enhances 5-HT neurotransmission via a modification of the properties of 5-HT neurones.

The increasing understanding of the different types of brain 5-HT receptor and their classification into $5\text{-}HT_1$-like and $5\text{-}HT_2$ with accompanying evidence for their functional correlations (Bradley et al., 1986) has brought to light interesting chronic effects of lithium (see Table 1.3). Chronic lithium administration enhances the $5\text{-}HT_1$-mediated behavioural syndrome produced by 8-hydroxy-2-dipropylaminotetralin (8-OH-DPAT) in the rat, attenuates the 8-OH-DPAT ($5\text{-}HT_{1A}$)-induced hypothermia in the mouse and decreases the $5\text{-}HT_2$-agonist-induced head-twitch in the mouse (Goodwin et al., 1986a,b).

A parsimonius explanation for the enhanced $5\text{-}HT_{1A}$-like syndrome produced by chronic lithium administration followed by an MAO inhibitor in the rat (Grahame-Smith and Green 1974) would be a combination of: (a) downregulation of somatodendritic $5\text{-}HT_{1A}$-inhibitory autoreceptors on 5-HT raphe cell bodies leading to increased 5-HT release; and (b) increased post-synaptic 5-HT_{1A} sensitivity, associated with predominantly 5-HT_1-like behavioural syndrome. These changes would result in an overall increase in post-synaptic 5-HT_{1A} functions in brain.

1.6 The Case for an Involvement of 5-HT in the Actions of Antidepressant Therapies

A great deal of attention has been paid to the down-regulation of β-receptor function produced by long-term antidepressant drug therapy and ECS as being a *unitary* mechanism for antidepressant activity. However, there is clear evidence that 5-HT function is altered by antidepressant therapy and ECT. These changes are tabulated in Table 1.4. The clearest and most consistent changes among antidepressants, monoamine oxidase inhibitors and repeated electroconvulsive shock is the attenuation by all of them of the 8-OH-DPAT hypothermic response in the mouse, which appears to be mediated through presynaptic, probably somatodendritic, inhibitory 5-HT_{1A} receptors (Goodwin *et al.*, 1985; Green *et al.*, 1986; Goodwin *et al.*, 1986a,b).

Table 1.4 Neurotransmitter interactions in the adaptive responses to anti-depressant drugs and ECS

5-HT–noradrenaline links
1. β_2-agonists enhance 5-HT_{1A} and 5-HT_2 functions.
2. α_2-agonists inhibit 5-HT_2 functions.
3. Noradrenergic lesions inhibit the enhancement of 5-HT_2 and dopamine function produced by ECS.
4. 5-HT lesions prevent the down-regulation of cortical β-adrenoceptors by antidepressant drugs and ECS.

5-HT–$GABA_B$ links (Gray and Green, 1986a,b; Godfrey *et al.*, 1987)
1. Up-regulation of $GABA_B$ receptors by antidepressants and ECS and increased sensitivity of inhibition of 5-HT release in brain slices to $GABA_B$ agonists.
2. Inhibition of 5-HT_2-induced phosphatidylinositol phosphate breakdown by $GABA_B$ agonists.

See Green and Goodwin, 1986; Heal *et al.*, 1986.

The case for an involvement of 5-HT in the action of antidepressant therapies is now impressive. The animal biochemical, pharmacological and behavioural evidence has been outlined. The clinical evidence is as follows:

(a) Non-selective and selective 5-HT-uptake blockers are effective in the treatment of depression.

(b) L-tryptophan with a monoamine oxidase inhibitor is an effective therapy for depression.

(c) Van Praag *et al.* (1973) have shown the efficacy of 5-hydroxytryptophan as an antidepressant.

(d) Shopsin *et al.* (1975, 1976) showed that the administration of parachloro-phenylalanine (which inhibits the synthesis of 5-HT) blocked the antidepressant affect of tranylcypromine and imipramine.

(e) If we consider the effects of lithium on 5-HT function then we can then invoke 5-HT function in the clinical enhancement by lithium of the antidepressant effects of antidepressant drugs (De Montigny and Blier, 1984).

1.7 Relevance of Neuropharmacological Adaptive Changes to the Actions of Antidepressant Treatments

What evidence is there that any of the adaptive changes seen in the rodent have a bearing upon the actions of antidepressant treatment in the depressed patient? Do they occur and if they occur are they part of the pharmacological action of these treatments upon which their therapeutic effect is exerted?

The first question to answer is whether any of these adaptive changes have an effect on overall synaptic transmission and neuronal function. De Montigny and Blier (1985) showed that during the administration to rats of zimelidine, a relatively specific 5-HT uptake blocker, the electrophysiological activity of 5-HT neurones in the raphe nucleus was reduced after two days of treatment, but had recovered after 14 days of treatment, probably because of desensitization of the somato-dendritic autoreceptor. Although radioligand binding studies suggest down-regulation of cortical 5-HT_2 receptors by chronic antidepressant drug administration, De Montigny's electrophysiological studies suggest that there is increased sensitivity of post-synaptic target neurones. He has found similar changes with repeated ECS.

Cowen *et al.* (1986) have shown that in normal subjects chronic treatment with desipramine for 16 days enhances the prolactin secretion response to infusion of L-tryptophan (assumed to act through increased 5-HT synthesis), suggesting that overall 5-HT trans-synaptic function is increased.

Cowen *et al.* (1983) studied the effect of chronic antidepressant admini-stration on β-adrenoceptor function of the rat pineal *in vivo* by examining effects on pineal melatonin. Repeated administration of antidepressant drugs resulted in reduced pineal 'post-synaptic' β-adrenoceptor sensitivity as judged by the response of pineal melatonin to β-agonists. However, the spontaneous physiological increase in plasma melatonin during the dark phase was unchanged following repeated desmethylimipramine administration. This implied that the reduced β-adrenoceptor sensitivity may be part of an adaptive process which maintains normal pineal function in the face of blockade of noradrenaline uptake.

A very similar investigation was therefore carried out in humans (Cowen *et al.*, 1985). In this investigation it was clearly shown that midnight plasma melatonin concentration in normal subjects increased initially during desmethylimipramine treatment. Then, as the treatment was continued, the midnight plasma melatonin concentrations began to fall after the fifth day of desmethylimipramine administration, suggesting adaptive changes, and by the third week of treatment they had approached the starting levels. This was interpreted as showing that the adaptive changes that occur in noradrenergic synapses during desmethylimipramine treatment do not decrease overall noradrenaline transmission below normal levels, but instead restore synaptic homeostasis in the presence of the drug. It was very interesting that a rebound increase in noradrenergic transmission, as reflected by midnight plasma melatonin levels, was seen on DMI withdrawal.

The findings in human beings were very similar to those in the rat. Of course, the noradrenergic synapse in the pineal is 'outside' the central nervous system, but the principles of adaptation probably apply.

It is very important to relate any 'up-' or 'down-regulation' of receptor number or function to overall synaptic function if physiological sense is to be made out of adaptive phenomena. Glue *et al.* (1986) have shown that 5-HT-mediated prolactin release in response to L-tryptophan loading in normal subjects was enhanced by subacute and chronic lithium treatment. This response is probably mediated by $5\text{-}HT_1$-like receptors and might indicate increased 5-HT function like that observed in rats treated with lithium.

The human evidence for an effect of ECT on neurotransmitter function in depressed patients is conflicting (see Checkley *et al.*, 1984). Costain *et al.* (1982) showed that growth hormone response to the dopamine agonist apomorphine was increased in patients with depression treated with ECT, which could indicate increased dopamine function such as that seen in the rat.

1.8 Neurotransmitter System Interrelationships in the Effects of Antidepressant Therapies and ECS

Over the past few years it has become apparent that one neurotransmitter function can profoundly effect the function of another, by acting either at closely situated receptor sites or at the neuronal system level, i.e. one neuronal system affecting the function of another. In addition, one neurotransmitter function may affect the way that another adapts to repeated antidepressant administration or electroconvulsive shock. Some interactions are shown in Table 1.4.

It is not yet clear how such interactions are responsible for changes in adaptive responses, nor has the precise neuroanatomy been defined upon which the functional linkage depends.

1.9 Conclusions

Several changes are cited which indicate adaptive changes of monoamine neuronal system functions to antidepressant drug therapy, electroconvulsive shock and lithium. The problem is whether these relate to the pharmacological actions upon which the therapeutic actions of the treatments depend. On the indirect evidence available, some of the changes seen in rodents may occur in the human being. There are, however, differences between the adaptive responses to antidepressant drug therapy and those to electroconvulsive shock which highlight differences in 5-HT$_2$-mediated and dopamine-mediated functions for the antidepressant effect of these two types of therapy.

We must always consider whether, when we find up- or down-regulation of a receptor, this indicates an increased or decreased function. The human studies quoted in the test, albeit of pineal function, show that the changes in β-receptor function may not be accompanied physiologically by changes in overall transsynaptic function, which indicates adaptation to *maintain* synaptic homeostasis.

Nevertheless, these studies on neuropharmacological adaptation in response to antidepressant drugs, ECT and lithium demonstrate a pattern of changes in monoamine function occurring in the brain during continued treatment with these therapies.

It seems quite plausible, in the absence of evidence to the contrary, that these changes might be important in the therapeutic effect of these treatments. It might also be that in the intrinsic functional pathology underlying the depressive state there is 'endogenous' neuropharmacological adaptation, so that even if the depressive state is triggered by one specific neurotransmitter defect then widespread adaptive changes might follow on from that that would require correction during therapy.

References

Atterwill, C. R., and Tordoff, A. F. C. (1982). Effects of repeated lithium administration on the subcellular distribution of 5-hydroxytryptamine in rat brain. *Br. J. Pharmacol.*, 76, 413–21.

Barbaccia, M. L., Gandolfi, O., Chuang, D. M., and Costa, E. (1983). Modulation of neuronal uptake by a putative endogenous ligand of imipramine recognition sites. *Proc. Nat. Acad. Sci.*, 80, 5134–8.

Berridge, M. J., Downes, C. P., and Hanley, M. R. (1982). Lithium amplifies agonist-dependent phosphatidylinositol responses in brain and salivary glands. *Biochem. J.*, 206, 587–95.

Blier, P., and De Montigny, C. (1985). Short-term lithium administration enhances serotonergic neurotransmission: Electrophysiological evidence in the rat CNS. *Europ. J. Pharmacol.*, 113, 69–77.

Bradley, P. B., Engel, G., Feniuk, W., Fozard, J. R., Humphrey, P. P. A., Middlemiss, D. N., Mylecharane, E. J., Richardson, B. P., and Saxena, P. R. (1986). Proposals for the classification and nomenclature of functional receptors for 5-hydroxytryptamine. *Neuropharmacology*, 25, 563–76.

Checkley, S. A., Meldrum, B. S., and McWilliam, J. R. (1984). Mechanism of action of ECT.

Neuroendocrine studies. In Lerer, B., Weiner, R. D., and Belmaker, R. H. (eds.), *ECT: Basic Mechanisms (Biological Psychiatry: New Prospects*, 1). Libbey, London, 101-6.

Costain, D. W., Cowen, P. J., Gelder, M. G., and Grahame-Smith, D. G. (1982). Electroconvulsive therapy in the brain: evidence for increased dopamine mediated responses. *Lancet*, ii, 400-4.

Cowen, P. J., Fraser, S., Grahame-Smith, D. G., Green, A. R., and Stamford, C. (1983). The effect of chronic antidepressant administration on β-adrenoceptor function of the rat pineal. *Br. J. Pharmac.*, 78, 89-96.

Cowen, P. J., Geaney, D. P., Schachter, M., Green, A. R., and Elliott, J. M. (1986). Desmethylimipramine treatment in normal subjects: effects on neuroendocrine responses to L-tryptophan and platelet 5HT related receptors. *Archives of General Psychiatry*, 43, 61-7.

Cowen, P. J., Green, A. R., Grahame-Smith, D. G., and Braddock, L. E. (1985). Plasma melatonin during desmethylimipramine treatment. Evidence for changes in noradrenergic transmission. *J. Clin. Pharmac.*, 19, 799-805.

De Montigny, C., and Blier, P. (1984). Effects of antidepressant treatments in 5HT neurotransmission: electrophysiological and clinical studies. In Usdin, E., Asberg, M., Bertilsson, L., and Sjoqvist, F. (eds.), *Frontiers in Biochemical and Pharmacological Research in Depression*. Raven, New York, 223-39.

De Montigny, C., and Blier, P. (1985). Electrophysiological aspects of serotonin neuropharmacology: implications for antidepressant treatments. In Green, A. R. (ed.), *Neuropharmacology of Serotonin*. Oxford University Press, Oxford, 181-217.

Fink, M. (1979). *Convulsive Therapy: Theory and Practice*. Raven, New York.

Glue, P. W., Cowen, P. J., Nutt, D. J., Kolakowska, T., and Grahame-Smith, D. G. (1986). The effects of lithium on 5-HT mediated neuroendocrine responses and platelet 5-HT receptors. *Psychopharmacology*, 90, 398-402.

Godfrey, P. P., Grahame-Smith, D. G., Gray, J. A., and McClue, S. J. (1987). GABA$_B$ receptor mediated inhibition of 5-HT stimulated phosphatidylinositol turnover in mouse cerebral cortex. *Br. J. Pharmacol.*, 90, 253.

Goodwin, G. M., De Souza, R. J., Wood, A. J., and Green, A. R. (1986a). Lithium decreases 5-HT$_{1A}$ and 5-HT$_2$ receptor, and α_2-adrenoceptor mediated function in mice. *Psychopharmacology*, 90, 482-7.

Goodwin, G. M., De Souza, R. J., Wood, A. J., and Green, A. R. (1986b). The enhancement by lithium of the 5-HT$_{1A}$ mediated serotonin syndrome produced by 8-OH-DPAT in the rat: evidence for a post-synaptic mechanism. *Psychopharmacology*, 90, 488-93.

Goodwin, G. M., De Souza, R. J., and Green, A. R. (1985). Presynaptic serotonin receptor mediated response in mice attenuated by antidepressant drugs and electroconvulsive shock. *Nature*, 317, 531-3.

Grahame-Smith, D. G., and Green, A. R. (1974). The role of 5-hydroxytryptamine in the hyperactivity produced in rats by lithium and monoamine oxidase inhibition. *Br. J. Pharmacol.*, 52, 19-26.

Grahame-Smith, D. G., Green, A. R., and Costain, D. W. (1978). Mechanism of the antidepressant action of electroconvulsive therapy. *Lancet*, i, 254-6.

Gray, J. A., and Green, A. R. (1986a). Increased GABA$_B$ receptor function in mouse frontal cortex after repeated administration of antidepressant drugs or electroconvulsive shocks. *Br. J. Pharmacol.*, 92, 357-62.

Gray, J. A., and Green, A. R. (1986b). Evidence for increased GABA$_B$ receptor function in mouse frontal cortex following antidepressant administration. *Br. J. Pharmacol.*, 89, 799.

Green, A. R. (1986a). Changes in GABA biochemistry and seizure threshold. *Ann. NY Acad. Sci.*, 462, 105-19.

Green, A. R. (1986b). Electroconvulsive therapy: a GABA-ergic mechanism? In Lloyd, K. G., Bartholini, G., and Morselli, P. (eds.) *GABA and Mood Disorders*. Raven, New York, 57-60.

Green, A. R., and Goodwin, G. M. (1986). Antidepressants and monoamines: actions and interactions. In Deakin, J. F. W. (ed.), *The Biology of Depression*. Gaskell, London, 175-89.

Green, A. R., Heal, D. J., and Goodwin, G. M. (1986). The effects of electroconvulsive therapy in antidepressant drugs on monoamine receptors in rodent brain – similarities and differences. CIBA Foundation Symposium 123, 'Antidepressants and Receptor Function'. Wiley, Chichester, 246–69.

Green, A. R., and Nutt, D. J. (1983). Antidepressants. In Grahame-Smith, D. G., and Cowen, P. J. (eds.), *Psychopharmacology 1, Part 1. Preclinical Psychopharmacology.* Excerpta Medica, Amsterdam, 1–37.

Green, A. R., and Nutt, D. J. (1985). Antidepressants. In Grahame-Smith, D. G., and Cowen, P. J. (eds.), *Psychopharmacology 2, Part 1. Preclinical Psychopharmacology.* Excerpta Medica, Amsterdam, 1–34.

Heal, D. J., Philpot, J., O'Shaughnessy, K. H., and Davis, C. L. (1986). The influence of central noradrenergic function on $5-HT_2$-mediated head-twitch responses in mice: possible implications for the actions of antidepressant drugs. *Psychopharmacology,* **89,** 414–20.

Lerer, B., Weiner, R. D., and Belmaker, R. H. (eds.) (1984). *ECT: Basic Mechanisms. (Biological Psychiatry: New Prospects),* **1,** Libbey, London.

Lloyd, K. G., Thuvet, F., and Pilc, A. (1985). Up-regulation of γ-aminobutyric acid $(GABA)_B$ binding sites in rat frontal cortex: a common action of repeated administration of different classes of antidepressants and electroshock. *J. Pharmac. Exp. Ther.,* **235,** 191–9.

Oswald, I., Brezinova, V., and Dunleavy, D. L. F. (1972). On the slowness of action of tricyclic antidepressant drugs. *Br. J. Psychiat.,* **120,** 673–7.

Porter, R., Boch, G., and Clark, S. (1986). *CIBA Foundation Symposium 123: Antidepressants and Receptor Function.* Wiley, London.

Raisman, R., Briley, M. S., and Langer, S. Z. (1979). Specific tricyclic antidepressant binding sites in rat brain. *Nature,* **281,** 148–9.

Rehavi, M., Paul, S. M., Skolnick, R., and Goodwin, F. (1980). Demonstration of specific high affinity binding sites for [^{3}H]-imipramine in human brain. *Life Sci.,* **76,** 2273–9.

Shopsin, B., Friedman, E., and Gershon, S. (1976). Parachlorophenylalanine reversal of tranylcypromine effects in depressed patients. *Arch. Gen. Psychiatry,* **33,** 811–19.

Shopsin, B., Gershon, M., Goldstein, M., Friedman, E., and Wilks, S. (1975). Use of synthesis inhibitors in defining a role for biogenic amines during imipramine treatment in depressed patients. *Psychopharmacol. Commun.,* **1,** 239–49.

Sugrue, M. F. (1983). Chronic antidepressant therapy and associated changed in central monoaminergic functioning. *Pharmac. Ther.,* **21,** 1–33.

Swerdlow, M. R., Lee, D., Koob, G. F., and Vaccarino, F. J. (1985). The effects of chronic dietary lithium on behavioural indices of dopamine; denervation supersensitivity in the rat. *J. Pharmacol. Expt. Therap.,* **235,** 325–9.

Trieser, S. L., Cascio, C. S., O'Donohue, T. L., Thoa, N. B., Jackobowitz, D. M., and Kellar, K. J. (1981). Lithium increases serotonin release and decreases serotonin receptors in hippocampus. *Science,* **213,** 1529–31.

Van Praag, H. M., Flentge, F., Korf, J., Dols, L. C. W., and Schut, T. (1973). A pilot study of the predictive value of the probenicid test in application of 5-hydroxytryptophan as an antidepressant. *Psychopharmacologia.* (Berl.), **33,** 141–51.

2

Modulation of 5-HT Autoreceptors Probably Contributes to the Antidepressant Action of 5-HT Uptake Blockers

M. Briley and C. Moret

2.1 Introduction

The modulation of 5-hydroxytryptamine (5-HT) neurotransmission is mediated through serotonergic autoreceptors (for review, see Moret, 1985). 5-HT itself and other serotonergic agonists decrease the release of 5-HT elicited by depolarising stimuli by a feedback mechanism. There is increasing evidence that the receptors involved in this autoregulation are located on the serotonergic nerve terminals and are of the 5-HT_{1B} subtype (Middlemiss, 1984). 5-HT autoreceptor antagonists, such as methiothepin, not only inhibit the effects of agonists but, by antagonising the inhibitory effect of endogenous 5-HT, provoke an increase in the release.

The action of the 5-HT autoreceptor has been shown by release studies in a varaety of brain areas both in slices and in synaptosomal preparations (Moret, 1985). The studies presented in this chapter have all been carried out in rat hypothalamic slices using electrical stimulation. The release of $[^3\text{H}]$-5-HT from superfused slices of rat hypothalamus, previously incubated with $[^3\text{H}]$-5-HT, can be provoked by electrical field stimulation at 3 Hz, 20 mA, 2 ms. Under these conditions a 2 min stimulation releases about 2% of the tissue radioactivity content. The ratio of the radioactivity released by two consecutive stimulations (S_2/S_1) separated by about 40 min is close to unity and the variation in this ratio is a convenient way of representing the effects of 5-HT release by a drug introduced between the two stimulations.

Using this system, lysergic acid diethylamine (LSD) has been shown to be a potent 5-HT autoreceptor agonist at concentrations of 0.01 to 1 μM (Table 2.1). This effect may be antagonised by the 5-HT autoreceptor antagonist, methiothepin, but not by the α-adrenoceptor antagonist, phentolamine, or the dopamine receptor antagonist, sulpiride (Langer and Moret, 1982). Thus, under these experimental conditions, LSD acts purely as a 5-HT autoreceptor agonist (Langer and Moret, 1982) in spite of its known affinity for noradrenergic and dopaminergic receptors. Methiothepin, when added alone, at concentrations of 0.1 or 1 μM, before the second stimulation, significantly increases the release of 5-HT as compared with the first stimulation (Table 2.1).

Table 2.1   Effect of LSD and Methiothepin on $[^3H]$-5-HT release elicited by electrical stimulation of rat hypothalamic slices

Concentration (μM)	S_2/S_1	
	+ LSD	+ Methiothepin
0	1.13 ± 0.01 (8)	
0.01	0.67 ± 0.11* (7)	1.23 ± 0.17 (5)
0.1	0.40 ± 0.09** (8)	1.91 ± 0.24** (9)
1	0.09 ± 0.06** (4)	2.93 ± 0.31** (8)

LSD or methiothepin was added to the superfusion medium 20 min before the second stimulation. The values presented are the means + SEM of (n) determinations. Values S_1 and S_2 are the fractions of the tissue radiactivity released by 2 min stimulations (3 Hz, 20 mA, 2 msec) applied 60 and 104 min after the end of the incubation with $[^3H]$-5-HT. *$p < 0.05$; **$p < 0.005$ compared with the release in the absence of drugs.

2.2 The Effect of 5-HT Uptake Inhibitors on the 5-HT Autoreceptor

5-HT uptake inhibitors, such as citalopram, by themselves have no effect on the release of 5-HT (Fig. 2.1). These compounds, however, attenuate the inhibitory effect of LSD on $[^3H]$-5-HT release induced by electrical stimulation, in a concentration-dependent manner (Langer and Moret, 1982; Galzin et al., 1985) (Fig. 2.2). Similar results have been found with tricyclic antidepressants, such as imipramine and amitriptyline, and non-tricyclic 5-HT uptake inhibitors, such as paroxetine (Galzin et al., 1985). The same effect is also seen when other 5-HT

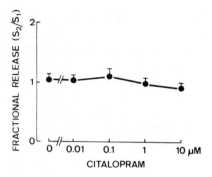

Fig. 2.1   Effect of citalopram on [^{3}H]-5-HT release elicited by electrical stimulation of rat hypothalamic slices. Citalopram was added to the superfusion medium 20 min before the second stimulation. The values presented are the means + SEM of (*n*) determinations. Values S_1 and S_2 are the fractions of the tissue radioactivity released by 2-min stimulations (3 Hz, 20 mA, 2 ms) applied 60 and 104 min after the end of the incubation with [^{3}H]-5-HT.

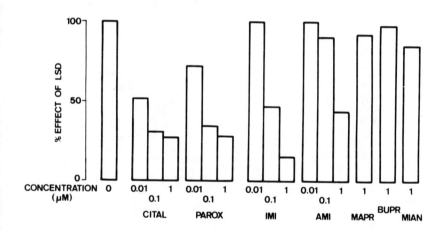

Fig. 2.2   Effect of various antidepressant drugs on the inhibition of stimulation evoked [^{3}H]-5 HT release elicited by 0.1 μM LSD. Antidepressants were added to the superfusion medium at the beginning of the superfusion period and remained present throughout the experiment. LSD (0.1 μM) was added 20 min before the second stimulation. The values presented are the percentage of the effect (inhibition) of LSD (0.1 μM) in the absence of antidepressants. Calculated from data in Langer and Moret (1982) and Galzin *et al.* (1985).

agonists, such as 5-methoxytryptamine (Galzin *et al.*, 1985) and dihydroergocristine (Moret and Briley, 1986a) are used instead of LSD. In these experiments none of the 5-HT uptake inhibitors modified, by themselves, the electrically evoked release of [^{3}H]-5-HT (Langer and Moret, 1982; Galzin *et al.*, 1985).

The compounds that attenuate the presynaptic agonist-induced inhibition of 5-HT release without affecting the release of 5-HT by themselves, all inhibit the uptake of 5-HT. Most of them are also proven or putative antidepressants. It appears, however, that the former property is the most important since antidepressants that do not inhibit 5-HT uptake, such as maprotiline, buproprione and mianserine, do not attenuate the presynaptic inhibition induced by LSD (Fig. 2.2). Furthermore, midalcipran, an antidepressant which inhibits both 5-HT and noradrenaline uptake (Moret *et al.*, 1985; Briley, 1986), has been shown to attenuate stereoselectively these autoreceptor effects (Moret and Briley, 1986b). The Z-form of the drug which inhibits uptake is active at attenuating the effect of LSD whereas the E-form which is inactive on 5-HT uptake is also inactive at the autoreceptor (Fig. 2.3).

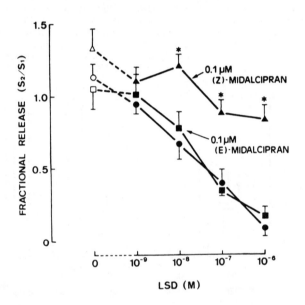

Fig. 2.3 Effect of the two enantiomers of midalcipran on the inhibition by LSD of the electrically evoked release of [³H]-5-HT. Z- or E-midalcipran was added to the superfusion medium at the beginning of the superfusion period and remained present throughout the experiment. LSD was added 20 min before the second stimulation. The values presented are the means + SEM of 4 to 8 determinations. Values S_1 and S_2 are the fractions of the tissue radioactivity released by 2 min stimulations (3 Hz, 20 mA, 2 ms) applied 60 and 104 min after the end of the incubation with [³H]-5-HT. *$p < 0.005$ compared with the corresponding values in the absence of midalcipran.

Finally, the potency with which the different 5-HT uptake inhibitors attenuate the effect of agonist at the autoreceptor appears to be related to their potency at inhibiting 5-HT uptake (Galzin *et al.*, 1985). Thus it seems clear that inhibition of 5-HT uptake interferes with the autoregulation of 5-HT release induced by 5-HT autoreceptor agonists. There are two general mechanisms by which this could occur. The increased levels of 5-HT in the synaptic gap which results from the inhibition of 5-HT uptake could saturate the autoreceptor such that the addition of an exogenous agonist would have little effect. Alternatively, a direct and specific interaction between the 5-HT uptake complex and the 5-HT auto-receptor could occur.

2.3 The Effect of Monoamine Oxidase Inhibitors on the 5-HT Autoreceptor

If the increase of synaptic 5-HT is the basis for the interaction described above then similar results would be expected with other compounds known to increase synaptic 5-HT, such as monoamine oxidase inhibitors. In contrast to the 5-HT uptake inhibitors, however, the monoamine oxidase inhibitor pargyline, when added to the superfusion medium before the second stimulation decreased, in a concentration-dependent manner, the electrically evoked release of $[^3H]$-5-HT (Moret and Briley, 1986b) (Fig. 2.4).

The serotonergic antagonist methiothepin shifted this concentration–response curve of pargyline to the right (Fig. 2.4). The α-adrenoceptor antagonist phentol-amine, at $1 \mu M$, also partially reduced the inhibitory effect of pargyline. The partial inhibition of pargyline-induced $[^3H]$-5-HT release by phentolamine is probably explained by the fact that pargyline also increases synaptic noradrenaline levels that by stimulating α-adrenoceptors on 5-HT terminals (Göthert and Huth, 1980; Galzin et al., 1984) would decrease $[^3H]$-5-HT overflow. Similar results have also been found with other monoamine oxidase inhibitors, such as the monoamine oxidase-A selective inhibitor clorgyline, and the monoamine oxidase-B selective inhibitor deprenyl (Table 2.2). Selectivity for the type A or type B enzyme does not seem to be particularly important for this effect.

In contrast with the 5-HT uptake inhibitors, pargyline does not modify the effect of 5-HT release of an autoreceptor agonist such as LSD (Galzin et al., 1985). The pargyline-induced inhibition of the $[^3H]$-5-HT release was, however, antagonised by the 5-HT uptake inhibitor citalopram from $0.1 \mu M$ (Fig. 2.4).

The results with pargyline suggest that its action is mediated through increased levels of synaptic 5-HT. Monoamine oxidase inhibitors decrease the metabolism of 5-HT and noradrenaline, increasing the synaptic levels of the neurotrans-mitters. The resulting increased stimulation of the 5-HT autoreceptor would cause a decreased evoked $[^3H]$-5-HT release. The antagonism of this inhibitory effect by methiothepin at $0.1 \mu M$, a concentration which inhibits the 5-HT autoreceptor (Langer and Moret, 1982), tends to confirm this interpretation.

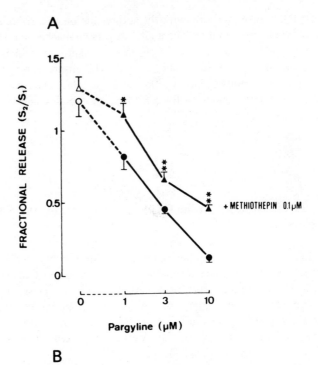

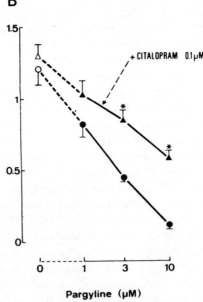

Fig. 2.4 *(caption opposite)*

Table 2.2   Effect of pargyline, deprenyl and clorgyline on $[^3H]$-5-HT release elicited by electrical stimulation of rat hypothalamic slices

	S_2/S_1
Control	1.21 ± 0.11 (5)
Pargyline 1 μM	0.82 ± 0.09* (6)
3 μM	0.45 ± 0.03** (5)
10 μM	0.12 ± 0.03** (4)
Deprenyl 1 μM	0.98 ± 0.06 (5)
3 μM	0.68 ± 0.10* (8)
10 μM	0.38 ± 0.09** (5)
Clorgyline 0.01 μM	0.65 ± 0.07* (4)
0.1 μM	0.37 ± 0.1** (6)

Pargyline, deprenyl or clorgyline was added to the superfusion medium 20 min before the second stimulation. The values presented are the means + SEM of (*n*) determinations. Values S_1 and S_2 are the fractions of the tissue radiactivity released by 2 min stimulations (3 Hz, 20 mA, 2 msec) applied 60 and 104 min after the end of the incubation with $[^3H]$-5-HT.

2.4 Discussion

These results present an interesting paradox in that when 5-HT levels are increased by an inhibitor of monoamine oxidase then the electrically evoked release of 5-HT is reduced but when 5-HT levels are increased by an inhibitor of 5-HT uptake then 5-HT release remains unaltered. Furthermore, the presence of a 5-HT uptake inhibitor is capable of reducing the effect of the monoamine oxidase inhibitor on 5-HT release. Thus, although both pargyline and citalopram both

---

Fig. 2.4   Effect of methiothepin (A) and citalopram (B) on the inhibition of the electrically evoked release of $[^3H]$-5-HT provoked by pargyline. Methiothepin or citalopram was added to the superfusion medium at the beginning of the superfusion period and remained present throughout the experiment. Pargyline was added 20 min before the second stimulation. The values presented are the means + SEM of 4 to 8 determinations. Values S_1 and S_2 are the fractions of the tissue radioactivity released by 2-min stimulations (3 Hz, 20 mA, 2 ms) applied 60 and 104 min after the end of the incubation with $[^3H]$-5-HT. *$p < 0.05$; **$p < 0.01$ compared with the corresponding values in the absence of methiothepin or citalopram.

increase synaptic 5-HT levels, they have very different effects on the 5-HT auto-receptor. Pargyline appears to act simply as an indirect autoreceptor agonist. Citalopram, on the other hand, has no effect by itself and attenuates the effects of the direct and indirect 5-HT autoreceptor agonists. These results suggest that the interaction between 5-HT uptake inhibition and 5-HT autoregulation does not occur via a modification of synaptic 5-HT levels but rather through a direct interaction between the uptake mechanism and the autoreceptor, both of which are situated on the presynaptic membrane.

Since there is evidence to suggest an influence of the activity of the 5-HT uptake complex on 5-HT autoregulation, the possibility that a reciprocal control may exist should also be considered. That is, is the uptake of 5-HT or its inhibi-tion by specific uptake inhibitors modified by 5-HT autoreceptor agonists and antagonists? Results show, however, that neither LSD nor methiothepin affect the uptake of 5-HT at concentrations which are active at the 5-HT autoreceptor (Briley and Moret, 1983). In addition, neither LSD nor methiothepin alter the inhibition of 5-HT uptake by citalopram (Briley and Moret, 1983). Thus there is no evidence to suggest any influence of the 5-HT autoreceptor on 5-HT uptake or its inhibition by the selective uptake inhibitor, such as citalopram.

In conclusion, there is now considerable evidence that inhibition of 5-HT uptake leads to a reduced negative-feedback control on the electrically evoked release of 5-HT. Since functional 5-HT autoreceptors have also been found in human brain (Schlicker et al., 1985), the therapeutic implications of the above interaction could be very important. The increased synaptic levels of 5-HT resulting from the inhibition of 5-HT uptake would normally be, at least par-tially, counteracted by a reduction in 5-HT release brought about through an increased stimulation of the 5-HT autoreceptors. This is the phenomenon which is clearly seen with the monoamine oxidase inhibitors as described above. With the 5-HT uptake inhibitors, however, the attenuation of the 5-HT autoreceptor activity allows the full effect of their inhibition of uptake to be felt. Further-more, the attenuation of 5-HT autoreceptor activity probably also leads to a reduction of the feedback control induced by the endogenous neurotransmitter. Indeed, it remains to be demonstrated which is the more important action of the 5-HT uptake inhibitors: their increase of synaptic 5-HT by uptake inhibition or their increase of synaptic 5-HT by the reduction of the 5-HT autoreceptor activity.

It is possible that the pharmacological phenomenon described above may have physiological importance as well. The [^{3}H]-imipramine binding site is asso-ciated with the uptake mechanism of 5-HT and is probably responsible for the modulation of its activity (for review see Briley, 1985). Certain authors have proposed that there may indeed be an endogenous ligand that physiologically regulates the uptake of 5-HT (Langer et al., 1984; Barbaccia and Costa, 1984). If this is the case then the results discussed here suggest that the activity of the 5-HT autoreceptor may be modulated in parallel and in the same direction as 5-HT uptake, via an interaction between the uptake complex and the autoreceptor. Depressed patients have been shown to have a reduced number of [³H]-imipramine binding sites on their platelets (Briley, *et al.*, 1980) and probably in their brains as well (Stanley *et al.*, 1982; Perry *et al.*, 1983). Since this deficit appears to be more trait-dependent than state-dependent (Baron *et al.*, 1986) it could reflect a reduced ability to modulate synaptic 5-HT levels, not only through the uptake of 5-HT but also by indirect modulation of the 5-HT autoreceptor. This reduced capacity to modulate 5-HT levels may be at the basis of their inability to cope with internal or external modifications that perturb 5-HT function and result in a depressive episode.

References

Barbaccia, M. L., and Costa, E. (1984). Autacoids for drug receptors: A new approach in drug development. Presynaptic modulation and presynaptic receptors in mental disease. *Ann. N.Y. Acad. Sci.*, **430**, 103-14.

Baron, M., Barkai, A., Gruen, R., Peselow, E., Fieve, R. R., and Quitkin, F. (1986). Platelet ³H-imipramine binding in affective disorders: trait versus state characteristics. *Am. J. Psychiatry*, **143**, 711-17.

Briley, M., Langer, S. Z., Raisman, R., Sechter, D., and Zarifian, E. (1980). Tritiated imipramine binding sites are decreased in platelets of untreated depressed patients. *Science*, **209**, 303-5.

Briley, M. (1985). Imipramine binding: its relationship with serotonin uptake and depression. In Green, A. R. (ed.), *Neuropharmacology of Serotonin*. Oxford University Press, Oxford, 21-49.

Briley, M. (1986). Midalcipran hydrochloride. *Drugs of the Future*, **11**, 21-23.

Briley, M., and Moret, C. (1983). Is 5-HT uptake regulated by the 5-HT autoreceptor? *Br. J. Pharmacol.*, **80**, 673.

Galzin, A. M., Moret, C., and Langer, S. Z. (1984). Evidence that exogenous but not endogenous norepinephrine activates the presynaptic alpha-2 adrenoceptors on serotonergic nerve endings in the rat hypothalamus. *J. Pharmacol. Exp. Ther.*, **228**, 725-32.

Galzin, A. M., Moret, C., Verzier, B., and Langer, S. Z. (1985). Interaction between tricyclic and nontricyclic 5-hydroxytryptamine uptake inhibitors and the presynaptic 5-hydroxytryptamine inhibitory autoreceptors in the rat hypothalamus. *J. Pharmacol. Exp. Ther.*, **235**, 200-11.

Göthert, M., and Huth, H. (1980). Alpha-adrenoceptor-mediated modulation of 5-hydroxytryptamine release from rat brain cortex slices. *Naunyn-Schmiedeberg's Arch. Pharmacol.*, **313**, 21-6.

Langer, S. Z., and Moret, C. (1982). Citalopram antagonizes the stimulation by lysergic acid diethylamide of presynaptic inhibitory serotonin autoreceptors in the rat hypothalamus. *J. Pharmacol. Exp. Ther.*, **222**, 220-6.

Langer, S. Z., Raisman, R., Taharoui, L., Scatton, B., Niddam, R., Lee, C., and Claustre, Y. (1984). Substituted tetrahydro-β-carbolines are possible candidates as endogenous ligands of the ³H-imipramine binding site. *Eur. J. Pharmacol.*, **98**, 153-4.

Middlemiss, D. N. (1985). The putative 5-HT₁ receptor agonist, RU 24969, inhibits the efflux of 5-hydroxytryptamine from rat frontal cortex slices by stimulation of the 5-HT autoreceptor. *J. Pharm. Pharmacol.*, **37**, 434-7.

Moret, C. (1985). Pharmacology of the serotonin autoreceptor. In Green, A. R. (ed.), *Neuropharmacology of Serotonin*. Oxford University Press, Oxford, 21-49.

Moret, C., and Briley, M. (1986a). Dihydroergocristine-induced stimulation of the 5-HT autoreceptor in the hypothalamus of the rat. *Neuropharmacol.*, **25**, 169-174.

Moret, C., and Briley, M. (1986b). Effects of 5-HT uptake blockers and monoamine oxidase inhibitors on 5-HT autoregulation. *Neurosc. Lett.*, *suppl.*, **26**, s234.

Moret, C., Charveron, M., Finberg, J. P. M., Couzinier, J. P., and Briley, M. (1985). Bio-
    chemical profile of midalcipran (F 2207), 1-phenyl-1-diethylaminocarbonyl-2-amino-
    methylcyclopropane (Z) hydrochloride, a potential fourth generation antidepressant
    drug. *Neuropharmacol.*, **24**, 1211–19.
Perry, E. K., Marshall, E. F., Blessed, G., Tomlinson, B. E., and Perry, R. H. (1983). De-
    creased imipramine binding in the brains of patients with depressive illness. *Br. J. Psychiat.*,
    142, 188–92.
Schlicker, E., Brandt, F., Classen, K., and Göthert, M. (1985). Serotonin release in human
    cerebral cortex and its modulation via serotonin receptors. *Brain Res.*, **331**, 337–41.
Stanley, M., Virgilio, J., and Gershon, S. (1982). Tritiated imipramine binding sites are
    decreased in the frontal cortex of suicides. *Science*, **216**, 1337–9.

3

Effects of Acute and Chronic Treatment with Imipramine on 5-Hydroxytryptamine and 5-Hydroxytryptamine Comodulators in Central 5-Hydroxytryptamine Neurons and on Glucocorticoid Receptors in Central Monoaminergic Neurons: a Morphometrical and Microdensitometrical Analysis

K. Fuxe, I. Kitayama, A.M. Janson, L.F. Agnati, A. Cintra, S.O. Ögren, A. Härfstrand, P. Eneroth and J.-Å. Gustafsson

3.1 Introduction

Central 5-hydroxytryptamine (5-HT) neurons represent targets of action for antidepressant drugs, as for example is demonstrated by the presence of high densities of [³H]-imipramine binding sites in the nerve cell membranes of the central 5-HT neurons (see Langer and Briley, 1981). Quantitative receptor autoradiography of [³H]-imipramine binding sites has indicated their presence in the nerve cell membrane of the 5-HT cell bodies, axons and nerve terminals (Fuxe *et al.*, 1983a). The density of [³H]-imipramine binding sites seems particularly high in the 5-HT nerve cell group of the nucleus raphe dorsalis (group B7; Dahlström and Fuxe, 1964). In view of the fact that a high secretion of cortisol has been demonstrated in patients with a severe depression (see Carroll, 1984), it is also of particular interest that strong glucocorticoid receptor (GR) immunoreactivity (IR) has been demonstrated in the vast majority of the 5-HT nerve cells of the lower brain-stem of the male rat (Fuxe *et al.*, 1985a, b; Härfstrand *et al.*, 1986a).

New morphometric and microdensitometric methods have been developed to analyse the effects of psychoactive drugs on transmitter-identified neurons and especially on the central monoamine neurons (Agnati *et al.*, 1984; Fuxe *et al.*, 1983b, 1985c, d; Agnati and Fuxe, 1985). Methods have also been developed for the quantitative evaluation of coexistence in nerve cell bodies and nerve terminals (Agnati *et al.*, 1982; Fuxe *et al.*, 1985d).

These new methods have been used in the present paper to study the effects of acute and chronic oral treatment with imipramine in clinically relevant doses on discrete 5-HT nerve cell body groups (Dahlström and Fuxe, 1964) and on the 5-HT nerve terminal systems of the ventral horn of the spinal cord (Dahlström and Fuxe, 1965) in view of the existence of substance P (SP) and thyroid hormone-releasing hormone (TRH) immunoreactivities in some of these 5-HT nerve terminals (Hökfelt *et al.*, 1978; Björklund *et al.*, 1979; Johansson *et al.*, 1981). In these analyses we have also included the studies on the effects of chronic imipramine treatment on GR immunoreactivity in various 5-HT nerve cell groups, in the locus coeruleus, and in various cortical regions in order to establish whether antidepressants influence not only membrane receptors but also intracellular receptor mechanisms. It should be noted that the 5-HT co-modulator SP in spinal cord membrane preparations has been shown to reduce the affinity and to increase the B_{max} values of 5-HT_1 binding sites (Agnati *et al.*, 1983). Furthermore, it was found that SP *in vitro* counteracts the effects of chronic imipramine treatment on the 5-HT_1 receptors and spinal cord membranes (Fuxe *et al.*, 1984). Thus, previous results in our laboratories indicate that chronic antidepressant treatment, at least chronic imipramine treatment, may antagonise the effects of a 5-HT comodulator in the spinal cord (Fuxe *et al.*, 1984). In line with these results it has been found that the 5-HT uptake-blocking agent zimelidine upon chronic treatment elevates SP levels in the ventral horn, an action which may be produced by reduced release of SP (see Brodin *et al.*, 1984; Iverfeldt *et al.*, 1986). The present article summarises our recent experiments on these issues (Kitayama *et al.*, 1987a, b).

3.2 Material and Methods

Male-specific, pathogen-free Sprague-Dawley rats were used. In the acute experiments 10 μmol/kg of imipramine was given orally (forced feeding with a size 3 feeding tube (Rüsch, FRG)) 2 h before sacrifice. In the chronic experiments imipramine was given orally, twice daily in a dose of 10 μmol/kg for 2 weeks. The rats were decapitated 2 h after the last treatment. A control group was treated acutely or chronically with saline in the same way as with imipramine.

3.2.1 Immunohistochemical Techniques

For details on the immunohistochemical technique, see Fuxe *et al.*, 1985c, d; Cintra *et al.*, 1986. A polyclonal rabbit 5-HT antiserum (code SER 1-16; Steinbusch *et al.*, 1978) was used in a dilution of 1 : 4000, a polyclonal rabbit SP antiserum (Amersham, Amersham, England) was used in a dilution of 1 : 750, a polyclonal rabbit TRH antiserum (antiserum 4319, Visser and Klootwijk, 1981) was used in a dilution of 1 : 750 and a monoclonal GR antiserum was used in a dilution of 1 : 3000 (see Okret *et al.*, 1984, for characterisation of this antibody). The staining was made by the use of the avidin–biotin immunoperoxidase system, Vectastain (Vector Laboratories, Burlingame, CA, USA) with 3-3'diaminobenzidine HCl (DAB, Sigma, St Louis, MO, USA) as chromogene, resulting in a brownish staining of the respective immunoreactivities in the nerve cells. As controls antisera which had been preabsorbed with the respective synthetic peptide or 5-HT (50 μg/ml diluted antiserum) were used. In the case of the GR antiserum absorption was made with a highly purified GR preparation. For further details, see Kitayama *et al.*, 1987a, b.

3.2.2 Biochemical Techniques

The determinations of 5-HT and 5-hydroxyindolacetic acid (5-HIAA) levels were performed according to the methods of Mayer and Shoup (1983) as modified by Hallman *et al.* (1984). Spinal cord SP immunoreactivity was also determined by radioimmunoassay (RIA) measurements (Fuxe *et al.*, 1985c). Furthermore, serum corticosterone and aldosterone levels were determined using standard RIA procedures (Nilsen *et al.*, 1980; Härfstrand *et al.*, 1986b).

3.2.3 Morphometric and Microdensitometric Procedures

Antigen immunoreactivity was semi-quantitatively determined in nerve cell bodies, nerve cell processes and in nerve terminals with a method based on the procedure previously described (Agnati *et al.*, 1978, 1984, 1987; Agnati and Fuxe, 1985; Fuxe *et al.*, 1985c, d; Zoli *et al.*, 1987) using the IBAS 2 image analyser (Zeiss, Kontron, FRG) linked with a video camera (Bosch, FRG). For further details, see Kitayama *et al.*, 1987a, b.

The microdensitometric procedure determining the immunoreactivity of the specifically stained nerve cell profiles is illustrated in Figs. 3.1 and 3.2. The morphometric characterisation included determination of the mean profile area (μm^2) and the profile number for the nerve cell bodies. These values should be considered relative and not absolute, since an unbiased stereological estimation using the dissector has not been performed (Sterio, 1984). The total field-area, that is the total immunoreactive area in the sampled field, for the specific immunoreactivity profiles ($(FA_c)_0$ for nerve cell body profiles; $(FA_n)_0$ for nuclear profiles; $(FA_t)_0$ for nerve terminal profiles) was determined and the

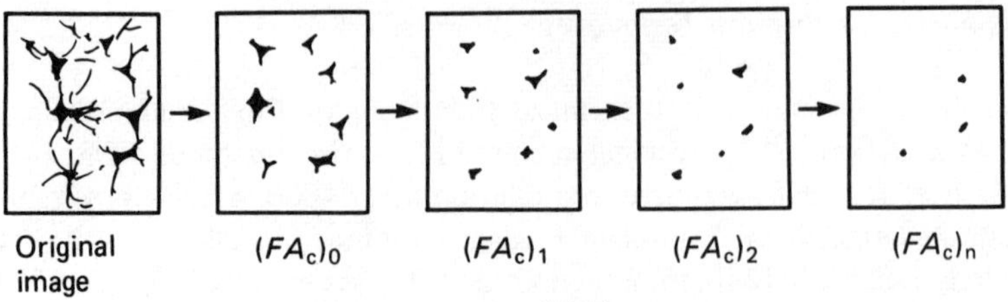

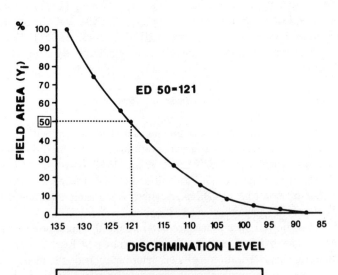

$(FA_c)_0$: total field area for the specific immunoreactive cell body profiles

$(FA_c)_i$: respective field area for parts of the specific immunoreactive cell body profiles discriminated at stepwise increased levels of discrimination

Y_i : respective per cent ratio of $(FA_c)_i/(FA_c)_0$

Fig. 3.1 A schematic representation of the procedure introduced to obtain a semi-quantitative evaluation of the antigen content in one sample of specific immunoreactivity in nerve cell body profiles. In the figure the effects of subsequent discrimination steps are illustrated. After each discrimination step the field area of positive immunoreactivity $((FA_c)_i)$ is measured. The percentage ratios, $Y_i = [(FA_c)_i/(FA_c)_0] \times 100$, are calculated. By means of these values the evaluation of the antigen contents is performed.

Fig. 3.2 (*caption opposite*)

corresponding grey-tone value, including the specific immunoreactive structures with the lowest absorbance, was also noted. The higher the grey-tone level the lower the absorption. Then, by subsequent discrimination steps, the field areas (FA_i) corresponding to more intensely stained structures were determined. The respective percentage ratios of the field area $(Y_i = FA_i/FA_0 \times 100)$ obtained at the discrimination steps were plotted on the Y-axis (Fig. 3.2). The grey-tone value reducing the FA_0 value by 50%, the GV_{50}, was then obtained. In one experiment the mean grey-tone value at the $(FA_c)_0$ level was determind, GV_{100}. The background grey-value was measured in an area near the sampled field of the section and where there were no specific immunoreactive nerve profiles. The median grey-value (Md) was calculated by deducting the GV_{50} value from the background grey-value. A basal grey-value was obtained in a similar way by subtracting the GV_{100} value from the background grey-value. An evaluation of the overall mean immunoreactivity (IR) (T–IR) was obtained by the formula: $T–IR = Md \times FA_0$.

The coexistence of a neurotransmitter and a peptide in the nerve terminal profiles was calculated using the occlusion method (Fuxe *et al.* 1985d; Agnati *et al.*, 1982) with the formula described in Fig. 3.3. The coexisting

$$\text{Coexistence of 5-HT/SP} = 100 \times \frac{FA(5\text{-HT}) + FA(SP) - FA(5\text{-HT} + SP)}{FA(5\text{-HT})}$$

$$\text{Coexistence of 5-HT/TRH} = 100 \times \frac{FA(5\text{-HT}) + FA(TRH) - FA(5\text{-HT} + TRH)}{FA(5\text{-HT})}$$

$FA(5\text{-HT})$: field area for 5-HT immunoreactivity
$FA(SP)$: field area for SP immunoreactivity
$FA(TRH)$: field area for TRH immunoreactivity
$\left.\begin{array}{l} FA(5\text{-HT+SP}) \\ FA(5\text{-HT+TRH}) \end{array}\right\}$: field area for the specific immunoreactivity obtained when 5-HT and SP or 5-HT and TRH antisera are mixed together

Fig. 3.3   The formulas used to calculate coexistence of neuronal messengers using the occlusion method. These formulas are applied for calculation of the coexistence of 5-HT/SP and 5 HT/TRH. An evaluation of the number of the immunoreactive nerve terminal profiles is obtained by measuring the total immunoreactive area for the respective antisera in the sampled field (field area).

Fig. 3.2   Illustration of the procedure for the semi-quantitative evaluation of relative antigen contents (see Fig. 3.1). The respective percentage ratios, $Y_i = [(FA_c)_i/(FA_c)_0] \times 100$, obtained at the subsequent discrimination steps ranging from 135 to 85 are plotted on the Y-axis. The higher the value the lower the absorption. From the 50% value the GV_{50} is obtained (121). The median grey-value (Md) is equal to the background grey value minus the GV_{50} value (i.e. $200 - 121 = 79$).

immunoreactive field area for specifically stained nerve terminal profiles was obtained by subtracting the field area found after incubation with the mixed antibodies from the sum of the field-areas found after incubation with each of the respective antibodies alone. Then, the coexistence was expressed as a percentage of the field-area obtained after staining with the 5-HT antiserum.

3.3 Results

3.3.1 Studies on 5-HT, SP and TRH Immunoreactivities

3.3.1.1 Effects of Acute Imipramine Treatment

The 5-HT, SP and TRH immunoreactivity in the nerve terminals of the ventral horn were not changed by acute oral dose of imipramine (10 μmol/kg) as evaluated from the median grey-values. However, the 5-HT immunoreactivity in group B7 (nucleus raphe dorsalis) but not in any other 5-HT nerve cell group studied was increased by acute treatment with imipramine (Table 3.1). Thus, a highly significant 40% increase in the $(FA_c)_0$ value was recorded as well as a significant increase in the total average immunoreactivity. The median grey-value (Md), however, is unchanged, and the increase in the total field-area of group B7 in acute imipramine-treated rats is explained by an increase in the mean profile area for 5-HT cell bodies (Fig. 3.4). The number of cell body profiles was not influenced. The mean profile area of group B1 was instead significantly reduced (Fig. 3.4).

The entity of 5-HT/SP and 5-HT/TRH coexisting nerve-terminal profiles in the sampled regions of the spinal cord was around 100% and no changes were noted after acute imipramine treatment.

3.3.1.2 Effects of Chronic Imipramine Treatment

Chronic treatment with imipramine caused a significant increase in SP immunoreactivity in the medial part of the ventral horn of the cervical and lumbar enlargements (Fig. 3.5) as evaluated from the median grey-tone value (Md) and the total average immunoreactivity (lumbar level). 5-HT and TRH immunoreactivity remained unchanged in the ventral horn of the spinal cord. Furthermore, following chronic imipramine treatment the morphometric parameters of group B7 were no longer significantly changed. This was also true for group B1 (Table 3.1). Instead, chronic treatment with imipramine selectively increased 5-HT immunoreactivity in the lateral part of group B3 (ventral part of the reticular gigantocellular nucleus).

As seen in Fig. 3.6, chronic treatment with imipramine did not influence the number of coexisting 5-HT/SP and 5-HT/TRH immunoreactive nerve terminal profiles in the ventral horn of the cervical and lumbar enlargements.

Table 3.1 Effects of acute and chronic imipramine treatment on 5-HT immunoreacitivty in 5-HT nerve cell groups

Region	Treatment	Acute imipramine			Chronic imipramine		
		Md	$(FA)_0/(\mu m^2)$	$T\text{-}IR$	Md	$(FA)_0/(\mu m^2)$	$T\text{-}IR$
B1 c	Saline	98 ± 5	$1\,420 \pm 240$	$138\,600 \pm 16\,700$	101 ± 14	$1\,890 \pm 390$	$180\,300 \pm 46\,400$
	Imipramine	106 ± 3	910 ± 140	$94\,600 \pm 12\,200$	102 ± 10	$2\,610 \pm 900$	$284\,100 \pm 114\,300$
B2 c	Saline	87 ± 8	$3\,050 \pm 80$	$264\,200 \pm 19\,100$	90 ± 14	$2\,940 \pm 390$	$285\,000 \pm 69\,700$
	Imipramine	98 ± 5	$3\,440 \pm 690$	$334\,200 \pm 60\,900$	89 ± 8	$2\,830 \pm 410$	$264\,400 \pm 52\,400$
B2 p	Saline	59 ± 8	$22\,140 \pm 740$	$1\,303\,900 \pm 179\,400$	67 ± 4	$21\,990 \pm 2\,930$	$1\,490\,500 \pm 230\,200$
	Imipramine	72 ± 8	$26\,040 \pm 3\,670$	$1\,861\,100 \pm 285\,800$	68 ± 4	$21\,170 \pm 2\,490$	$1\,454\,900 \pm 205\,400$
B3M c	Saline	84 ± 5	$4\,420 \pm 900$	$377\,100 \pm 85\,400$	84 ± 11	$4\,710 \pm 1\,030$	$432\,100 \pm 121\,400$
	Imipramine	90 ± 7	$4\,950 \pm 320$	$445\,700 \pm 50\,300$	99 ± 15	$4\,730 \pm 950$	$501\,800 \pm 147\,000$
B3L c	Saline	95 ± 5	$2\,970 \pm 630$	$273\,400 \pm 45\,400$	$88 \pm 14^*$	$2\,580 \pm 210$	$216\,800 \pm 31\,800$
	Imipramine	103 ± 5	$3\,440 \pm 730$	$346\,100 \pm 67\,000$	102 ± 15	$2\,370 \pm 180$	$244\,000 \pm 43\,000$
B7 c	Saline	95 ± 10	$14\,600 \pm 1\,270^{**}$	$1\,349\,300 \pm 83\,700^*$	95 ± 17	$17\,320 \pm 3\,780$	$1\,837\,900 \pm 534\,900$
	Imipramine	92 ± 8	$21\,000 \pm 1\,730$	$1\,912\,400 \pm 195\,100$	97 ± 17	$20\,280 \pm 4\,070$	$2\,039\,800 \pm 570\,300$

For details on treatment with imipramine see text. Sampled regions are shown in Fig. 3.6. All groups are evaluated with respect to cell body profiles (c). In group B2 also the profiles of cell processes are evaluated (p). By means of the microdensitometric analysis (see Figs. 3.1 to 3.3) the median grey value (Md), the total IR area for profiles $(FA)_0$ and an overall evaluation of the total average IR $(T\text{-}IR = Md \times (FA)_0)$ was performed. Means $\pm$ SEM are shown. Acute imipramine: $N = 3$ to 4 rats, chronic imipramine: $N = 5$ to 6 rats. The values from each rat represent the mean of 2 to 3 adjacent coronal 25 μm sections (see text). Statistical analysis was performed with paired Student's t-test. $* = p < 0.05$; $** = p < 0.01$.

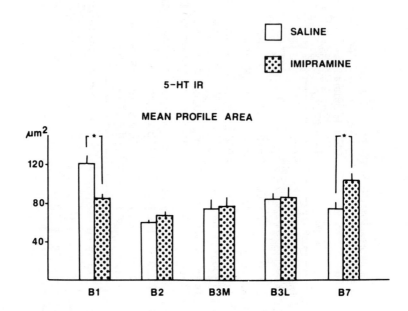

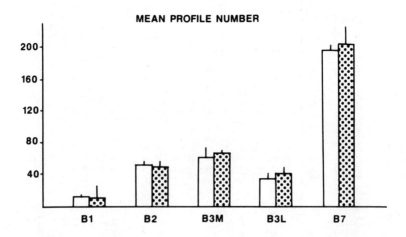

Fig. 3.4 Effects of acute imipramine treatment on the morphometric characteristics of 5-HT immunoreactive (IR) nerve cell bodies of groups: B1, B2, B3M, B3L and B7. Means ± SEM are shown; $n = 3$ to 4 rats. The values from each rat represent the mean of 2 to 3 adjacent coronal sections. A two-tailed paired Student's t-test was used. $*p < 0.05$; $**p < 0.01$.

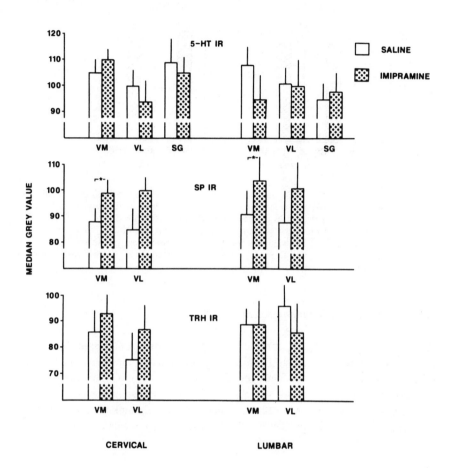

Fig. 3.5 Effects of chronic imipramine treatment on 5-HT, SP and TRH immunoreactivity (IR) in nerve terminal profiles of the cervical and lumbar enlargements of the spinal cord in the male rat. All three substances were analysed in the medial (VM) and lateral (VL) parts of the ventral horn and 5-HT was also determined in the substantia gelatinosa (Sb) of the dorsal horn. Means ± SEM are shown; n = 5 rats. The values from each rat represent the mean of the left and the right side of 2 to 3 adjacent coronal 25 μm sections. Two-tailed paired Student's t-test was used. *p < 0.05.

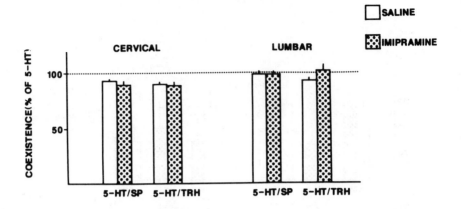

Fig. 3.6 The effects of chronic imipramine treatment on the coexisting 5-HT/SP and 5-HT/TRH nerve terminals in the medial part of the ventral horn of the cervical and lumbar enlargements of the spinal cord in the male rat. Means ± SEM are shown; $n = 7$ rats. The values from each rat represent the mean of the left and right side of 2 to 3 adjacent triplets of coronal 25 μm sections. The values are expressed as a percentage of the number of 5-HT nerve terminal profiles. No significant effects were found with a two-tailed paired Student's t test and the values are close to the 100% value.

3.3.2 Studies on GR Immunoreactivities

As seen in Figs. 3.7 and 3.8, chronic imipramine treatment increased the median grey-value of GR immunoreactive nuclear profiles in the medial and lateral part of group B3 and within the locus coeruleus. The number of GR immunoreactive profiles was not changed. As seen, no significant changes in the microdensitometric parameters were observed following chronic imipramine treatment in the CRF-rich region of the paraventricular hypothalamic nucleus or in the cortical areas analysed.

3.3.3 Biochemical Studies

The results showed that the ratio of 5-HIAA/5-HT was significantly reduced in the ventral horns of the cervical and lumbar enlargements, but the ratio was un-affected in the dorsal horn. However, the 5-HT levels were unaltered by the chronic imipramine treatment (Kitayama *et al.*, 1987a). Furthermore, chronic imipramine treatment produced a marked and significant rise of SP immuno-reactivity in the dorsal horn of the lumbar enlargement (Kitayama *et al.*, 1987a). Finally, the chronic imipramine treatment as evaluated two hours following the last administration did not significantly change the basal corticosterone and aldosterone serum levels (Kitayama *et al.*, 1987b).

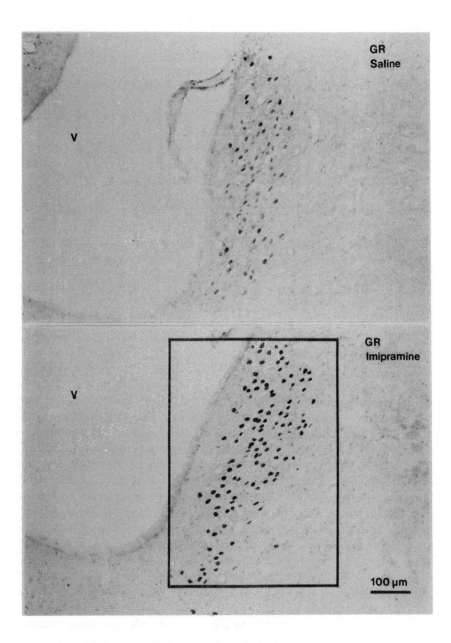

Fig. 3.7 Examples of photographs taken in paired sections of group A6 (locus coeruleus) (200 X). A = control; B = imipramine treatment. The sampled region for the measurement of GR immunoreactivity covers an area of 250 000 μm^2 (600 × 425 μm) which is enclosed by the solid line in the photograph. The centre of the region is situated 300 μm ventral from the lateral border of the fourth ventricle.

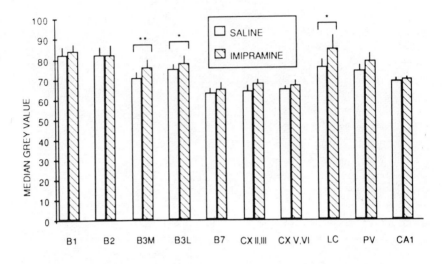

Fig. 3.8   Effects of imipramine treatment on the median grey value (*Md*) of GR immuno-reactivity in various brain regions. Means ± SEM are shown. Number of rats = 10 to 12. For further details, see Table 3.1.

3.4 Discussion

The studies on coexistence of 5-HT/SP and 5-HT/TRH immunoreactivity show that coexistence occurs in all 5-HT nerve terminals in the medial part of the ventral horn and also following acute and chronic imipramine treatment (Kitayama et al., 1987a). Furthermore, the available evidence indicates that chronic imipramine treatment in clinically relevant doses reduces 5-HT utilisation and increases SP immunoreactivity in the 5-HT, SP and TRH costoring nerve terminals of the ventral horn without modulation of TRH immunoreactivity. It seems possible that the increases of SP immunoreactivity observed following chronic imipramine treatment reflect a reduced release of SP from the costoring nerve terminals secondary to a reduced firing-rate (see also Iverfeldt et al., 1986). Thus, evidence for reduced 5-HT utilisation in the costoring terminals of the ventral horn was observed. These results indicate that in fact one of the 5-HT comodulators, in this case SP, can be affected by chronic imipramine treatment, indicating the possibility that also some of the 5-HT comodulators in the ascending 5-HT neurons, e.g. galinin, may be affected by chronic imipramine treatment and play a role in the therapeutic activity of antidepressant drugs. It is of substantial interest that SP immunoreactivity is differentially affected as compared with TRH immunoreactivity. The interpretation given above, that chronic imipramine treatment reduces SP release, is in line with previous findings, showing that chronic imipramine treatment produces a small reduction in the number of

5-HT binding sites and a small increase in their affinity as evaluated in spinal cord membranes (Fuxe *et al.*, 1984). Thus, such an effect can be related to reduced SP release, since *in vitro* SP counteracts the effects of chronic imipramine treatment on the 5-HT$_1$ receptor binding characteristics in spinal cord membranes by increasing the K_D and B_{max} values (Fuxe *et al.*, 1984; see also Agnati *et al.*, 1983).

Of substantial interest is the present observation that acute imipramine treatment can selectively increase the field-area, the total 5-HT immunoreactivity and the mean profile-area of the 5-HT immunoreactivity in group B7 without influencing the median grey-value. It seems possible that this action is related to an ability of acute imipramine treatment to depress the firing-rate of the 5-HT neurons of nucleus raphe dorsalis (Sheard *et al.*, 1972; dé Montigny and Blier, 1984). However, chronic treatment with zimelidine, which does not result in an inhibition of the firing-rate of the B7 neurons (Blier and de Montigny, 1980) also increases 5-HT immunoreactivity in group B7 (Fuxe *et al.*, 1984), as evaluated by means of semiquantitative microfluorometry (Fuxe *et al.*, 1985c). Thus, a reduction of firing-rate in the B7 5-HT neurons and increases in 5-HT immunoreactivity in group B7 are not always correlated. It is instead suggested that the demonstrated increase in the volume of the B7 5-HT cell bodies by acute imipramine treatment is caused by a reduction in fast axoplasma transport. Thus, it seems possible that the large number of [³H]-imipramine binding sites found in the membrane of the 5-HT nerve cell bodies and dendrites of group B7 (Fuxe *et al.*, 1983a) can control the activity of proteinkinases via regulation of the transmembrane ionic transport mechanisms (see Langer and Galzin, 1987). These proteinkinases may regulate the phosphorylation of the soluble protein translocators with ATPase activity, which are of importance in rapid anterograde axonal transport (Schnapp and Reese, 1986). Upon chronic imipramine treatment, no increase in the mean profile area of group B7 has been observed, owing possibly to a down-regulation of [³H]-imipramine binding sites in group B7, leading to restoration of activity in fast axonal transport. However, it also seems possible that the failure to see an increase in the mean profile-area of group B7 upon chronic imipramine treatment reflects the slowing of the general metabolic activity of the 5-HT cell bodies to match a maintained reduction in the fast axonal transport. The fact that upon chronic imipramine treatment it was possible to observe increases in 5-HT immunoreactivity in the lateral part of group B3 does not support the existence of a down-regulation of the [³H]-imipramine binding sites at the level of the 5-HT cell bodies. Also, chronic zimelidine treatment increases 5-HT immunoreactivity in group B7 (Fuxe *et al.*, 1983b). It is suggested that a major site for the antidepressant action of imipramine and zimelidine is the 5-HT cell bodies of group B7.

Group B1 is richly innervated by noradrenaline nerve terminals which may exert an inhibitory influence on 5-HT metabolism (Dahlström and Fuxe, 1964; 1965). This property of the group B1 may explain its ability to respond to acute imipramine treatment by a significant reduction of the mean profile-area of

5 HT immunoreactivity. These results may be explained by a preferential reduction of 5-HT synthesis in this group, especially since acute antidepressant treatment is known to reduce 5-HT synthesis and utilisation (Carlsson and Lindqvist, 1978; Corrodi and Fuxe, 1969; Svensson 1978). Such a reduction of 5-HT synthesis may in this case be caused mainly by the ability of imipramine to block noradrenaline uptake in the noradrenaline terminals innervating group B1.

It is also clear from the results reported that chronic imipramine treatment can produce a significant increase in GR immunoreactivity within the locus coeruleus and in the medial and lateral part of the 5-HT cell-group B3 without a change in corticosterone and aldosterone serum levels (see Kitayama *et al.*, 1987b). Thus, the number of GR in these neurons may be increased by chronic imipramine treatment. It seems possible that chronic imipramine treatment, by producing adaptive changes in monoamine receptor mechanisms in the locus coeruleus and in the 5-HT cell group B3, can influence the gene expression of the GR, so that the transcription rates are increased, leading to an increased formation of GR. Of substantial interest is the demonstration of increases of GR immunoreactivity in the locus coeruleus, since this noradrenergic system directly innervates all the cortical regions of the brain (see Fuxe *et al.*, 1970; Ungerstedt 1971; Olson and Fuxe, 1971). Furthermore, an important action of chronic treatment with imipramine is probably a down-regulation of cortical β-adrenergic receptors (Sulser, 1984), and GR in the cortical regions is of importance in the control of the decoding mechanism of the noradrenergic signal (Mobley and Sulser, 1980a, b). By increasing the amount of GR within the noradrenergic cell bodies of the locus coeruleus, chronic imipramine treatment may counteract the possible down-regulation of GR in the locus coeruleus by tonic hypersecretion of glucocorticoids as found in depressed patients. In this way the regulation by GR of the neuronal and metabolic activity of the locus coeruleus can be maintained, which may for instance be of importance for the appropriate regulation of noradrenaline and noradrenaline comodulator synthesis and release (see Fuxe *et al.*, 1985d).

Acknowledgements

This work has been supported by a grant (MH25504) from the NIH and by a grant (04X-715) from the Swedish Medical Research Council. For excellent secretarial assistance we are grateful to Anne Edgren.

References

Agnati, L. F., Benfenati, F., Cortelli, P., and D'Alessandro, R. (1978). A new method to quantify catecholamine stores visualized by means of the Falck-Hillarp technique. *Neurosci. Lett.*, **10**, 11–17.
Agnati, L. F., Fuxe, K., Locatelli, V., Benfenati, F., Zini, I., Panerai, A. E., El Etreby, M. F.,

and Hökfelt, T. (1982). Neuroanatomical methods for the quantitative evaluation of coexistence of transmitters in nerve cells. Analysis of the ACTH- and beta-endorphin immunoreactive nerve cell bodies of the mediobasal hypothalamus of the rat. *J. Neurosci. Methods*, 5, 203-14.

Agnati, L. F., Fuxe, K., Benfenati, F., Zini, I., and Hökfelt, T. (1983). On the functional role of coexistence of 5-HT and substance P in bulbospinal 5-HT neurons. Substance P reduces affinity and increases density of ^{3}H-5-HT binding sites. *Acta Physiol. Scand.*, 117, 299-301.

Agnati, L. F., Fuxe, K., Benfenati, F., Zini, I., Zoli, M., Fabbri, L., and Härfstrand, A. (1984). Computer assisted morphometry and microdensitometry of transmitter identified neurons with special reference to the mesostriatal dopamine pathway. I. Methodological aspects. *Acta Physiol. Scand.*, 120, 621-4.

Agnati, L. F., and Fuxe, K. (1985). *Quantitative Neuroanatomy in Transmitter Research*, Macmillan, Basingstoke.

Agnati, L. F., Fuxe, K., Zoli, M., Zini, I., Härfstrand, A., Toffano, G., and Goldstein, M. (subm.). Morphometrical and microdensitometrical studies on phenylethanolamine-N-methyltransferase and neuropeptide γ-immunoreactive neurons in the rostral medulla oblongata of the adult and old male rat. *Neuroscience*.

Björklund, A. J., Emson, P. C., and Gilbert, R. F. T. (1979). Further evidence for the possible coexistence of 5-hydroxytryptamine and substance P in medullary raphe neurones of rat brain. *Br. J. Pharmacol.*, 66, 112-13.

Blier, P., and de Montigny, C. (1980). Effect of chronic tricyclic antidepressant treatment on the serotoninergic autoreceptor. A microiontophoretic study in the rat. *Naunyn Schmiedeberg's Arch. Pharmacol.*, 314, 123-8.

Brodin, E., Peterson, L-L., Ögren, S-O., and Bartfai, T. (1984). Chronic treatment with serotonin uptake inhibitor zimelidine elevates substance P levels in the rat spinal cord. *Acta Physiol. Scand.*, 122, 209-11.

Carlsson, A., and Lindqvist, M. (1978). Effects of antidepressant agents on the synthesis of brain monoamines. *J. Neural. Transm.*, 43, 73-91.

Carroll, B. J. (1984). Dexamethasone suppression test for depression. In *Advances in Biochemical Psychopharmacology*, vol. 39, Raven, New York, 179-88.

Cintra, A., Fuxe, K., Härfstrand, A., Agnati, L. F., Miller, L. S., Greene, J. L., and Gustafsson, J.-A. (1986). On the cellular localization and distribution of estrogen receptors in the rat tel- and diencephalon using monoclonal antibodies to human estrogen receptor. *Neurochem. Int.*, 8, 585-95.

Corrodi, H., and Fuxe, K. (1969). Decreased turnover in central 5-HT nerve terminals induced by antidepressant drugs of the imipramine type. *Eur. J. Pharmacol.*, 7, 56-9.

Dahlström, A., and Fuxe, K. (1964). Evidence for the existence of monoamine containing neurons in the central nervous system. I. Demonstration of monoamines in the cell bodies of brainstem neurons. *Acta Physiol. Scand.*, 62, 1-55.

Dahlström, A., and Fuxe, K. (1965). Evidence for the existence of monoamine containing neurons in the central nervous system. II. Experimentally induced changes in the intraneuronal amine levels. *Acta Physiol. Scand.*, 64, 1-36.

de Montigny, C., and Blier, P. (1984). Effects of antidepressant treatments on 5-HT neurotransmission: Electrophysiological and clinical studies. *Adv. Biochem. Psychopharmacol.*, 39, 223-41.

Fuxe, K., Hökfelt, T., and Ungerstedt, U. (1970). Morphological and functional aspects of central monoamine neurons. *International Review of Neurobiology*. Academic, New York, 13, 93-126.

Fuxe, K., Calza, L., Benfenati, F., Zini, I., and Agnati, L. F. (1983a). Quantitative autoradiographic localization of ^{3}H-imipramine binding sites in the brain of the rat: Relationship to ascending 5-hydroxytryptamine neuron systems. *Proc. Natl. Acad. Sci.*, 80, 3836-40.

Fuxe, K., Agnati, L. F., Andersson, K., Calza, L., Benfenati, F., Zini, M., Battistini, N., Köhler, C., Ögren, S.-O., and Hökfelt, T. (1983b). In Ackenheil, M., and Matussek, N. (eds.), *Special Aspects of Psychopharmacology*, Expansion Scientifique Française, Paris, 13-32.

Fuxe, K., Ögren, S.-O., Benfenati, F., and Agnati, L. F. (1984). In Usdin, E., Asberg, M., Bertilsson, L., and Sjöqvist, F. (eds.), *Frontiers in Biochemical and Pharmacological*

Research in Depression, Raven, New York, 271–84.

Fuxe, K., Wikström, A.-C., Okret, S., Agnati, L. F., Härfstrand, A., Yu, Z.-Y., Granholm, L., Zoli, M., Vale, W., and Gustafsson, J.-A. (1985a). Mapping of glucocorticoid receptor immunoreactive neurons in the rat tel- and diencephalon using a monoclonal antibody against rat liver glucocorticoid receptor. *Endocrinology*, 177, 1803–12.

Fuxe, K., Härfstrand, A., Agnati, L. F., Yu, Z.-Y., Cintra, A., Wikström, A.-C., Okret, S., Cantoni, E., and Gustafsson, J.-A. (1985b). Immunocytochemical studies on the localization of glucocorticoid receptor immunoreactive nerve cells in the lower brain stem and spinal cord of the male rat using a monoclonal antibody against rat live glucocorticoid receptor. *Neurosci. Lett.*, 60, 1–6.

Fuxe, K., Agnati, L. F., Zoli, M., Härfstrand, A., Grimaldi, R., Bernardi, P., Camurri, M., and (1985c). In Agnati, L. F., and Fuxe, K. (eds.), *Quantitative Neuroanatomy in Transmitter Research*, Macmillan, Basingstoke, 331–48.

Fuxe, K., Agnati, L. F., Zoli, M., Härfstrand, A., Grimaldi, R., Bernardi, P., Camurri, M. and Goldstein, M. (1985d). In Agnati, L. F., and Fuxe, K. (eds.), *Quantitative Neuroanatomy in Transmitter Research*, Macmillan, Basingstoke, 157–74.

Hallman, H., Jonsson, G. and Sundström, E. (1984). Effects of the noradrenaline neurotoxin DSP4 on monoamine neurons and their transmitter turnover in rat CNS. *J. Neural Transm.*, 60, 89–102.

Härfstrand, A., Fuxe, K., Cintra, A., Agnati, L. F., Zini, I., Wikström, A.-C., Okret, S., Yu, Z.-Y., Goldstein, M., Steinbusch, H., Verhofstad, A., and Gustafsson, J.-A. (1986a). Glucocorticoid receptor immunoreactivity in monoaminergic neurons of rat brain. *Proc. Natl. Acad. Sci.*, 83, 9779–83.

Härfstrand, A., Fuxe, K., Agnati, L. F., Eneroth, P., Zini, I., Zoli, M., Andersson, K., von Euler, G., Terenius, L., Mutt, V., and Goldstein, M. (1986b). Studies on neuropeptide γ-catecholamine interactions in the hypothalamus and in the forebrain of the male rat. Relationship to neuroendocrine function. *Neurochem. Int.*, 8, 355–76.

Hökfelt, T., Ljungdahl, A., Steinbusch, H., Verhofstad, A., Nilsson, G., Brodin, E., Pernow, B., and Goldstein, M. (1978). Immunohistochemical evidence of substance P-like immunoreactivity in some 5-hydroxytryptamine-containing neurons in the rat central nervous system. *Neuroscience*, 3, 517–38.

Iverfeldt, K., Peterson, L.-L., Brodin, E., Ögren, S.-O., and Bartfai, T. (1986). Serotonin type-2 receptor mediated regulation of substance-P release in the ventral spinal cord and the effects of chronic antidepressant treatment. *Arch. Pharmacol.*, 333, 1–6.

Johansson, O., Hökfelt, T., Pernow, B., Jeffcoate, S. L., White, N., Steinbusch, H. W. B., Verhofstad, A. A. L., Emson, P. C., and Spindel, E. (1981). Immunohistochemical support for three putative transmitters on one neuron: Coexistence of 5-hydroxytryptamine, substance P- and thyrotropin releasing hormone-like immunoreactivity in medullary neurons projecting to the spinal cord. *Neuroscience*, 6, 1857–81.

Kitayama, I., Jansson, A. M., Fuxe, K., Agnati, L. F., Cintra, A., Ögren, S.-O., Härfstrand, A., Eneroth, P., Tsutsumi, T., Jonsson, G., Steinbusch, H. W. M., and Visser, T. J. (1987a). Effects of acute and chronic treatment with imipramine on 5-hydroxytryptamine nerve cell groups and on bulbospinal 5-hydroxytryptamine/substance P/thyrotropin releasing hormone immunoreactive neurons in the rat. A morphometric and microdensitometric analysis. *J. Neural Transm.*

Kitayama, I., Jansson, A. M., Cintra, A., Fuxe, K., Agnati, L. F., Ögren, S.-O., Härfstrand, A., Eneroth, P., and Gustafsson, J.-A. (1987b). Effects of chronic imipramine treatment on glucocorticoid receptor immunoreactivity in various regions of the rat brain. Evidence for selective increases of glucocorticoid receptor immunoreactivity in the locus coeruleus and in the nucleus raphe magnus. *J. Neural. Transm.*

Langer, S. Z., and Briley, M. (1981). High affinity ^{3}H-imipramine binding: A new biological tool for studies in depression. *Trends Neurosci.*, 4, 28–31.

Langer, S. Z., and Galzin, A.-M. (1987). In Fuxe, K., and Agnati, L. F. (eds.), *Receptor-receptor interactions: a new intramembrane integrative mechanism*, Macmillan, Basingstoke, in press.

Mayer, G. S., and Shoup, R. E. (1983). Simultaneous multiple electrode liquid chromatographic-electrochemical assay for catecholamines, indolamines and metabolites on brain tissues. *J. Chromatography*, 255, 533–44.

Mobley, P. L., and Sulser, F. (1980a). Adrenal corticoids regulate sensitivity of noradrenaline receptor coupled adenylate cyclase in brain. *Nature*, **286**, 608–9.

Mobley, P. L., and Sulser, F. (1980b). Adrenal steroids affect the norepinephrine sensitive adenylate cyclase system in rat limbic forebrain. *Eur. J. Pharmacol.*, **65**, 321–3.

Nilsen, O. G., Toftgård, R., and Eneroth, P. (1980). Effects of acrylnitrile on rat liver cytochrome P-450, benzo(a)-pyrene metabolism and serum hormone levels. *Tox. Lett.*, **6**, 399–404.

Okret, S., Wikström, A.-C., Wrange, Ö., Andersson, B., and Gustafsson, J.-A. (1984). Monoclonal antibodies against the rat liver glucocorticoid receptor. *Proc. Natl. Acad. Sci.*, **81**, 1609–13.

Olson, L., and Fuxe, K. (1971). On the projections from the locus coeruleus noradrenaline neurons: the cerebellar innervation. *Brain Res.*, **28**, 165–71.

Schnapp, B. J., and Reese, T. S. (1986). New developments in understanding rapid axonal transport. *Trends Neurosci.*, **9**, 155–62.

Sheard, M. H., Zolovick, A., and Aghajanian, G. K. (1972). Effect of tricyclic antidepressant drugs. *Brain Res.*, **43**, 690–94.

Steinbusch, H. W. M., Verhofstad, A. A. J., and Joosten, H. W. J. (1978). Localization of serotonin in the central nervous system by immunohistochemistry. *Neuroscience*, **3**, 811–19.

Sterio, D. C. (1984). The unbiased estimation of number and sizes of arbitrary particles using the disector. *J. Microsc.*, **134**, 127–36.

Sulser, F. (1984). In *Advances in Biochemical Psychopharmacology*, vol. 39, Raven, New York, 249–61.

Svensson, T. H. (1978). Attenuated feed-back inhibition of brain serotonin synthesis following chronic administration of imipramine. *Naunyn Schmiedeberg's Arch. Pharmacol.*, **302**, 115–18.

Ungerstedt, U. (1971). Stereotaxic mapping of the monoamine pathways in the rat brain. *Acta Physiol. Scand.*, **367**, 1–48.

Visser, T. J., and Klootwijk, V. (1981). Approaches to a markedly increased sensitivity of the radioimmunoassay for the thyrotropin-releasing hormone by derivatization. *Biochem. Biophys. Acta*, **673**, 454–66.

Zoli, M., Agnati, L. F., Fuxe, K., Zini, I., Merlo Pick, E., Grimaldi, R., Härfstrand, A., Wikström, A. C., and Gustafsson, J.-A. (1987). Morphometrical and microdensitometrical studies on phenylethanolamine-*N*-methyltransferase and neuropeptide γ-immunoreactive nerve terminals and on glucocorticoid receptor immunoreactive nerve cell nuclei in the paraventricular hypothalamic nucleus in adult and old male rats. *Neuroscience*, submitted.

4

Molecular Interactions of Antidepressants with the Serotonergic Receptor 5-HT$_{1D}$ Coupled to a High-affinity Adenylate Cyclase Activity: Importance of the Site Labelled by [3H]-Minaprine

G. Fillion, S. Dufois, C. Fayolle, M. P. Fillion, P. Oudar and P. Barone

4.1 Introduction

Several neurochemical theories of major affective disorders have been presented during the last decades. Initially, the fact that patients treated with reserpine developed symptoms which resemble certain forms of depression suggested that biogenic amines may play an important role in the disease (Freis, 1954; Achor *et al.*, 1955; Muller *et al.*, 1955; Lemieux *et al.*, 1956). It is known that reserpine depletes brain tissues not only in dopamine and in noradrenaline but also in serotonin (5-hydroxytryptamine, 5-HT) (Pletscher *et al.*, 1956); therefore the hypothesis has been proposed that depression might be related to a deficit in those amines, and, in particular, may involve 5-HT metabolite disturbances (Coppen, 1967; Murphy *et al.*, 1978; van Praag, 1982). However, Crow *et al.* (1984) did not observe any changes in serotonin metabolites in individuals committing suicide.

Various studies have also examined the neurotransmitter receptors which were potentially involved in that pathology. In particular, the recognition sites for biogenic amines have been determined either by classical biochemical approaches or by autoradiography using post-mortem human brain tissues in normal or depressed individuals (Wander *et al.*, 1986).

In parallel, many studies have been designed to examine the molecular and cellular mechanisms of action of antidepressant drugs. Interesting observations have been reported: long-term antidepressant treatment induced a down-regulation of β-adrenergic receptors (Schildkraut et al., 1967; Banerjee et al., 1977; Kellar et al., 1981; Maggi et al., 1980; Peroutka and Snyder, 1980; Sugrue, 1983) which was probably coupled with a subsensitivity of noradrenaline-induced adenylate cyclase activation (Sulser et al., 1978; Charney et al., 1981; Garcha et al., 1985). These results suggested a prominent role of β-adrenergic receptors. However, all tricyclic antidepressants did not induce these effects (Mishra et al., 1980; Sugrue, 1983), suggesting that the β-receptor down-regulation was presumably not a basic phenomenon in the mechanism of action of antidepressants. Other amine receptors might be involved in antidepressant activities (see Sugrue, 1983): e.g. 5-HT receptors have been extensively studied with regard to antidepressant activity. The classical theory postulated that antidepressants act as uptake inhibitors or as inhibitors of monoamine oxidases, thus possibly leading after long-term treatments to the regulation of the number of 5-HT receptors. The results presented in the literature do not allow a precise conclusion as to a particular mechanism, since long-term antidepressant treatments have led to various and contradictory results (see Sugrue, 1983). The variety of these results might be explained by the presence of multiple subclasses of 5-HT sites, possibly regulated in different ways by antidepressant treatments.

The fact that some antidepressants of the new generation are devoid of any inhibiting effect on the uptake of neurotransmitters, or that they specifically inhibit 5-HT or NA uptake, suggested that a mechanism different from a single presynaptic action was likely. A direct effect of antidepressants at the serotonergic postsynaptic receptor site was suggested by several authors (Ogren et al., 1979; Aprison and Hintgen, 1981; Fillion and Fillion, 1981; Fuxe et al., 1983). Therefore, it might be useful to summarise briefly the present situation concerning the 5-HT receptors. Indeed, a number of results have led to the concept of a variety of serotonergic receptors. A recent review by Bradley et al. (1986) has tentatively proposed a classification for these receptors: three classes of receptors exist corresponding to 5-HT$_1$, 5-HT$_2$ and 5-HT$_3$ receptors. The last class is involved in peripheral physiological phenomena inhibited very low concentrations of cocaine or cocaine derivatives; the 5-HT$_3$ binding site has not yet been observed. 5-HT$_2$ receptors are responsible for physiological responses in the periphery and in the central nervous system (in particular the 5-HT behavioural syndrome); the corresponding binding site is labelled by antagonists with a nanomolar affinity and by 5-HT itself with a low affinity (μM). The 5-HT$_1$ sites possess a high affinity (nM) for [^{3}H]-5-HT; these sites are divided into pharmacologically distinct subclasses, 5-HT$_{1A}$, 5-HT$_{1B}$ and 5-HT$_{1C}$. We demonstrate herein the existence of a 5-HT$_{1D}$ subclass related to the stimulation of an adenylate cyclase activity.

Finally it has been shown, in addition to these different classes, that a site was able to recognise [^{3}H]-5-HT with an intermediate affinity (10 to 15 nM)

(Fillion *et al.*, 1976, 1979; Segawa *et al.*, 1979; Whitaker-Azmitia and Azmitia, 1986).

In the present chapter, we report experimental results illustrating the direct interaction of antidepressants with a particular functional serotonergic receptor (5-HT$_{1D}$) coupled with a high-affinity serotonin-stimulated adenylate cyclase. The interaction mechanism may involve a specific receptor labelled by [^{3}H]-minaprine, an antidepressant devoid of any activity on monoamine (including 5-HT) uptake (Bizière *et al.*, 1985; Worms *et al.*, 1986).

4.2 Material and Methods

4.2.1 Tissue Preparation

Male Sprague-Dawley rats (180 to 230 g) were sacrificed by decapitation and their brains dissected on ice. Cerebral tissue was homogenised in an ice-cold buffer (30 mg tissue per ml) containing tris-HCl (5 mM), pH 7.4, sucrose (0.32 M), EGTA (2 mM), phenylmethylsulfonylfluoride (PMSF) (0.1 mM) and aprotinin (5 units/l), using a Potter glass–Teflon homogeniser. The homogenate was centrifuged for 5 min at 4 °C and 1000 g. The resulting pellet was resuspended and recentrifuged. Supernatants were added and centrifuged for 5 min at 20 000 g; the resulting pellet was resuspended and lysed under magnetic stirring for 1 h in a cold tris-HCl buffer (5 mM), pH 8.2, containing EGTA (2 mM) and protease inhibitors (PMSF 0.1 mM, aprotinin 5 units/l). Membranes were centrifuged (20 000 g for 10 min) resuspended in the same buffer and incubated for 10 min at 37 °C, to remove endogenous 5-HT.

4.2.2 Binding Assays

Membranes were resuspended in a tris-HCl buffer (50 mM), pH 7.4, containing pargyline (1 μM) and when specified (see text) ascorbate (0.1%) and CaCl$_2$ (4 mM). The aliquots of the membranal material were incubated at 22 °C for 30 min, in the presence of [^{3}H]-5-HT or [^{3}H]-minaprine. Spiperone (1 μM), propranolol (3 μM) or increasing concentrations of the tested drugs were added as indicated in the text. The non-specific binding was defined in the presence of unlabelled 5-HT (0.1 mM). The aliquots were filtered under vacuum through a Whatman GF/B filter and washed twice with a 5 ml ice-cold tris-HCl buffer (50 mM). Radioactivity was measured by liquid scintillation in OCS (New England Nuclear) (4 ml).

Thin-layer chromatography (TLC) has been used to test the purity of [^{3}H]-5-HT and whether, under our experimental conditions, oxydative processes led to degraded metabolites. Tritiated 5-HT was assayed using a TLC system, cellulose F 254 DC Alufolian plates (Merck); the solvent consisted of butanol–acetic acid–water (25 : 5 : 10). Samples (25 μl of 1 μM solution) were spotted without warming and the migration was performed in the dark. The solvent front was usually situated at 18 cm from the depot. Chromatograms were analysed using a radioactivity scanner coupled to a microcomputer. Each band was analysed for 5 minutes. Tritiated 5-HT incubated for 30 min at 22 °C in the usual incubation medium except for membrane material corresponded to a single major peak (95 to 99%) of radioactivity characterised by a very similar R_F (0.43) to the one observed for native [^{3}H]-5-HT (R_F = 0.41). In the presence of membrane material, the same pattern was observed for the chromatogram; no oxidised metabolites could be detected (a full study is in preparation).

4.2.3 Adenylate Cyclase Activity Measurements

In this study, adenylate cyclase activity was evaluated through the production of cyclic adenosine monophosphate (cyclic AMP) in cortical tissue preparation.

The membrane preparation was diluted (16 times) and centrifuged for 10 min at 20 000 g; the corresponding pellet was resuspended in a tris–HCl buffer (50 mM), pH 7.4, containing Mg^{2+} (4 mM) EGTA (0.5 mM) and isobutylmethyl-xanthine (IBMX) (0.1 mM). The adenylate cyclase activity was determined at 30 °C for 10 min in an incubation mixture containing: adenosine triphosphate (ATP) (1 mM); guanosine triphosphate (GTP) (0.1 mM), creatine phosphate (20 mM) and creatine phosphokinase (0.2 mg/ml). The reaction was initiated by the addition of membrane (1 to 1.2 mg/ml final protein concentration) and stopped by boiling for 4 min and addition of ethanol (1 ml) which was also used to extract cyclic AMP. Samples were cooled down in ice and lyophilised. The resulting solid extract was resuspended in NaH_2PO_4 (0.2 M), $NaClO_4$ (0.1 M), pH 5, and methanol (10% v/v) and centrifuged for 10 min at 5000 g. The supernatant was chromatographed using an HPLC technique (C 18 reversed-phase column 250 × 4 mm; ID particle size 5 μm), with an isocratic elution (mobile phase: NaH_2PO_4 (0.2 M), $NaClO_4$ (0.1 M), pH 5, and methanol (10% v/v)). Cyclic AMP was quantified by u.v. detection at 254 nM.

During measurement of the effect of various drugs on the 5-HT-induced adenylate cyclase activation, the tested drug was added in the medium prior to the 5-HT.

4.2.4 Protein Measurements

Proteins were measured according to the method described by Lowry *et al.* (1951).

4.2.5 Drugs

[^{3}H]-5-HT (24.4 Ci/mmol) was obtained from New England Nuclear. The following compounds were generous gifts: TVXQ 7821 (Dr Traber, Troponwerke GmbH), MDL 72222 (Dr Fozard, Merrell Dow Research Institute), mesulergine

(Dr Palacios, Sandoz), mianserin (Dr Erhard, Organon), 5-carboxyamidotrypt-amine (5-CONH$_2$ T) (Dr Humphrey, Glaxo). The other drugs were obtained from commerical sources.

4.3 Results

4.3.1 Existence of a Serotonergic Receptor Coupled to a High-affinity Adenylate Cyclase

4.3.1.1 Binding of [^{3}H]-5-HT to a High-affinity Site 5-HT$_{1D}$ Different From 5-HT$_{1A}$, 5-HT$_{1B}$ or 5-HT$_{1C}$

The binding of [^{3}H]-5-HT was assayed at low concentrations (1 to 6 nM) using rat brain cortex tissue; it corresponded to the well-known 5-HT$_1$ population of sites (Bennett and Snyder, 1976; Fillion et al., 1976; Bradley et al., 1986) able to bind [^{3}H]-5-HT with a high affinity (K_D = 3 nM). To determine the presence of 5-HT$_{1A}$ and 5-HT$_{1B}$ in the preparation, binding assays have been performed successively in the presence of spiperone (1 μM), which at that concentration inhibits specifically 5-HT$_{1A}$ sites, and propranolol (3 μM), which suppresses 5-HT$_{1B}$ sites. Mesulergine (0.1 μM) was also used to inhibit 5-HT$_{1C}$ sites. The binding of [^{3}H]-5-HT to 5-HT$_1$ in the presence of these antagonists was still signifi-cant (40% of the total reversible binding), indicating the existence of a population of sites different from the 5-HT$_{1A}$, 5-HT$_{1B}$ or 5-HT$_{1C}$ sites. Under these con-ditions, [^{3}H]-5-HT bound to 5-HT$_1$-like sites, which apparently correspond to a single population of sites having a high affinity constant (K_D = 2.3 ± 0.9 nM) (Fig. 4.1 (top)). The corresponding number of sites was close to 0.09 pmol/mg protein. The pharmacological analysis showed that these sites correspond to the 5-HT$_1$ class; moreover, it indicated that they were not 5-HT$_2$ or 5-HT$_3$, as ketanserin and MDL 72222, 5-HT$_2$ and 5-HT$_3$ antagonists, respectively, only poorly displaced the observed [^{3}H]-5-HT binding.

The binding of [^{3}H]-5-HT to these sites was displaced by agonists such as 5-HT, bufotenin and trifluoromethylphenylpiperazine (TFMPP). 5-methoxytryp-tamine was 100 times less potent, whereas 8-hydroxy-2-dipropylaminotetralin (8-OH-DPAT, a 5-HT$_{1A}$ agonist) was only a weak displacer.

LSD inhibited the binding with a K_i close to 10 nM, whereas methysergide and dihydroergotamine were 10 to 50 times less potent; mianserin and cinanserin were active only in the micromolar range. TVXQ 7821 was poorly recognised (K_i = 10 μM). RU 24969 displaced [^{3}H]-5-HT with a low affinity (K_i = 5 μM), although in some assays part of the binding was inhibited with a high affinity (K_i close to 10 nM). The latter part corresponded presumably to remaining 5 HT$_{1A}$ and/or $_{1B}$ sites selectively inhibited by RU 24969 as shown by Hamon et al. (1984).

GTP, at concentrations which are known to interact with adenylate cyclase activity, reduced the binding of [^{3}H]-HT observed in the presence of spiperone (1 μM) and propranolol (3 μM).

4.3.1.2 Adenylate Cyclase Activation Induced by 5-HT

The activation of adenylate cyclase was determined by measuring the cyclic AMP production with an HPLC method. 5-HT was able to increase the production of cyclic AMP with two distinct activities.

The basal rate of the cyclic AMP production (the mean of 15 experiments) was 340 ± 78 pmoles of cyclic AMP/mg protein min^{-1}. Nanomolar concentrations of 5-HT activated adenylate cyclase; the cyclic AMP production could reach 460 ± 24 pmoles of cyclic AMP per mg protein min^{-1}, which corresponded to an increase of 40 ± 14% ($n = 15$) of the basal activity (Fig. 4.1 (bottom)). The apparent activation constant (K_{act}) was 0.8 ± 0.05 nM (Fig. 4.1 (bottom)). A second type of activation was induced by 5-HT at higher concentrations with an apparent activation constant (K_{act} = 0.15 μM). The cyclic AMP production increased to 650 ± 20 pmol/mg protein min^{-1}, which coresponded to 50 ± 6% ($n = 10$) of the basal level after the subtraction of the nanomolar activity. Like 5-HT, serotonergic agonists also stimulated the high-affinity adenylate cyclase activity. Thus the tryptamine derivatives = 5-methoxy-N,N-dimethyltryptamine (5-MeO-N,N-DMT), bufotenin and 5-methoxytryptamine (5-MeOT) showed K_{act} of 1.5 ± 0.8, 0.5 ± 0.02 and 2 ± 0.3 nM respectively, and trifluoromethyl phenylpiperazine (TFMPP) showed a K_{act} of 0.62 ± 0.04 nM (Table 4.1). LSD, as a partial agonist, had also a stimulating effect, corresponding to a high-affinity constant (pK_{act} = 9.22 ± 0.02).

Spiperone (10 nM to 1 mM), propranolol (up to 0.1 mM) or mesulergine (up to 0.1 μM) did not modify the maximal effect of nanomolar concentrations of 5-HT nor the apparent activation constant.

On the contrary, spiperone (1 μM) and propranolol (3 μM) markedly inhibited the enzymatic activation induced by high concentrations of 5-HT. These results showed that the two types of cyclase activation were distinct. 8-OH-DPAT also had a 5-HT-like effect at higher concentrations (K_{act} = 69 ± 21 nM). This effect was inhibited by spiperone (1 μM).

The cyclase activation induced by nanomolar concentrations of 5-HT was inhibited by serotonergic antagonists (dihydroergotamine, methysergide, cinanserin, mianserin). This activation was not inhibited by naloxone, phenoxybenzamine or phentolamine, thus indicating that the effect was mediated by 5-HT receptors.

4.3.1.3 5-HT$_1$ Binding Sites and High-affinity Adenylate Cyclase Activity Induced by 5-HT

The correlation existing between the effects of various drugs on the adenylate

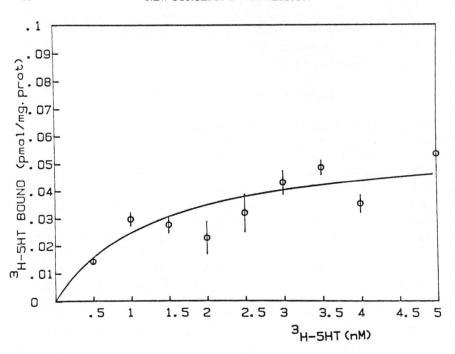

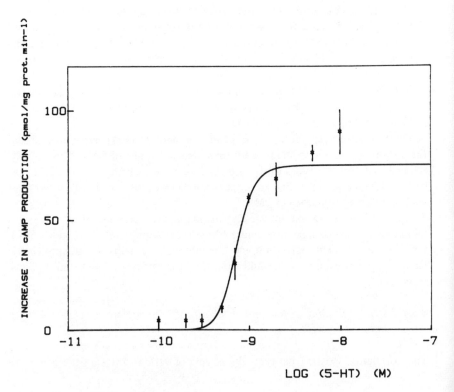

Table 4.1   Effects of various drugs on adenylate cyclase activity and 5-HT$_{1D}$ binding on membranal fractions in rat cortex

Agonists	Adenylate cyclase pK_{act}	5-HT$_{1D}$ Binding pK_I
5-HT	9.06 ± 0.06	8.40 ± 0.25
Bufotenin	9.30 ± 0.02	8.71 ± 0.15
8-OH-DPAT	6.82 ± 0.04	5.31 ± 0.23
5-MeOtryptamine	8.70 ± 0.06	7.21 ± 0.11
TFMPP	6.80 ± 0.02	5.59 ± 0.17
LSD	9.22 ± 0.02	7.37 ± 0.22
5-CONH$_2$-tryptamine	5.31 ± 0.05	6.22 ± 0.08
RU 2469	6.15 ± 0.12	5.32 ± 0.26
Antagonists	pK_I	pK_I
Methysergide	7.40 ± 0.30	7.04 ± 0.12
Metitepin	7.63 ± 0.22	5.27 ± 0.14
Cinanserin	6.10 ± 0.30	6.11 ± 0.19
TVXQ 7821	6.30 ± 0.17	4.88 ± 0.20
Ketanserin	5.00 ± 0.11	4.94 ± 0.22
Dihydro-ergotamine	8.13 ± 0.04	7.98 ± 0.16
MDL 72222	4.40 ± 0.02	4.00 ± 0.29
Mesulergine	5.00 ± 1.30	5.50 ± 0.11
Mianserin	6.58 ± 0.05	5.98 ± 0.07
Cocaine	< 4	< 4

Binding experiments were performed on cortical homogenates prepared as described in section 4.2.

The aliquots of the homogenate were incubated at 22 °C for 30 min in the presence of [^{3}H]-5-HT (2 nM), spiperone (1 μM), propranolol (3 μM) and increasing concentrations of the tested substances (10^{-10} to 10^{-4} M); the binding of [^{3}H]-5-HT was determined as described in section 4.2.

The effect of agonists and antagonists on the serotonergic activation of the adenylate cyclase was determined after incubating the membrane fractions in the presence of the tested substances. Data are expressed as pK_{act} (−log concentration of agonist which produces half-maximal stimulation) and pK_I. The latter values were calculated from IC$_{50}$ derived from computer analysis.

The values are presented as the means ± SEM of at least three independent experiments for each tested drug.

Fig. 4.1 (opposite) Binding of [^{3}H]-5-HT and stimulation of adenylate cyclase activity in membranes prepared from rat cerebral cortex.

(Top) Binding of [^{3}H]-5-HT was measured as described in section 4.2 using [^{3}H]-5-HT (1 to 6 nM) in the presence of spiperone (1 μm) and propranol (3 μM).

Each point corresponds to the mean (± SEM) of triplicate determinations. The calculation of the binding parameters was done by computerised non-linear regression analysis. In the present assay, a single class of binding site was observed with the following parameters: K_D = 1.38 nM, B_{max} = 0.059.

(Bottom) Stimulation of the adenylate cyclase was measured using a 10-min incubation of the membrane preparation in the presence of increasing concentrations of 5-HT (0.1 to 10 nM final concentration). In this assay, the basal cyclic AMP production was 250 pmol/mg protein min^{-1}. The maximal activation was observed with an activation constant K_{act} = 0.7 nM; it was equivalent to a 32% increase of the basal level. Each point of the curve refers to the mean ± SEM of triplicate determinations.

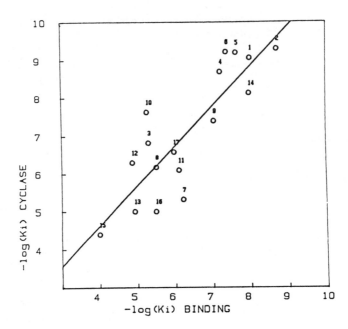

Fig. 4.2 The correlation between pK_i values calculated from binding experiments and pK_{act} and pK_i values calculated from adenylate cyclase activation experiments. The drugs studied in the corresponding assays were:

1 5-HT	10 metitepine
2 bufotenin	11 cinanserin
3 8-OH-DPAT	12 TVXQ 7821
4 5-MeOtryptamine	13 ketanserin
5 TFMPP (trifluoromethylphenylpiperazine)	14 dihydroergotamine
6 LSD (lysergic acid diethylamide)	15 MDL 72222
7 5 CONH$_2$-tryptamine	16 mesulergine
8 RU 24969	17 mianserin
9 methysergide	

A linear regression analysis was used to calculate the parameters of the curve. The correlation coefficient was $r = 0.85$; Student's t-test gave $t = 6.07$ and $p < 0.001$.

cyclase activity and their inhibition constant (K_i) when displacing [^{3}H]-5-HT from the 5-HT$_{1D}$ sites is illustrated in Fig. 4.2. The values of the correlation coefficient (0.85) strongly suggest the existence of a link between these binding sites and the enzyme activity.

4.3.2 Interaction of Antidepressants with the 5-HT$_1$ Binding and with the High-affinity Adenylate Cyclase Activity

4.3.2.1 Effect of Antidepressants on [^{3}H]-5-HT Binding In Vitro

The binding of [^{3}H]-5-HT to cortex was measured in tissue homogenate in the absence of selective serotonergic antagonist; therefore, the whole 5-HT$_1$ specific serotonergic binding was observed. The dissociation constant was K_D = 3.13 ± 0.24 nM and the corresponding B_{max} was 0.108 ± 0.033 pmol/mg protein.

Tricyclic (chlorimipramine, doxepine), tetracyclic (mianserin) and other antidepressants (nomifensin, trazodone) at 10 nM were able to increase the binding of [^{3}H]-5-HT to its sites. The increase was modest but significant, varying from 20 to 30% of the control for the weakest effects to 80 to 100% for the highest effects. The affinity constant was not significantly modified or a slight shift toward a lower affinity (K_D = 6 to 7 nM) was observed. The concentrations of the various antidepressants used in these experiments (10 nM) were never able to decrease the binding of [^{3}H]-5-HT.

On the other hand, non-antidepressant drugs were not able to induce the same enhancement of [^{3}H]-5-HT binding: they had no effect or slight decreased the binding when tested at high concentrations (10 to 100 μM) (diazepam, clonazepam, clobazam, haloperidol).

4.3.2.2 Effect of Antidepressants on the Adenylate Cyclase Activation Induced by 5-HT

The effects of antidepressants have been tested *in vitro* using cortical membranal preparations isolated from rat brain. It was observed that at a low concentration (10 nM) antidepressants stimulated the effect of 5-HT on the adenylate cyclase activity. Chlorimipramine, mianserin and citalopram favoured the serotonergic activation; the apparent activation constant was decreased (K_{act} control = 0.8 nM, K_{act} antidep. = 0 : 2 nM). The V_{max} of the enzymatic reaction was either not modified or slightly increased (+ 20 to 30%). However, for higher concentrations, the opposite effect was observed; the antidepressants inhibited the adenylate cyclase activation induced by 5-HT.

Therefore, it appears that antidepressants are able, *in vitro*, to interact with the binding of [^{3}H]-5-HT to its 5-HT$_1$ sites, and, in parallel, modify the adenylate cyclase activity specifically induced by 5-HT. These effects presumably correspond to a direct interaction of antidepressants with the 5-HT receptor.

4.3.3 Binding of [^{3}H]-Minaprine to Membrane Preparation

Minaprine is a 6-phenyl-3-aminopyridazine derivative and represents a new class of antidepressant (Worms *et al.*, 1986) (Fig. 4.3). It has been shown in clinical

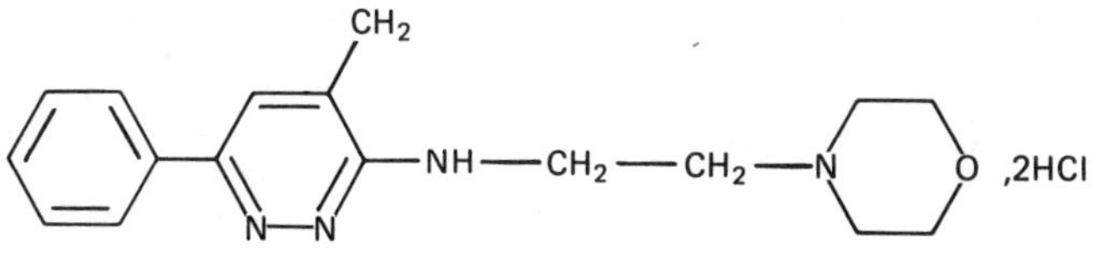

Fig. 4.3 Minaprine: formula.

studies to be more effective than placebo (Jouvent *et al.*, 1984) and comparable to imipramine (Bohacek *et al.*, 1986) or maprotiline (Radmayr *et al.*, 1986).

4.3.3.1 Biochemical Characteristics

The binding of [³H]-minaprine has been tested using the same membrane material as that used for [³H]-5-HT binding studies. A similar medium was used (tris-HCl buffer, pH 7.4, containing aprotinin 5 units/1, PMSF 0.1 mM and EGTA 2 mM). In a first series of experiments it was shown that the binding equilibrium was observed after 10 to 15 min at 22 °C, at a 10 nM concentration; the saturation curve observed for [³H]-minaprine at increasing concentration (1 to 30 nM) corresponded to a saturable, reversible binding having an affinity constant close to 8 nM (K_D = 8.3 ± 2). It appeared to correspond to a non-michaelian interaction under the experimental conditions used in that series of assays.

Figure 4.4 illustrates the binding curve observed in rat brain cortex. Similar results have been obtained using horse brain cortex. The apparent number of

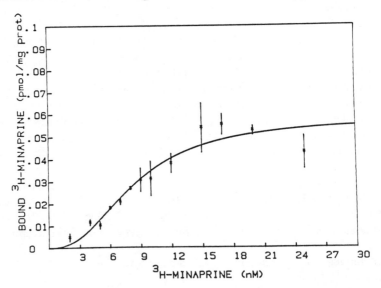

Fig. 4.4 Binding of [³H]-minaprine to membrane material isolated from rat hippocampus. Binding assays were performed as described in section 4.2. A crude mitochondrial fraction isolated from hippocampus was lysed for 1 h using a hypoosmotic tris–HCl buffer, centrifuged at 20 000g. The resulting pellet was incubated at 37 °C for 10 min and centrifuged for 10 min at 20 000g, resuspended in tris–HCl buffer, pH 7.4, and washed. Aliquots of the membrane material were incubated at 22 °C for 30 min in the presence of [³H]-minaprine (1 to 25 nM final concentration). Free and bound radioactivities were separated by rapid filtration and the binding measured using liquid scintillation counting.

The binding parameters were calculated from a nonlinear regression analysis using a computerised calculation.

In the present assay, the affinity constant was K_D = 8.35 nM and the B_{max} = 0.057 pmol/mg protein. Each point is the mean ± SEM of triplicate determinations.

sites was 0.057 ± 0.015 pmol/mg protein in rat brain cortex and corresponded to a lower value in horse cortical tissue (0.025 ± 0.09 pmol/mg protein).

The regional distribution of these sites in rat brain was heterogenous for the three areas tested. The hippocampus (0.065 ± 5 pmol/mg protein) corresponded to the highest capacity of binding. The striatum contained 0.032 ± 0.005 pmol/mg protein.

4.3.3.2 Pharmacological Characteristics

In a series of preliminary assays, the pharmacological properties of that binding have been examined. It was shown that low concentrations of antidepressants (10^{-9} to 5.10^{-8} M) decreased markedly the binding of [^{3}H]-minaprine. The fact that [^{3}H]-minaprine bound in a non-michaelian manner, presumably positively co-operative, did not allow a precise determination of the mode of interaction, in particular whether it represented a competitive displacement or not. Nevertheless, chlorimipramine, indalpine, fluoxetine, mianserin and amoxapine inhibited the binding of [^{3}H]-minaprine, whereas non-antidepressant drugs (TVXQ 7821, haloperidol, 8-OH-DPAT or clonazepam) were ineffective (Fig. 4.5).

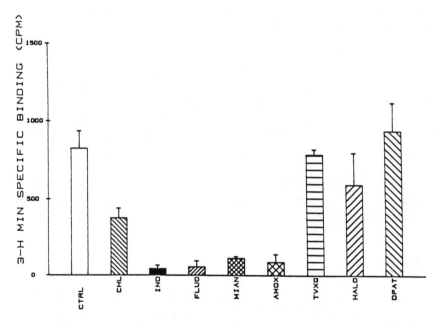

Fig. 4.5 Effects of various drugs on [^{3}H]-minaprine binding. Binding of [^{3}H]-minaprine (10 nM) has been measured in the presence of various drugs (50 nM). Membrane material was incubated for 30 min at 22°C and bound and free radioactivities were separated by rapid filtration. The bars shown the means $\pm$ SEM of the binding of [^{3}H]-minaprine in the presence of the studied drugs in at least three independent assays. CTRL, control; CHL, chlorimipramine; IND, indalpine; FLUO, fluoxetine; MIAN, mianserin; AMOX, amoxapin; TVXQ, TVXQ 7821; HALO, haloperiodol; DPAT, 8-OH-DPAT.

It was of interest to examine whether 5-HT had any interaction with the binding of [^{3}H]-minaprine. The amine clearly interacted with the binding of the antidepressant. In particular, at nanomolar concentrations 5-HT was able to decrease [^{3}H]-minaprine binding. This effect was observed precisely at 5-HT concentrations which correspond to the affinity constant of the amine for its 5-HT$_1$ site.

Methysergide did not modify the binding of [^{3}H]-minaprine up to 1 μM, but reversed the inhibiting effect of nanomolar concentrations of 5-HT. This result strongly suggests that the recognition site for [^{3}H]-minaprine is distinct from that for [^{3}H]-5-HT.

Therefore the binding interaction shown in these experiments presumably involves two distinct sites, possibly localised on the same protein macromolecule. These two sites appear related through a complex mechanism affecting the macromolecule(s), i.e. an allosteric mechanism which remains to be demonstrated.

4.3.4 Effect of Chronic Antidepressant Treatments on the Binding of [^{3}H]-5-HT to the 'Intermediate Affinity' Site (K_D = 10 to 15 nM)

The binding of [^{3}H]-5-HT in brain tissue not only involves 5-HT$_1$ sites having a nanomolar affinity for the amine (K_D = 3 to 4 nM), but also involves a population of sites characterised by a somewhat lower affinity (K_D = 10 to 15 nM) (Robaut et al., 1985).

An examination has been made of the effects of a chronic treatment with antidepressants or electroconvulsive shock (ECT) upon the binding of [^{3}H]-5-HT to these sites. Chronic treatment with mianserin, trimeprimine and chlorimipramine, or with repeated (6 times) ECT in rat, resulted in an increase of the binding of [^{3}H]-5-HT. The enhancement was an increase in B_{max} (60 to 110%) without significant changes in the affinity constant (Table 4.2).

Citalopram had no effect, suggesting that a different mechanism is involved for this substance (data not shown). It is also interesting to note that this phenomenon has been obtained in hippocampus, but was not observed in parallel assays using cortex (Table 4.2) or striatum preparations.

4.4 Discussion

A multiplicity of binding types for 5-HT has already been demonstrated (5-HT$_1$, 5-HT$_2$, 5-HT$_3$), and three subtypes of 5-HT$_1$ sites have been proposed (Bradley et al., 1986): it appears that a new 5-HT$_{1D}$ subtype plays an important role in the serotonergic function, as it is probably related to a physiological effector, namely an adenylate cyclase activated by 5-HT with a high apparent affinity constant. The good correlation observed for the potencies of a series of drugs to inhibit the binding of [^{3}H]-5-HT to the 5-HT$_{1D}$ site and those able to modify the high-affinity adenylate cyclase strongly suggests that the observed serotonergic

Table 4.2   Effect of chronic antidepressant treatment on the binding of [^{3}H]-5-HT to the site of intermediate affinity in rat brain

Treatment	n	$K_D \pm$ SEM (nM)	$B_{max} \pm$ SEM (pmol/mg protein)	Variation % of control B_{max}
Hippocampus				
Untreated rats	(12)	8.22 ± 4.14	0.29 ± 0.05	—
NaCl	(18)	7.61 ± 3.12	0.32 ± 0.05	—
Sham ECT	(3)	8.40 ± 4.92	0.30 ± 0.01	—
ECT	(3)	15.80 ± 7.17	0.63 ± 0.20	+ 110
Chlorimipramine	(3)	11.30 ± 3.78	0.50 ± 0.05	+ 56
Mianserin	(3)	14.30 ± 5.3	0.51 ± 0.05	+ 59
Cortex				
Untreated rats	(6)	10.56 ± 6.95	0.34 ± 0.09	—
NaCl	(18)	14.12 ± 8.25	0.35 ± 0.12	—
Sham ECT	(6)	9.27 ± 3.1	0.27 ± 0.04	—
ECT	(6)	8.04 ± 4.51	0.25 ± 0.07	− 26
Chlorimipramine	(6)	12.30 ± 7.69	0.38 ± 0.18	+ 8
Mianserin	(6)	7.65 ± 2.61	0.30 ± 0.02	− 14

Effect of various chronic antidepressant treatments on binding of [^{3}H]-5-HT to 5-HT (intermediate affinity) binding sites in the rat hippocampus and cortex.

Rats were injected daily with chlorimipramine, mianserin, trimeprimine (10 mg/kg) or with the vehicle (NaCl) for two weeks. ECT was delivered every second day for two weeks. Animals were sacrificed 48 hours after the last injection.

entity corresponds to a functional serotonergic receptor (Fillion *et al.*, submitted). Previously it had been shown that the adenylate cyclase activity stimulated by nanomolar concentration of 5-HT was not presynaptically located on serotonergic terminals but was likely to be present on postsynaptic neurones (Fillion *et al.*, 1979).

Moreover, several experimental results suggest that this receptor may play a role in the modulatory activity of 5-HT upon other neurotransmitters functions. Thus 5-HT has been reported to inhibit the release of acetylcholine from superfused brain striatum (Vizi *et al.*, 1981; Gillet *et al.*, 1985; Maura and Raiteri 1986).

The results presented here indicate that antidepressants interact with a 5-HT$_1$ serotonergic receptor. *In vitro*, they increase the high-affinity binding, and in parallel they favour the stimulating effect of 5-HT on the high-affinity adenylate cyclase activity. Previously we reported similar findings indicating that antidepressants favoured the high-affinity binding for [^{3}H]-5-HT (Fillion and Fillion, 1981); the interpretation of these results led to the hypothesis that antidepressants induced a structural change of the 5-HT receptor protein from a low-affinity to a high-affinity conformation. It is interesting to note that antidepressants in low concentrations also favour the adenylate cyclase stimulation induced by 5-HT. Moreover, this interaction is observed *in vitro* and therefore corresponds to a direct effect of antidepressant at the 5-HT receptor. This effect is not a competitive phenomenon at the serotonergic site, i.e. it corresponds to an increase in B_{max} without a significant change in the affinity constant for the high-affinity binding; a competitive effect would correspond to a decrease in binding with a change in K_D. Therefore these results indicate that antidepressants are able to modify the binding of 5-HT to its receptors using a distinct but interacting site.

Note also that typical and atypical antidepressants interact with the $5-HT_1$ binding, suggesting that their effect is initially independent of a presynaptic uptake-inhibiting property. It is also interesting to note that MAO inhibitors do not interact directly at the postsynaptic receptor; it is not excluded that they would act at that level after long-term treatment.

Assuming that antidepressants act at a site distinct from the 5-HT binding site, it was interesting to study the characteristics of that site. Minaprine, a substance whose antidepressant activities have been reported (Radmayr et al., 1986; Bohacek et al., 1986) was available. It is devoid of any presynaptic effects, i.e. it does not inhibit NA, DA or 5-HT uptake. Moreover, it could be labelled by tritium (Bizière et al., 1985; Worms et al., 1986).

Sites labelled by [^{3}H]-minaprine have been observed in various areas of the rat brain. Although the distribution studies have still to be extended, the number of these sites appears to be higher in the hippocampus than in the cortex or striatum. The binding parameters correspond to a high-affinity constant which is precisely in the range of minaprine concentrations (10 nM) which interact with the 5-HT receptor.

The fact that typical and atypical antidepressants displace [^{3}H]-minaprine with a high apparent affinity constant, whereas non-antidepressant drugs do not, suggests an interesting role for this population of sites in the molecular mechanisms involved in the effects of antidepressant drugs. This role has now to be more precisely defined.

It is of particular interest to note that 5-HT is able to interact with the binding of [^{3}H]-minaprine. Indeed, 5-HT, at nanomolar concentrations which precisely correspond to the affinity constant of 5-HT for the $5-HT_{1D}$ receptor, clearly displaces the binding of this antidepressant. These results favour the hypothesis suggesting that distinct but interacting sites bind 5-HT and antidepressants respectively. The molecular mechanism which regulates the interaction phenomenon is not yet elucidated. Among speculations which could be presented, the existence of allosteric regulations cannot be excluded. Moreover, as previously suggested by Fuxe et al. (1983), cotransmitters like substance P might be involved in the effects of antidepressants after a long-term treatment; it is not excluded that these endogenous substances may directly affect the interactions between antidepressants and 5-HT function. This hypothesis has to be tested.

All the results described in the present report are related to 'in-vitro' experiments. Assuming that they represent interaction phenomena between antidepressants and 5-HT receptors they can, at most, correspond only to acute effects of antidepressants. Then the relevance of the phenomenon to the clinical property of antidepressants has to be questioned, as it is well known that antidepressant properties are related to the 'therapeutic delay' of the treatment. Among the multiple observations which have been reported following long-term antidepressant treatments it has not been possible to determine a particular phenomenon corresponding to a basic mechanism involved in the therapeutic effect of the antidepressants. Many changes which have been reported (see Sugrue, 1983) may proceed from indirect and non-relevant effects. The complexity of the results leads to conclusions that generally suggest that several types of neurotransmitters are involved.

The interest of the observations reported above concerning molecular interactions of antidepressants in acute experiments resides in the fact that these effects may be linked to measurable and specific regulations observed after long-term treatments. Indeed, the long-term blockade or stimulation of functional receptors generally corresponds to reactive changes involving regulation mechanisms.

Thus the present observations present a double interest: the first is fundamental and suggests that 5-HT$_{1D}$ receptors may play a crucial role in the pathology of depression; the second, therapeutic, tends to suggest that the sites binding [^{3}H]-minaprine represent a possible initial and basic target of antidepressant drugs. These results may help to open a new direction of research for the design of original chemical structures efficient in the treatment of depression.

References

Achor, R. W P., Hanson, N. O., and Grifford, R. W. (1955). Hypertension treated with *Rauwolfia serpentina* (whole root) and with reserpine. *J. Am. Med. Ass.*, 159, 841–5.

Aprison, M. W., and Hintgen, J. N. (1981). Hypersensitive serotonergic receptors: a new hypothesis for one subgroup of unipolar depression derived from an animal model. In Haber, B., Gabay, S., Issidorides, D. R., and Alivisator, S. (eds.), *Serotonin: Current Aspect of Neurochemistry and Function*, Plenum, New York, 627–55.

Banerjee, S. P., Kuhn, L. S., Riggi, S. J., and Chander, S. K. (1977). Development of beta-adrenergic receptor subsensitivity by antidepressants. *Nature*, 268, 455–6.

Bennett J. P., and Snyder, S. H. (1976). Serotonin and lysergic acid diethylamide binding in rat brain membranes: relationship to postsynaptic serotonin receptors. *Mol. Pharmacol*, 12, 373–89.

Bizière, K., Worms, P., Kan, J. P., Mandel, P., Garattini, S., and Roncucci, R. (1985). Minaprine, a new drug with antidepressant properties. *Drugs Exp. Clin. Res.*, 11, 831–40.

Bohacek, N., Ravic, M., and Bizière, K. (1986). A double-blind comparison of minaprine and imipramine in the treatment of depressed patients. *J. Clin. Psychopharmacol.*, 6, 320–1.

Bradley, P. B., Engel, G., Feniuk, W., Fozard, J. R., Humphrey, P. P. A., Middlemiss, D. N., Mylecharane, E. J., Richardson, B. P., and Saxena, P. R. (1986). Proposals for the clarification and nomenclature of functional receptors for 5-HT. *Nueropharmacol.*, 25, 563–76.

Charney, D. S., Menkes, D. B., and Heninger, G. R. (1981). Receptor sensitivity and the mechanism of action of antidepressant treatment. *Archs gen. Psychiat.*, 38, 1160–5.

Coppen, A. J. (1967). The biochemistry of affective disorders. *Br. J. Psychiat.*, 113, 1407–11.

Crow, T. J., Cross, A. J., Cooper, S. J., Deakin, J. F. W., Ferrier, I. N., Johnson, J. A., Joseph, M. H., Owen, F., Poulter, M., Lofthouse, R., Corsellis, J. A. N., Chambers, D. R., Blessed, G., Perry, E. K., Perry, R. H., and Tomlinson, B. E. (1984). Neurotransmitter receptors and monoamine metabolites in the brains of patients with alzheimer-type dementia and depression, and suicides. *Neuropharmacol.*, 23, 1561–9.

Fillion, G., Fillion, M. P., Spirakis, C., Bahers, J. M., and Jacob, J. (1976). 5-hydroxytryptamine binding to synaptic membranes from rat brain. *Life Sci.*, 18, 65–74.

Fillion, G., Beaudoin, D., Rousselle, J. C., Deniau, J. M., Fillion, M. P., Dray, F., and Jacob, J. (1979). Decrease of [³H]-5-HT high affinity binding and 5-HT adenylate cyclase activation after kainic acid lesion in rats brain striatum. *J. Neurochem.*, 33, 567–70.

Fillion, G., and Fillion, M. P. (1981). Modulation of affinity of postsynaptic serotonin receptors by antidepressant drugs. *Nature*, 292, 349–51.

Freis, E. (1954). Mental depression in hypertensive patients treated for long periods with large doses of reserpine. *New Eng. J. Med.*, 251, 1006–8.

Fuxe, K., Ogren, S. O., Agnati, L. F., Benfenati, F., Fredholm, B., Andersson, K., Zini, I., and Eneroth, P. (1983). Chronic antidepressant treatment and central 5-HT synapses. *Neuropharmacol.*, 22, 389–400.

Garcha, G., Smokcum, R. W. J., Stephenson, J. D., and Weeramantri, T. B. (1985). Effects of some atypical antidepressants of beta-adrenoreceptors binding and adenylate cyclase activation in the rat forebrain. *Eur. J. Pharmacol.*, 108, 1–7.

Gillet, G., Ammor, S., and Fillion, G. (1985). Serotonin inhibits acetylcholine release from rat striatum slices: Evidence for a presynaptic receptor mediated effect. *J. Neurochem.*, 45, 1687–91.

Hamon, M., Bourgoin, S., Gozlan, H., Hall, M. D., Goetz, C., Artaud, F., and Horn, A. S. (1984). Biochemical evidence for the 5-HT agonist properties of PAT (8-hydroxy-2-(Di-n-Propyl-amino)tetralin) in the rat brain. *Eur. J. Pharmac.*, 100, 263–76.

Jouvent, R., Lancrenon, S., Patay, M., and Widlocher, D. A. (1984). A controlled study: minaprine versus placebo in inhibited depressed out-patients. In *Recent Advances in Psychiatric Treatment*. First European Conference. Vienna.

Kellar, K. J., Cascio, C. S., Butler, J. A., and Kurtzke, R. N. (1981). Differential effects of electroconvulsive shock and antidepressant drugs on serotonin₂ receptors in rat brain. *Eur. J. Pharmacol.*, 69, 515–18.

Lemieux, G., Davignon, A., and Genest, J. (1956). Depressive states during rauwolfia therapy for arterial hypertension. A report of 30 cases. *Can. Med. Ass. J.*, 74, 522–26.

Lowry O. H., Rosebrough, N. S., Farr, A. L., and Randall, R. J. (1951). Protein measurement with the Folin phenol reagent. *J. Biol. Chem.*, 193, 265–75.

Maggi, A., U'Prichard, D. C., and Enna, S. J. (1980). Differential effects of antidepressant treatment on brain monoaminergic receptors. *Eur. J. Pharmacol.*, 61, 91–8.

Maura, G., and Raiteri, M. (1986). Cholinergic terminals in rat hippocampus possess 5-HT$_{1B}$ receptors mediating inhibition of acetylcholine release. *Eur. J. Pharmacol.*, 129, 333–7.

Mishra, R., Janowsky, A., and Sulser, F. (1980). Action of mianserin and zimelidine on the norepinephrine receptor coupled adenylate cyclase system in brain: subsensitivity without reduction in beta-adrenergic receptor binding. *Neuropharmacol.*, 19, 983–7.

Muller, L., Pryor, W. W., Gibbons, J. E., and Orgain, E. S. (1955). Depression and anxiety occurring during rauwolfia therapy. *J. Am. Med. Ass.*, 159, 836–9.

Murphy, D. L., Camphell, I., and Costa, J. L. (1978). Current status of the indoleamine hypothesis of the affective disorders. In Lipton, M. A., Dimascio, A., and Killam, K. F. (eds.), *Psychopharmacology: A Generation of Progress*. Raven, New York, 1235–47.

Ogren, S. O., Fuxe, K., Agnati, L. F., Gustafsson, J. A., Jonsson, G., and Holm, A. C. (1979). Reevaluation of the indoleamine hypothesis of depression. Evidence for a reduction of functional activity of central 5-HT systems for antidepressant drugs. *J. Neurol. Trans.*, 46, 85–103.

Peroutka, S. J., and Snyder, S. H. (1980). Regulation of serotonin 5-HT₂ receptors labelled with [³H]-spiroperidol by chronic treatment with the antidepressant amitriptyline. *J. Pharmacol. Exp. Ther.*, 215, 582–7.

Pletscher, A., Shore, P. A., and Brodie, B. B. (1956). Serotonin as a mediator of reserpine action in the brain. *J. Pharmacol.*, 116, 84–9.

Radmayr, K , Bizière, K., Bentel, U. (1986). Minaprine and maprotiline in endogenous depression. A double-blind controlled study. *Clin. Trials J.*, 23, 100–9.

Robaut, C., Fillion, M. P., Dufois, S., Fayolle-Bauguen, C., Rousselle, J. C., Gillet, G., Benkirane, S., and Fillion, G. (1985). Multiple high affinity binding sites for 5-hydroxytryptamine: a new class of sites distinct from 5-HT$_1$ and S$_2$. *Brain Res.*, 346, 250–62.

Schildkraut, J. J., Schamberg, S. M., Breese, G. R., and Kopin, I. J. (1967). Norepinephrine metabolism and drugs used in the affective disorders: a possible mechanism of action. *Am. J. Psychiatry*, 124, 600–5.

Segawa, T., Mizuta, T., and Nomura, Y. (1979). Modification of central 5-hydroxytryptamine binding sites in synaptic membranes from rat brain after long-term adminstration of tricyclic antidepressants. *Eur. J. Pharmacol.*, 58, 75–83.

Sugrue, M. F. (1983). Chronic antidepressant therapy and associated changes in central monoaminergic receptor functioning. *Pharmacology and Therapeutics*, 21, 1–33.

Sulser, F., Vetulani, J., and Mobley (1978). Mode of action of antidepressant drugs. *Biochem. Pharmacol.*, 27, 257–61.

Van Praag, H. M. (1982). Neurotransmitters and CNS disease: depression. *Lancet*, ii, 1264–7.

Vizi, E. S., Harsing, G., and Zsilia, G. (1981). Evidence of the modulatory role of serotonin in acetylcholine release from striatal interneurons. *Brain Research*, 212, 89–9.

Wander T. J., Nelson, A., Haruo, O., and Richelson, E. (1986). Antagonism by antidepressants of serotonin S$_1$ and S$_2$ receptors of normal human brain in vitro. *Eur. J. Pharmacol.*, 132, 115–21.

Whitaker-Azmitia, P., and Azmitia, E. C. (1986). [^{3}H]-5-hydroxytryptamine binding to brain astroglial cells: differences between intact and homogenized preparation and mature and immature cultures. *J. Neurochem.*, 46, 1186–89.

Worms, P., Kan, J. P., Perio, A., Wermuth, G. G., Bizière, K., and Roncucci, R. (1986). Profil pharmacologique d'un psychotrope original, la minaprine: comparaison avec six antidépresseurs de référence. *J. Pharmacol.* (Paris), 17, 126–38.

5

In-vivo Identification of the Serotonin (5-HT) Autoreceptor in the Rat Suprachiasmatic Nucleus (SCN)

K. F. Martin and C. A. Marsden

There is considerable evidence that disturbances in the mechanisms controlling circadian rhythms play an important part in the aetiology of depression (Hallonquist *et al.*, 1986). For instance, Carrol *et al.* (1976) reported that 88% of bipolar and 50% of unipolar depressives demonstrated early escape from overnight dexamethasone suppression. Wehr *et al.* (1983) suggested that this phenomenon could be explained by a resetting of the 'biological clock'. Thus if, as they observed, circadian rhythms of depressives are phase-advanced compared with control subjects, one might expect an early escape since the drug will have been given later in the circadian cycle of the depressives.

The consensus of opinion in the literature is that circadian rhythms are controlled by a system within the central nervous system (CNS), the suprachiasmatic nuclei (SCN) of the hypothalamus being the site of major importance (for review see Moore, 1983). Unfortunately, little evidence is available to suggest the mechanisms involved within the SCN by which control is exerted. The SCN receives a rich serotoninergic innervation and circumstantial evidence has led to the hypothesis that serotonin (5-HT may play a part in the control of circadian rhythms (Wirz-Justice *et al.*, 1982). There is, however, little information about the control of 5-HT neuronal activity in the SCN.

Several different recognition sites have been identified on neurones within the central nervous system for the neurotransmitter serotonin (5-HT). The initial binding studies of Peroutka and Snyder (1979) revealed two sites which they designated 5-HT_1 and 5-HT_2 receptors. More recent evidence has suggested that the 5-HT_1 binding site can be further subdivided into 5-HT_{1A} and 5-HT_{1B} subtypes (Pedigo et al., 1981; Schellman et al., 1984) and that certain 5-HT agonists bind preferentially to a particular subtype. For instance, the tetralin derivative 8-hydroxy-2-(n-dipropylamino) tetralin (DPAT) is reported to be a selective ligand for the $5\text{-}HT_{1A}$ binding site (Middlemiss and Fozard, 1983) and the piperidinyl indole derivative 5-methoxy-3-[1,2,3,6-tetrahydro-4-pyridinyl]-1H indole (RU 24969) has been proposed as a selective ligand for the $5\text{-}HT_{1B}$ site (Sills et al., 1984; Doods et al., 1985). It has generally been accepted on the basis of in-vitro studies that the pre-junctional 5-HT autoreceptor is a $5\text{-}HT_1$ receptor (for review see Moret, 1985). However there has been controversy as to whether it is a $5\text{-}HT_{1A}$ or $5\text{-}HT_{1B}$ receptor.

We have investigated the regulation of 5-HT release and metabolism in the SCN using carbon fibre microelectrodes implanted into the SNC and have studied the effects of selective 5-HT receptor agonists and antagonists on the height of the indole peak recorded in an attempt to identify the receptors involved in the regulation of 5-HT release in these nuclei. Our carbon fibre microelectrodes are particularly suited for use in small nuclei like the SCN as the tip diameter is only 20 μm.

In common with other workers (Faradji et al., 1983) we have found that the size of the oxidation peak recorded at approximately +0.3 V ('peak 3') increased as the electrode was lowered towards the SCN. However, there was a noticeable decrease upon entry, a phenomenon we have used as an indicator of electrode position prior to histological verification (Martin and Marsden, 1986a).

Intraperitoneal injection of the $5\text{-}HT_1$ receptor agonist RU 24969 was associated with a transient rise in the size of peak 3 (5-HIAA) followed by a prolonged and marked decrease two hours after administration. This decrease lasted for up to six hours and was similar to the results obtained by Brazell et al. (1985) where a working electrode or an intracerebral dialysis probe was implanted in the frontal cortex. The decrease in the size of peak 3 was probably the result of decreased 5-HT release and subsequent metabolism to 5-HIAA following stimulation of the $5\text{-}HT_1$ autoreceptor that is thought to regulate 5-HT release (Middlemiss, 1985, 1984). The non-selective 5-HT receptor antagonist methiothepin prevented the RU 24969-mediated decrease in peak 3 while on its own the antagonist increased the size of peak 3 by 20 ± 2%, 75 min after administration, but the selective $5\text{-}HT_2$ receptor antagonist ketanserin did not affect the response to RU 24969 (Martin and Marsden, 1986a). These results are similar to those obtained in the frontal cortex with RU 24969 and the 5-HT antagonist metergoline and support the view that 5-HT release in the SCN is under the control of a $5\text{-}HT_1$ autoreceptor (Brazell et al., 1985). RU 24969 not only decreases 5-HIAA but also 5-HT in the frontal cortex when extracellular levels are monitored using intracerebral dialysis (Brazell et al., 1985).

DPAT, when given intravenously, decreased 5-HT metabolism in the SCN such that 60 minutes after DPAT administration, peak 3 height had decreased by 33 ± 3% (Marsden and Martin, 1986; Fig. 5.1; $n = 4$). This finding is in general agreement with those of Hjorth et al. (1982), who reported that DPAT dose-

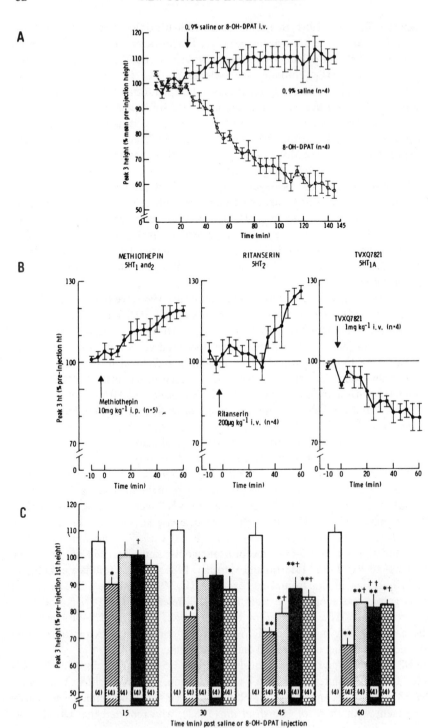

dependently decreased tissue levels of 5-HIAA. In order to determine the 5-HT receptor involved in this response to DPAT we administered methiothepin 5 minutes before DPAT. At a dose which would block the response to RU 24969 (Martin and Marsden, 1986a) we were able only to attenuate the response to DPAT. The selective $5\text{-}HT_2$ receptor antagonist ritanserin also appeared to attenuate the response to DPAT; however, when its own effect on peak 3 height was taken into consideration (20% increase 60 min post-administration) it became doubtful whether $5\text{-}HT_2$ receptors were involved in the response to DPAT.

In addition to DPAT, isapirone (TVX Q 7821) has been reported to be a selective ligand for the $5\text{-}HT_{1A}$ binding site (Dompert et al., 1985; Schuuman et al., 1984) where it is reported to have partial agonist properties (Martin et al., 1986). In our experimental protocol we observed that isapirone was able to block the effect of DPAT on peak 3 height recorded in the SCN, while it also had some agonist effects (Fig. 5.1). Thus we were able to conclude that the effects of DPAT involved $5\text{-}HT_{1A}$ receptors and also that isapirone may be a partial agonist at $5\text{-}HT_{1A}$ receptors (Marsden and Martin, 1986).

The cardiovascular responses to peripheral administration of DPAT have been suggested to involve α_2-adrenoceptors (Fozard and McDermott, 1985). In order to determine whether α_2-adrenoceptors were involved in the neurochemical responses to DPAT described above, we attempted to block the effects of DPAT with the selective α_2-adrenoceptor antagonist idazoxan (Doxey et al., 1983). Interestingly, at a dose which had no effect on peak 3 height alone, idazoxan completely abolished the response to DPAT (Fig. 5.2). These data indicated that the effects of i.v. DPAT involved not only $5\text{-}HT_{1A}$ receptors but also α_2-adrenoceptors.

To determine where these $5\text{-}HT_1$ receptor agonists were acting to decrease 5-HT release and metabolism in the SCN, i.e. in nerve-terminal region (the SCN)

Fig. 5.1 (opposite) (A) Effect of 0.9% w/v NaCl solution (saline 1 ml kg^{-1} i.v., •, n = 4) 8-hydroxy-2-(n-dipropylamino)tetralin (8OOH-DPAT, 0.1 mg kg^{-1} i.v., o, n = 4) on the height of peak 3 recorded in the suprachiasmatic nucleus (SCN). Each point represents the mean and the SEM is illustrated by the vertical lines.

(B) The effect of methiothepin (10 mg kg^{-1} i.p., n = 5) ritanserin (0.2 mg kg^{-1} i.v., n = 4) and TVXQ 7821 (1 mg kg^{-1} i.v., n = 4) on the height of peak 3 recorded in the SCN. Each point represents the mean and the SEM is also shown. Note the decrease in peak 3 height following injection TVXQ 7821.

(C) The effect of 0.9% w/v NaCl solution (saline 1 ml kg^{-1} i.v., open columns) 8-hydroxy-2-(n-dipropylamino)tetralin (8-OH-DPAT, 0.1 mg kg^{-1} i.v., hatched columns) on the height of peak 3 recorded in the SCN 15, 30, 45 and 60 min after their injection. The effect of administration of methiothepin (1 mg kg^{-1} i.v., stippled columns) ritanserin (0.2 mg kg^{-1}, solid columns) TVXQ 7821 (1 mg kg^{-1} i.v., honeycombed columns) 5 min before an injection of 8-OH-DPAT (0.1 mg kg^{-1} i.v.) is also shown. Each column represents the mean of 4 observations and the SEM is shown by the vertical lines. *p < 0.05, **p < 0.01 compared with saline. †p < 0.05, ††p < 0.01 compared with 8-OH-DPAT.

A

B

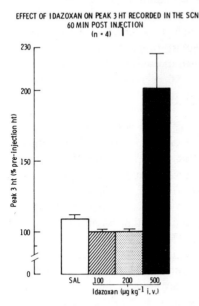

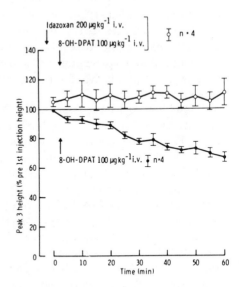

Fig. 5.2 (A) The effect of 0.9% w/v NaCl solution (saline 1 ml kg^{-1}, open columns) and idazoxan (0.1 mg kg^{-1} i.v., hatched columns; 0.2 mg kg^{-1} i.v., stippled columns and 0.5 mg kg^{-1} i.v., solid columns) on peak 3 height recorded in the suprachiasmatic nucleus (SCN). Each column represents the mean and the SEM is shown by the vertical lines. The number of animals in each group is shown in parentheses at the bottom of each column.

(B) The effect of idazoxan (0.2 mg kg^{-1} i.v., o, $n = 4$) 5 min before 6-hydroxy-2-(n-dipropylamino)tetralin (8-OH-DPAT, 0.1 mg kg^{-1} i.v.) and the effect of 8-OH-DPAT (0.1 mg kg^{-1} i.v., •, $n = 4$) on peak 3 height recorded in the SCN of the chloral hydrate anaesthetised rat. Each point represents the mean and the SEM is shown by the vertical lines.

or on the cell bodies (the dorsal raphe nucleus), we have administered RU 24969 and DPAT directly into both of these nuclei while recording from the SCN.

When RU 24969 was infused directly into the dorsal raphe in doses of up to 10 μg in 0.5 μl of saline, the size of the indole oxidation peak was unchanged. However, RU 24969 injected into the SCN contralateral to the one containing the recording electrode was associated with a dose-dependent decrease in the height of peak 3. The peak height decreased by 26 ± 7% one hour after 5 μg and by 81 ± 7% one hour after a further 5 μg (Fig. 5.3; Marsden and Martin, 1985a). These results strongly suggest that the 5-HT$_1$ receptor regulating 5-HT release and metabolism in the 5-HT nerve terminals of the SCN that RU 24969 acts upon is located on those terminals and not on the cell bodies within the dorsal raphe nucleus.

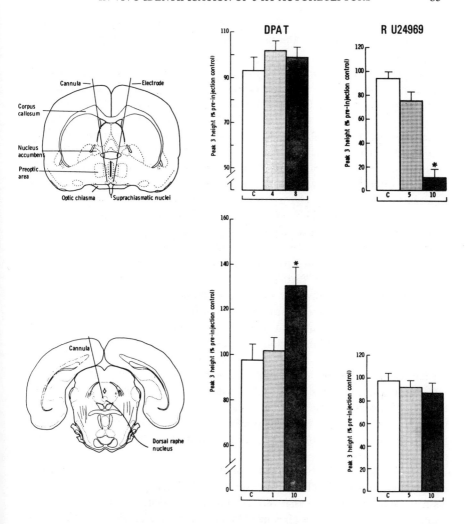

Fig. 5.3 Diagram illustrating the effect of infusion of DPAT or RU 24969 into the SCN (upper panels) or the DRN (lower panels) on peak 3 height recorded in the SCN one hour after infusion. The open histobars (labelled C) represent the height of peak 3 after infusion of saline. The numbers at the bottom of each histobar indicate the quantity of drug infused (μg) in 0.5 μl of saline over one minute. Each histobar represents the mean ± SEM of at least 4 observations. *$p < 0.05$ compared with appropriate saline control (Student's t-test).

The results obtained following local injection of DPAT into the SCN or in the dorsal raphe nucleus were in marked contrast to those obtained following local injection of RU 24969 described above. Infusion of DPAT (4 or 8 μg) into the SCN had no effect on the height of peak 3 recorded in the SCN (Fig. 5.3) (Marsden and Martin, 1985b). This observation led us to conclude that the presynaptic autoreceptor in the rat was in fact a 5-HT_{1B} receptor, a finding which is in agreement with the previously reported *in vitro* data (Middlemiss, 1984; Ennis, 1986).

Several groups have now reported that 5-HT_{1A} receptor agonists such as DPAT inhibit the firing of 5-HT neurones in the dorsal raphe nuclei (e.g. de Montigny *et al.*, 1984; Wilkinson, L. O., Abercrombie, E., Rasmussen, K., and Jacobs, B. L., in preparation 1987). On the basis of these findings and our own, following i.v. injection of DPAT described above, one might expect local infusion of DPAT into the dorsal raphe nuclei to be associated with a decrease in the height of peak 3 recorded in the SCN. However, we observed the exact opposite of this predicted effect. The lowest dose we used (1 μg) had no significant effects, whereas the highest dose (10 μg) was actually associated with a significant increase in peak 3 height (31 ± 8%, $n = 5$). Thus, although decreased serotonergic unit activity is probably associated with a decrease in 5-HT release, quite clearly this is not reflected by similar changes in 5-HT metabolism. Thus neurone firing may not be directly coupled to 5-HT metabolism in certain situations and this possibility is the subject of further investigations in our laboratory.

Finally, we have carried out behavioural studies to determine whether the 5-HT_{1B} receptors we have identified in the SCN are involved in the control of circadian rhythms. We continuously infused either saline (0.5 μl/h) or RU 24969 (2.5 μg in 0.5 μl/h) into the region of the SCN for 14 days while simultaneously monitoring the locomotor activity of the animal throughout the day–night cycle. We observed that the normal circadian pattern of activity was unaffected by an infusion of saline whereas the activity pattern of those rats which had received RU 24969 was abnormal, in that there appeared to be a loss of entrainment to the light–dark cycle (Martin and Marsden, 1986b). This pattern of activity across the circadian cycle resembled the disturbed circadian rhythms sometimes seen in depressed patients.

In conclusion, using *in vivo* voltammetry we have confirmed the *in vitro* observations that the 5-HT autoreceptor is of the 5-HT_{1B} subtype. In addition, we have obtained evidence that the serotonergic innervation of the SCN may be important in the control of circadian rhythms. This may provide a link between the apparently diverse hypotheses that have implicated 5-HT and circadian rhythm generating systems in the aetiology of affective disorder, and is worthy of further investigation.

Acknowledgements

KFM is a Wellcome Trust Research Fellow in Mental Health and CAM is a Wellcome Senior Lecturer. We thank the MRC for additional financial support. Generous supplies of DPAT (ICI plc), RU 24969 (Roussell-Uclaf), isapirone (Tropenwerke) and ritanserin (Janssen) are gratefully acknowledge.

References

Brazell, M. P., Marsden, C. A., Nisbet, A. P., and Routledge, C. (1985). The 5-HT receptor agonist RU 24969 decreases 5-hydroxytryptamine (5-HT) release and metabolism in the rat frontal cortex *in vitro* and *in vivo*. *Br. J. Pharmacol.*, 86, 209–18.

Carroll, B. J., Curtis, G. C., and Mendels, J. (1976). *Arch. Gen. Psychiat.*, 33, 1039–48.

de Montigny, C., Blier, P., and Chaput, Y. (1984). Electrophysiologically-identified serotonin receptors in the rat CNS. Effect of antidepressant treatment. *Neuropharmacology*, 23, 1511–20.

Dompert, W. U., Glaser, T., and Traber, J. (1985). [^{3}H]-TVX Q 7821: identification of 5-HT$_1$ binding sites as a target for a novel putative anxiolytic. *Naunyn-Schmiedeberg's Arch. Pharmacol.*, 328, 467–70.

Doods, H. N., Kalkman, H. O., Dejonge, A., Thooler, M. J. M. C., Wilffert, B., Timmermans, P. B. M. W. M., and Vanzwieten, P. (1985). Differential selectivities of RU 24969 and 8-OH-DPAT for the purported 5-HT$_{1A}$ and 5-HT$_{1B}$ binding sites, correlation between 5-HT$_{1A}$ affinity and hypotensive activity. *Eur. J. Pharmacol.*, 112, 363–70.

Doxey, J. C., Roach, A. G., and Smith, C. F. C. (1983). Studies on RX 781094: a selective, potent and specific antagonist of α_2-adrenoceptors. *Br. J. Pharmacol.*, 78, 489–505.

Ennis, C. (1986). The 5-HT autoreceptor in the rat hypothalamus resembles a 5-HT$_{1B}$ receptor. *Br. J. Pharmacol.*, 88, 370P.

Faradji, H., Cespuglio, R., and Jouvet, M. (1983). Voltammetric measurements of 5-hydroxyindole compounds in the suprachiasmatic nucleus: circadian fluctuations. *Brain Res.*, 279, 111–19.

Fozard, J. R., and McDermott, I. (1985). The cardiovascular response to 8-hydroxy-2-(di-n-propylamino) tetralin (8-OH-DPAT) in the rat. *Br. J. Pharmacol.*, 84, 69P.

Hallonquist, J. D., Goldberg, M. A., and Brandes, J. S. (1986). Affective disorders and circadian rhythms. *Can. J. Psychiatry*, 31, 259–72.

Hjorth, S., Carlsson, A., Lindberg, P., Sanchez, D., Wikstrom, H., Arvidssen, L.-E., Hacksell, U., and Nilsson, J. L. G. (1982). 8-Hydroxy-2-(di-n-propylamino) tetralin, (8-OH-DPAT) a potent and selective simplified argot congener with central 5-HT-receptor stimulating activity. *J. Neural. Trans.*, 55, 169–88.

Marsden, C. A., and Martin, K. F. (1985a). RU 24969 decreases 5-HT release in the SCN by acting on 5-HT receptors in the SCN but not the dorsal raphe. *Br. J. Pharmacol.*, 85, 219P.

Marsden, C. A., and Martin, K. F. (1985b). *In vivo* voltammetric evidence that the 5-HT autoreceptor is not of the 5-HT$_{1A}$ sub-type. *Br. J. Pharmacol.*, 86, 445P.

Marsden, C. A., and Martin, K. F. (1986). Involvement of 5-HT$_{1A}$ and α_2 receptors in the decreased 5-hydroxytryptamine release and metabolism in rat suprachiasmatic nucleus after intravenous 8-hydroxy-2-(n-dipropylamino) tetralin. *Br. J. Pharmacol.*, 89, 277–86.

Martin, K. F., and Marsden, C. A. (1986a). *In vivo* voltammetry in the suprachiasmatic nucleus of the rat: Effects of RU 24969, methiothepin and ketanserin. *Eur. J. Pharmacol.*, 121, 135–40.

Martin, K. F., and Marsden, C. A. (1986b). Pharmacological manipulation of the serotonergic input to the SCN – an insight into the control of circadian rhythms. *Ann. N.Y. Acad. Sci.*, 473, 542–5.

Martin, K. F., Mason, R., and McDougall, H. (1986). Electrophysiological evidence that isapirone (TVX Q 7821) is a partial agonist at 5-HT$_{1A}$ receptors in the rat hippocampus. *Br. J. Pharmacol.*, 89, 729P.

Middlemiss, D. N. (1984). 8-Hydroxy-2-(di-n-propylamino) tetraline is devoid of activity at the 5-hydroxytryptamine autoreceptor in rat brain. Implications for the proposed link between the autoreceptor and the [^{3}H]-5-HT recognition site. *Naunyn-Schmiedeberg's Arch. Pharmacol.*, 327, 18–22.

Middlemiss, D. N. (1985). The putative 5-HT$_1$ receptor agonist, RU 24969, inhibits the efflux of 5-hydroxytryptamine from rat frontal cortex slices by stimulation of the 5-HT autoreceptor. *J. Pharm. Pharmacol.*, 37, 434–7.

Middlemiss, D. N., and Fozard, J. R. (1983). 8-Hydroxy-2-(di-n-propylamino) tetralin discriminates between subtypes of the 5-HT recognition site. *Eur. J. Pharmacol.*, 90, 151–3.

Moore, R. Y. (1983). Organisation and function of a central nervous system circadian oscillator: the suprachiasmatic hypothalamic nuclei. *Fed. Proc.*, **42**, 2783–9.

Moret, C. (1985). Pharmacology of the serotonin autoreceptor. In Green, A. R. (ed.), *Neuropharmacology of Serotonin*. Oxford University Press, Oxford, 21–49.

Pedigo, N. W., Yamamura, H. J., and Nelson, D. L. (1981). Discrimination multiple [^{3}H]-5 hydroxytryptamine binding by neuroleptic spiperone in rat brain. *J. Neurochem.*, **36**, 220–6.

Peroutka, S. J., and Snyder, S. H. (1979). Multiple serotonin receptors: Differential binding of [^{3}H]-5 hydroxytryptamine, [^{3}H]-lysergic acid diethylamide and [^{3}H]-spiroperidol. *Mol. Pharmacol.*, **16**, 687–99.

Schnellman, R. G., Waters, S. J., and Nelson, D. L. (1984). [^{3}H]-5-Hydroxytryptamine binding sites: species and tissue variation. *J. Neurochem.*, **42**, 65–70.

Schuuman, T., Davies, M. A., Dompert, W. U., and Traber, J. (1984). TVX Q 7821: a new nonbenzodiazepine putative anxiolytic. *9th Int. Congr. Pharmacol.*, London, 1463.

Sills, M. A., Wolfe, B. B., and Frazer, A. (1984). Determination of selective and nonselective compounds for the 5-HT$_{1A}$ and 5-HT$_{1B}$ receptor subtypes in rat frontal cortex. *J. Pharmacol. exp. Ther.*, **231**, 480–7.

Wehr, T. A., Sack, D., Rosenthal, N., Duncan, W., and Gillin, J. C. (1983). Circadian rhythm disturbances in manic-depressive illness. *Fed. Proc.*, **42**, 2809–14.

Wirz-Justice, A., Groos, G. A., and Wehr, T. A. (1982). The neuropharmacology of circadian timekeeping in mammals. In Aschoff, J., Daan, S., and Groos, G. A. (eds.), *Vertebrate Circadian Systems, Structure and Physiology*, Springer, Berlin, 183–93.

6

Thyrotrophin-realeasing Hormone (TRH) and 5-Hydroxytryptamine (5-HT) Interactions and Their Involvement in the Pharmacology of Antidepressants

C. A. Marsden, C. Lighton, R. M. Edwards, K. Fone and G. W. Bennett

6.1 Summary

Several studies have demonstrated that both antidepressant drugs and electro-convulsive shock (ECS) treatment alter 5-hydroxytryptamine (5-HT) receptor number and responsiveness. Furthermore, the down-regulation of β-adrenoceptors produced by antidepressant treatments is dependent upon intact 5-HT neurones. There is, however, little information about the factors involved in the regulation of 5-HT receptor function. This chapter investigates the possible role of thyrotrophin-releasing hormone (TRH) in the long-term regulation of 5-HT receptors. TRH coexists with 5-HT and substance P in neurones innervating the ventral horn of the spinal cord. Lesions of the 5-HT neurones to the nucleus accumbens and the septal region not only reduce 5-HT but also TRH, as does inhibition of tryptophan hydroxylase. 5,7-dihydroxytryptamine lesions also decrease the TRH-receptor-induced locomotor hyperactivity (monitored using the TRH analogue CG3509) but not the reversal of pentobarbitone sleep-time. Chronic intracerebroventricular infusion of a purified lgG fraction of TRH antiserum enhances the behavioural responses produced by CG3509 (sleep-time reversal and hyperactivity), prolongs pentobarbitone-induced sleep and also increases the behaviour syndrome produced by the 5-HT agonist 5-methoxy-N, N-dimethyltryptamine. These results indicate a functional interaction between central nervous system 5-HT and TRH neuronal systems.

Chronic amitriptyline treatment (15 mg/kg, twice daily for 15 days) increases levels of TRH in the accumbens and ventral spinal cord while decreasing the CG3509 induced behavioural responses and 5-HT$_2$ receptor number. The change in TRH is not seen in rats lesioned with 5,7-dihydroxytryptamine. In contrast, ECS decreases TRH in the accumbens and ventral spinal cord while increasing the CG3509-induced behaviour and 5-HT$_2$ receptor number.

The results suggest that TRH may have a role in the long-term adaptation of 5-HT receptor function produced by antidepressant treatments. It remains to be determined whether the changes in β-adrenoceptors also involve TRH and whether TRH analogues given together with conventional antidepressants speed up the antidepressant-induced changes in amine receptor function.

6.2 General Introduction

There is now convincing evidence that chronic treatment with either antidepressant drugs or electroconvulsive shock treatment (ECS) alters both the number and functional responsiveness of 5-hydroxytryptamine (5-HT) receptors and adrenoceptors in the rat brain (Green et al., 1986). Thus, prolonged treatment with many conventional and newer antidepressant drugs decreases 5-HT$_2$ (Peroutka and Snyder, 1980) and 5-HT$_{1A}$ receptors (Green et al., 1986). In contrast, ECS enhances 5-HT$_2$ (Green et al., 1983) but attenuates 5-HT$_{1A}$ receptor-mediated responses (Goodwin et al., 1985). Both antidepressant treatments down-regulate β-adrenoceptors (Sulser and Mobley, 1981) and attenuate α_2-receptor-mediated behaviour (Heal et al., 1981, 1983; Sugrue, 1981). The importance of amine receptor adaptation by antidepressant treatments in their clinical efficacy is not established. Equally, there is little information available about the mechanisms by which amine receptors undergo adaptation in response to long-term drug treatment or the effects of such treatments on the biochemical transducer mechanisms associated with the receptors.

During the past few years numerous studies have indicated that neuropeptides in the brain interact in functional terms with amine neuronal systems, either in the short term by altering such factors as amine release (e.g. both TRH and substance P influence 5-HT and dopamine release (Heal and Green, 1979; Sharp et al., 1982; Mitchell and Fleetwood-Walker, 1981)), or in the long term by acting as trophic factors (Jonsson and Hallman, 1982; Schmidt-Achert et al., 1984). Such studies have led to the concept of neuropeptides acting as neuromodulators in the CNS and particular attention has been given to those peptides that coexist with conventional amine neurotransmitters. The present chapter discusses the evidence that thyrotrophin-releasing hormone (TRH) is involved in the adaptive processes that occur following antidepressant drug treatment. No definitive answers can be given, but we hope that expressing ideas about an area that is very much in its infancy will generate both further work and understanding of the mechanisms involved in amine receptor adaptation.

6.1.1 Brain TRH: Coexistence with 5-HT

TRH is present in the brain in several regions other than the hypothalamus, the site of its neuroendocrine role; these include limbic areas such as the nucleus accumbens and the septum as well as the ventral horn of the spinal cord. In these regions, high levels of TRH immunoreactivity (Hokfelt *et al.*, 1975; Lighton *et al.*, 1984a) and saturable TRH binding sites (Ogawa *et al.*, 1984, Sharif and Burt, 1983) are found and Ca^{2+}-dependent release of TRH can be demonstrated *in vitro* (Shaeffer *et al.*, 1977; Sharp *et al.*, 1982). In the spinal cord TRH immunoreactivity is found in the same descending medullary raphe neurones as 5-HT and substance P. Evidence for this comes from the observation that administration of the serotonergic neurotoxins 5,7- and 5,6-dihydroxytryptamine (5,7- and 5,6-DHT) results in the loss of TRH and substance P together with 5-HT (Johansson *et al.*, 1981; Gilbert *et al.*, 1982). 5-HT and the two peptides also have similar electrophysiological effects on motor neurones within the spinal cord (White, 1985) and some data are consistent with the view that TRH and 5-HT interact at the receptor level to facilitate spinal motor neurone function (Barbeau and Bedard, 1981).

There is also evidence that TRH and 5-HT interact, though they do not necessarily coexist, within certain brain areas. Thus 5-7-DHT lesions reduce TRH levels in the nucleus accumbens but not in other brain regions, and a similar selective loss of TRH is observed after inhibition of tryptophan hydroxylase to lower 5-HT levels (Lighton *et al.*, 1984a). Such information has obviously raised the question of whether co-release of TRH might be involved in the adaptive changes to 5-HT binding sites produced by drug treatments. This is particularly relevant to antidepressant treatments, as there have been several reports over the years concerning the antidepressant properties of TRH; some indicate a positive effect of the neuropeptide while others have been less enthusiastic (see Metcalf, 1982, for review).

Any investigation of the functional interactions between TRH and 5-HT is hampered by the lack of readily available ligands for TRH binding sites and analogues or drugs that selectively antagonise the receptor-mediated effects of TRH. In the work described in this chapter we have attempted to overcome these problems, first by measuring the behavioural responses produced by stable analogues of TRH, such as CG3509 (orotyl-histidyl-prolineamide, Fig. 6.1) (Metcalf, 1982), as an index of TRH receptor function. Second, we have developed a technique for continuously infusing a purified IgG fraction of TRH antibodies intracerebroventricularily so as to remove extracellular TRH in the brain (Lighton *et al.*, 1986).

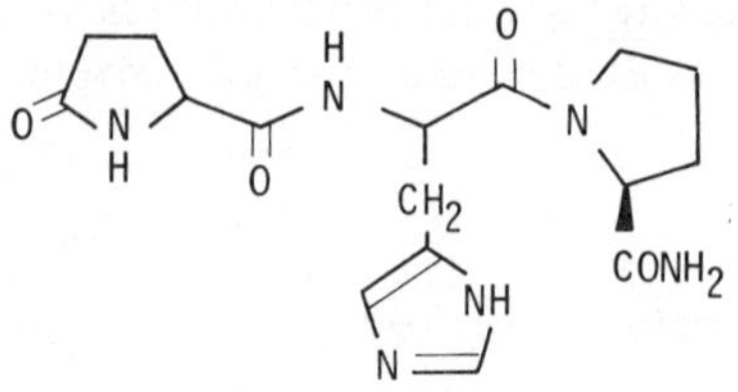

TRH (Pyroglutamyl - Histidyl - Proline Amide)

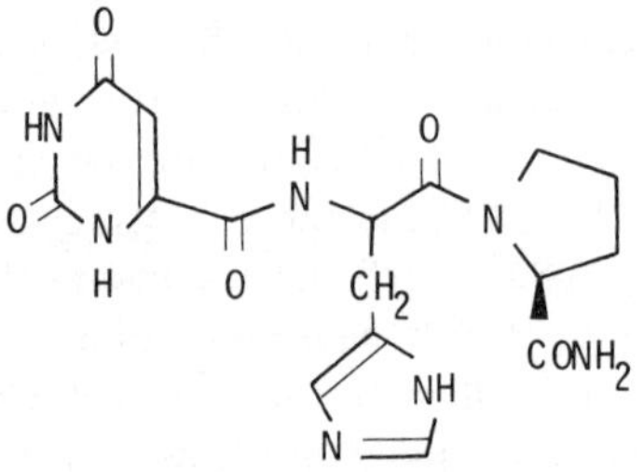

CG 3509 (Orotyl - Histidyl - Proline Amide)

Fig. 6.1 Chemical structures of TRH and the stable analogue of TRH, CG3509 (orotyl-histidyl-prolineamide).

6.2 Behavioural Effects of TRH Analogues

6.2.1 Pentobarbitone Sleep-time

Several studies have shown that systemically administered TRH reverses sleep-time induced by pentobarbitone (Bhargava, 1981; Breese *et al.*, 1975) and similar effects are observed when TRH is injected into either the nucleus accumbens or the septum, suggesting that these brain areas are important in the analeptic effects of TRH. We have shown that the stable TRH analogue CG3509 (2 µg) also reduced pentobarbitone sleep-time when injected into the nucleus accumbens or septum but not the striatum. CG3509 not only reversed pentobarbitone sleep-time but also pentobarbitone-induced hypothermia and decreased respiration (Sharp *et al.*, 1984c). Present evidence indicates that these effects involve septohippocampal cholinergic neurones (Kalivas and Horita, 1980).

6.2.2 Locomotor Effects

Central and peripheral administration of TRH or CG3509 produced clear enhancement of locomotor activity in rats (Heal and Green, 1979; Sharp et al., 1984b; Kalivas et al., 1987) consistent with TRH acting as an endogenous ergotropic substance in the CNS (Metcalf, 1982). This effect is also observed when either TRH (5 to 20 μg) or CG3509 (0.01 to 5 μg) is injected directly into the nucleus accumbens (Fig. 6.2(A); Sharp et al., 1984b) and appears to relate to increased dopamine release in the nucleus accumbens but not the striatum (Sharp et al., 1982; Sharp et al., 1984a). The effect of the analogue is more potent and longer lasting than that of TRH (Sharp et al., 1984b), which is consistent with the view that the analogues have greater biological stability (Metcalf, 1982).

6.2.3 Wet-dog Shakes

Intrathecal injection of TRH or CG3509 (Bennett et al., 1986b; Fone et al., in press) produces dose-related shaking behaviour and wet-dog shakes (Fig. 6.2(C)). The distribution of iodinated TRH following its intrathecal injection is consistent with brain-stem or spinal mechanisms being involved in this response (Fone et al., in press). Furthermore, the effect is antagonised by α_1-adrenoceptor antagonists (e.g. prazosin (2 mg/kg) and phenoxybenzamine (2 and 5 mg/kg)), and prevented by depletion of spinal catecholamines using the tyrosine hydroxylase inhibitor α-methyl-p-tyrosine (300 mg/kg i.p.) (Fone et al., in press; Fig. 6.2(C)). It is worth noting that 5-HT$_2$ receptors have been suggested to be involved in wet-dog shake behaviour in rats (Yap and Taylor, 1983), which is of interest in view of the coexistence of TRH and 5-HT in the spinal cord; though Drust and Connor (1983) consider that shaking behaviour induced by TRH and 5-HT are mediated by different mechanisms.

These three behavioural models have been used in the present studies to monitor changes in TRH-receptor responsiveness in the nucleus accumbens (locomotor activity), medial septum (pentobarbitone sleep-time) or the spinal cord (wet-dog shakes) following chronic drug treatment.

6.2.4 Behavioural Tests of 5-HT Receptor Function

There are now several selective agonists of the 5-HT receptor subtypes available that produce characteristic behavioural responses. In the present work we have used 5-methoxy-N,N-dimethyltryptamine (5-MEODMT; 2.5 mg/kg i.p.), a 5-HT agonist which effects both 5-HT$_{1A}$ (Sills et al., 1984) and 5-HT$_2$ receptors (Heal et al., 1985), though in the rat the 5-HT$_{1A}$ action appears to predominate (Sills et al., 1984). The behavioural effects in the rat consist of forepaw treading, flat

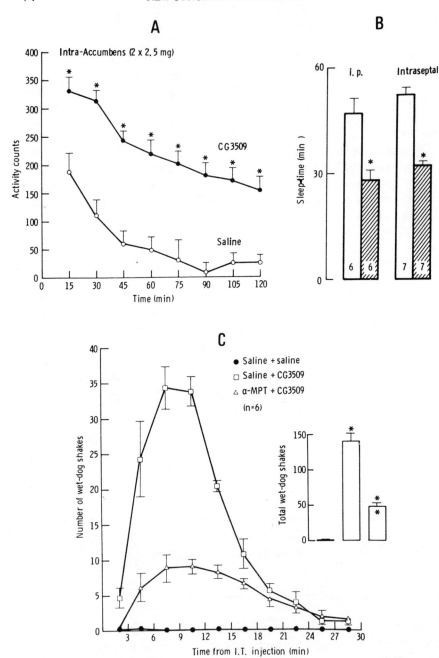

Fig. 6.2 (*caption opposite*)

body posture and hindlimb abduction. Lesions of the 5-HT neurones using 5,7-DHT enhance the behavioural response and this correlates with the decrease in brain 5-HT (Nisbet and Marsden, 1984), and increased $5\text{-}HT_2$ receptor number (Heal et al., 1985), indicating that the 5-HT receptors involved are post-synaptic. In the first experiments we determined the effects of 5,7-DHT lesions on the TRH- and 5-HT-receptor-mediated responses in the brain.

6.3 Effects of 5,7-DHT Lesions on TRH- and 5-HT-Receptor-Mediated Responses

When CG3509 (4.5 mg/kg i.p.) was given 15 days after 5,7-DHT (75 μg into each lateral ventricle), the locomotor response produced by the TRH analogue was significantly reduced compared with saline-injected controls, but there was no effect on the reversal of pentobarbitone (40 mg/kg i.p.)-induced sleep when this was tested on day 16 using the same dose of CG3509 (Fig. 6.3). In contrast, the behavioural response produced by 5-MEODMT (2.5 mg/kg i.p.) was significantly increased (Fig. 6.3), which supports previous evidence that 5,7-DHT lesions produce supersensitivity of the $5\text{-}HT_2$ receptors stimulated by 5-MEODMT (Heal et al., 1985). Thus, loss of 5-HT innervation results in a decreased response in the dopamine-mediated increase in locomotor activity produced by TRH but not in the cholinergically mediated reversal of pentobarbitone-induced sleep (Kalivas and Horita, 1980). The 5,7-DHT-induced decrease in TRH hyperactivity response could result from supersensitivity of 5-HT receptors involved in the control of dopamine neuronal function, as previous studies have indicated that stimulation of these receptors decreases dopamine release (Costall et al., 1976) and consequently the supersensitivity may result in decreased CG3509-induced release of dopamine. In addition, loss of 5-HT neurones may have a direct effect on TRH

Fig. 6.2 Effect of CG3509 on locomotor activity (A), pentobarbitone sleep-time (B) and wet-dog shakes (C) in the rat.

(A) CG3509 (•; 2.5 μg into each nucleus accumbens) or 0.9% saline (○; 2 μl into each nucleus accumbens) was administered and activity counted (doppler shift radar) for the following 120 min (data from Sharp et al., 1984b). *$p < 0.05$ compared with controls; $n = 6$ in each case.

(B) The effects of CG3509 (hatched) or 0.9% saline (unhatched) on sleep-time induced by pentobarbitone (40 mg/kg i.p.). CG3509 was given either i.p. administration (4.5 mg/kg) or directly into the septal region (2 μg into each septum); CG3509 or saline were administered 20 min after the induction of sleep (loss of righting reflex). *$p < 0.05$ compared with controls. (Data from Bennett et al., 1986a, in press.)

(C) Time-course of the effects of intrathecal CG3509 (□, 2 μg) or 0.9% saline (•; 10 μl) on the number of wet-dog shakes in the rat. Another group of rats were given α-methyl-p-tyrosine (△, 300 mg/kg) 18 h before the injection of CG3509 (2 μg intrathecally). Inset: the results expressed as total shakes over the recording period. Note the production of wet-dog shakes by CG 3509 and the decrease in this response in catecholamine-depleted rats. (Data from Fone et al., in press.)

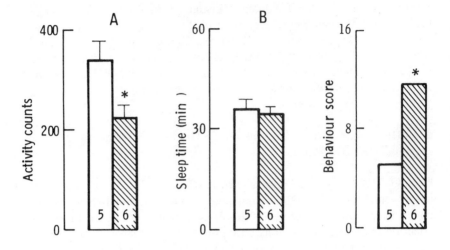

Fig. 6.3 Effect of 5,7-DHT (hatched; 75 μg into each lateral ventricle) and 0.9% saline (un-hatched) on CG3509 (4.5 mg/kg i.p.)-induced hyperactivity, and pentobarbitone (40 mg/kg i.p.)-induced sleep-time and the behavioural syndrome produced by 5-MEODMT (2.5 mg/kg i.p.). Note the decreased hyperactivity response with CG3509, no change in the sleep-time, and the increased 5-MEODMT response. 5,7-DHT was given on day one and the rats tested with 5-MEODMT on day 10 and CG3509 on day 12 (hyperactivity) and day 15 (sleep-time). *$p < 0.05$ compared with saline treated controls.

receptor number, since a previous study has demonstrated that 5,7-DHT lesions produce a 40% increase in the binding of a labelled TRH analogue to saturable sites in the spinal cord (Sharif *et al.*, 1983), increased facilitation of spinal reflexes by TRH (Barbeau and Bedard, 1981; Clarke and Stirk, 1983) and the enhancement of respiration in the cat (Mueller *et al.*, 1984). In our experiments the locomotor response produced by CG3509 in the nucleus accumbens was reduced by 5,7-DHT in contrast to results from the spinal cord. This conflict may reflect the complex relationship between 5-HT, dopamine and TRH receptor function in this area of the brain.

Further work is required to fully determine the effects of 5,7-DHT on dopamine and TRH receptors as well as the various 5-HT receptor subtypes. For example, it is not clear which 5-HT receptor subtype mediates the effects on dopamine release. In this respect it is interesting that chronic treatment with a selective 5-HT$_2$ antagonist, such as ritanserin, does not increase 5-HT$_2$ receptor number, as one would predict on the basis of data obtained with dopamine receptors, but decreases the number (Leysen *et al.*, 1986). It is clear that more information is needed on the factors regulating changes in 5-HT receptor number with respect to the different receptor subtypes.

6.4 Effects of TRH-antibody Infusion on CG3509- and MEODMT-Induced Behaviour

The results in the previous section demonstrate that 5-HT neuronal loss alters not only 5-HT receptor agonist but also TRH receptor agonist responsiveness, though the mechanism is not understood. An alternative approach to understanding the relationship between 5-HT and TRH receptor changes is to look at the effects of altering the brain peptide level or receptor activity on 5-HT and TRH responses. Such an approach is hindered by the lack of selective TRH receptor antagonist drugs. A number of previous studies have shown that the action of endogenous brain peptides can be antagonised by passive immunisation following acute intracerebroventricular (i.c.v.) administration of peptide antiserum (Chihara et al., 1978; Leshner et al., 1978; Prasad et al., 1980). We have extended this approach by chronically (1 or 2 weeks) infusing into the ventricles purified IgG fractions of TRH antiserum (Lighton et al., 1986). Preliminary results showed that purified antibody decreased the in vitro release of TRH produced by potassium (55 mM) from brain region slices by over 70% without altering the tissue levels of TRH (Lighton et al., 1986).

The TRH antibodies were raised in sheep at Nottingham (Lighton et al., 1984a), fully characterised and demonstrated to cross-react only with peptides which contain both N- and C-terminal residues of synthetic TRH. Both the TRH antibody (TRH-AS) and control antisera (C-AS) were partially purified by retaining the γ-globulin fraction while removing the high level of plasma albumin using ammonium sulphate precipitation and dialysis (Lighton et al., 1986). The binding of TRH to the purified TRH-AS was compared with that to the unpurified TRH-AS and no significant difference was found (Bennett et al., in press). Most importantly, the purified IgG fraction of TRH-AS, unlike the unpurified TRH-AS, did not produce mortalities or obvious abnormal neuroanatomical or behavioural effects when infused chronically.

When the purified TRH-AS was chronically infused, using osmotic minipumps, (Alzet 2-week pumps, model 2002) into both lateral ventricles for 14 days (Fig. 6.4) there was a significant increase in the length of pentobarbitone (40 mg/kg) sleep-time and the reversal of this sleep-time by CG3509 when the analogue was either administered i.p. (4.5 mg/kg) or directly into the medial septum (5 μg) (Fig. 6.5(A)). The CG3509 (4.5 mg/kg i.p.) locomotor response was also significantly increased (Fig. 6.5(B)) when tested on day 12. In both cases, control rats were infused with C-AS in an identical manner. Chronic TRH-AS also significantly enhanced the behavioural syndrome produced by 5-MEODMT (2.5 mg/kg i.p.) given on day 10 (Fig. 6.5(C)). The above results suggest that chronic infusion of TRH-AS alters not only the sensitivity of central TRH receptors but also those of 5 HT. In the converse of these experiments it has been shown that chronic i.c.v. administration of TRH or TRH analogues down-regulates TRH receptors and causes behavioural tolerance (Simasko and Horita, 1985; Ushijima et al., 1986). Recently we have shown that repeated intrathecal administration of

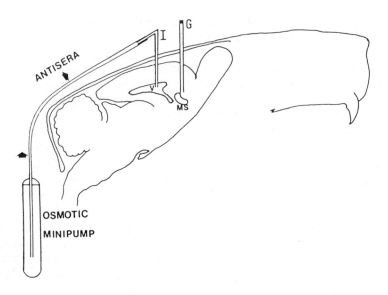

Fig. 6.4 System for the chronic 14-day infusion of TRH antibodies into the ventricles of the rat using an osmotic minipump (Alzet model 2002). The minipump was inserted under the skin behind the scapula. Two pumps were placed into each animal with cannulae (I) inserted into both ventricles. Injection cannulae (G) were placed into the medial septal regions on both sides of the brain for the subsequent injection of CG3509 on days 12 and 15.

CG3509 significantly attenuates the wet-dog shake response produced by this analogue (Table 6.4). The enhanced response to CG3509 following TRH-AS infusion supports the conclusion reached in the *in vitro* release studies that the antibodies decrease extracellular TRH subsequently causing supersensitivity of TRH receptors. Similarly, the increased sleep-time produced by pentobarbitone may reflect decreased extracellular levels of the ergotropic TRH, as previous studies have shown that increased extracellular TRH decreased pentobarbitone sleep-time (Prange *et al.*, 1974) (Fig. 6.6). An alternative explanation for these results might be that the TRH-AS infusion alters hypothalamic TRH and hence pituitary TSH, prolactin release and circulating thyroid hormones. These hormones can feed back onto the brain, so altering extrahypothalamic TRH responsiveness and CNS function. Previous studies have shown that central 5-HT receptors are involved in the regulation of hypothalamic TSH output (Schettini *et al.*, 1983). This endocrine mediation seems an unlikely mechanism, however, as we have found no changes in plasma-free T4 levels following either infusion (14 days) or repeated (twice daily for 5 days) intra-accumbens injections of TRH-AS.

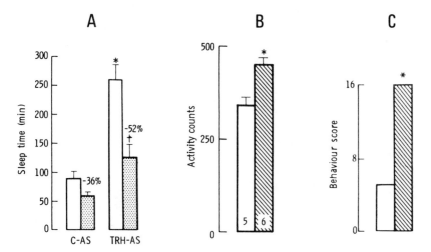

Fig. 6.5 (A) Effect of i.c.v. infusion of TRH antisera (TRH-AS) or control antisera (C-AS) for 14 days on the sleep-time induced by pentobarbitone (40 mg/kg i.p.) and its reversal by CG3509 (stippled; 2 μg into each septum) compared with saline injection (unstippled; 2 μl) tested on day 15. Note the prolonged sleep-time in the rats given TRH-AS and challenged with saline compared with rats given C-AS and the increased reversal of the sleep-time by CG3509 after TRH-AS (data from Lighton *et al.*, 1986).

(B) Effect of TRH-AS (hatched) compared with C-AS (unhatched) on the hyperactivity response produced by CG3509 (4.5 mg/kg i.p.). Note the increased response to CG3509 after chronic (12 days) TRH-AS. *$p < 0.05$ compared with C-AS. (Student's t-test.)

(C) Effect of TRH-AS (hatched) compared with C-AS (unhatched) on the 5-MEODMT (2.5 mg/kg i.p.)-induced behavioural response. Note the increased 5-MEODMT response after 10 days' infusion with TRH-AS. *$p < 0.05$ compared with C-AS (Mann–Whitney U-test).

TRH-AS also increased the responsiveness of the 5-HT agonist 5-MEODMT. The addition of TRH to membrane preparations of the nucleus accumbens 30 min before the addition of 3-H-ketanserin decreases the number of 5-HT$_2$-specific binding sites (Metz, A., and Green, A. R., unpublished; Table 6.1), suggesting that TRH is involved in the adaptation of 5-HT$_2$ receptors. The present finding that decreases in extracellular TRH enchance 5-HT agonist responsiveness would support this view. A possible way to further test this hypothesis would be to observe the effects on brain TRH levels of antidepressant drugs, which down-regulate 5-HT$_2$ receptors, and ECS, which increases 5-HT$_2$ but decreases 5-HT$_1$ receptor number. If TRH is involved in the regulation of 5-HT$_2$ receptors then the drugs would be expected to increase the peptide levels while ECS should decrease them.

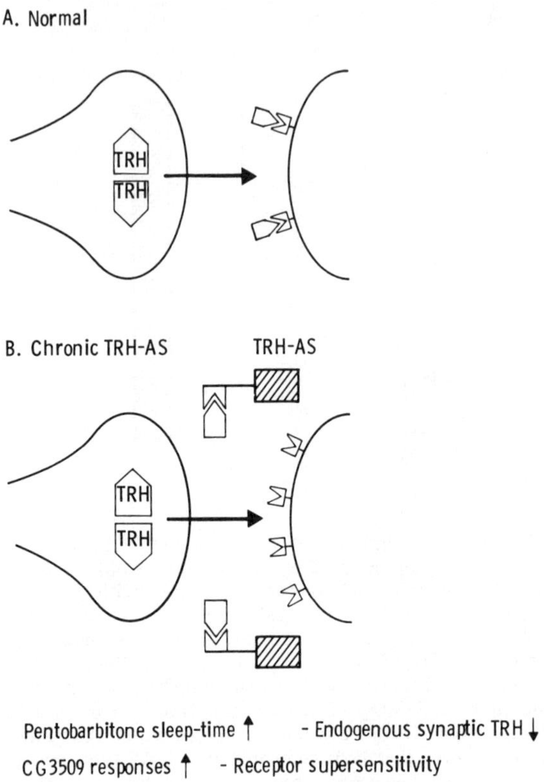

A. Normal

B. Chronic TRH-AS　　　　　TRH-AS

Pentobarbitone sleep-time ↑　　　- Endogenous synaptic TRH ↓
CG3509 responses ↑　　- Receptor supersensitivity

Fig 6.6　Possible mechanism for the effects observed after chronic TRH antisera (TRH-AS) infusion.
　(A) In the normal situation TRH is released from nerve endings and it can then bind to TRH receptors. Analogues such as CG3509 can also bind to the TRH receptors.
　(B) During TRH-AS infusion the antibodies remove TRH released into the extracellular space, which results in a compensatory increase in the number of TRH receptors. Removal of endogenous TRH results in enhanced pentobarbitone sleep-time but the TRH receptor supersensitivity potentiates the effects of the directly acting TRH analogue CG3509.

6.5 Effects of Chronic Antidepressant Drugs or ECS on TRH Levels in the Brain and *In-vitro* Release

Chronic administration twice daily for 15 days of amitriptyline (15 mg/kg), chlorimipramine (15 mg/kg), mianserin (2 mg/kg) or metergoline (2 mg/kg) all increase TRH levels in the nucleus accumbens and the ventral spinal cord, but not other brain regions. The most marked increases were seen following amitriptyline administration (Table 6.2). When endogenous TRH release was measured

Table 6.1   Effects of TRH on [^{3}H]-ketanserin binding in homogenates of the rat nucleus accumbens

	B_{max} (fmol/mg)	K_D (nM)
Control (n)	331 ± 9	1.75 ± 0.20
TRH (5 × 10^{-5} M)	253 ± 7*	1.38 ± 0.05

The homogenates were pre-incubated for 30 min in the presence of TRH before the addition of [^{3}H]-ketanserin. *$p < 0.025$ compared with controls. Data supplied by Drs. A. Metz and A. R. Green.

Table 6.2   Effects of chronic treatment with amitriptyline or electroconvulsive shock (ECS) on the levels and potassium stimulated release of TRH in the rat nucleus accumbens and lumbar spinal cord

	Level		Release	
	*Drug	†ECS	Drug	ECS
Nucleus accumbens	+124%(6)	−42%(17)	+40%(6)	−47%(8)
Lumbar cord (16 or 17)	+130%(6)	−40%(16)	+53%(6)	ND

*Amitriptyline (15 mg/kg twice daily) or 0.9% saline were given for 14 days and the rats killed 4 h after the last injection and the tissue levels of TRH measured in various brain regions (medium eminence, suprachiasmatic nucleus, septal nuclei, nucleus accumbens and lumbar spinal cord). The increase was only observed in the nucleus accumbens, lumbar cord and the suprachiasmatic nucleus. In separate rats the release of TRH in response to 55 mM potassium was measured using brain slices (for method see Lighton et al., 1984b).

†Male rats were given repeated electro-shocks (125 V, 50 Hz sinusoidal for 1 sec) under halothane anaesthesia. 5 shocks were given over 10 days and the rats killed 24 h after the last shock. Tissue levels and release were measured as in the amitriptyline experiment (ND = not done). Data taken from Lighton et al., 1984b, 1985.

in brain region slices obtained from rats after 14 days' treatment with amitriptyline there was increased release in response to elevated potassium ions (55 mM) only in the nucleus accumbens and ventral spinal cord in comparison with saline-injected controls (Table 6.2) (Lighton et al., 1985). In contrast, ECS (5 times over 10 days) decreased TRH levels, and release in the same brain regions as amitriptyline had the opposite effects (Table 6.2) (Lighton et al., 1984b).

These results indicate that chronic antidepressant drug treatment increases the releasable pool of TRH in the ventral spinal cord where TRH coexists with 5-HT (Gilbert et al., 1982) and the nucleus accumbens where 5,7-DHT lesions and p-chlorophenylalanine decrease both TRH and 5-HT (Lighton et al., 1984a). Iverfeldt et al. (1986) have reached a similar conclusion with regard to substance P in the ventral spinal cord where this peptide also coexists in the same neurones as 5-HT and TRH (Hokfelt et al., 1978; Gilbert et al., 1982). Again, chronic treatment with antidepressant drugs (zimelidine and imipramine) increased the levels and potassium-stimulated release of the neuropeptide. One explanation for the increase in both TRH and substance P is that the antidepressant drugs decrease 5-HT neuronal firing (de Montigny *et al.*, 1981) and hence release of 5-HT and the coexisting peptides, resulting in an increase in the releasable pools of the peptides. This explanation would suggest that neuronal levels of TRH would increase but extracellular levels of the peptide *in vivo* would decrease. To test this idea we determined the effects of chronic amitriptyline treatment on the behavioural responses produced by CG3509. In contrast to the antidepressant drugs, ECS reduced TRH levels in the nucleus accumbens and lumbar spinal cord and *ex vivo* release; again, this could indicate decreased levels of releasable TRH and hence increased extracellular levels *in vivo*. If these assumptions are correct then the antidepressant drugs should cause supersensitivity of TRH-induced responses and ECS would decrease the responses.

6.6 Effects of Antidepressant Drugs and ECS on CG3509-induced Responses

Chronic amitriptyline (15 mg/kg) treatment (twice daily for 14 days) reduced the locomotor response produced by bilateral intra-accumbens injection of CG3509 ($2 \times 2.5 \mu g$). Comparable to this effect is the increase in pentobarbitone sleep-time, but decrease in the reversal by CG3509 of pentobarbitone-induced sleep-time and pentobarbitone-induced hypothermia and decreased respiration (Bennett *et al.*, 1986a) (Table 6.3). These observations indicate that chronic amitriptyline, rather than decreasing extracellular TRH, as a consequence of lowered neuronal firing, as suggested above, increases these levels, resulting in down-regulation of TRH receptors and subsequent decreased responsiveness. In contrast, repeated ECS significantly increased the CG3509-induced hyperactivity and the degree of reversal of pentobarbitone-induced hypothermia and respiratory depression, indicating that this treatment may decrease extracellular TRH *in vivo*.

There are problems in interpreting the results obtained with the pentobarbitone sleep-time, as amitriptyline enhances the level of anaesthesia attained with the 40 mg/kg dose of pentobarbitone (Lin 1978), but the opposite effects of the drug and ECS on the CG3509-mediated responses would support the view that these two treatments affect TRH receptor sensitivity in opposite directions, which in turn may reflect the changes in TRH levels and *ex vivo* release observed after amitriptyline and ECS treatment (Lighton *et al.*, 1984b, 1985).

Table 6.3   Summary of the effects of 5,7-DHT induced 5-HT lesions, TRH antibody infusion, chronic antidepressant drug treatment and repeated electroconvulsive shock (ECS) on TRH and 5-HT receptor mediated responses

	Pentobarbitone sleep	TRH CG 3509 Sleep reversal	Activity	5-HT 5-MEODMT behaviour	5-HT2 receptor binding
5,7-DHT	?	−	↑	↑	↑
TRH-AS	↑	↑			?
Antidepressants	↓	↓	↓	↓	↓
ECS	−	−	↑	↓	↓

See text for details of the tests. ↑ = increase, ↓ = decrease, − = no change, ? = not known. Note that antidepressant drugs and ECS produce opposite effects on both 5-HT- and TRH-mediated responses. Data summarised from: Stolz *et al.*, 1983; Green *et al.*, 1983; Bennett *et al.*, 1986a; Bennett *et al.*, in press.

6.7 TRH and Long-term 5-HT Receptor Adaptation

Fuxe *et al.* (1983) suggested that some of the adaptive changes in 5-HT receptors induced by chronic antidepressant treatments are mediated via modulatory co-factors. The previously mentioned observation, that under certain conditions TRH decreases 5-HT$_2$ ligand binding in the nucleus accumbens (Metz, A., and Green, A. R., unpublished; Table 6.1), combined with other data in this chapter showing reciprocal changes in 5-HT$_2$ and TRH receptor responsiveness under a variety of situations, raises the possibility that TRH may act directly on post-synaptic 5-HT$_2$ receptors to regulate binding and responses elicited by the receptors. That the changes in TRH and 5-HT function induced by antidepressants in the nucleus accumbens and lumbar spinal cord may be associated comes from a recent observation by us that the increase in TRH level in the two regions produced by amitriptyline is not seen in rats lesioned with 5,7-DHT (Fig. 6.7). Other workers have demonstrated that similar lesions prevent the antidepressant drug-induced down-regulation of β-receptors (Barbaccia *et al.*, 1983; Nimgaonker *et al.*, 1985). It is not clear whether 5-HT$_1$ or 5-HT$_2$ receptors are involved in the β-receptor down-regulation, but the observation that antidepressant drugs and ECS affect 5-HT$_2$ receptors in opposite directions but both down-regulate β-receptors would appear to rule out 5-HT$_2$ receptor involvement. ECS and the drugs decrease 5-HT$_1$ receptors (Goodwin *et al.*, 1985; Green *et al.*, 1986) so these receptors could be involved in the β-receptor down-regulation. It remains to be determined, however, whether TRH is involved in the adaptation of the 5-HT$_1$ receptors or indeed whether the down-regulation of the β-receptors is dependent on the antidepressant-induced changes in TRH levels. It will be

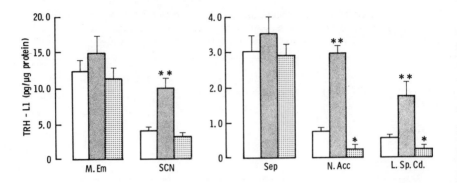

Fig. 6.7   Effects of 5,7-DHT (75 μg into each lateral ventricle after pretreatment with desipramine 15 mg/kg i.p.) on the chronic amitriptyline (15 mg/kg i.p. twice daily for 14 days)-induced increase in TRH in the suprachiasmatic nucleus (SCN), nucleus accumbens (N. Acc) and lumbar spinal cord (L. Sp. Cd). M. Em = median emincence. Unstippled: 0.9% saline twice daily for 14 days. Darker stippling: amitriptyline. Lighter stippling: 5,7-DHT plus amitriptyline. The rats were killed 4 hours after the last amitriptyline injection. Note the rise in TRH in the SCN, N. Acc and L. Sp. Cd. but not the M. Em following amitriptyline treatment and the absence of this increase in rats pretrated with 5,7-DHT to lesion the 5-HT neurones, before the start of the amitriptyline treatment. $**p < 0.0001$ compared with saline controls. $*p < 0.05$ compared with saline controls (Student's t-test).

necessary to determine more precisely the effects of TRH pn the various 5-HT receptor subtypes. 5-MEODMT lacks selectivity for these subtypes and the experiments need to be repeated using more selective 5-HT agonists such as 8-hydroxy-2-(di-n-propylamino) tetralin (8-OH-DPAT) which is selective for 5-HT$_{1A}$ receptors (Middlemiss and Fozard, 1983). TRH could also interact directly with adrenoceptors and Heal $et\ al.$ (1987) have demonstrated that TRH enhances release of noradrenaline in the hypothalamus.

   Alternatively, the β-receptor changes may not be dependent on 5-HT receptors but on 5-HT itself. Sulser (1986) found that β-receptor down-regulation by desipramine does not occur when 5-HT is depleted by inhibiting tryptophan hydroxylase with p-chlorophenylalanine (PCPA), though Nimgaonker and co-workers (1985) found that only 5,7-DHT lesions and not PCPA prevented down-regulation of β-adrenoceptors. This point obviously requires clarification, but a possible explanation is that 5,7-DHT lesions result in the loss of a receptor modulator and TRH is an important candidate. It is important to know whether depletion of extracellular TRH, using TRH-AS, prevents the amitriptyline-induced rise in brain TRH and β-adrenoceptor down-regulation. Another question is whether combined TRH analogue and antidepressant treatment 'speeds up' the changes in amine receptors produced by antidepressants.

   Finally, there is increasing evidence that TRH has long-term regulatory functions apart from acute behavioural effects. Thus it has a trophic effect on the enzyme choline acetyltransferase (ChaT) in cultured motoneurones (Schmidt-

Achert *et al.*, 1984), an effect we have observed *in vivo* (Fone *et al.*, in press). In the latter case this was accompanied by a highly significant increase in ventral cord 5-HT (Table 6.4). The results presented in this chapter indicate that TRH

Table 6.4 Effect of repeated intrathecal administration of CG3509 on wet-dog shakes, 5-HT and choline acetyltransferase activity (ChaT) in the spinal cord

	Wet-dog shakes (number/30 min)	5-HT (ng/mg protein)	ChaT (mol ACh formed/h/g)
Control (0.9% saline (8)	0	5.69 ± 0.56	2.06 ± 0.10
1st injection CG3509 (8)	157 ± 11		
5th injection CG3509 (8)	67 ± 9†		
9th injection CG3509 (8)	68 ± 5†	9.34 ± 0.61*	2.79 ± 0.21*

CG3509 (2 µg) or saline (10 µl) was administered twice daily for 5 days. Wet-dog shakes were counted (Fone *et al.*, in press) after the 1st, 5th and 9th injection. ChaT activity (Fonnum, 1975) and 5-HT levels (Lighton *et al.*, 1984a) in the ventral lumbar cord were determined after the 9th injection. †Significantly decreased compared with 1st injection ($p < 0.05$). *Significantly increased compared with controls ($p < 0.05$). Data compared using Student's t-test. Figures in brackets refer to number of animals.

may have a role in the long-term adaptation of monoamine receptors, in particular those for 5-HT, a role that may help explain the changes in receptor number and function reported following chronic 5-HT$_2$ antagonist (Blackshear *et al.*, 1983; Leysen *et al.*, 1986) and antidepressant drug treatment. Such information should help our understanding of the mechanisms involved in amine receptor adaptation and could lead to the development of faster-acting treatments for depression.

Acknowledgements

We thank the Mental Health Foundation, Wellcome Trust and MRC for financial support. Dr Richard Green (Astra) provided the expertise for the ECS experiments; C. A. Marsden is a Wellcome Senior Lecturer. We also thank Philippa Dix for providing some of the unpublished data presented.

References

Barbaccia, M. L., Brunello, N., Chuang, D. M., and Costa, E. (1983). On the mode of action of imipramine: Relationship between serotonergic axon terminal function and down regulation of β-adrenergic receptors. *Neuropharmacology*, 22, 373–84.

Barbeau, H., and Bedard, P. (1981). Similar motor effects of 5HT and TRH in rats following chronic spinal transection and 5,7-dihydroxytryptamine injection. *Neuropharmacology*, 20, 477–81.

Bennett, G. W., Green, A. R., Lighton, C., and Marsden, C. A. (1986a). Changes in the behavioural response to a TRH analogue following chronic amitryptyline treatment and repeated electroconvulsive shock in the rat. *Br. J. Pharmac.*, 88, 129–40.

Bennett, G. W., Fone, K. C. F., and Marsden, C. A. (1986b). Prazosin antagonises the wet-dog shake behaviour produced by intrathecal administration of a TRH analgoue, CG 3509. *Br. J. Pharmac.*, 88, 300.

Bennett, G. W, Edwards, R. M., Lighton, C., and Marsden, C. A. (in press). Thyrotrophin releasing hormone-5-hydroxytryptamine interactions in the brain studied using chronic immunization and chemical lesioning techniques. *J. Receptor Research*.

Bhargava, H. N. (1981). Antagonism of ketamine-induced anaesthesia and hypothermia by thyrotrophin releasing hormone and cyclo (his-pro). *Neuropharmacology*, 20, 699–702.

Blackshear, M. A., Friedman, R. L., and Sanders-Bush, E. (1983). Acute and chronic effects of serotonin (5-HT) antagonists on serotonin binding sites. *Naunyn-Schmiedeberg's Arch. Pharmacol.*, 324, 125–9.

Breese, G. R., Cott, J. M., Cooper, B. R., Prange, A. J., Lipton, M. A., and Plotnikoff, N. P. (1975). Effects of thyrotrophin-releasing hormone (TRH) on the actions of pentobarbital and other centrally acting drugs. *J. Pharmac. Exp. Ther.*, 193, 11–22.

Chihara, K., Arimura, A., Chihara, M., and Schally, A. V. (1978). Effects of intraventricular administration of anti-somatostatin-globulin on the lethal dose-50 of strychnine and pentobarbital in rats. *Endocrinology*, 103, 912–16.

Clarke, K. A., and Stirk, G. (1983). Motoneurone excitability after administration of a thyrotrophin releasing hormone analogue. *Br. J. Pharmac.*, 80, 561–5.

Costall, B., Naylor, R. J., Marsden, C. D., and Pycock, C. J. (1976). Serotonergic modulation of the dopamine response from the nucleus accumbens. *J. Pharm. Pharmac.*, 28, 523–6.

de Montigny, C., Blier, P., Caile, G., and Koussi, E. (1981). Pre- and post-synaptic effects of zimelidine and norzimelidine on the serotoninergic system: single cell studies in the rat. *Acta. psychiatr. scand.*, 63, suppl. 290, 79–90.

Drust, E. G., and Connor, J. D. (1983). Pharmacological analysis of shaking behaviour induced by enkephalins, thyrotropin-releasing hormone or serotonin in rats: evidence for different mechanisms. *J. Pharmac. Exp. Ther.*, 224, 148–54.

Fone, K. C. F., Bennett, G. W. and Marsden, C. A. (in press). Involvement of catecholaminergic neurones and -adrenoceptors in the wet-dog shake and forepaw locking behaviours produced by the intrathecal injection of a TRH analogue, CG 3509. *Neuropharmacology*.

Fone, K. C. F., Dix, P., Bennett, G. W., and Marsden, C. A. (in press). Chronic intrathecal TRH analogue (CG3509) alters wet-dog shakes, spinal cord choline actyltransferase and indoleamine levels. *Br. J. Pharmac.*

Fonnum, F. (1975). A new and rapid radiochemical method for the determination of choline acetyltransferase. *J. Neurochem.*, 24, 407–9.

Fuxe, K., Ogren, S. O., Agnati, L. F., Benfenati, F., Fredholm, B., Anderson, K., Zini, I., and Eneroth, P. (1983). Chronic antidepressant treatment and central 5HT synapses. *Neuropharmacology*, 22, 398–400.

Gilbert, R. F., Emson, P. C., Hunt, S. P., Bennett, G. W., Marsden, C. A., Sandberg, B. E. B., and Steinbusch, H. W. (1982). The effects of monoamine neurotoxins on peptides in the rat spinal cord. *Neuroscience*, 7, 69–87.

Goodwin, G. M., De Souza, R. J., and Green, A. R. (1985) Presynaptic serotonin receptor mediated response in mice attenuated by antidepressant drugs and electroconvulsive shock. *Nature* (Lond.) 317, 531–3.

Green, A. R., Heal, D. J., Johnson, P., Laurence, B. E., and Nimgaonkar, V. L. (1983). Antidepressant treatments: effects in rodents on dose-response curves of 5-hydroxy-tryptamine- and dopamine-mediated behaviours in 5-HT$_2$ receptor number in frontal cortex. *Br. J. Pharmac.*, **80**, 377–85.

Green, A. R., Heal, D. J., and Goodwin, G. M. (1986). The effects of electroconvulsive therapy and antidepressant drugs on monoamine receptors in rodent brain – similarities and differences. In *Antidepressants and Receptor Function*, CIBA Foundation Symposium 123. Wiley, Chichester, 246–58.

Heal, D. J., and Green, A. R. (1979). Administration of thyrotrophin releasing hormone (TRH) in rats releases dopamine in n. accumbens but not n. caudatus. *Neuropharmacology*, **18**, 23–31.

Heal, D. J., Akagi, H., Bowdler, J. M., and Green, A. R. (1981). Repeated electroconvulsive shock attenuates clonidine-induced hypoactivity in rodents. *Eur. J. Pharmac.*, **75**, 231–7.

Heal, D. J., Lister, S., Smith, S. L., Davies, C. L., Molyneux, S. G., and Green, A. R. (1983). The effects of acute and repeated administration of various antidepressant drugs on clonidine-induced hypoactivity in mice and rats. *Neuropharmacology*, **22**, 983–92.

Heal, D. J., Philpot, J., Molyneux, S. G., and Metz, A. (1985). Intracerebroventricular administration of 5,7-dihydroxytryptamine to mice increases both head-twitch response and the number of cortical 5-HT$_2$ receptors. *Neuropharmacology*, **24**, 1201–6.

Heal, D. J., Stoodley, N., Elliott, J. M., Marsden, C. A., Bennett, G. W., and Youdim, M. B. H. (1987). Behavioural and biochemical evidence for noradrenaline release in mouse brain by TRH and some of its biologically stable analogues. *Neuropharmacology*, **26**, 313–22.

Hokfelt, T., Fuxe, K., Johansson, O., Jeffcoate, S., and White, N. (1975). Distribution of thyrotrophin releasing hormone (TRH) in the CNS as revealed by immunohistochemistry. *Eur. J. Pharmacol.*, **34**, 389–92.

Hokfelt, T., Ljunfdahl, A., Steinbusch, H., Verhofstad, A., Nilsson, G., Brodin, E., Pernow, B., and Goldstein, M. (1978). Immunohistochemical evidence of substance P-like immunoreactivity in some 5-hydroxytryptamine-containing neurons in the rat central nervous system. *Neuroscience*, **3**, 517–38.

Iverfeldt, K., Peterson, L.-L., Brodin, E., Ogren, S.-O., and Bartfai, T. (1986). Serotonin type-2 receptor mediated regulation of substance P release in ventral spinal cord and the effects of chronic antidepressant treatment. *Naunyn-Schmiedeberg's Arch. Pharmac.*, **333**, 1–6.

Johansson, O., Hokfelt, T., Pernow, B., Jeffcoate, S. L., White, N., Steinbusch, H. W. M., Verhofstad, A. A. J., Emson, P. C., and Spindel, E. (1981). Immunohistochemical support for three putative transmitters in one neurone: co-existence of 5-hydroxytryptamine, substance P and thyrotrophin releasing hormone-like immunoreactivity in medullary neurones projecting to the spinal cord. *Neuroscience*, **6**, 1857–81.

Jonsson, G., and Hallman, H. (1982). Substance P counteracts neurotoxin damage on norepinephrine neurons in rat brain during ontogeny. *Science*, **215**, 75–7.

Kalivas, P. W., and Horita, A. (1980). Thyrotropin releasing hormone: Neurogenesis of actions in the pentobarbital narcotized rat. *J. Pharmac. Exp. Ther.*, **212**, 202–10.

Kalivas, P. W., Stanley, D., and Prange, A. J. (1987). Interaction between thyrotropin-releasing hormone and the mesolimbic dopamine system. *Neuropharmacology*, **26**, 33–8.

Leshner, A. I., Hofstein, R., Samuel, D., and Gireidanau, T. B. V. W. (1978). Intraventricular injection of anti-vasopressin serum blocks learned helplessness in rat. *Biochem. Pharmacol. Behav.*, **9**, 889–92.

Leysen, J. E., Van Gompel, P., Gommeren, W., Woestenborghs, B., Janssen, P. A. J. (1986). Down-regulation of serotonin-S$_2$ receptors in rat brain by chronic treatment with the serotonin-S$_2$ antagonists ritanserin and setoperone. *Psychopharmacology*, **88**, 434–44.

Lighton, C., Marsden, C. A., and Bennett, G. W. (1984a). The effects of 5,7-dihydroxytryptamine and *p*-chlorophenylalanine on thyrotrophin. *Neuropharmacology*, **23**, 55–60.

Lighton, C., Marsden, C. A., Bennett, G. W., Minchin, M., and Green, A. R. (1984b). Decrease in thyrotrophin releasing hormone (TRH) in the n. accumbens and lumbar spinal cord following repeated electroconvulsive shock. *Neuropharmacology*, **23**, 963–6.

Lighton, C., Bennett, G. W., and Marsden, C. A. (1985). Increase in levels and *ex vivo* release of thyrotrophin releasing hormone (TRH) in specific regions of the rat CNS by chronic antidepressant treatment. *Neuropharmacology*, 24, 401–6.

Lighton, C., Bennett, G. W., and Marsden, C. A. (1986). Chronic immunization of endogenous thyrotrophin releasing hormone (TRH) in brain alters the behavioural response to pentobarbital and a TRH analogue. *Brain Res.*, 378, 385–9.

Lin, M. T. (1978). Effects of specific inhibitors of 5-hydroxytryptamine uptake on thermoregulation in rats. *J. Physiol.*, 284, 147–54.

Metcalf, G. (1982). Regulatory peptides as a source of new drugs — the clinical prospects for analogues of TRH which are resistant to metabolic degradation. *Brain Res. Rev.*, 4, 389–408.

Middlemiss, D. M., and Fozard, J. R., (1983). 8-hydroxy-2-(di-n-propylamino) tetralin discriminates between sub-types of the 5-HT$_1$ recognition site. *Eur. J. Pharmac.*, 90, 151–3.

Mitchell, R., and Fleetwood-Walker, S. (1981). Substance P, but not TRH, modulates the 5-HT autoreceptor in vental lumbar spinal cord. *Eur. J. Pharmac.*, 76, 119–20.

Mueller, R. A., Towle, A. C., and Brees, G. R. (1984). Supersensitivity to the respiratory stimulatory effect of TRH in 5,7-dihydroxytryptamine-treated rats. *Brain Res.*, 298, 370–73.

Nimgaonkar, V. L., Goodwin, G. M., Davies, C. L., and Green, A. R. (1985). Down regulation of β-adrenoceptors in rat cortex by repeated administration of desipramine, electroconvulsive shock and clenbuterol requires 5-HT neurones but not 5-HT. *Neuropharmacology*, 24, 279–83.

Nisbet, A., and Marsden, C. A. (1984). Increased behavioural response to 5-methoxy-N,N-dimethyltryptamine but not to RU-24969 after intraventricular 5,7-dihydroxytryptamine administration. *Eur. J. Pharmac.*, 104, 177–80.

Ogawa, N., Yamawaki, Y., Kuroda, H., Nukina, I., Ota, Z., Fujino, M., and Yanaihara, N. (1982). Characteristics of thyrotrophin-releasing hormone (TRH) receptors in rat brain. *Peptides*, 3, 669–77.

Peroutka, S. J., and Snyder, S. H. (1980). Chronic antidepressant treatment lowers spiroperidol-labelled serotonin receptor binding. *Science*, 210, 88–90.

Prange, A. J., Breese, G. R., Cott, J. H., Martin, B. R., Cooper, B. R., Wilson, I. C., and Plotnikoff, N. P. (1974). Thyrotrophin releasing hormone: Antagonism of pentobarbital in rodents. *Life Sci.*, 14, 447–55.

Prasad, C., Jacobs, J. J., and Wilber, J. F. (1980). Immunological blockade of endogenous thyrotrophin releasing hormone produces hypothermia in rats. *Brain Res.*, 193, 580–3.

Schettini, G., Di Renzo, G., Amoroso, S., Annunziato, L., and Quattrone, A. (1983). Chemical denervation produces supersensitivity of central serotonergic receptors involved in the control of TSH secretion in the rat. *Brain Res.*, 261, 349–52.

Schmidt-Archert, K. M., Askanas, U., and Engel, W. K. (1984). Thyrotropin-releasing hormone enhances choline acetyltransferase and creatine kinase in cultured spinal ventral horn neurones. *J. Neurochem.*, 43, 586–9.

Shaeffer, J. M., Axelrod, J., and Brownstein, M. J. (1977). Regional difference in dopamine-mediated release of TRH-like material from synaptosomes. *Brain Res.*, 138, 571–4.

Sharif, N. A., and Burt, D. A. (1983). Receptors for thyrotrophin releasing hormone (TRH) in rabbit spinal cord. *Brain Res.*, 270, 259–64.

Sharif, N. A., Burt, D. A., Towle, A. C., Mueller, R. A., and Breese, G. R. (1983). Co-depletion of serotonin and TRH induces apparent supersensitivity of spinal TRH receptors. *Eur. J. Pharmac.*, 95, 301–4.

Sharp, T., Bennett, G. W., and Marsden, C. A. (1982). TRH analogues increase dopamine release from slices of rat brain. *J. Neurochem.*, 39: 1763–66.

Sharp, T., Brazell, M. P., Bennett, G. W., and Marsden, C. A. (1984a). The TRH analogue CG 3509 increases *in vivo* catechol/ascorbate oxidation in the n. accumbens but not the striatum of the rat. *Neuropharmacology*, 23, 617–23.

Sharp, T., Bennett, G. W., Marsden, C. A., and Tulloch, I. F. (1984b). A comparison of the locomotor effects induced by centrally injected TRH and TRH analogues. *Regulatory Peptides*, 9, 305–15.

Sharp, T., Tulloch, I. F., Bennett, G. W., Marsden, C. A., Metcalf, G., and Dettmar, P. W. (1984c). Analeptic effects of centrally injected TRH and TRH analogues in the pentobarbitone-anaesthetised rat. *Neuropharmacology*, **23**, 339–48.

Sills, M. A., Wolfe, B. B., and Frazer, A. (1984). Determination of selective and non-selective compounds for the $5-HT_{1A}$ and $5-HT_{1B}$ receptor subtypes in rat frontal cortex. *J. Pharmac. exp. Ther.*, **231**, 480–7.

Simasko, S. M., and Horita, A. (1985). Treatment of rats with the TRH analogue MK-771. Down regulation of TRH receptors and behavioural tolerance. *Neuropharmacology*, **24**, 157–66.

Stolz, J. F., Marsden, C. A., and Middlemiss, D. N. (1983). Effect of chronic antidepressant treatment and subsequent withdrawal on [^{3}H]-5-hydroxytryptamine and [^{3}H]-spiperone binding in rat frontal cortex and serotonin-mediated behaviour. *Psychopharmacology*, **80**, 150–5.

Sugrue, M. F. (1981). Effects of acutely and chronically administered antidepressants on the clonidine-induced decrease in rat brain 3-methoxy-4-hydroxyphenylethyleneglycol sulphate content. *Life Sci.*, **28**, 377–83.

Sulser, F. (1986). Discussion in *Antidepressants and receptor function. CIBA Foundation Symposium 123*. Wiley, Chichester, 263.

Sulser, F., and Mobley, P. L. (1981). Regulation of central noradrenergic receptor function: new vistas on the mode of action of antidepressant treatment. In Usdin, E. (ed.), *Neuroregulators: Basic and Clinical Aspects*. Wiley, Chichester, 55–83.

Ushijima, I., Mizuki, Y., Hara, T., Watanabe, K., Hirano, H., Yamada, M., and Glavin, G. B. (1986). Effects of acute and long-term treatments with thyrotropin-releasing hormone on locomotor activity and jumping behaviour in mice. *Pharmac. Biochem. Behav.*, **24**, 1423–8.

White, S. R. (1985). A comparison of the effects of serotonin, substance P and thyrotropin-releasing hormone on excitability of rat spinal motoneurones *in vivo*. *Brain Res.*, **335**, 63–70.

Yap, C. Y., and Taylor, D. A. (1983). Involvement of $5-HT_2$ receptors in the wet-dog shake behaviour induced by 5-hydroxytryptophan in the rat. *Neuropharmacology*, **22**, 801–4.

7

Selective Antagonism by Serotonin Uptake Inhibitors of H 75/12-Induced Hyperthermia in Rats

P. Worms, N. Coutou and K. Biziere

The administration of H75/12 (3-hydroxy-4-methyl-alpha-ethyl-phenethyl-amine) to rats leads to a marked enhancement of body temperature (Christensen *et al.*, 1977). This hyperthermic effect is thought to be due to a specific displacement of serotonin (5-HT) from serotonergic neurons, after selective uptake of H75/12 by serotonergic terminals (Carlsson *et al.*, 1969; Maitre *et al.*, 1980). It has been shown that 5-HT uptake inhibitors such as citalopram, CGP6085A or midalcipran are able to antagonise both the neuronal depletion in 5-HT and the hyperthermia induced by H75/12 (Christensen *et al.*, 1977; Maitre *et al.*, 1980; Moret *et al.*, 1985).

The aim of the present study was to characterise the pharmacology of H75/12-induced hyperthermia and to assess a potential selectivity of this model for 5-HT uptake inhibitors.

7.1 Material and Methods

Male Sprague-Dawley rats (Charles River; France), weighing 180 to 220 g, were used. The method used was that described by Christensen *et al.* (1977), modified as follows: test-drugs or vehicle were administered 30 min (intraperitoneally, i.p.) or 60 min (orally, p.o.) before a subcutaneous (s.c.) injection of H75/12 (40 mg/kg). The rats were isolated in macrolon test cages (20 x 30 cm), placed in a temperature-controlled laboratory (20 ± 1 °C) and allowed to adjust for 1 h before drug administration. Rectal temperature was measured by means of a thermoelectric probe (YSI423) immediately before drug administration and every 30 min for 3 h after the injection of H75/12. The mean (± SEM) differences between pre- and post-drug values were calculated.

For statistical analysis, the areas under the time-response curves (AUCs) were calculated for each treatment, and their means were compared using the Mann-Whitney U-test.

The following drugs were used (sources within parenthesis): H75/12 (Labkemi, Sweden), citalopram hydrochloride (Lündbeck, Denmark), indalpine (Pharmuka, France), norzimelidine 2 hydrochloride (Astra, Sweden), imipramine hydrochloride (Ricerchemica, Italy), chlormipramine hydrochloride (CMI) and desipramine hydrochloride (DMI) (Ciba-Geigy, Switzerland), (±) fenfluramine hydrochloride and amineptine hydrochloride (Servier, France), nomifensine maleate (extracted from Alival R, Hoechst-Roussel, France). SR 95191 and moclobemide were synthesised at the laboratory of Organic Chemistry (Sanofi Recherche).

7.2 Results

When injected s.c. at a dose of 40 mg/kg, H75/12 induced a clear rise in rectal temperature, which lasted approximately 3 h. Maximal increase in rectal temperature was observed 1 to 1.5 h post-injection, and varied from $+ 2\,^{\circ}C$ to $+ 2.5\,^{\circ}C$.

As shown in Table 7.1, the selective 5-HT uptake inhibitors citalopram (3 to

Table 7.1   Antagonism of H75/12 hyperthermia by 5-HT uptake inhibitors

Drugs	Doses (mg/kg)	Route	Increase in rectal temperature ($^{\circ}C$)	
			H75/12	Combination
Citalopram	3	s.c.	2.0 ± 0.2	0.6 ± 0.2*
	10	s.c.	2.0 ± 0.2	0.4 ± 0.2*
Indalpine	3	i.p.	2.0 ± 0.2	0.6 ± 0.2*
	10	i.p.	2.0 ± 0.2	0.8 ± 0.1*
	30	i.p.	2.0 ± 0.2	0.2 ± 0.2*
Norzimelidine	3	i.p.	2.0 ± 0.2	0.6 ± 0.1*
	10	i.p.	2.0 ± 0.2	0.6 ± 0.2*†

Data are expressed as mean (± SEM) increases of rectal temperature ($^{\circ}C$) as compared with pre-injection values. *$p < 0.01$ versus H75/12 controls. †Significant rise in temperature induced by the test drug itself.

10 mg/kg s.c.), indalpine (3 to 30 mg/kg i.p.) and norzimelidine (3 to 10 mg/kg i.p.) markedly antagonised H75/12-induced hyperthermia. None of these drugs affected rectal temperature by itself, with the exception of norzimeldine, which induced a slight increase in rectal temperature at the highest dose tested (0.7 ± 0.2 °C; $p < 0.05$).

The tricyclic antidepressants, imipramine (15 to 30 mg/kg p.o.), chlorimipramine (10 to 30 mg/kg i.p.) and desmethylimipramine (10 to 30 mg/kg i.p.), also blocked the effect of H75/12, without affecting body temperature by themselves (Table 7.2).

As shown in Table 7.3, nomifensine, a mixed dopamine (DA) and noradrenaline (NA) uptake inhibitor (10 to 30 mg/kg i.p.) and amineptine, a selective DA uptake inhibitor (30 to 60 mg/kg i.p.) did not antagonise H75/12 hyperthermia, and even induced a significant hyperthermia by themselves (+ 0.6 ± 0.1 °C to + 2.0 ± 0.3 °C; $p < 0.01$). Similarly, the 5-HT releaser (±) fenfluramine (10 to 30 mg/kg p.o.) increased rectal temperature by itself (+ 0.7 ± 0.3 °C at 30 mg/kg; $p < 0.05$), but failed to affect the hyperthermic effect of H75/12 (Table 7.3).

Table 7.2   Antagonism of H75/12 hyperthermia by tricyclic antidepressant drugs

Drugs	Doses (mg/kg)	Route	Increase rectal temperature (°C)	
			H75/12	Combination
CMI	10	i.p.	2.0 ± 0.2	0.3 ± 0.2*
	30	i.p.	2.0 ± 0.2	0 ± 0.1*
Imipramine	15	p.o.	1.7 ± 0.1	0.5 ± 0.2*
	30	p.o.	1.7 ± 0.1	0.1 ± 0.3*
DMI	10	i.p.	2.1 ± 0.1	0.8 ± 0.3*
	30	i.p.	2.1 ± 0.1	0.1 ± 0.2*

See explanation below Table 7.1. *$p < 0.05$ compared with H75/12 controls.

The selective monoamine oxidase-A inhibitors moclobemide and SR 95191 did not antagonise, and even potentiated, H75/12-induced hyperthermia. Neither compound, *per se*, affected rectal temperature (Table 7.3).

Finally, the antipyretic aspirin failed to antagonise the effect of H75/12 (H75/12 controls: + 2.3 ± 0.1 °C; combination with 30 mg/kg p.o.: + 2.0 ± 0.2, (non-significant); with 100 mg/kg p.o.: + 3.2 ± 0.1 °C, $p < 0.05$).

Table 7.3 Effect of catecholamine uptake inhibitors, (±) fenfluramine and monoamine oxidase-A inhibitors, on H75/12-induced hyperthermia.

Drugs	Doses (mg/kg)	Route	Increase in rectal temperature (°C) H75/12	Combination
Nomifensine	10	i.p.	2.1 ± 0.2	2.6 ± 0.4†
	30	i.p.	2.1 ± 0.2	2.7 ± 0.6†
Amineptine	30	i.p.	2.0 ± 0.2	2.6 ± 0.1†
	60	i.p.	2.0 ± 0.2	2.7 ± 0.3†
(±) Fenfluramine	10	p.o.	1.9 ± 0.1	1.7 ± 0.3
	30	p.o.	1.9 ± 0.1	1.4 ± 0.3†
Moclobemide	10	p.o.	2.3 ± 0.1	2.4 ± 0.3
	30	p.o.	2.3 ± 0.1	3.0 ± 0.5
SR 95191	30	p.o.	2.3 ± 0.2	1.7 ± 0.3
	60	p.o.	2.3 ± 0.2	2.8 ± 0.3*

See explanation below Table 7.1. *$p < 0.05$ compared with H75/12 controls. †Significant rise in temperature induced by the test drug itself.

7.3 Discussion

The present data indicate that compounds which inhibit the neuronal uptake of 5 HT, either selectively (citalopram: Christensen et al., 1977; indalpine: Le Fur and Uzan, 1977; norzimelidine; CMI) or non-selectively (imipramine, DMI), all antagonise the hyperthermic effect of the 5-HT displacer H75/12. These results are in agreement with those previously reported for citalopram, imipramine or midalcipran (Christensen et al., 1977; Moret et al., 1985). They also fit in with the fact that 5-HT uptake inhibitors, including those tested in the present study, all antagonise the neuronal depletion in 5-HT induced by H75/12 in the rat (Carlsson et al., 1969; Maitre et al., 1980; Mouget-Goniot and Worms, unpublished results). It must be noted that although DMI is usually considered to be a more selective inhibitor of NA than of 5-HT, it has been shown to inhibit 5-HT uptake at high doses, similar to those used in the present study.

In contrast, the selective inhibitors of NA and/or DA uptake, nomifensine (Brogden et al., 1979) and amineptine (Samanin et al., 1977), do not affect H75/12-induced hyperthermia, suggesting a certain selectivity of this model for 5-HT uptake inhibition. This statement is reinforced by the lack of activity of the 5-HT releaser (±) fenfluramine (although its own hyperthermic effect may well interfere with the test procedure), as well as that of the selective monoamine oxidase-A inhibitors moclobemide (Da Prada et al., 1983) and SR 95191

Table 7.4 Comparison between the data obtained in various hyperthermia models in rats and the data obtained in the model of potentiation of 5-HTP-induced tremor in rats

| Drugs | Range of active doses | | | ED 50 |
	H75/12	Fenfluramine*†	PCA*	5-HTP‡
Citalopram	3 to 10 s.c.	20 i.p.	20 i.p.	12 i.p.
Indalpine	3 to 30 i.p.	–	–	8 i.p.
CMI	10 to 30 i.p.	10 to 20 i.p.	20 i.p.	20 i.p.
Nomifensine	Inactive	–	–	Inactive
Moclobemide	Inactive	–	–	1.3 p.o.
SR 95191	Inactive	–	–	10.3 p.o.

Data are expressed as active doses (antagonism of hyperthermia) or ED_{50} values (5-HTP) in mg/kg. *Taken from Pawlowski *et al.*, 1981. †Taken from Sugrue, 1984. ‡Taken from Worms *et al.*, 1987. Abbreviations: PCA: parachloroamphetamine; 5-HTP: 5-hydroxytryptophane.

(Worms *et al.*, 1987). This latter result is particularly interesting as, in another classical model used for the selection of 5-HT uptake inhibitors, namely the potentiation of 5-HTP-induced behaviours (Ortmann *et al.*, 1980), both mono-amine oxidase inhibitors *and* 5-HT uptake inhibitors are active (see the summary in Table 7.4).

Finally, it is noteworthy that the antipyretic (anti-hyperthermic) drug aspirin is unable to antagonise this type of 5-HT-dependent hyperthermia.

The comparison with the results obtained in other models designed for the characterisation of 5-HT uptake inhibition (fenfluramine- and parachloroamphet-amine-induced hyperthermia) (see summary in Table 7.4), shows a good agreement between these results (Pawlowski *et al.*, 1981; Sugrue, 1984) and those reported here for the antagonism of H75/12. However, only few studies have been devoted to the characterisation of these two other models, and it is thus difficult to compare all these models in terms of selectivity.

In conclusion, the preliminary data reported here suggest that the antagonism of H75/12-induced hyperthermia in rats may well represent a selective model for the study of 5-HT uptake inhibitors. However, additional work remains to be done to further characterise this potential 'selectivity'. This includes the study of 5-HT receptor blockers as well as that of non-serotonergic drugs which are known to induce a marked hypothermia (i.e. reserpine, oxotremorine, apo-morphine).

References

Brogden, R. N., Heel, R. C., Speight, T. M., and Avery, G. S. (1979). *Drugs*, **18**, 1–24.
Carlsson, A., Corrodi, H., Fuxe, K., and Hokfelt, T. (1969). *Eur. J. Pharmacol.*, **5**, 357–65.
Christensen, A. V., Fjalland, B., Pedersen, V., Samsal, P. D., and Svendsen, O. (1977). *Eur. J. Pharmacol.*, **41**, 153–62.

Da Prada, M., Kettler, R., and Haefely, W. E. (1983). *Mod. Probl. Pharmacopsychiat.*, 19, 231–45.

Le Fur, G., and Uzan, A. (1977). *Biochem. Pharmacol.*, 26, 497–503.

Maitre, L., Moser, P., Baumann, P. A., and Waldmeier, P. C. (1980). *Acta Psychiat. Scand.*, 61, 97–110.

Moret, C., Charveron, M., Finberg, J. P. M., Couzinier, J. P., and Briley, M. (1985). *Neuropharmacol.*, 24, 1211–19.

Ortmann, R., Waldmeier, P. C., Radeke, E., Felner, A., and Delini-Stula, A. (1980). *Naunyn-Schmiedeberg's Arch. Pharmacol.*, 311, 185–92.

Pawlowski, L., Ruczinska, J., and Gorka, Z. (1981). *Psychopharmacology*, 74, 161–5.

Samanin, R., Jori, A., Bernasconi, S., Morpugo, E., and Garattini, S. (1977). *J. Pharm. Pharmacol.*, 29, 555–68.

Sugrue, M. F. (1984). *Br. J. Pharmac.*, 81, 651–7.

Worms, P., Kan, J. P., Wermuth C. G., Roncucci, R., and Biziere, K. (1987). *J. Pharmacol. Exp. Ther.*, 240, 241–250.

8

Beyond Nosology in Biological Psychiatry. 5-HT Disturbances in Mood, Aggression and Anxiety Disorders

H. M. van Praag, R. S. Kahn, G. M. Asnis, S. Wetzler, S. L. Brown, A. Bleich and M. L. Korn

8.1 5-HT, a Neurotransmitter of All Seasons?

5-HT disorders have been reported in depression, anxiety states, schizophrenia and alcoholism. The increasing number of psychiatric states in which serotonin (5-hydrotryptamine; 5-HT) apparently can be disturbed seems bewildering. The situation has been called chaotic, the findings themselves non-specific. Van Kammen (1987) called 5-HT, ironically, a neurotransmitter of all seasons. We do not concur with either statement and in this chapter we explain why. First we discuss the available data; then we try to bring them into a conceptual frame-work.

8.2 5-HT in Depressive Disorders

8.2.1 5-HT Disturbances

Direct evidence of disordered 5-HT metabolism in depressive disorder is provided by the occurrence of lowered levels of 5-hydroxindoleacetic acid (5-HIAA) in cerebrospinal fluid (CSF), under baseline conditions (Fig. 8.1) and after probenecid loading (Fig. 8.2). This finding was reported by most investigators, though not all (reviewed in van Praag, 1982a). Low baseline and post-probenecid

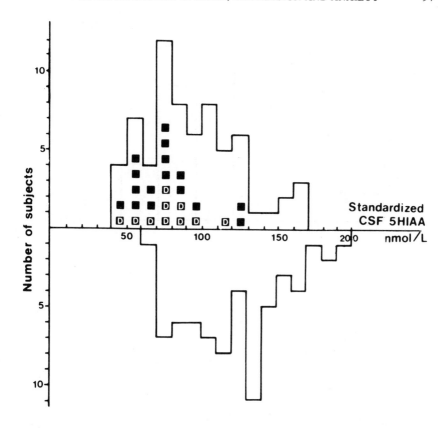

Fig. 8.1 Standardised concentrations of CSF 5-HIAA in patients who have attempted suicide (upward) and healthy volunteer control subjects (downward). ■, suicide attempts by a violent method (any method other than a drug overdose, taken by mouth, or a single wrist cut). D, a subject who subsequently died from suicide, in all cases but one within 1 year after the lumbar puncture (Asberg *et al.*, 1984).

CSF 5-HIAA is indicative of lowered 5-HT metabolism in the central nervous system (CNS). Low CSF 5-HIAA is more likely to occur in major depression, melancholic type (endogenous or vital depression (van Praag *et al.*, 1965)), in severe depression, in psychotic depression and in depression precipitated by life events, than in dysthymic disorder (neurotic or personal depression (van Praag *et al.*, 1965)), mild depression, non-psychotic depression, and 'spontaneous' depression, respectively. In most studies, no more than 30 to 40% of patients with melancholic depression showed the CSF signs of 5-HT disturbances.

Peripheral signs of 5-HT disturbances have also been reported in subgroups of depressive patients (reviewed in van Praag, 1984a). First, those pertaining to

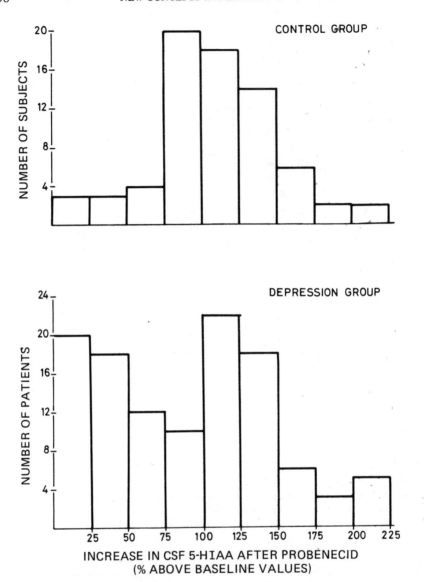

Fig. 8.2 Increase of CSF 5-HIAA concentration after probenecid in patients suffering from vital (endogenous; major) depression (bottom) and in a non-psychiatric control group (top). The columns indicate the number of patients showing the increase in concentration given at the bottom of the column. The distribution in the depression group is bimodal. There is a significant increase in individuals with low CSF 5-HIAA accumulation after probenecid (van Praag, 1982b).

blood platelets, in which 5-HT content, 5-HT uptake and density of imipramine binding sites were found to be lowered. Though the platelet is considered to be a reasonable model of serotonergic nerve endings in the CNS, it remains unknown whether platelet abnormalities in depression signify comparable disturbances in the brain.

Several authors, moreover, found in depression the plasma ratio of tryptophan versus aminoacids competing for the same carrier mechanisms into the CNS to be lowered. Under those conditions the influx of tryptophan into the CNS can be expected to be diminished and herewith 5-HT synthesis.

Finally, challenge tests have been used to gather information on the responsiveness of post-synaptic 5-HT receptors. The principal challengers used so far have been the 5-HT precursors tryptophan and 5-hydroxytryptophan (5-HTP) and fenfluramine, a 5-HT releaser and uptake inhibitor. The serotonergically modulated 'output' being measured consisted of hormone release, particularly that of prolactin, growth hormone and cortisol, and of temperature regulation. The hormonal data have been ambiguous, owing mainly to non-specificity of the challengers, all of which have measurable influences on central catecholamines (CA) as well (review in van Praag et al., 1987a). A new generation of compounds selective for 5-HT receptors or even for particular 5-HT receptor subtypes is being developed and holds great promise for 5-HT studies in psychiatry.

As was the case with low CSF 5-HIAA, peripheral 5-HT disturbances have only been found in subgroups of the depressive population. The subgroups, however, are ill defined. Little is known, moreover, about the intercorrelation of the various peripheral 5-HT disturbances among themselves and with CSF 5-HIAA levels.

8.2.2 Hypothesis 1: Biochemical Heterogeneity of Depression

On the basis of the occurrence of low baseline and post-probenecid CSF 5-HIAA in a subgroup of depression, we postulated the existence of a 5-HT-related subtype of depression, introducing herewith the concept of biochemical heterogeneity of psychiatric disorders (van Praag et al., 1970; van Praag and Korf, 1971b). Disparate pathophysiological processes, we suggested, might result in the same syndrome: in this case, the depressive syndrome, occurring with and without demonstrable disturbances in central 5-HT. Biochemical heterogeneity would have profound implications for treatment: '5-HT depressions', for example, would be the natural candidates for selective 5-HT agonists. As an analogy we referred to the anaemia syndrome. Clinically, anaemic patients look pretty much alike. Pathogenetically they are very different and so is their treatment.

8.2.3 Hypothesis 2: 5-HT Disturbances Related to Particular Psychopathological Dimensions

An alternative explanation, however, has to be considered. 5-HT disturbances are not linked to a particular subtype of depression but to a particular component of that syndrome that might be part of it but might be absent. A related possibility is the 5-HT disorders being related to a personality trait functioning as a vulnerability factor for depression or for a component of that syndrome, but not discernible in all depressive patients.

We found evidence arguing against the concept of a '5-HT depression' as well as evidence favouring the alternative hypothesis relating 5-HT disorders to particular psychopathological dimensions. The two sets of data are discussed in the next sections.

8.3 Data Arguing Against the Concept of a '5-HT Depression'

Selective 5-HT reuptake inhibitors have generally been found to possess antidepressant properties (Lemberger et al., 1985). However, no subgroup of depression has been demarcated that responds preferentially or exceptionally strongly, as could have been expected if a subgroup of '5-HT depressions' had existed. The strength of this argument weakens, however, if one acknowledges that the compound most frequently used, zimelidine, affects in humans both 5-HT and NA (Potter et al., 1985). Other allegedly selective 5-HT reuptake inhibitors have not been studied in this manner.

A more convincing argument provided our studies with the 5-HT precursor 5-hydroxytryptophan (5-HTP) in depression (review in van Praag and Lemus, 1986). We showed the drug to have antidepressant properties. This compound, however, increases not only 5-HT metabolism but also that of noradrenaline (NA). This effect is probably due to 5-HTP penetrating catecholaminergic (CA-ergic) neurons, where it is transformed in 5-HT. 5-HT acts in these cells as a false transmitter, leading to compensatory increase of NA metabolism. The net effect of these two opposing forces, i.e. false transmitter formation and augmentation of NA production, is, in all likelihood, an increase in NA activity.

In approximately 25% of the 5-HT responders the therapeutic effect tends to subside in the second month of treatment, albeit generally not completely. We demonstrated that the decline in therapeutic response is paralleled by a normalisation of NA metabolism with 5-HT metabolism remaining increased (Fig. 8.3). If decline of therapeutic efficacy and normalisation of NA metabolism are related, we reasoned, renewed augmentation of NA metabolism should restore the therapeutic effect. Adding tyrosine, the precursor of NA, to the 5-HTP regime indeed had that effect. It restored not only the therapeutic effect of 5-HTP but also the heightened level of NA metabolites (Fig. 8.4), a strong indication that simultaneously increasing 5-HT *and* NA metabolism provides

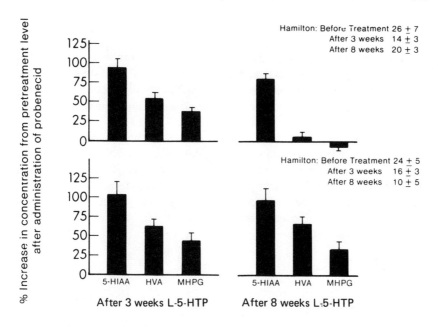

Fig. 8.3 Augmenting effect of L-5-HTP (200 mg/day in combination with carbidopa, 150 mg/day) on CA metabolism is transient in patients who relapsed after the first month of 5-HTP treatment (top). In the first month of treatment, there is a substantial increase of HVA and MHPG in CSF after a probenecid load. In the second treatment month, the levels of those metabolites have returned to normal. The 5-HIAA response remains increased over time. In patients in whom the therapeutic response to 5-HTP continued, the effect on CA metabolites in CSF did not subside (bottom) (van Praag, 1983b).

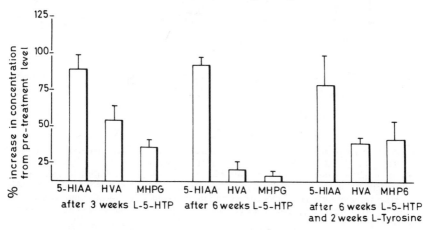

Fig. 8.4 Influence of L-5-HTP and the combination of L-5-HTP and L-tyrosine on post-probenecid CSF 5-HIAA and HVA and baseline MHPG. After 3 weeks of 5-HTP treatment, the concentration of the three metabolites had significantly increased. After 6 weeks of 5-HTP, CSF HVA and MHPG had 'habituated'. Both concentrations rose again after adding tyrosine. 5-HIAA remained high during the entire treatment period (van Praag, 1983b).

better conditions for antidepressant activity than increasing 5-HT metabolism alone.

In the same direction point data collected with the precursor of 5-HT, i.e. tryptophan (review in van Praag and Lemus, 1986; van Praag, 1984b). It is inactive in severe depression and weakly therapeutic in mild depression, it being unknown whether the improvement is based on a true antidepressant effect or on sedation.

Tryptophan increases 5-HT metabolism in man, without increasing that of CA. Administered in high doses it even decreases CA metabolism, probably by competing with tyrosine for entrance in the CNS (van Praag et al., 1987a) (Fig. 8.5). If the lack of antidepressant efficacy were related to tryptophans' inability to raise CA synthesis then one could expect tyrosine to raise tryptophan's efficiency above the significance level. This is indeed what we have demonstrated to occur (van Praag, 1985).

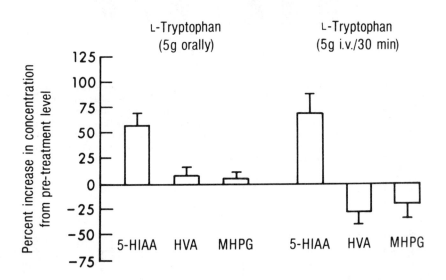

Fig 8.5 Percentage increase in the concentration of 5-HIAA, HVA, and MHPG in lumbar CSF after administration to five test subjects of a single dose of 5 g L-tryptophan either orally or intravenously. 5-HIAA concentration rose significantly on both occasions and to the same extent. After oral administration, the changes in HVA and MHPG were insignificant; after i.v. administration both concentrations dropped significantly. Lumbar CSF was withdrawn after probenecid loading (5 g/5 h), 8 h after starting the load (van Praag et al., 1987a).

We *conclude* that the data discussed are hard to reconcile with the concept of a subgroup of predominantly 5-HT-related depressions. They rather permit the following interpretations: selective 5-HT agonists are weak antidepressants, or, alternatively, they are partial antidepressants, active only against certain components of the depressive syndrome. Several lines of evidence argue in favour of the latter hypothesis; aggression-, anxiety-, and mood-disregulation being the arguably 5-HT-related psychopathological dimensions.

8.4 Data Suggesting 5-HT Disorders Being Related to Particular Psychopathological Dimensions

8.4.1 Aggression Regulation

Asberg et al. (1976) reported that in depression low CSF 5-HIAA occurs preferentially in patients who had recently attempted suicide, had done so with violent means (all means, apart from drug overdose and superficial wrist cutting) and had acted impulsively rather than premeditating the deed (Asberg et al., 1986) (Fig. 8.1). The first observation has been repeatedly, though not universally, confirmed; the second has been contested (review in van Praag, 1986a). Moreover, the contention that the violence of the suicide attempt reflects the strength of the wish to die is not justified. Seriousness of suicide attempt and seriousness of suicide intent are not strongly correlated (van Praag et al., in preparation). The observation that low CSF 5-HIAA relates to deficient impulse-control is intriguing but has so far been made in only two studies (Linnoila et al., 1983; Lidberg et al., 1985) and awaits confirmation.

Subsequently several groups of observations specified the relationship between 5-HT and suicide.

(a) The risk of suicide attempts in depressed patients is not evenly distributed (van Praag and Plutchik, submitted). Some patients resort to it, the majority do not. In the group of depressed patients with a lifetime history of at least one suicide attempt, the attempt frequency is skewed as well, a minority of patients being responsible for the majority of the attempts. In other words: a subgroup of depressed patients attempt suicide regularly, the majority of patients do so sporadically or never. This conclusion holds for both the groups of major depression (Fig. 8.6) and that of dysthymic disorders (Fig. 8.7). Attempt frequency, moreover, was found to be independent of depression frequency. It was in the group of repeated suicide attempters that we found CSF 5-HIAA most frequently to be decreased, indicating this variable indeed to be related to strong or imbalanced autoagressive impulses.

(b) Lowered CSF 5-HIAA was found to occur not only in depressed but also in non-depressed suicide attempters (Traskman et al., 1981) (Fig. 8.8), i.e. in individuals with personality disorders (Brown et al., 1979, 1982) and in schizophrenics ordered to suicide by 'voices' (Fig. 8.9) (van Praag, 1983a; Ninan et al., 1984). 5-HT disorders thus seem to relate to suicidal behaviour irrespective of diagnosis.

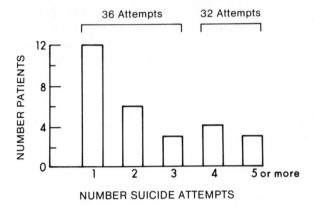

Fig. 8.6 Distribution of number of suicide attempts in a group of 29 patients with major depression who had made at least one suicide attempt during their lifetime. The total number of attempts was 68 and 7 patients (24%) carried the weight of 32 (47%) of the attempts (van Praag and Plutchik, submitted).

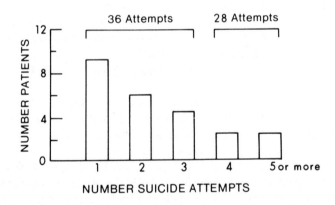

Fig. 8.7 Distribution of number of suicide attempts in a group of 26 patients with dysthymic disorder and at least one suicide attempt during lifetime. The total number of attempts numbered 64. Six patients (23%) carried the weight of 28 (44%) of the attempts (van Praag and Plutchik, submitted).

(c) In low-CSF-5-HIAA depressives we found not only an increased rate of suicide attempt but also multiple signs of augmented outward-directed aggression (van Praag, 1986b) (Table 8.1). This finding indicates low CSF 5-HIAA being related to disturbed aggression regulation rather than to increased suicidality as such.

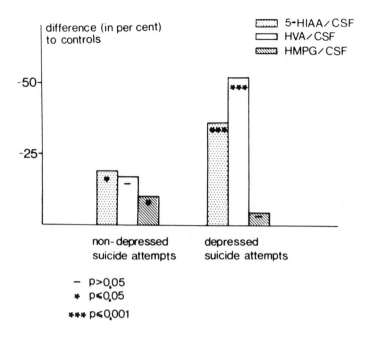

Fig. 8.8 Differences in CSF monoamine metabolite levels (adjusted for age and height) between controls and depressed and non-depressed suicide attempters (Traskman et al., 1981).

(d) Low CSF 5-HIAA has been found to occur in individuals with pathologically increased outward-directed aggression without signs of depression (Brown et al., 1979, 1982; Bioulac et al., 1980; Linnoila et al., 1983; Lidberg et al., 1984, 1985). Individuals with a variety of severe personality disorders have been studied, some of them delinquents. Admittedly, the number of aggression/ 5-HT studies is still small and studies of this kind are fraught with methodological pitfalls; nevertheless, they all point in the same direction: lowered metabolism of 5-HT in the CNS (Table 8.2). No negative study has so far been reported.

The data reported here seem to justify the *conclusion* that in humans, like in animals (Valzelli, 1981), serotonergic regulation is involved in aggression regulation. The amount of aggression displayed in a given situation is dependent on three factors: strength of the aggressive impulses, strength of the countervailing forces (Plutchik et al., in press) and the ability to control and balance these impulses. What is unknown is which of those variables is 5-HT-dependent. Preliminary data suggest deficient impulse control to be the behavioural correlate of diminished 5-HT metabolism (Linnoila et al., 1983; Lidberg et al., 1985). Intriguing as this hypothesis may be — relating a biological variable to what

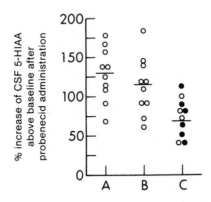

A = Non-psychiatric control group

B = Schizophrenic without suicidal
    history

C = Schizophrenic with suicidal history

O = Non-violent suicide

● = Violent suicide

Fig. 8.9 Post-probenecid CSF 5-HIAA in non-depressed schizophrenic patients. CSF 5-HIAA was significantly lower in the schizophrenic patients who had made recent suicide attempts, than in those without lifetime history of suicide attempts and then in a control group (van Praag 1983a).

Table 8.1 Low-5-HIAA depressives compared with normal-5-HIAA depressives present (van Praag, 1986)

Finding	p
More suicide attempts	< 0.01
Greater number of contacts with police	< 0.05
Increased arguments with	
relatives	< 0.05
spouse	< 0.01
colleagues	< 0.05
friends	< 0.05
More hostility at interview	< 0.05
Impaired employment history (arguments)	< 0.05

seems to be a very basic constituent of the human behavioural repertoire – the hypothesis is a very preliminary one. Moreover, under the premise of this hypothesis one would expect 5-HT to be disturbed in other disorders in which impulse control is diminished, such as compulsive gambling and firesetting. In these individuals, however, CSF 5-HIAA was reported to be normal (Linnoila, 1986).

Table 8.2 Studies on CSF 5-HIAA and aggression*

Reference	No.	Sex	Diagnosis	Measurement aggression	Assay CSF 5-HIAA	Postprobenecid or baseline 5-HIAA	Other MA metabolites in CSF
Brown et al. (1979)	26	M	Personality disorder	Checklist lifetime history of aggressive acts	Flurometrically	Baseline	HVA unchanged MHPG increased
Brown et al. (1982)	12	M	Borderline personality	Checklist lifetime history of aggressive acts Buss–Durkes Inventory MMPI	Mass fragmentography	Baseline	HVA unchanged MHPG unchanged
Bioulac et al. (1980)	6	M	xyy Personality disorder	Lifetime history of aggressive behaviour	Fluorometrically	Postprobenecid	HVA unchanged MHPG not measured
Linnoila et al. (1983)†	36	M	Severe personality disorders	21 had killed; 15 had made attempts to kill; all were alcohol abusers	Liquid chromatography	Baseline	HVA unchanged MHPG unchanged
Lidberg et al. (1984)	1 F, 2 M		Depression	Killed own child; subsequently attempted suicide	Not stated	Baseline	Not stated

*The two variables were negatively correlated in all studies. †Low CSF 5-HIAA in impulsive violent offenders as opposed to those who had premeditated their acts.

Aggression is not a unitary concept. This has been recognised in animal research and several schemes have been proposed to classify aggressive actions (Rodgers and Waters, 1985). Different neural circuitries and neurochemical patterns have been associated with different forms of aggression (Daruna, 1978; Adams, 1979). The non-unitary nature of human aggression is obvious but no useful classification has as yet been developed. Hence, the question whether disturbed 5-HT relates to disturbed aggression in general, or to particular types of aggression, has not yet been studied.

Finally, decreased 5-HT metabolism in the brain can reflect two different functional states. First, it may indicate primary serotonergic hypoactivity; alternatively, it could indicate primary serotonergic hyperactivity having led to compensatory decrease of 5-HT metabolism. In the first case, one would expect 5-HT potentiators to be helpful in aggressive disorders, in the latter cases one would expect this from 5-HT attenuators. Data in humans are extremely scarce. Morand *et al.* (1983) found tryptophan in high dosages to reduce aggression in schizophrenics. To our knowledge, no other controlled studies of 5-HT potentiators in states of increased aggression have been published.

In animals selective anti-aggressive effects have been reported with the so-called serenics, piperazine derivatives with a selective effect on particular sets of 5-HT receptors (Oliver and Mos, 1986). Since it is unknown whether these receptors reside pre- or post-synaptically, it is unknown whether they decrease (pre-synaptic stimulation) or increase (post-synaptic stimulation) 5-HT activity.

8.4.2 Anxiety Regulation

Biological findings in depression have generally been attributed to the state of depression. The inclination to investigate their relationship to, say, the anxiety component of the depressive syndrome is minimal. Hopes of finding disease-related markers and the fear of losing disease-relatedness of certain biological variables were so strong as to prevent it. The concept of specificity was linked to syndromal of nosological entities. A specific link of a biological variable to, say, anxiety would have stamped it as non-specific. Of the many studies of CSF 5-HIAA in depression, only three have analysed the CSF 5-HIAA/anxiety relationship. All three reported a negative correlation (Banki, 1977; Rydin *et al.*, 1982; Redmond *et al.*, 1986). We could not confirm this conclusion, though we did note that patients with the highest anxiety scores tended to gravitate to the low post-probenecid CSF 5-HIAA levels (Fig. 8.10). It should be added, however, that the data were analysed *post hoc*, and the only anxiety measure available was the anxiety score on the Hamilton Depression Scale.

Several other groups of data suggest a relation of 5-HT to anxiety or to anxiety states (review in Kahn *et al.*, in press). Most of the data are psychopharmacological in nature, indicating that drugs interfering with central 5-HT can have an ameliorating effect on pathological anxiety. The tricyclic anti-depressant clomi-

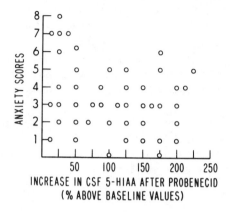

Fig. 8.10 Relation between post-probenecid 5-HIAA in CSF and anxiety ratings in 44 patients with non-psychotic major depression, melancholic type. There is no significant correlation, though the 6 patients with the highest anxiety scores clustered in the group with very low 5-HIAA responses. The anxiety scores are the summation of scores on the items 'anxiety psychic' and 'anxiety somatic' on the Hamilton Depression Scale.

pramine has consistently been found to exert a favourable effect in *obsessive compulsive disorder* (OCD). (Thoren *et al.*, 1980; Marks *et al.*, 1980; Montgomery, 1980). Clomipramine has a strong effect on 5-HT; its major metabolite desmethylclomipramine, however, is an uptake inhibitor of NA. It is the former effect, however, that is probably responsible for the therapeutic effects. Tricyclics with no or less effect on 5-HT, such as desipramine, are ineffective in OCD (Insel *et al.*, 1985; Zohar and Insel, in press). Moreover, clinical improvement on clomipramine is correlated with plasma levels of the drug itself, not with the concentration of its metabolite, and also with reduction of CSF 5-HIAA (Stern *et al.*, 1980; Insel *et al.*, 1983; Thoren *et al.*, 1980). Other more selective 5-HT-potentiating drugs, finally, such as tryptophan and zimelidine, have also been shown to exert anti-obsessional and anti-compulsive effects (Yaryuria-Tobias and Bhagavan, 1977; Kahn *et al.*, 1984).

In *panic disorder* (PD) drugs increasing the availability of 5-HT in the brain have been shown to exert both anti-anxiety and anti-panic effects; the most notable are 5-HTP, clomipramine and the selective 5-HT reuptake inhibitors zimelidine and fluvoxamine (Kahn and Westenberg, 1985; Kahn *et al.*, in press; Den Boer *et al.*, in press; Evans *et al.*, 1986).

In *generalised anxiety disorder* (GAD), a new, recently marketed drug, buspirone, has profound effects on central 5-HT (Taylor *et al.*, 1985). It exerts reportedly both agonistic and antagonistic effects on 5-HT_{1A} receptors, the net effect probably being decreased 5-HT function. Preliminary data indicate that ritanserin, a selective 5-HT$_2$ antagonist, is an effective agent in GAD (Ceulemans et al., 1985).

The findings in GAD suggest that, by decreasing 5-HT activity, anxiety symptoms are ameliorated. This hypothesis is supported by data derived from the PD studies alluded to above. The effect of the indirect 5-HT agonists was reportedly biphasic (Kahn and Westenberg, 1985). Initially, the patients deteriorated, i.e. anxiety and panic increased. After 2 to 4 weeks the deterioration gradually gave way to improvement. This biphasic response has been tentatively ascribed to hypersensitivity of post-synaptic 5-HT receptors in (certain) anxiety states. Increasing 5-HT availability would initially worsen the condition, but owing to down-regulation of the receptor system the therapeutic response would gradually ensue.

The hypothesis relating hypersensitivity of postsynaptic 5-HT receptors to (certain forms of) anxiety receives additional support from studies with the selective 5-HT$_1$ receptor agonist m-chlorophenylpiperazine (MCPP). We demonstrated that relatively low oral doses of MCPP (0.25 mg/kg) increased anxiety and panic attacks in PD patients with or without major depression. In normal controls and in patients with major depression but without PD the drug did not influence anxiety levels (Kahn et al., in press, submitted) (Fig. 8.11). The release of cortisol after an MCPP challenge was also augmented in PD patients (Figs. 8.12 and 8.13). Other researchers using higher doses of MCPP, i.e. 0.5 mg/kg,

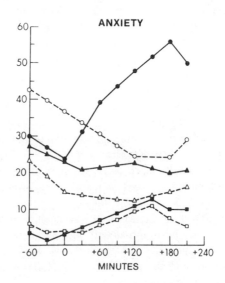

Fig. 8.11 Anxiety as measured on the profiles of moods states, before and after administration of placebo and MCPP (0.25 mg/kg). □, normal controls, placebo; ■, normal controls, MCPP; ○, panic disorder, placebo; ●, panic disorder, MCPP; △, major depression, placebo; ▲, major depression, MCPP.

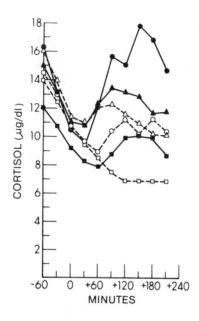

Fig 8.12 Cortisol serum levels, before and after administration of placebo and MCPP (0.25 mg/kg). □, normal controls, placebo; ■, normal controls, MCPP; ○, panic disorder, placebo; ●, panic disorder, MCPP; △, major depression, placebo; ▲, major depression, MCPP.

did not report induction of anxiety in normal subjects either (Mueller *et al.*, 1985, 1986; Zohar and Insel, in press). Administered i.v., in a dose of 0.1 mg/kg, MCPP did induce anxiety and panic in PD patients, but also in normal controls (Woods, 1986). These findings can be explained by assuming differences in receptor sensitivity. If in PD 5-HT receptor hypersensitivity exists then one would expect low doses of MCPP to deteriorate the condition but to be ineffectual in normals. A bolus dose, i.v. administered, flooding 5-HT receptors with the agonist and inducing a sudden increase in 5-HT activity, could conceivably increase the anxiety level in normals as well.

One study concluded 5-HT receptor sensitivity to be normal in PD patients, a conclusion based on the tryptophan/prolactin test (Charney and Heninger, 1986). The validity of this test, however, is questionable. Tryptophan is not an appropriate 5-HT challenger, especially when given in high (i.v.) doses. It competes with tyrosine, the precursor of DA and NA, for the same carrier mechanism to enter the brain (Wurtman, 1982), and therefore tyrosine's influx in the brain diminishes. Consequently, assessment of prolactin release after high i.v. doses of tryptophan might reflect the resultant of changes in DA function and 5-HT function (van Praag *et al.*, 1987a).

In summary, several lines of evidence suggest serotonergic hyperactivity to be an anxiogenic mechanism. No data are as yet available as to whether the 5-HT

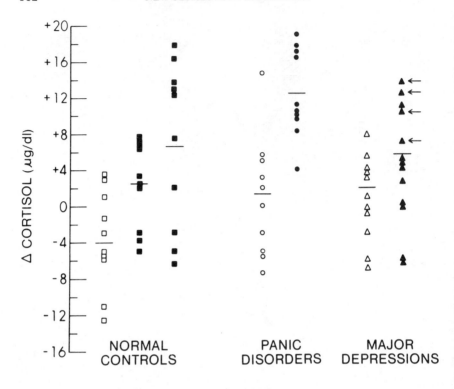

Fig. 8.13 Delta cortisol (peak minus baseline), after administration of placebo and MCPP. □, normal controls, placebo; ■, normal controls, 0.25 mg/kg MCPP; ■, normal controls, 0.50 mg/kg MCPP; ○, panic disorder, placebo; ●, panic disorder, MCPP (0.25 mg/kg); △, major depression, placebo; ▲, major depression, MCPP (0.25 mg/kg); → (arrow indicates patients with major depression and a history of panic disorder/attacks).

disturbances relate to a particular anxiety disorder or to the psychopathological dimension anxiety as such.

8.4.3 Mood Regulation

5-HT disturbances were initially linked to depressive *disorder* (van Praag *et al.*, 1970; van Praag and Korf, 1971b). Now it seems much more likely that they relate to heightened anxiety/aggression as it might occur in depression, but in many other psychiatric disorders as well. Depression is a particular disorder of mood accompanied by numerous other psychological dysfunctions. Disorders of mood are not unique for depression, but occur in many psychiatric disorders. Is 5-HT involved in the regulation of mood? The question remains moot. Some observations speak in favour of such a relationship. In normal volunteers a diet low in tryptophan (the precursor of 5-HT) led to lowering of mood (Young *et al.*, 1985), while tryptophan has been shown to possess therapeutic qualities in mild depression (Thomson *et al.*, 1982). Inhibiting the synthesis of 5-HT blocked the therapeutic effect of tricyclic antidepressants (Shopsin *et al.*, 1976). Moreover, CSF 5-HIAA has also found to be lowered in depressives (as yet) without suicidal history and without undue aggression (van Praag, 1986a). Finally, the lowest levels of CSF 5-HIAA have been found in *depressed* patients with recent suicide attempts (Fig. 8.8).

An observation arguing against 5-HT's involvement in mood regulation is that MCPP did not clearly effect mood state in major depression, nor in normals. It should be added, however, that the effects of this drug have so far been studied only after single administration. An obvious way to collect new data relevant to this problem would be to study 5-HT status in individuals with lowering of mood but no full depressive syndrome. Bereaved people and certain schizophrenics would qualify, but no data have been published. In a small sample of drug-free schizophrenics, not qualifying for the DSM III diagnosis of major depression, we found no correlation between mood lowering and CSF 5-HIAA.

In summary, available data do not allow conclusions about 5-HT's involvement in mood regulation. On balance, the data so far seem to hint that such a relation indeed exists, at least in depressive disorders.

8.5 Discussion

8.5.1 Interpretation of Data

Available evidence indicates that low baseline and post-probenecid CSF 5-HIAA, indicative of decreased 5-HT metabolism in the CNS, is not, as initially suggested, a characteristic of certain forms of depression but of a particular set of psychopathological dimensions, i.e. heightened aggression and anxiety, irrespective of syndromal or nosological diagnosis. In depression these dimensions might be pronounced or insignificant, providing an explanation why reduced CSF 5-HIAA occurs in some but is absent in other depressives. It is unknown whether 5-HIAA concentration in CSF varies with the intensity of manifest aggression and anxiety.

A related possibility is that low CSF 5-HIAA relates not directly to increased anxiety and aggression, but rather to personality traits responsible for an increased propensity towards aggression and anxiety under certain stimulus conditions. Deficient impulse control could be such a trait. In favour of the latter hypothesis speaks the finding that several studies have shown lowered CSF 5-HIAA to be state-independent (i.e. persistent after disappearance of the symptoms) (van Praag, 1977; Traskman-Bendz *et al.*, 1984) and that this biological variable is accompanied by an increased risk of depression (van Praag and de Haan, 1979) and suicide (Traskman *et al.*, 1981).

Whether mood regulation is another dimension under serotonergic control is much less certain. On balance, however, the evidence seems strong enough to hypothesise such a relationship to exist.

As to the kind of relationship between serotonergic regulation and the various psychopathological dimensions, one can conceive of two different models. First, each of the three dimensions mentioned could relate independently to the serotonergic system. Ascending 5-HT projections from the medial and dorsal raphe nuclei innervate a variety of forebrain structures, such as cortex, hippocampus, septum, amygdala and hypothalamus. Different 5-HT projections could be involved in the regulation of anxiety, aggression and mood, much the same as we have, for example, accepted the nigrostriatal dopamine (DA) system to be primarily involved in motor regulation, the mesolimbic and mesocortical DA system predominantly in emotional regulation.

An alternative model could be that 5-HT dysregulation is linked to only one psychopathological dimension, the others being its consequences. For example, if it were the anxiety level that was serotonergically controlled, raising the anxiety level could conceivably lead to changes in aggression and lowering of mood. So far, the clinical 5-HT data do not indicate the centrality of any one of the three psychopathological dimensions. Rather, they suggest that in probands with lowered CSF 5-HIAA each of the dimensions can be primary or predominant.

The former possibility seems not only more likely but also more appealing, since it provides a biological explanation for the clinical observation that disregulations of mood, anxiety and aggression tend to cluster (review in Kahn *et al.*, in press). Panic disorder and obsessive compulsive disorder, for example, are frequently accompanied by major depression, and depressed patients have an increased incidence of panic attacks, generalised anxiety and obsessive compulsive symptoms. Similarly, depression and aggression dysregulation are linked. Depression is a common precursor of suicidal behaviour, and suicidal behaviour and outward-directed aggression are also correlated. In individuals with histories of violent behaviour, suicide rates were found to be increased. The interrelation between anxiety and aggression has been less well studied. It seems clear, however, that strong aggressive impulses can either induce or suppress fear and apprehension. Induction of fear by aggressive impulses is seen in certain phobias (e.g. fear of knives) and obsessions (e.g. fears of killing one's children). Suppression of fear by aggressive impulses occurs in certain forms of antisocial personality disorder. What is unknown is whether anxiety disorders are accompanied by heightened (auto) aggression. Natural fear, of course, can either unleash aggression or inhibit it.

Due to the development of selective 5-HT drugs (reuptake inhibitors; agonists and antagonists of particular 5-HT receptor subpopulations) testing of the revised 5-HT hypothesis has come within reach. If the hypothesis were justified one would expect drugs that selectivity affect 5-HT to be indicated in states of augmented anxiety and aggression (possibly accompanied by mood lowering), irrespective of the syndromal or nosological framework. This would then be the first instance of a psychotropic drug prescribed for a functional state, rather than on the basis of a particular diagnosis (van Praag *et al.*, 1987b).

8.5.2 Functional Psychopathology

The fact that 5-HT disorders do not selectively relate to particular disease entities does not mark them as non-specific. They seem specific on a functional level, that is related to particular psychological dysfunctions. This interpretation has, as mentioned above, therapeutic implications, but theoretical implications as well. Up to now, psychiatry has been virtually obsessed with the search for markers of disease entities, such as depression, schizophrenia and panic disorder. Over the years we have advocated another approach and named it functional psychopathology (van Praag and Leijnse, 1965; van Praag *et al.*, 1975). Most parsimoniously formulated, it consists of three components: (a) dissection of a given psychopathological syndrome in its component parts, i.e. the psychological dysfunctions; (b) measurement of these dysfunctions; and (c) analysis of possible correlations between biological and psychological dysfunctions. This approach was formulated as a complement to, not as an alternative for, the nosological/syndromal one. Psychological dysfunctions, such as disturbances in perception, information processing, mood regulation, etc., that are syndromally non-specific, are observable in a variety of psychiatric disorders. Hence one would assume the same to be true for concomitant biological dysfunctions. As these are specific for a particular (set of) psychological dysfunction(s), one would expect them to be syndromally non-specific. The 5-HT studies in depression illustrate the validity of this approach. 5-HT disturbances were successively related to depression, a subtype of endogenous depression, suicidality in depression, suicidality in general, aggression dysregulation and (possibly) impulse control. These are typical examples of denosologisation of a biological variable in favour of a functional behavioural correlate. It is not the only example. Low CSF HVA, originally thought to be a sign of Parkinson's disease, is more likely correlated to states of hypoactivity and lack of initiative, irrespective of diagnosis (van Praag and Korf, 1971a). Diminished somatostatin levels, initially reported in Alzheimer's disease, seem however to be linked to certain cognitive disturbances, across diagnoses (Bissette *et al.*, 1986).

In short, biological psychiatry would be well served, we think, if it loosened its rigid nosological orientation and included the functional viewpoint as a complementary frame of reference. 5-HT research has served as a powerful catalyst of that process. Rather than being a 'transmitter of all seasons,' 5-HT seems to herald a new epoch of research in biological psychiatry.

8.6 Summary

5-HT disorders have been reported to occur in a variety of psychiatric disorders. The situation has been called chaotic, the disturbances non-specific. We reject this viewpoint. 5-HT disturbances are non-specific only from a nosological-categorical vantage point; they seem rather specific from a functional–dimensional point of view, correlating as they do with particular psychopathological dimensions, i.e. aggression-, anxiety- and possibly mood-disregulation, across diagnosis. The evolution of 5-HT research in psychiatry illustrates the importance of what we have called the functional approach, implying dissection of a given psychopathological syndrome in its component parts, i.e. the psychological dysfunctions, and searching for correlations between biological and psychological dysfunctions. The rigid preoccupation of biological psychiatry with the search for markers of disease entities has hampered progress. The functional approach should be incorporated in biological psychiatry, not as an alternative for the nosological approach but as its complement.

References

Adams, D. B. (1979). Brain mechanisms for offence, defense and submission. *Behav. Brain. Sci.*, **2**, 201–41.

Asberg, M., Traskman, L., and Thoren, P. (1976). 5-HIAA in the cerebrospinal fluid: A biochemical suicide predictor? *Arch. Gen. Psychiatr.*, **33**, 1193–7.

Asberg, M., Bertilsson, L., Martensson, B., Scalia-Thomba, G.-P., Thoren, P., and Traskman, L. (1984). CSF monoamine metabolites in melancholia. *Acta. Psychiatr. Scand.*, **69**, 201–19.

Asberg, M., Nordstrom, L., and Traskman-Bendz, L. (1986). *Biological factors in suicide*. In Roy, A. (ed.), *Suicide*. Williams and Wilkins, Baltimore.

Banki, C. M. (1977). Correlation of anxiety and related symptoms with cerebrospinal fluid 5-hydroxyindoleacetic acid in depressed women. *J. Neural. Transm.*, **41**, 135–43.

Bioulac, B., Benezich, M., Renaud, B., Noel, B., and Roche, D. (1980). Serotonergic functions in 47, XYZ syndrome. *Biol. Psychiatr.*, **15**, 917.

Bissette, G., Widerlov, E., Walleus, H., Karlsson, I., Eklund, K., Forsman, A., and Nemeroff, C. B. (1986). Alterations in cerebrospinal fluid concentrations of somatostatinlike immunoreactivity in neuropsychiatric disorders. *Arch. Gen. Psychiatr.*, **43**, 1148–51.

Brown, G. L., Ebert, M. E., Goyer, P. F., Jimerson, D. C., Klein, W. J., Bunney, W. E., and Goodwin, F. K. (1982). Aggression, suicide and serotonin: Relationships to CSF amine metabolites. *Am. J. Psychiatr.*, **139**, 741–6.

Brown, G. L., Goodwin, F. K., Ballenger, J. C., Goyer, P. F., and Major, L. F. (1979). Aggression in humans correlates with cerebrospinal fluid metabolites. *Psychiatr. Res.*, **1**, 131–9.

Ceulemans, D. L. S., Hoppenbrouwers, M. L. J. A., Gelders, Y. G., and Reyntjens, A. J. M. (1985). The influence of ritanserin, a serotonin antagonist, in anxiety disorders: A double-blind placebo-controlled study versus lorazepam. *Pharmacopsychiatr.*, **18**, 303–5.

Charney, D. S., and Heninger, G. R. (1986). Serotonergic function in panic disorders. *Arch. Gen. Psychiatr*, **43**, 1059–65.

Daruna, J. H. (1978). Patterns of monoamine activity and aggressive behavior. *Neurosci. Biobehav. Rev.*, **2**, 101–13.

Den Boer, J. A., Westenberg, H. G. M., Kamerbeek, W. D. J., Verhoeven, W. M. A., and Kahn R. S. (in press). Effect of serotonin uptake inhibitors in anxiety disorders; a double-blind comparison of clomipramine and fluvoxamine. *Int. Clin. Psychopharm.*

Evans, L., Kenardy, J., Schneider, P., and Hoey, H. (1986). Effect of a selective serotonin uptake inhibitor in agoraphobia with panic attacks. *Acta Psychiatr. Scand.*, **73**, 49–53.

Insel, T. R., Murphy, D. L., Cohen, R. M., Alterman, I., Kilts, C., and Linnoila, M. (1983). Obsessive compulsive disorder: A double blind trial of clomipramine and clorgyline. *Arch. Gen. Psychiatr.*, **40**, 605–12.

Insel, T. R., Mueller, E. A., Alterman, I., Linnoila, M., and Murphy, D. L. (1985). Obsessive-compulsive disorder and serotonin: Is there a connection? *Biol. Psychiatr.*, **20**, 1174–88.

Kahn, R. S., Westenberg, H. G. M., and Jolles, J. (1984). Zimelidine treatment of obsessive-compulsive disorder. *Acta Psychiatr. Scand.*, **69**, 259–61.

Kahn, R. S., and Westenberg, H. G. M. (1985). l-5-hydroxytryptophan in the treatment of anxiety disorders. *J. Affect. Disord.*, **8**, 197–200.

Kahn, R. S., Westenberg, H. G. M., Verhoeven, W. M. A., Gispen-de Wied, C. C., and Kamerbeek, W. D. J. (in press). Effect of a serotonin precursor and uptake inhibitor in anxiety disorders; a double-blind comparison of 5-hydroxytryptophan, clomipramine and placebo. *Int. Clin. Psychopharm.*

Kahn, R. S., van Praag, H. M., Wetzler, S., Asnis, G. M., and Barr, J. (in press). Serotonin and anxiety revisited. *Biol. Psychiatr.*

Kahn, R. S., Westzler, S., van Praag, H. M., and Asnis, G. M. (subm.). Indication for serotonergic supersensitivity in patients with panic disorder.

Lemberger, L., Fuller, R. W., and Zerbe, R. L. (1985). Review. Use of specific serotonin uptake inhibitors as antidepressants. *Clinical Neuropharmacol.*, **8**, 299–317.

Lidberg, L., Asberg, M., and Sundquist-Stensman, U. B. (1984). 5-Hydroxyindoleacetic acid in attempted suicides who killed their children. *Lancet*, ii, 928.

Lidberg, L., Tuck, J. R., Asberg, M., Scalia-Tomba, G. P., and Bertilsson, L. (1985). Homicide, suicide and CSF 5-HIAA. *Acta Psychiatr. Scand.*, **71**, 230–6.

Linnoila, M., Virkhunen, M., Scheinin, M., Nuutila, A., Rimon, R., and Goodwin, F. K. (1983). Low cerebrospinal fluid 5-hydroxyindoleacetic acid concentration differentiates impulsive from nonimpulsive violent behavior. *Life Sci.*, **33**, 2609–14.

Linnoila, M. (1986). Monoamines and impulse control in humans. Paper read at the American College of Neuropsychopharmacology, Washington.

Marks, I. M., Stern, R. S., Mawson, D., Cobb, J., and McDonald, R. (1980). Clomipramine and exposure for obsessive-compulsive rituals. *Br. J. Psychiatr.*, **136**, 1–25.

Montgomery, S. A. (1980). Clomipramine in obsessional neurosis: A placebo controlled trial. *Pharm. Med.*, **1**, 189–92.

Morand, C., Young, S. N., and Ervin, F. R. (1983). Clinical response of aggressive schizophrenics to oral tryptophan. *Biol. Psychiatr.*, **18**, 575–8.

Mueller, E. A., Sunderland, T., and Murphy, D. L. (1985). Neuroendocrine effects of m-CRP, a serotonin agonist, in humans. *J. Clin. Endocrinol. Metab.*, **61**, 1179–84.

Mueller E. A., Murphy, D. L., and Sunderland, T. (1986). Further studies of the putative serotonin agonist, m-chlorophenylpiperazine: Evidence for a serotonin receptor mediated mechanisms of action in humans. *Psychopharmacol.*, **89**, 388–91.

Ninan P. T., van Kammen, D. P., Scheinin, M., Linnoila, M., Bunney, W. E., and Goodwin, F. K. (1984). CSF 5-hydroxyindoleacetic acid levels in suicidal schizophrenic patients. *Am. J. Psychiatr.*, **141**, 566–9.

Oliver, B., and Mos, J. (1986). Serenics and aggression. *Stress and Med.*, **2**, 197–209.

Plutchik, R., van Praag, H. M., and Conte, H. (in press). Suicide and violence risk in psychiatric patients. *Arch. Gen. Psychiatr.*

Potter W. Z., Scheinin, M., Golden, R. N., Rudorfer, M. V., Cowdry, R. W., Calil, H. M., Ross, R. J., and Linnoila, M. (1985). Selective antidepressants and cerebrospinal fluid, Lack of specificity on norepinephrine and serotonin metabolites. *Arch. Gen. Psychiatr.*, **42**, 1171–7.

Redmond, D. E., Katz, M. M., Maas, J. W., Swann, A., Casper, R., and Davis, J. M. (1986). Cerebrospinal fluid amine metabolites: Relationships with behavioural measurements in depressed, manic and healthy control subjects. *Arch. Gen. Psychiatr.*, **43**, 938–47.

Rodgers, R. J., and Waters, A. J. (1985). Benzodiazepines and their antagonists: A pharmacoethological analysis with particular reference to effects on 'aggression.' *Neurosci. Behav. Rev.*, **9**, 21–35.

Rydin, E., Schalling, D., and Asberg, M. (1982). Rorschach ratings in depressed and suicidal patients with low CSF 5-HIAA. *Psychiatr. Res.*, 7, 229-43.

Shopsin, B., Gershon, S., and Friedman, E. (1976). PCPA reversal of tranylcypromine effects in depressed patients. *Arch. Gen. Psychiatr.*, 33, 811-19.

Stern, R. S., Marks, I. M., and Mawson, D. (1980). Clomipramine and exposure for compulsive rituals: Plasma levels, side effects and outcome. *Br. J. Psychiatr.*, 136, 161-6.

Taylor, D. P., Eison, M. S., Riblet, L. A., and Vandermaelen, C. P. (1985). Pharmacological and clinical effects of buspirone. *Pharmacol. Biochem. Behav.*, 23, 687-94.

Thomson, J., Rankin, H., Ashcroft, J. W., Gates, C. M., McOneea, J. K., and Cummings, J. W. (1982). The treatment of depression in general practice: A comparison of l-tryptophan, amitriptyline and a combination of l-tryptophan and amitriptyline with placebo. *Psychiatr. Res.*, 12, 741-51.

Thoren P., Asberg, M., Cronholm, B., Jornestedt, L., and Traskman, L. (1980). Clomipramine treatment of obsessive compulsive disorder: I. A controlled clinical trial. *Arch. Gen. Psychiatr.*, 37, 1281-9.

Traskman, L., Asberg, M., Bertillson, L., and Sjostrand, L. (1981). Monoamine metabolites in CSF and suicidal behavior. *Arch. Gen. Psychiatr.*, 38, 631-6.

Traskman-Bendz, L., Asberg, M., Bertelsson, L., and Thoren, P. (1984). CSF monoamine metabolites of depressed patients during illness and recovery. *Acta. Psychiatr. Scand.*, 69, 333-42.

Valzelli, L. (1981). *Psychobiology of Aggression and Violence.* Raven, New York.

van Kammen, D. P. (1987). 5-HT, a neurotransmitter for all seasons? *Biol. Psychiatr.*, 22, 1-3.

van Praag, H. M. (1977). Significance of biochemical parameters in the diagnosis, treatment and prevention of depressive disorders. *Biol. Psychiatr.*, 12, 101-31.

van Praag, H. M. (1982a). Neurotransmitters and CNS disease: depression. *Lancet*, ii, 1259-64.

van Praag, H. M. (1982b). Depression, suicide and the metabolism of serotonin in the brain. *J. Affect. Disor.*, 4, 275-90.

van Praag, H. M. (1983a). CSF 5-HIAA and suicide in non-depressed schizophrenics. *Lancet*, ii, 977-8.

van Praag, H. M. (1983b). In search of the action mechanism of antidepressants, 5-HTP/tyrosine mixtures in depression. *Neuropharmacol.*, 22, 433-40.

van Praag, H. M. (1984a). Depression, suicide and serotonin metabolism in the brain. In Post, R. M., and Ballinger, J. C. (eds.), *Neurobiology of Mood Disorders.* Williams and Wilkins, Baltimore, 601-18.

van Praag, H. M. (1984b). Studies in the mechanism of action of serotonin precursors in depression. *Psychopharmacol. Bull.*, 20, 599-602.

van Praag, H. M. (1985). Serotonin precursors with and without tyrosine in the treatment of depression. In Shadgrass, C., Josias, W., Bridger, K., Weiss, D., Stoff, D., and Simpson, J. (eds.), *Proc. IV World Congr. of Biological Psychiatry.* Elsevier, New York, 1986, 77-99.

van Praag, H. M. (1986a). Biological suicide research. Outcome and limitations. *Biol. Psychiatr.*, 21, 1305-23.

van Praag, H. M. (1986b). (Auto) aggression and CSF 5-HIAA in depression and schizophrenia. *Psychopharmacol. Bull.*, 2, 669-73.

van Praag, H. M., and Leijnze, B. (1965). Neubewertung des sydroms. Skizze einer funktionellen pathologie. *Psychiatr. Neurol. Neurochir.*, 68, 50-66.

van Praag, H. M., Uleman, A. M., and Spitz, J. C. (1965). The vital syndrome interview. A structured standard interview for the recognition and registration of the vital depressive symptom complex. *Psychiatr. Neurol. Neurochir.*, 68, 329-46.

van Praag, H. M., Korf, J., and Puite, J. (1970). 5-hydroxyindoleacetic acid levels in the cerebrospinal fluid of depressive patients treated with probenecid. *Nature*, 225, 1259-60.

van Praag, H. M., and Korf, J. (1971a). Retarded depression and the dopamine metabolism. *Psychopharmacol.*, 19, 199-203.

van Praag, H. M., and Korf, J. (1971b). Endogenous depressions with and without disturbances in the 5-hydroxytryptamine metabolism: A biochemical classification? *Psychopharmacol.*, 19, 148-52.

van Praag, H. M., Korf, J., Lakke, J. P. W. F., and Schut, T. (1975). Dopamine metabolism in depression, psychoses and Parkinson's disease: The problem of the specificity of biological variables in behaviour disorders. *Psychol. Med.*, **5**, 138–46.

van Praag, H. M., and de Haan, S. (1979). Central serotonin metabolism and frequency of depression. *Psychiatr. Res.*, **1**, 219–24.

van Praag, H. M., and Lemus, C. (1986). Monoamine precursors in the treatment of psychiatric disorders. In Wurtman, J. J., and Wurtman, R. J. (eds.). *Nutrition and the Brain*. Raven, New York.

van Praag, H. M., and Plutchik, R. (subm.). Increased suicidality in depression. Group or sub-group characteristic.

van Praag, H. M., Lemus, C., and Kahn, R. (1987a). Hormonal probes of central serotonergic activity. Do they really exist? *Biol. Psychiatr.*, **22**, 86–98.

van Praag, H. M., Plutchik, R., and Korn, M. (in prep.). Relatedness of seriousness of suicide intent and seriousness of suicide attempt.

van Praag, H. M., Kahn, R., Asnis, G. M., Lemus, C. Z., and Brown, S. (1987b). Therapeutic indications for serotonin-potentiating compounds: A hypothesis. *Biol. Psychiatr.*, **22**, 205–12.

Woods, S. W. (1986). Drug and phobic exposure induced anxiety states. American Psychiatric Association, 139th Annual Meeting, Washington DC.

Wurtman, R. J. (1982). Nutrients that modify brain functions. *Sci. Am.*, **246**, 42–51.

Yaryuria-Tobias, J. S., and Bhagavan, H. N. (1977). L-Tryptophan in obsessive compulsive disorders. *Am. J. Psychiatr.*, **134**, 1298–9.

Young, S. N., Smith, S. E., Pihl, R. O., and Ervin, F. R. (1985). Tryptophan depletion causes a rapid lowering of mood in normal males. *Psychopharmacol.*, **87**, 173–7.

Zohar, J., and Insel, T. R. (in press). Obsessive compulsive disorder; psychobiological approaches to diagnosis, treatment and psychophysiology. *Biol. Psychiatr.*

9

5-HT and Depression: the Present Position

A. Coppen and C. Swade

Depressive illness is characterised by periods of depression usually starting in the early forties. If the patient is not treated the episode will last from six to eighteen months and then spontaneously remit. A characteristic is the relapsing nature of the illness, with over 60% of patients suffering recurrent episodes of depression. It is more common in women than men, and there is evidence of a strong genetic factor (Smeraldi *et al.*, 1977).

Owing to the natural history of the illness, it is good clinical practice to treat an episode with antidepressants for at least six months after apparent response to the drug because of the long period of an episode of depression. It is also good practice to start prophylactic therapy, usually with lithium or an anti-depressant, if a patient has had three or more episodes of depression, two of which have occurred in the last five years. The modern management of depression has resulted in a very significant decrease in the considerable morbidity that was suffered by these patients before the advent of antidepressant drugs.

Anyone reviewing the pathology of depression is confronted by a daunting mass of literature, some of it contradictory. This chapter does not purport to be a comprehensive review of the field, but is a selection based on our own research interests. Some of the contradictions are probably due to failure to properly define the type of patients studied. Recently, differences due to seasonal variation have been recognised that were not previously allowed for. A growing complication is the fact that depression is being diagnosed and treated early, and it is becoming difficult to find patients to study who have not received medication.

There are two groups of biochemical factors to be considered in studies of the chemical pathology of depressive illness. First, there are changes related to the onset and duration of an episode of depression. Second, there may be trait abnormalities in these patients that may make them vulnerable to these episodic changes. It is therefore essential that depressive patients should be studied both during an episode of depression before drug treatment and again after recovery from the illness when the patients have discontinued drug therapy. The results should be compared with those obtained from control subjects, representative of the normal healthy population, matched for age and sex, and tested under the same conditions as the patients (Coppen, 1974).

Another approach is to study the ways that drugs that are effective in treating depression alter the biochemical functioning or composition of patients, normal control subjects, or experimental animals (Green and Costain, 1979). These results should be interpreted with caution since biochemical changes produced by a drug may be unrelated to its therapeutic action.

Early investigations into the biochemistry of depressive illness were prompted by observations of the effects of various drugs on mood or behaviour. The structural similarity between the hallucinogenic drug lysergic acid diethylamide (LSD) and the neurotransmitter 5-hydroxytryptamine (5-HT) led Woolley and Shaw (1954) to propose that 5-HT might be involved in the regulation of mental processes. The antihypertensive drug reserpine was observed to cause severe depression in some patients (Harris, 1957). Reserpine and related compounds produce a marked depletion of monoamines from the mammalian central nervous system (CNS) and from peripheral tissues by interfering with the intracellular vesicle storage of these amines (Carlsson et al., 1957). Conversely, elevation of mood was reported in tuberculosis patients treated with isoniazid and iproniazid. These drugs were found to be inhibitors of monoamine oxidase (MAO), an enzyme involved in the catabolism of monoamines (Zeller et al., 1955; Pare and Sandler, 1959). The chance observation that certain tricyclic compounds have an antidepressant action was followed by the finding that they inhibit the re-uptake of released monoamines in brain slices and synaptosome preparations (Carlsson et al., 1969). These observations led to the formulation of hypotheses of depression postulating absolute or relative deficiencies of various monoamines in the brains of depressive patients (Schildkraut, 1965; Coppen, 1967). The role of the monoamines in depressive illness has been a matter of speculation and investigation for over a quarter of a century, and the 5-HT hypothesis of depression has been of surprising durability.

The first direct observation linking depressive illness and 5-HT was the finding that tryptophan potentiated the antidepressant activity of a monoamine oxidase inhibitor (MAOI) (Fig. 9.1; Coppen et al., 1963). This potentiation was considerable and significant, and indicated that a powerful new antidepressant activity was present with the combined medication. This observation has been replicated in other studies (Pare, 1963; Glassman and Platman, 1969; Gutierrez and Lopez-Ibor, 1971). The simplest explanation for these findings is that the combination

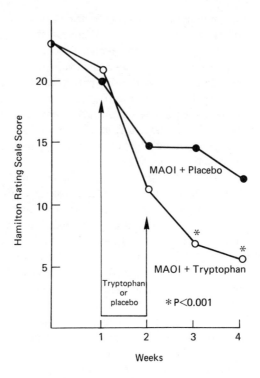

Fig 9.1 Potentiation of the antidepressive effect of an MAOI by tryptophan (after Coppen *et al.*, 1963).

of tryptophan and MAOI acts by increasing the amount of brain 5-HT. This led to the formation of the 5-HT hypothesis of depressive illness which postulates that depressive illness is associated with a deficiency of 5-HT in the central nervous system of depressed patients.

Pare (1965) measured the post-mortem levels of brain 5-HT in patients who had been given a MAOI for varying periods before they died, and found that the drug had to be administered for at least 2 weeks before the levels of 5-HT in the brain tissue began to rise. This period corresponds to the time taken for a MAOI to exert its maximum antidepressant effect. In animals, the increase in brain 5-HT that occurs with the administration of a MAOI may be considerably enhanced by feeding the animal large doses of tryptophan, the precursor of 5-HT (Hess and Doepfner, 1961). In rats, administration of tryptophan alone increases the rate of brain 5-HT synthesis but does not affect behaviour. Pretreatment of the animals with a MAOI results in behavioural changes (Grahame-Smith, 1971).

5-HT is synthesised from the essential amino acid tryptophan. The active transport of amino acids across the blood–brain barrier is saturable and stereo-specific (Pardridge and Oldendorf, 1977). The hydroxylation of tryptophan is the rate-limiting step in 5-HT synthesis in the brain as tryptophan-5-hydroxylase is unsaturated with respect to its substrate (Curzon, 1975).

As the synthesis of 5-HT is limited in the brain by tryptophan availability, the rate of 5-HT synthesis will rise or fall with changes in the plasma concentration of tryptophan, and so depends at least partly on nutritional status (Fernstrom, 1973). Depression is a symptom in certain types of malnutrition, for example pellagra (Dickerson and Wiryanti, 1978).

The synthesis of brain 5-HT is only a minor pathway of tryptophan metabolism, as peripheral metabolism accounts for about 98% of the total tryptophan metabolism. Thus only a small proportion of tryptophan enters the brain (Hagen and Cohen, 1966). An important peripheral step in the metabolism occurs in the liver. The enzyme tryptophan pyrrolase can be induced by its substrate, tryptophan, and by corticosteroids (Knox and Auerbach, 1955). Increased activity of tryptophan pyrrolase would reduce the amount of tryptophan available for 5-HT formation, and also increase the plasma levels of kynurenine, which may compete with tryptophan for transport into the brain (Green and Curzon, 1970). This may be important in depression, as depressive patients may have raised concentrations of steroids in their plasma (Curzon, 1969; Lapin and Oxenkrug, 1969; Sachar et al., 1973). It may also affect 5-HT receptor interactions, as the administration of kynurenine has a marked effect on 5-HT-induced head-twitches in mice (Handley and Miskin, 1977).

It has been reported that female depressed patients excrete significantly more kynurenine than female controls after administration of tryptophan, which suggests that the activity of tryptophan pyrrolase may be increased in depression (Curzon and Bridges, 1970). However, without the artificial conditions of a tryptophan load there is no measurable difference between depressive patients and control subjects either in the plasma concentration of kynurenine (Wood et al., 1978) or in the urinary excretion of kynurenine (Frazer et al., 1973). These results, together with those of Møller and colleagues (1976), suggest that hepatic tryptophan pyrrolase activity is not significantly increased during a depressive illness. However, the presence of kynurenine in rat brain (Joseph, 1977), and evidence of a brain enzyme with pyrrolase activity (Gal, 1974), suggest the possibility of interaction between 5-HT and pyrrolase pathway metabolites such as kynurenine in the brain. There is pharmacological evidence to suggest that this may occur (Gould and Handley, 1978), so it is possible that kynurenine has some physiological role in the regulation of tryptophan and 5-HT pathways within the CNS.

The clinical efficacy of tryptophan with or without a MAOI (Coppen et al., 1967) directed attention to tryptophan concentrations in the plasma of depressive patients. Tryptophan is bound to albumin in the plasma, and the free (non-bound) fraction is only 10 to 20% of the total plasma tryptophan (McMenamy and Oncley, 1958). There are reports of lowered concentrations of free tryptophan in depression (Coppen et al., 1973; Baumann et al., 1975; Kishimoto and Hama, 1976; Nakaya, 1976; Curzon et al., 1979; Fiore et al., 1979; Schmid-Burgk *et al.*, 1981), although others have reported normal levels of free tryptophan in depression (Garfinkel *et al.*, 1976; Peet *et al.*, 1976; Riley and Shaw, 1976; Sepping *et al.*, 1977; Chouinard *et al.*, 1979; Møller *et al.*, 1979; Thomson *et al.*, 1982). There is even one report of higher plasma-free tryptophan levels in depression (Niskanen *et al.*, 1976).

There are a number of possible explanations for these discrepancies in the reported level of free tryptophan in depression. Different groups have used different methods for the separation of the free tryptophan from the plasma, and different methods for the assay of tryptophan, and this could account for at least part of the variation in the reported values for the absolute concentration of free tryptophan in plasma (Wood *et al.*, 1977). Problems of psychiatric classification of depression may also underlie some of the discrepancies. In an attempt to explain conflicting reports on plasma-free tryptophan, we divided our patients into three groups according to their Newcastle scale score (Carney *et al.*, 1965), in which high scores are associated with depression of a predominantly endogenous type. While there were no significant differences in the levels of free or total tryptophan there was a trend towards lower plasma-free tryptophan levels in patients with features more characteristic of endogenous depression. It may be that the general practitioner now has relatively effective antidepressant treatments at his disposal for endogenous forms of depression, but not for non-endogenous forms of the illness, and that patients of the latter kind are contributing more substantially to in-patient research material. Yet another source of discrepancy may be the timing of sample collection, since there is evidence for seasonal variation in plasma tryptophan concentration (Swade and Coppen, 1980; Handley *et al.*, 1980).

There are a number of biochemical factors which influence tryptophan binding in plasma. The binding of tryptophan to albumin is weakened by non-esterified fatty acids (NEFA) (Curzon *et al.*, 1973), and it has been reported that percentage of free tryptophan and NEFA concentration are positively correlated (Curzon *et al.*, 1974). However, results from our laboratory have not found any such correlation. On the contrary, we have found raised NEFA levels in depressed patients (Wood and Coppen, 1978), which would, if anything, increase rather than decrease free tryptophan concentration.

Plasma NEFA levels are reduced by insulin (Manowitz *et al.*, 1977). As well as lowering blood glucose levels, insulin also causes a decrease on plasma levels of most amino acids, with the exception of tryptophan, which is increased (Fernstrom, 1973). Thus, the administration of insulin, or the consumption of a carbohydrate meal, causes an increase in the concentration of tryptophan in the rat brain (Tagliamonte *et al.*, 1975). There is also an increase in rat brain content of 5-HT and of its principal metabolite 5-hydroxyindoleacetic acid (5-HIAA) following a carbohydrate-rich, protein-free meal (Fernstrom and Wurtman, 1971). The administration of a glucose drink in conjunction with tryptophan has been shown to be of benefit in the treatment of depression (Coppen *et al.*, 1967).

There is evidence of an association between depression and decreased plasma folate levels. In a study of 100 consecutive admissions with severe depression, 24 patients had low serum folate (Reynolds *et al.*, 1970). In a group of 107 patients with recurrent affective disorders receiving long-term lithium therapy, those with lower plasma folate concentrations had a higher affective morbidity than those with higher folate concentrations, both at the time of folate determination and during the previous two years. The association was not due to weight change or to concomitant use of other drugs (Coppen and Abou-Saleh, 1982). We subsequently carried out a double-blind trial to investigate the effect on affective morbidity of a daily supplement of 200 μg of folic acid in patients on lithium therapy. During the trial the patients with the highest plasma folate concentrations showed a significant reduction in their affective morbidity (Coppen *et al.*, 1986). Leeming and colleagues (1982) showed a connection between folate and tetrahydrobiopterin (BH_4), in that folic acid in the form of 5-methyl-tetrahydrofolate increases the biosynthesis of BH_4. BH_4 is a cofactor for the hydroxylation of tryptophan in a rate-limiting step in the biosynthesis of 5-HT (Levitt *et al.*, 1965). BH_4 synthesis in brain preparations from depressed patients has been found to be lower than in control subjects (Blair *et al.*, 1984). In patients receiving lithium therapy there is evidence of a reduction in BH_4 synthesis, which is probably due to folate deficiency (Blair *et al.*, in press).

Direct evidence about the biochemical composition of the brain in depressive patients is hard to come by, and is dependent on the examination of the brains of patients who have committed suicide. There are a number of factors which make it difficult to interpret the results of post-mortem brain tissue studies. There is a problem in diagnosis, which must often be made retrospectively, since not all suicides are caused by depressive illness. The nutritonal state and the type and quantity of drugs taken before death are usually not known. It may be difficult to ascertain the time of day when the subject died, and it is known that many biochemical variates show circadian concentration variations. Also, the storage time between death and biochemical assay can significantly affect the results obtained (Coppen, 1974; Beskow *et al.*, 1976).

In spite of these limitations there have been a number of reports on the concentration of 5-HT and 5-HIAA in the brains of suicides. The first investigation was from our laboratory, and here it was found that depressive suicides had a significantly lower hindbrain 5-HT concentration than a control group of subjects who died from other means (Shaw *et al.*, 1967). Similar results have been reported by some groups (Bourne *et al.*, 1968; Pare *et al.*, 1969; Lloyd *et al.*, 1974), although others have not been able to replicate these findings (Beskow *et al.*, 1976; Cochran *et al.*, 1976). More recently, studies have concentrated on receptor density in the brains of suicides. The high-affinity binding sites for imipramine in brain tissue are associated with the neuronal uptake system for 5-HT (Rehavi *et al.*, 1983). There are reports of a reduction in the number of imipramine binding sites in the brains of suicides (Stanley *et al.*, 1982; Perry *et al.*, 1983). This could indicate a deficiency of 5-HT neuronal transport in the brains of depressive patients.

There have been many studies of the biochemistry of the cerebrospinal fluid (CSF) of depressive patients. Tryptophan has been found by some groups to be reduced in the CSF of depressives compared with normal controls (Coppen, 1974; Bridges et al., 1976), but others have reported normal CSF tryptophan levels in depressives (Ashcroft et al., 1973). Several groups have reported reduced CSF levels of 5-HIAA in depressed patients, which may suggest an impairment of 5-HT synthesis or metabolism in depression (Papeschi and McLure, 1971; Coppen et al., 1972; Åsberg et al., 1975; Bridges et al., 1976), although there are also reports of normal levels of 5-HIAA in CSF from depressives (Bowers et al., 1969; Vestergaard et al., 1978). Åsberg and colleagues (1976) found a bimodal distribution of 5-HIAA levels in CSF samples from depressed patients. In the subgroup characterised by a low level of 5-HIAA in the CSF, there was a negative correlation between 5-HIAA concentration and severity of depression. Also, the patients in this subgroup attempted suicide significantly more often than those in the subgroup with normal 5-HIAA levels, and they used more violent means.

The administration of probenecid has been shown to cause an increase in the concentration of free tryptophan in plasma by displacing tryptophan from its binding sites on plasma albumin. In rats probenecid causes an increase in brain tryptophan concentration (Tagliamonte et al., 1971), but the administration of probenecid in human subjects has no effect on CSF tryptophan concentration (Young et al., 1975). However, probenecid does cause an increase in human CSF concentrations of 5-HIAA by blocking the transport of 5-HIAA out of the CSF, and possibly also by causing an increase in 5-HT synthesis, since the increase in plasma free tryptophan may cause an increase in brain tryptophan concentration which might be reflected in increased production of 5-HT rather than an increase in brain tryptophan alone. It has been shown that the increase in CSF concentration of 5-HIAA after probenecid is much less in depressed patients than in control subjects, which may be due to a reduction in 5-HT synthesis in depression (Sjöström and Roos, 1972; van Praag et al., 1973; Goodwin et al., 1973).

There is, however, some dispute as to the relevance of neurotransmitter metabolites in lumbar CSF to neurotransmitter availability and function in the brain. Only some of the 5-HIAA has been functionally active in nerve transmission, since some of the 5-HIAA is produced as a result of intraneuronal 5-HT metabolism. Thus changes in CSF 5-HIAA concentration may indicate a change in 5-HT metabolism but not necessarily in 5-HT function. There is evidence for a spinal origin for some of the CSF 5-HIAA (Curzon et al., 1971; Garelis and Sourkes, 1973). The concentration of 5-HIAA in CSF can vary widely from day to day (van Praag, 1976). It has been reported that cerebral 5-HIAA passes directly into the blood (Meek and Neff, 1973) and it is not known if this proportion (about 90%) is constant.

Owing to the many difficulties involved in studies on brain tissue and CSF, researchers in the field of biological psychiatry have been attracted to the use of the blood platelet as a model for the central serotonergic neurone. Platelets are easily and repeatedly obtainable by venepuncture. Many of the properties of the brain 5-HT presynaptic terminal and of platelets are similar: both have active transport mechanisms for tryptophan and 5-HT, both have 5-HT storage granules and catabolise 5-HT by MAO, and both have high-affinity binding sites for α- and β-adrenoceptor ligands, 5-HT ligands and [^{3}H]-imipramine (Sneddon, 1973; Stahl, 1977; Maitre et al., 1980).

No consistent change has been reported in 5-HT content of platelets from depressed patients, but the variations between 'normal' values of different investigators is so great that small differences between patients and controls may have been obscured (Sneddon, 1973). Results from our laboratory showed that the concentration of 5-HT in whole blood (i.e., effectively platelet 5-HT, since very little 5-HT is detectable in the blood outside the platelets) was significantly lower during depression, but returned to normal after recovery (Coppen et al., 1976).

Kinetic analysis using low substrate concentrations and short incubation periods in order to measure the initial uptake rate has shown that the rate of up-take of 5-HT into the blood platelets of depressed patients is decreased. This seems to be one of the most consistently found abnormalities in biological psychiatry (Tuomisto and Tukiainen, 1976; Coppen et al., 1978; Malmgren et al., 1981; Meltzer et al., 1981; Stahl et al., 1983; Rausch et al., 1986). However, this abnormality is not specific for depressive illness, since a reduction in platelet 5-HT uptake has been observed in other disorders, including schizophrenia (Rotman et al., 1979; Giret et al., 1980), migraine (Coppen et al., 1979), and cirrhosis and hypertension (Ahtee et al., 1974).

The Michaelis constant (K_m) of platelet 5-HT uptake is essentially identical in both drug-free depressed patients and control subjects. The rate of transport of 5-HT through the platelet membrane (V_{max}) is, however, significantly lower in depressed patients. This suggests that the binding of 5-HT to platelet membrane binding sites is normal in depressed patients, but that the transport of 5-HT through the platelet membrane is impaired. This abnormality would appear to be trait- rather than state-dependent, since similar results are also found in depressive patients after recovery (Coppen et al., 1978), and no correlation has been found between severity of depression and rate of platelet 5-HT uptake (Coppen et al., 1979).

If the assumption that the kinetics of platelet 5-HT uptake are similar to the kinetics of 5-HT transport across synaptic membranes is valid for human tissues, then these observations are consistent with the 5-HT hypothesis of depressive illness since they suggest a reduced availability or turnover of neuronal 5-HT. The reduced rate of 5-HT uptake in depressive patients leads to a low platelet 5-HT content (Coppen et al., 1976). A low rate of transport in the brains of depressed patients may be related to the reduced 5-HT concentrations found in the brains of suicides (Shaw et al., 1967; Bourne et al., 1968; Pare et al., 1969; Lloyd et al., 1974).

Platelets maintain a low internal sodium concentration by means of a Na^+/K^+ ATPase in the membrane. The active uptake of 5-HT by platelets shows an absolute dependence on the extracellular sodium concentration and so is coupled to the activity of Na^+/K^+ ATPase. In the absence of sodium there is no net 5-HT uptake (Lingjaerde, 1969). There are reports of decreased Na^+/K^+ ATPase activity in membrane preparations from depressed patients (Choi et al., 1977; Hesketh et al., 1977; Naylor et al., 1980), and this might account for the reduced rate of 5-HT uptake by platelets from depressive patients. This is supported by a report of a correlation between platelet 5-HT uptake and platelet 5-HT content (Wirz-Justice et al., 1977). One group has measured not only the activity of the enzyme but also the number of sodium pump sites per erythrocyte, which was found to be similar in control subjects and depressed patients (Naylor et al., 1980). This might explain the similar K_m values for 5-HT uptake in controls and patients.

In both control subjects and depressive patients there is a marked seasonal variation in the rate of platelet 5-HT uptake (V_{max}). The lowest rates are observed in late spring and early summer (Swade and Coppen, 1980). This coincides with the time of year of greatest incidence of depression and the peak in the suicide rate.

Platelet 5-HT uptake is inhibited by tricyclic antidepressants. Inhibition is caused by interference with 5-HT binding to the transport molecule, reducing the affinity and thereby causing an increase in the value of K_m of 5-HT uptake. The majority of these drugs do not significantly affect V_{max}. In patients receiving uptake inhibitor drugs, correlations have been found between the increase in K_m of platelet 5-HT uptake and plasma drug concentrations. However, the total lack of correlation between platelet 5-HT uptake inhibition and clinical improvement is striking (Coppen et al., 1979). These results cast doubt on the common assumption that these drugs owe their antidepressant effect to uptake inhibition. By contrast, in depressive patients receiving prophylactic treatment with lithium the rate of uptake of 5-HT by platelets has been shown to be increased to control values (Coppen et al., 1980).

Recently there has been increasing interest in investigations into the characteristics of imipramine binding sites both in brain membrane preparations and on blood platelets. There are probably both high- and low-affinity binding sites (Reith et al., 1983). The high-affinity binding sites in brain tissue are associated with the neuronal uptake system for 5-HT (Reith et al., 1983; Rehavi et al., 1983). There are reports of a reduction in numbers of imipramine binding sites per platelet, though not in the affinity, in depressed patients (Briley et al., 1980; Gay et al., 1983). A reduction in binding sites, but normal affinity, has also been reported for the brains of suicides (Stanley et al., 1982; Perry et al., 1983). If the imipramine binding site is closely associated with the 5-HT transport site, then these findings might be taken as validation of the use of the platelet as a neuronal model in humans.

Two distinct 5-HT receptors have been identified in mammalian brain on the basis of radioligand binding assays (Peroutka and Snyder, 1982). The binding to 5-HT$_1$ receptors, which are labelled by [^{3}H]-5-HT and [^{3}H]-LSD, is regulated by guanine nucleotides. Binding to 5-HT$_2$ receptors occurs with [^{3}H]-spiro-peridol, [^{3}H]-mianserin and [^{3}H]-LSD. These receptors are not affected by guanine nucleotides, but are sensitive to chronic treatment with antidepressants and mediate the behavioural syndrome following central 5-HT stimulation. After one week of treatment with amitriptyline there is a significant decrease in the number of 5-HT$_2$ sites, and the effect is maximal after 3 to 6 weeks of chronic treatment (Peroutka and Snyder, 1980). Since this decrease is observed at clinically effective doses, alterations in 5-HT receptors may have important implications for the role of 5-HT in the affective disorders. It has been reported that there is a significantly greater number of 5-HT$_2$ receptors, but not 5-HT$_1$ receptors, in the frontal cortex of suicides compared with a control group (Stanley and Mann, 1983). It is possible that antidepressants may exert their therapeutic effect by reducing the number of 5-HT$_2$ receptors to normal levels.

5-HT induces a shape change in blood platelets, which may then lead to aggregation. Since ketanserin, a 5-HT$_2$ antagonist, blocks 5-HT-induced aggre-gation, the platelet aggregation receptor may be classified as 5-HT$_2$ (Schäcker and Grahame-Smith, 1982). Aggregatory techniques have been used to monitor the responsiveness of platelet 5-HT$_2$ receptors in depressed patients. Healey and colleagues (1983) reported that platelet receptor responsiveness was lower in depressed patients than in control subjects, and increased in those patients who responded to antidepressant treatment. However, we have found the functional activity system of the 5-HT$_2$ receptor system to be normal in our depressed patients (Wood et al., 1984). We found a significant positive correlation between the patients' HRS depression scores and two of the variates of the aggregatory response. It is possible that more severely depressed patients would have a higher aggregatory response than less depressed patients, but this would not account for the discrepancy between our results and those of Healey's group, since the mean HRS scores were similar in the two investigations. We have subsequently found an increased 5-HT-induced platelet aggregatory response in both bipolar and unipolar patients who were being treated with lithium prophylactically, indicat-ing that platelet 5-HT receptors may be functionally supersensitive in patients undergoing prophylactic lithium treatment (Wood et al., 1985). The results could not be reproduced by the addition of lithium in vitro. The supersensitivity was not related to the patients' plasma lithium concentration, duration of lithium treatment, or the affective morbidity of the patients. Hence the effect may be due to the low morbidity of these patients, rather than to any effect of lithium treatment, which would agree with the results of Healey and colleagues (1983) and would indicate that clinical improvement or remission from an affective illness is associated with enhanced 5-HT$_2$ receptor activity.

Certain endocrine abnormalities are associated with depressive illness. Myxoedema is a well established cause of depression, and can be diagnosed early by using a sensitive test of thyroid-stimulating-hormone (TSH). It has been shown that the antidepressant action of tricyclics can be enhanced by giving small doses of T3 (Prange *et al.*, 1969; Goodwin *et al.*, 1982). In our patients on long-term lithium therapy, the affective morbidity was twice as high in those patients with a moderately raised TSH compared with those patients with normal TSH (Coppen *et al.*, 1983). It has been shown that thyroid function can profoundly affect 5-HT-mediated behavioural responses in rats (Atterwell, 1981).

5-HT stimulates the release of prolactin. Intravenous infusion of the 5-HT precursor tryptophan produces an increase in plasma concentration of both prolactin and growth hormone in healthy subjects (MacIndoe and Turkingdon, 1973; Cowen *et al.*, 1985). However, in depressed patients the prolactin response to i.v. tryptophan is much less marked than in control subjects (Heninger *et al.*, 1984), indicating that serotonergic function is impaired in depressed patients. A new 5-HT receptor antagonist, ritanserin, is a potent and highly selective antagonist at 5-HT_2 receptors (Leysen *et al.*, 1985), which enters the brain well. Administration of ritanserin prior to infusion of tryptophan significantly enhances the prolactin response, but not the growth hormone response, in healthy subjects (Charig *et al.*, 1986). This suggests that endocrine responses to tryptophan are mediated by 5-HT_1 rather than 5-HT_2 receptors, and that 5-HT_2 receptor antagonists may increase 5-HT_1-mediated responses in the brain. Blunted prolactin response in depressed patients may be due to deficient 5-HT_1- or excessive 5-HT_2-mediated neurotransmission.

In conclusion, the 5-HT hypothesis of depression has stood the test of time. However, the biochemical changes in affective disorders are complex, and the metabolism and function of 5-HT is influenced by many factors. Much work remains to be done before we will be able to predict which individuals are liable to become depressed, and, having identified these subjects, the factors which will precipitate an episode of depression. The sought-for marker for depressive illness remains elusive, although it is probable that it will be found to have more than a remote connection with some aspect of the functioning of 5-HT.

References

Ahtee, L., Pentikäinen, L., Pentikäinen, P., and Paasonen, M. (1974). 5-hydroxytryptamine in blood platelets of cirrhotic and hypertensive patients. *Experientia*, **30**, 1328-9.

Asberg, M., Thóren, P., Träskman, L., Bertilsson, L., and Ringberger, V. (1975). Serotonin depression – a biochemical subgroup within the affective disorders? *Science*, **191**, 478-80.

Asberg, M., Träskman, L., and Thóren, P. (1976). 5-HIAA in the cerebrospinal fluid. A biochemical suicide predictor? *Arch. Gen. Psychiat.*, **33**, 1193-7.

Ashcroft, G. W., Blackburn, I. M., Eccleston, D., Glen, A. I. M., Hartley, W., Kinloch, N. E., Lonergan, M., Murray, L. G., and Pullar, I. A. (1973). Changes on recovery in the concentrations of tryptophan and the biogenic amine metabolites in the cerebrospinal fluid of patients with affective illness. *Psychol. Med.*, **3**, 319-25.

Atterwell, C. K. (1981). Effect of acute and chronic T_3 administration to rats on central 5-HT and dopamine-mediated behavioural responses and related brain biochemistry. *Neuropharmacol.*, **20**, 131-44.

Baumann, P., Schmocker, M., Reyero, F., and Heimann, H. (1975). Free and bound tryptophan in the blood of depressives. *Acta vitamin enzymol.*, **29**, 255-61.

Beskow, J., Gottfries, C. G., Roos, B. E., and Winblad, B. (1976). Determination of monoamine and monoamine metabolites in the human brain: post-mortem studies in a group of suicides and in a control group. *Acta Psychiatr. Scand.*, **53**, 7-20.

Blair, J. A., Morar, C., Hamon, C. G. B., Barford, P. A., Pheasant, A. E., Whitburn, S. B., Leeming, R. J., Reynolds, G. P., and Coppen, A. (1984). Tetrahydrobiopterin metabolism in depression. *Lancet*, **ii**, 163.

Bourne, H. R., Bunney, W. E., Colburn, R. W., Davis, J. M., Davis, J. N., Shaw, D. M., and Coppen. A. (1968). Noradrenaline, 5-hydroxytryptamine and 5-hydroxyindole acetic acid in hindbrains of suicidal patients. *Lancet*, **ii**, 805-8.

Bowers, M. B., Heninger, G. R., and Gerbode, F. (1969). Cerebrospinal fluid 5-hydroxyindole acetic acid and homovanillic acid in psychiatric patients. *Int. J. Neuropharmacol.*, **8**, 255 (1969).

Bridges, P. K., Bartlett, J. R., Sepping, P., Kantameneni, B. D., and Curzon, G. (1976). Precursors and metabolites of 5-hydroxytryptamine and dopamine in the ventricular cerebrospinal fluid of psychiatric patients. *Psychol. Med.*, **6**, 399-405.

Briley, M. S., Langer, S. Z., Raisman, R., Sechter, D., and Zarifian, E. (1980). Tritiated imipramine binding sites are decreased in platelets of untreated depressed patients. *Science*, **209**, 303-5.

Carlsson, A., Corrodi, H., Fuxe, K., and Hökfelt, T. (1969). Effects of some antidepressant drugs on the depletion of intraneuronal brain catecholamine stores caused by 4-α-dimethylmetatyramine. *Europ. J. Pharmac.*, **5**, 367-73.

Carlsson, A., Rosengreen, E., Bertler, A., and Nilsson, J. (1957). Effect of reserpine on the metabolism of catecholamines. In Garattini, S., and Ghetti, V. (eds.), *Psychotropic Drugs*, Elsevier, Amsterdam, 363.

Carney, M. W. P., Roth, M., and Garside, R. F. (1965). The diagnosis of depressive symptoms and the prediction of ECT responses. *Br. J. Psychiat.*, **111**, 659-74.

Charig, E. M., Anderson, I. M., Robinson, J. M., Nutt, D. J., and Cowen, P. J. (1986). L-tryptophan and prolactin release: evidence for interaction between 5-HT_1 and 5-HT_2 receptors. *Human Psychopharmacol.*, **1**, 93-7.

Choi, S. J., Taylor, M. A., and Abrams, R. (1977). Depression, ECT and erythrocyte adenosine triphosphatase activity. *Biol. Psychiat.*, **12**, 75-81.

Chouinard, G., Young, S. N., Annable, L., and Sourkes, T. L. (1979). Tryptophan-nicotinamide, imipramine and their combination in depression. *Acta psychiat. Scand.*, **59**, 395-414.

Cochran, E., Robins, E., and Grote, S. (1976). Regional serotonin levels in brain: a comparison of depressive suicides and alcoholic suicides with controls. *Biol. Psychiat.*, **11**, 283-94.

Coppen, A. (1967). The biochemistry of affective disorders. *Br. J. Psychiat.*, **113**, 1237-64.

Coppen, A. (1974). Serotonin in the affective disorders. In Kline, N. S. (ed.), *Factors in Depression*. Raven, New York, 33-4.

Coppen, A., and Abou-Saleh, M. T. (1982). Plasma folate and affective morbidity during long-term lithium therapy. *Br. J. Psychiat.*, **141**, 87-9.

Coppen, A., Abou-Saleh, M., Milln, P., Bailey, J., and Wood, K. (1983). Decreasing lithium dosage reduces morbidity and side-effects during prophylaxis. *J. Affect. Dis.*, **5**, 353-62.

Coppen, A., Chaudhry, S., and Swade, C. (1986). Folic acid enhances lithium prophylaxis. *J. Affect. Dis.*, **10**, 9-13.

Coppen, A., Eccleston, E., and Peet, M. (1973). Total and free tryptophan concentration in the plasma of depressive patients. *Lancet*, **ii**, 60-3.

Coppen, A., Prange, A. J., Whybrow, P. C., and Noguerra, R. (1972). Abnormalities of indoleamines in affective disorders. *Arch. Gen. Psychiat.*, **26**, 474-8.

Coppen, A., Rao, V. A. R., Swade, C., and Wood, K. (1979). Inhibition of 5-hydroxytryptamine reuptake by amitriptyline and zimelidine and its relationship to their therapeutic action. *Psychopharmacol.*, **63**, 125-9.

Coppen, A., Shaw, D. M., and Farrell, J. P. (1963). Potentiation of the antidepressive effect of a monoamine oxidase inhibitor by tryptophan. *Lancet*, **i**, 79–81.

Coppen, A., Shaw, D. M., Herzberg, B., and Maggs, R. (1967). Tryptophan in the treatment of depression. *Lancet*, **ii**, 1178–80.

Coppen, A., Swade, C., and Wood, K. (1978). Platelet 5-hydroxytryptamine accumulation in depressive illness. *Clin. Chim. Acta.*, **87**, 165–8.

Coppen, A., Swade, C., and Wood, K. (1980). Lithium restores abnormal platelet 5-HT transport in patients with affective disorders. *Br. J. Psychiat.*, **136**, 235–8.

Coppen, A., Swade, C., Wood, K., and Carroll, J. D. (1979). Platelet 5-hydroxytryptamine accumulation and migraine. *Lancet*, **ii**, 914.

Coppen, A., Turner, P., Rowsell, A. R., and Padgham, C. (1976). 5-hydroxytryptamine (5-HT) in the whole-blood of patients with depressive illness. *Postgrad. Med. J.*, **52**, 156–8.

Cowen, P. J., Gadhvi, H., Gosden, B., and Kolakowska, T. (1985). Responses of prolactin and growth hormone to L-tryptophan infusion: effects in normal subjects and schizophrenic patients receiving neuroleptics. *Psychopharmacol.*, **86**, 164–9.

Curzon, G. (1969). Tryptophan pyrrolase – a biochemical factor in depressive illness? *Br. J. Psychiat.*, **115**, 1367.

Curzon G. (1975). The control of tryptophan metabolism. In Parke, D. V. (ed.), *Basic Life Sciences, vol. 6: Enzyme Induction*. Plenum, New York, 169–84.

Curzon, G. (1979). Relationships between plasma, CSF and brain tryptophan. *J. Neural Trans.*, suppl. 15, 81–92.

Curzon, G., and Bridges, P. K. (1970). Tryptophan metabolism in depression. *J. Neurol. Neurosurg. Psychiat.*, **33**, 698–704.

Curzon, G., Friedel, J., Katamaneni, B., Greenwood, M. H., and Lader, M. H. (1974). Unesterified fatty acids and the binding of tryptophan in human plasma. *Clin. Sci. Mol. Med.*, **47**, 415–24.

Curzon, G., Friedel, J., and Knott, P. J. (1973). The effect of fatty acids on the binding of tryptophan to plasma protein. *Nature*, **242**, 198–200.

Curzon, G., Gumpert, E. J. W., and Sharpe, D. M. (1971). Amine metabolites in the lumbar cerebrospinal fluid of humans with restricted flow of cerebrospinal fluid. *Nature*, **231**, 189.

Curzon, G., Kantamaneni, B. D., Lader, M. H., Greenwood, M. H. (1979). Tryptophan disposition in psychiatric patients before and after stress. *Psychol. Med.*, **9**, 457–63.

Dickerson, J. W. T., and Wiryanti, J. (1978). Pellagra and mental disturbance. *Proc. Nutr. Soc.*, **37**, 167–71.

Fernstrom, J. D. (1973). The control of brain serotonin concentration by the diet. In Ferin M., Halberg, F., Richart, R. M., and Van de Wiele, R. L. (eds.), *Biorhythms and Human Reproduction*, Wiley, New York, 513–26.

Fernstrom, J. D. (1979). Diet induced changes in plasma amino acid pattern: effects on the brain uptake of large neutral amino acids and on brain serotonin synthesis. *J. Neural. Trans.*, suppl. 15, 55–67.

Fernstrom, J. D., and Wurtman, R. J. (1971). Brain serotonin content: increase following ingestion of carbohydrate diet. *Science*, **174**, 1023–25.

Fiore, C. E., Malatino, L. S., and Petrone, G. (1979). Differences between plasma tryptophan patterns in endogenous and neurotic depression. *IRCS Med. Sci.*, **7**, 525.

Frazer, A., Pandey, G. N., and Mendels, J. (1973). Metabolism of tryptophan in depressive disease. *Arch. Gen. Psychiat.*, **29**, 528.

Gal, E. M. (1974). Cerebral tryptophan-2,3-dioxygenase (pyrrolase) and its induction in rat brain. *J. Neurochem.*, **22**, 861–3.

Garelis, E., and Sourkes, T. L. (1973). Sites of origin in the central nervous system of monoamine metabolites measured in human cerebrospinal fluid. *J. Neurol. Neurosurg. Psychiat.*, **34**, 625.

Garfinkel, P. E., Warsh, J. J., Stancer, H. C., and Sibony, D. (1976). Total and free plasma tryptophan levels in patients with affective disorders. *Arch. Gen. Psychiat.*, **33**, 1462–6.

Gay, C., Langer, S. Z., Loo, H., Raisman, R., Sechter, D., and Zarifian, E. (1983). ^{3}H-imipramine binding in platelets: a state-dependent or independent biological marker in depression? *Br. J. Pharmacol.*, **78**, Proc. Suppl., 57.

Giret, M., Launay, J. M., Loo, H., Dreux, C., Benycoub, A., and Zarifian, E. (1980). Modifications of biochemical parameters in blood platelets of schizophrenic and depressive patients. *Neuropsychobiology*, 6, 290–6.

Glassman, A., and Platman, S. R. (1969). Potentiation of a monoamine oxidase inhibitor by tryptophan. *J. Psychiat. Res.*, 7, 83–8.

Goodwin, F. K., Post, R. M., Dunner, D. L., and Gordon, E. K. (1973). Cerebrospinal fluid amine metabolites in affective illness: the probenecid technique. *Am. J. Psychiat.*, 130, 73–9.

Goodwin, F. K., Prange, A. J., Post, R. M., Muscettola, G., and Lipton, M. A. (1982). Potentiation of antidepressant effects by L-triiodothyronine in tricyclic nonresponders. *Am. J. Psychiat.*, 139, 34–8.

Gould, S. E., and Handley, S. L. (1978). Dose-dependent dual action of kynurenine, a tryptophan metabolite, in the turnover of 5-hydroxytryptamine. *Proc. Br. J. Pharmacol.*, 55.

Grahame-Smith, D. G. (1971). Studies *in vivo* on the relationship between brain tryptophan, brain 5-HT synthesis and hyperactivity in rats treated with monoamine oxidase inhibitor and l-tryptophan. *J. Neurochem.*, 18, 1053–60.

Green, A. R., and Costain, D. W. (1979). The biochemistry of depression. In Paykel, E. S., and Coppen, A. (eds.), *Psychopharmacology of Affective Disorders*. Oxford University Press, Oxford.

Green, A. R., and Curzon, G. (1970). The effect of tryptophan metabolites on brain 5-hydroxytryptamine metabolism. *Biochem. Pharmacol.*, 19, 2061–8.

Gutierrez, J. L. A., and Lopez-Ibor, A. J. J. (1971). Tryptophan and a MAOI (Nialamide) in the treatment of depression. *Int. Pharmacopsychiat.*, 6, 92–7.

Hagen, P. B., and Cohen, L. H. (1966). Biosynthesis of indolealkylamines: physiological release and transport of 5-hydroxytryptamine. In Erspamer, V. (ed.), *Handbook of Experimental Pharmacology*, 19, Springer, Berlin, 182.

Handley, S. L., Dunn, T. L., Waldron, G., and Baker, J. M. (1980). Tryptophan, cortisol and puerperal mood. *Br. J. Psychiat.*, 136, 498–508.

Handley, S. L., and Miskin, R. C. (1977). The interaction of some kynurenine pathway metabolites ith 5-hydroxytryptophan and 5-hydroxytryptamine. *Psychopharmacol.*, 51, 305–9.

Harris, T. H. (1957). Depression induced by Rauwolfia compounds. *Am. J. Psychiat.*, 113, 950–63.

Healey, D., Carney, P. A., and Leonard, B. E. (1963). Monoamine-related markers of depression – changes following treatment. *J. Psychiat. Res.*, 17, 251–60.

Heninger, G. R., Charney, D. S., and Sternberg, D. E. (1984). Serotonergic function in depression. Prolactin response to intravenous tryptophan in depressed patients and healthy subjects. *Arch. Gen. Psychiat.*, 41, 398–402.

Hesketh, J. E., Glen, A. I. M., and Reading, H. W. (1977). Membrane ATPase activities in depressive illness. *J. Neurochem.*, 28, 1401–2.

Hess, S. M., and Doepfner, W. (1961). Behavioural effects and brain amine content in rats. *Arch. Intern. Pharmacodyn.*, 134, 89–99.

Joseph, M. H. (1977). The determination of kynurenine by gas-liquid chromatography; evidence for its presence in rat brain. *Br. J. Pharmacol.*, 59, 525.

Kishimoto, H., and Hama, Y. (1976). The level and diurnal rhythm of plasma tryptophan and tyrosine in manic-depressive patients. *Yokohama Med. Bull.*, 27, 89–97.

Knox, W. E., and Auerbach, V. H. (1955). The hormonal control of tryptophan peroxidase in rat. *J. Biol. Chem.*, 214, 307–13.

Lapin I. P., and Oxenkrug, G. E. (1961). Intensification of the central serotonergic processes as a possible determinant of the thymoleptic effect. *Lancet*, i, 132.

Leeming, R. J., Harpey, J.-P., Brown, S. M., and Blair, J. A. (1982). Tetrahydrofolate and hydroxycobolamin in the management of dihydropteridine reductase deficiency. *J. Ment. Defic. Res.*, 26, 21–5.

Levitt, M., Spector, S., Sjoerdsman, P., and Udenfried, S. (1965). Elucidation of the rate-limiting step in norepinephrine biosynthesis in the perfused guinea pig heart. *J. Pharmacol. Exp. Ther.*, 148, 1–8.

Leysen, J. E., Gommeren, W., Van Gompel, P., Wynants, J., Janssen, P., and Laduron, P. M.

(1985). Receptor binding properties *in vitro* and *in vivo* of ritanserin, a very potent and long acting serotonin-S_2 antagonist. *Mol. Pharmacol.*, **27**, 600–11.

Lingjaerde, O. (1969). Uptake of serotonin in blood platelets: dependence on sodium and chloride and inhibition by choline. *FEBS Letters*, **3**, 103–6.

Lloyd, K. J., Farley, I. J., Deck, J. H. N., and Hornykiewicz, O. (1974). Serotonin and 5-hydroxyindoleacetic acid in discrete areas of the brainstem of suicide victims and control patients. *Adv. Biochem. Psychopharmac.*, **11**, 387–97.

MacIndoe, J. H., and Turkingdon, R. W. (1973). Stimulation of human prolactin secretion by intravenous L-tryptophan. *J. Clin. Invest.*, **52**, 1972–8.

McMenamy, R. H., and Oncley, J. L. (1958). The specific binding of L-tryptophan to serum albumin. *J. Biol. Chem.*, **233**, 1436–47.

Maitre, L., Moser, P., Baumann, P. A., and Waldmeier, P. C. (1980). Amine uptake inhibitors: criteria of selectivity. *Acta. Psychiat. Scand.*, **61**, suppl. 280, 97–110.

Malmgren, R., Åsberg, M., Olsson, P., Tornling, G., and Unge, G. (1981). Defective serotonin transport mechanism in platelets from endogenously depressed patients. *Life Sci.*, **29**, 2649–58.

Manowitz, P., Menna-Perper, M., Mueller, P. S., Rochford, J., and Swartzburg, M. (1977). Effect of insulin on human plasma tryptophan and non-esterified fatty acids. *Proc. Soc. Exp. Biol. Med.*, **156**, 402–5.

Meek, J. L., and Neff, N. H. (1973). Is cerebrospinal fluid the major avenue for the removal of 5-hydroxyindoleacetic acid from the brain? *Neuropharmacol.*, **12**, 497.

Meltzer, H. Y., Ramesh, C. A., Barber, R., and Tricou, B. J. (1981). Serotonin uptake in blood platelets of psychiatric patients. *Arch. Gen. Psychiat.*, **38**, 1322–6.

Møller, S. E., Kirk, L., and Fremming, K. H. (1976). Plasma amino acids as an index for subgroups in manic depressive psychosis: correlation to effect of tryptophan. *Psychopharmacol.*, **49**, 205–13.

Møller, S. E., Kirk, L., and Honoré, P. (1979). Free and total plasma tryptophan in endogenous depression. *J. Affect. Dis.*, **1**, 69–76.

Nakaya, K. (1976). Serum free tryptophan concentration. The effects on the brain serotonin metabolism and its relationship to the mental diseases. *Psychiatrica Neurol. Jap.*, **78**, 132–45.

Naylor, G. J., Smith, A. H. W., Dick, E. G., Dick, D. A. T., McHarg, A. M., and Chambers, C. A. (1980). Erythrocyte membrane cation carrier in manic depressive psychosis. *Psychol. Med.*, **10**, 521–5.

Niskanen, P., Huttunen, M., Tamminen, T., and Jääskeläinen, J. (1976). The daily rhythm of plasma tryptophan and tyrosine in depression. *Br. J. Psychiat.*, **128**, 67–73.

Papeschi, R., and McLure, D. J. (1981). Homovanillic acid and 5-hydroxyindoleacetic acid in cerebrospinal fluid of depressed patients. *Arch. Gen. Psychiat.*, **25**, 354–358.

Pardridge, W. M., and Oldendorf, W. H. (1977). Transport of metabolic substrates through the blood-brain barrier. *J. Neurochem.*, **28**, 5–12.

Pare, C. M. B. (1963). Potentiation of monoamine oxidase by tryptophan. *Lancet*, **ii**, 527.

Pare, C. M. B. (1965). Some clinical aspects of antidepressant drugs. In Marks, J., and Pare, C. M. B. (eds.) *The Scientific Basis of Drug Therapy in Psychiatry*. Oxford University Press, Oxford.

Pare, C. M. B., and Sandler, M. (1959). A clinical and biochemical study of a trial of iproniazid in the treatment of depression. *J. Neurol. Neurosurg. Psychiat.*, **22**, 247–51.

Pare, C. M. B., Young, D. P. H., Price, K., and Stacey, R. S. (1969). 5-hydroxytryptamine noradrenaline and dopamine in brainstem, hypothalamus and caudate nucleus of controls and patients committing suicide by coal gas poisoning. *Lancet*, **ii**, 133–6.

Peet, M., Moody, J. P., Worrall, E. P., Walker, P., and Naylor, G. J. (1976). Plasma tryptophan concentration in depressive illness and mania. *Br. J. Psychiat.*, **128**, 255–8.

Peroutka, S. J., and Snyder, S. H. (1980). Long-term antidepressant treatment decreased spiroperidol-labelled serotonin receptor binding. *Science*, **210**, 88–90.

Peroutka, S. J., and Snyder, S. H. (1982). Recognition of multiple serotonin binding sites. In Ho, B. T., Schoolar, J. C., and Usdin, E. (eds.), *Serotonin in Biological Psychiatry* (Advances in Biochemical Psychopharmacology, vol. 34). Raven, New York, 155–72.

Perry, E. K., Marshall, E. F., Blessed, G., Tomlinson, B. E., and Perry, R. H. (1983). Decreased imipramine binding in the brains of patients with depressive illness. *Br. J. Psychiat.*, **142**, 188–92.

Prange, A. J., Wilson, I. C., and Rabon, A. M. (1969). Enhancement of imipramine anti-depressant activity by thyroid hormone. *Am. J. Psychiat.*, 126, 457-69.

Rausch, J. L., Janowsky, D. S., Risch, S. C., and Huey, L. Y. (1986). A kinetic analysis and replication of decreased platelet serotonin uptake in depressed patients. *Psychiatry Research*, 19, 105-12.

Rehavi, M., Skolnick, P., and Paul, S. M. (1983). Subcellular distribution of high affinity ³H-serotonin uptake in rat brain. *Europ. J. Pharmacol.*, 87, 335-9.

Reith, M. E. A., Sershen, H., Allen, D., and Lajtham, A. (1983). High- and low-affinity binding of ³H-imipramine in mouse cerebral cortex. *J. Neurochem.*, 40, 389-95.

Reynolds, E. H., Preece, J. M., Bailey, J., and Coppen, A. (1970). Folate deficiency in depressive illness. *Br. J. Psychiat.*, 117, 287-92.

Riley, G. J., and Shaw, D. M. (1976). Total and non-bound tryptophan in unipolar illness. *Lancet*, ii, 1249.

Rotman, A., Modai, I., Munitz, H., and Wifsenbeek, H. (1979). Active uptake of serotonin by blood platelets of schizophrenic patients. *FEBS Letters*, 101, 134-6.

Sachar, E. J., Hellman, L., Roffwarg, H. P., Halpern, F. S., Fukushima, D. K., and Gallagher, T. F. (1973). Disrupted 24-hour pattern of cortisol secretion in psychotic depression. *Arch. Gen. Psychiat.*, 28, 19-24.

Schächter, M., and Grahame-Smith, D. G. (1982). 5-hydroxytrypamine and the platelet-specific binding and uptake. In De Clerk, F., and Vanhoutte, P. M. (eds.), *5-Hydroxy-tryptamine in Peripheral Reactions*. Raven, New York, 83-94.

Schildkraut, J. J. (1965). The catecholamine hypothesis of affective disorders: a review of supporting evidence. *Am. J. Psychiat.*, 122, 509-522.

Schmid-Burgk, W., Kim, J. S., Lischewski, R., and Rassman, W. (1981). Levels of total and free tryptophan in the plasma of endogenous and neurotic depressives. *Arch. Psychiat. Nervkrankh.*, 231, 35-9.

Sepping, P., Wood, W., Bellamy, C., Bridges, P. K., O'Gorman, P., Bartlett, J. R., and Patel, V. K. (1977). Studies on endocrine activity, plasma tryptophan and catecholamine excretion on psychosurgical patients. *Acta psychiat. Scand.*, 56, 1-14.

Shaw, D. M., Camps, F. E., and Eccleston, E. (1967). 5-hydroxytryptamine in the hind-brains of depressive suicides. *Br. J. Psychiat.*, 113, 1407-11.

Sjöström, R., and Roos, B. E. (1972). 5-hydroxyindoleacetic acid and homovanillic acid in cerebrospinal fluid in manic-depressive psychosis. *Eur. J. Clin. Pharmac.*, 4, 170.

Smeraldi, E., Negri, F., and Melica, A. M. (1977). A genetic study of affective disorders. *Acta Psychiat. Scand.*, 56, 382-98.

Sneddon, J. M. (1973). Blood platelets as a model for monoamine-containing neurones. *Progr. Neurobiol.*, 1, 151-98.

Stahl, S. M. (1977). The human platelet – a diagnostic and research tool for the study of biogenic amines in psychiatric and neurologic disorders. *Arch. Gen. Psychiat.*, 34, 509-16.

Stahl, S. M., Woo, D. J., Mefford, I. N., Berger, P. A., and Ciaranello, R. D. (1983). Hyper-serotonemia and platelet serotonin uptake and release in schizophrenia and affective disorders. *Am. J. Psychiat.*, 140, 26-30.

Stanley, M., and Mann, J. J. (1983). Increased serotonin-2 binding sites in frontal cortex of suicide victims. *Lancet*, i, 214-16.

Stanley, M., Virgilio, J., and Gershon, S. (1983). Tritiated imipramine binding sites are decreased in the frontal cortex of suicides. *Science*, 216, 1337-9.

Swade, C. (1983). Platelet 5-hydroxytryptamine uptake in affective disorders. Ph. D. Thesis, University of Surrey.

Swade, C., and Coppen, A. (1980). Seasonal variations in biochemical factors related to depressive illness. *J. Affect. Dis.*, 2, 249-55.

Tagliamonte, A., Demontis, M. G., Olianas, M., Onali, P. L., and Gessa, G. L. (1975). Possible role of insulin in the transport of tyrosine and tryptophan from blood to brain. *Pharmacol. Res. Comm.*, 7, 493-9.

Tagliamonte, A., Tagliamonte, P., Perez-Cruet, J., Stern, S., and Gessa, G. L. (1971). Effect of psychotropic drugs on tryptophan concentration in rat brain. *J. Pharmacol. Exp. Ther.*, 177, 475-80.

Thomson, J., Rankin, H., Ashcroft, G. W., Yates, C. M., McQueen, J. K., and Cummings, S.

W. (1982). The treatment of depression in general practice. A comparison of 1-tryptophan, amitriptyline, and a combination of 1-tryptophan and amitriptyline with placebo. *Psychol. Med.*, **12**, 741–51.

Tuomisto, J., and Tukiainen, E. (1976). Decreased uptake of 5-hydroxytryptamine in blood platelets from depressed patients. *Nature*, **262**, 596–8.

van Praag, H. M. (1977). *Depression in Schizophrenia*, Spectrum, New York.

van Praag, H. M., Korf, J., and Schut, T. (1973). Cerebral monoamines and depression. An investigation with the probenecid technique. *Arch. Gen. Psychiat.*, **28**, 827–3.

Vestergaard, P., Sørensen, T., Hoppe, E., Rafaelsen, O. J., Yates, C. M., and Nicholaou, N. (1978). Biogenic amine metabolites in cerebrospinal fluid of patients with affective disorders. *Acta Psychiat. Scand.*, **58**, 83–96.

Wirz-Jutice, A., Lichsteiner, M., and Feer, H. (1977). Diurnal and seasonal variations in human platelet serotonin. *J. Neur. Trans.*, **41**, 7–15.

Wood, K., and Coppen, A. (1978). The effect of clofibrate on total and free plasma tryptophan in depressed patients. *Neuropharmacol.*, **17**, 417–31.

Wood, K., Harwood, J., and Coppen, A. (1978). The effect of antidepressant drugs on plasma kynurenine in depressed patients. *Psychopharmacol.*, **59**, 263–6.

Wood, K., Swade, C., Abou-Saleh, M., and Coppen, A. (1984). Peripheral serotonergic receptor sensitivity in depressive illness. *J. Affect. Dis.*, **7**, 59–65.

Wood, K., Swade, C., Abou-Saleh, M., and Coppen, A. (1985). Apparent supersensitivity of platelet 5-HT receptors in lithium-treated patients. *J. Affect. Dis.*, **8**, 69–72.

Wood, K., Swade, C., Harwood, J., Eccleston, E., Bishop, M., and Coppen, A. (1977). Comparison of methods for the determination of total and free tryptophan in plasma. *Clin. Chim. Acta.*, **80**, 299–303.

Woolley, D. W., and Shaw, E. (1954). Some neurophysiological aspects of serotonin. *Br. Med. J.*, **ii**, 122.

Young, S. N., Lal, S., Sourkes, T. L., Feldmuller, F., Arnoff, A., and Martin, J. B. (1975). Relationships between tryptophan in serum and CSF, and 5-hydroxyindole-acetic acid in CSF in man: effect of cirrhosis of liver and probenecid administration. *J. Neurol. Neurosurg. Psychiat.*, **38**, 322–30.

Zeller, E. A., Barsky, J., and Berman, E. R. (1955). Inhibition of monoamine oxidase by 1-isonicotinyl-2-isopropylhydrazine. *J. Biol. Chem.*, **214**, 267.

10

Platelet [³H]-Imipramine Binding Differentiates Major Depression from Alzheimer's Disease in Elderly

B. Suranyi-Cadotte, S. Gauthier, F. Lafaille, S. DeFlores, T. V. Dam, N. P. V. Nair and R. Quirion

10.1 Introduction

The tricyclic antidepressant imipramine binds with high affinity to specific sites in brain (Raisman et al., 1979a, b; 1980; Rehavi et al., 1980; Langer et al., 1981a) and blood platelets (Briley et al., 1979; Paul et al., 1980), which are believed to be associated to the uptake of serotonin (Langer et al., 1981b; Paul et al., 1981; Dumbrille-Ross and Tang, 1981; Sette et al., 1981). In both brain and platelets, the characteristics of [³H]-imipramine binding sites are very similar (Langer et al., 1981b; Paul et al., 1981). Furthermore, these binding sites are decreased in the central nervous system (Stanley et al., 1982) and platelets (Langer et al., 1981b; Briley et al., 1980; Paul et al., 1981; Suranyi-Cadotte et al., 1983) of depressed patients. Hence, platelet [³H]-imipramine binding may be a useful laboratory adjunct to differentiate major depression from other conditions. This may apply particularly to depression in the elderly, where the diagnostic distinction from primary degenerative dementia can be very difficult (McAllister, 1983). Both syndromes can coexist in the same individual (Reifler et al., 1982), and depression itself can present with cognitive impairment in the elderly. An erroneous diagnosis of a non-treatable dementia in a depressed patient has major therapeutic and prognostic implications. The objective of the present study was to investigate the utility of platelet [³H]-imipramine binding in the differential diagnosis of depression from dementia in the elderly.

10.2 Subjects and Methods

Our sample consisted of 12 young patients with major depressive disorder (4 males, 8 females, mean age ± SEM = 42 ± 7 years), 17 elderly patients with major depressive disorder (6 males, 11 females, mean age = 65 ± 5 years), 10 patients with primary degenerative dementia, Alzeimer type (4 males, 6 females; mean age 70 ± 4 years); 14 young healthy controls (mean age = 38 ± 8 years) and 12 elderly healthy controls (mean age = 67 ± 7 years). All depressed patients met research diagnostic criteria (RDC; Ferghner et al., 1972) for major depressive disorder and had Hamilton Depression Rating Scores of equal to or greater than 20 (mean Hamilton Depressive Score was 24 ± 4). Diagnosis of Alzheimer's disease was made according to criteria of the third edition of the *Diagnostic and Statistical Manual of Mental Disorders* (1980), CT scans, and the absence of treatable causes of dementia. The two control groups were physically and mentally healthy subjects, with no family history of major psychiatric or neurological illness, and who denied the use of psychotropic drugs. Depressed and Alzheimer disease patients were medication-free for at least 4 weeks prior to platelet $[^3H]$-imipramine binding assays. The study was conducted from November to February, 1984.

Platelet $[^3H]$-imipramine binding was measured as follows: blood samples were collected in ethylenediamine tetra-acetate (EDTA) vacutainers between 8 and 9 a.m. in the fasting state. Platelets were obtained from platelet-rich plasma by centrifugation at 18 000g for 10 min and washed twice with buffer (5 mM tris-HCl, 20 mM EDTA, 150 mM NaCl, pH 7.5). The preparation of platelet membranes by hypotonic lysis, homogenisation and centrifugation, and $[^3H]$-imipramine (30 to 50 Ci/mmol; New England Nuclear) binding assays were carried out as previously described (Briley et al., 1980; Wood et al., 1983). The lysed membranes were incubated with 0.3 + 10 nM $[^3H]$-imipramine at 4 °C for 60 minutes. Specific $[^3H]$-imipramine binding was determined as binding inhibited in the presence of 100 μM desipramine. The K_D and B_{max} of $[^3H]$-imipramine binding were calculated by linear regression of Scatchard plots. Protein assays and statistics (Neuman-Keuls) were performed as described previously (Wood and Peloquin, 1982).

10.3 Results

Specific binding of $[^3H]$-imipramine to platelet membranes represented 70 to 80% of total binding at 2.5 nM of $[^3H]$-imipramine. No statistical differences between males and females were observed, either in normal subjects or in depressed or Alzheimer disease patients. Figure 10.1 illustrates the individual platelet $[^3H]$-imipramine binding density (B_{max}) values in the two groups of healthy subjects, in young and elderly patients with major depression and in patients with Alzheimer's disease. Mean B_{max} of platelet $[^3H]$-imipramine binding was

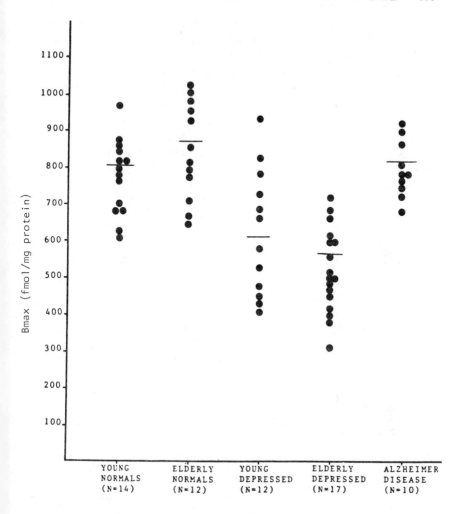

Fig. 10.1 The density (B_{max}) of platelet [³H]-imipramine binding sites in young and elderly normal subjects, in young and elderly patients with major depressive disorder and in patients with Alzheimer's disease.

only slightly, and non-significantly, higher in elderly (mean B_{max} ± SEM = 870 ± 48 fmol/mg protein) compared with younger (812 ± 47) normal subjects. In Alzheimer's disease patients, mean B_{max} values (825 ± 38) were comparable to normal subjects. In contrast, both young and elderly depressed patients had mean B_{max} values (young depressed = 602 ± 52; elderly depressed = 562 ± 47) which were significantly lower than their age matched controls (young = $p < 0.01$). Mean B_{max} values of both depressed groups were also significantly lower than that of Alzheimer disease patients ($p < 0.02$). As has been reported previously (Briley *et al.*, 1980; Langer *et al.*, 1981b; Wood *et al.*, 1983a), there was a considerable degree of overlap in B_{max} values between younger depressed and control groups (Fig. 10.1). However, interestingly, in elderly depressed patients B_{max} values showed little overlap with either normal subjects or patients with Alzheimer's disease. In elderly depressed patients mean B_{max} value was lower than the lowest value for either controls or Alzheimer disease subjects. Only 5 out of 17 elderly depressed patients had B_{max} values that overlapped with the lowest values of either normal or Alzheimer's disease subjects. Clinically, there were no distinguishing features among the 5 patients that could account for their higher B_{max} values. The affinity (K_D, nM) of [^{3}H]-imipramine for its binding site to platelets did not differ significantly between patients (young depressed = 2.8 ± 0.3; elderly depressed = 2.4 ± 0.4; Alzheimer = 3.0 ± 0.8) and controls (young = 2.7 ± 0.4; elderly = 2.5 ± 0.7).

10.4 Discussion

Previous results from this (Suranyi-Cadotte *et al.*, 1983; Wood *et al.*, 1983a) and other laboratories (Ahtee *et al.*, 1981; Kamal *et al.*, 1984) indicated that a reduction in the number (B_{max}) of platelet [^{3}H]-imipramine binding sites may occur in patients with major depressive disorder, but not in other psychiatric or non-psychiatric medical conditions. Our study of platelet [^{3}H]-imipramine binding in young and elderly depressed patients, their age-matched controls and patients with Alzheimer's disease further support the unique relationship between reduced platelet [^{3}H]-imipramine binding and major depressive disorder. The density (B_{max}) of platelet [^{3}H]-imipramine binding sites was significantly lower in depressed patients than normal subjects, as has been reported previously (Asarch *et al.*, 1981; Paul *et al.*, 1981; Suranyi-Cadotte *et al.*, 1982; Wood *et al.*, 1983b). The lower B_{max} of platelet [^{3}H]-imipramine binding observed here in elderly depressives is similar to that previously reported in young depressed populations (Suranyi-Cadotte *et al.*, 1982, 1983; Wood *et al.*, 1983a,b). Furthermore, this reduction in B_{max} values does not appear to be dependent on patient age. B_{max} values in normal elderly subjects were not lower than that of the normal younger groups; rather, a trend towards increased values was noted in the elderly. These results differ from initial reports (Langer *et al.*, 1980) of a negative correlation of B_{max} with age, but are consistent with more recent data of an age-related trend toward increased B_{max} of [^{3}H]-imipramine binding sites (Severson *et al.*, 1985). Further studies are required to determine the effect of age on platelet [^{3}H]-imipramine binding. However, the normal B_{max} values of age-matched Alzheimer's disease patients observed in the present study suggests that in elderly depressives the low density of platelet [^{3}H]-imipramine binding sites is not likely to depend on patient age.

Although B_{max} values in younger depressives were significantly lower than in age-matched healthy subjects, this reduction is only statistical, since there was a considerable degree of overlap with that of controls. Of considerable interest, however, was the little overlap in B_{max} values between elderly depressives and age-matched healthy and Alzheimer disease subjects. This data is suggestive of a considerable diagnostic applicability of platelet [³H]-imipramine binding in discriminating depression from Alzheimer's disease in the elderly. In a preliminary study of elderly depressed and Alzheimer disease patients, Knight et al. (1986) found a similar robust decrease in platelet [³H]-imipramine binding in elderly depressives, providing further evidence for the utility of platelet [³H]-imipramine binding in the differential diagnoses of depression and dementia.

[³H]-imipramine binding sites appear to be related to the uptake of serotonin in brain and platelets (Langer et al., 1981; Paul et al., 1981; Sette et al., 1981; Sette et al., 1983). Furthermore, in both tissues the pharmacological profile of [³H]-imipramine binding appears to be very similar (Briley et al., 1979; Paul et al., 1980; Rehavi et al., 1980). However, previous observations from this (Wood et al , 1983a) and other (Ahtee et al., 1981; Kamal et al., 1984) laboratories suggest that while uptake of serotonin may be reduced in a variety of psychiatric and non-psychiatric medical conditions, a reduction in the density of [³H]-imipramine binding sites may be specifically related to depressive disorders. Recently, several independent groups have reported the presence of endogenous inhibitors of the [³H]-imipramine binding site in brain (Barbaccia et al., 1983; Rehavi et al., 1985) and plasma (Angel and Paul, 1984; Brusov et al., 1985). The abnormally low density of [³H]-imipramine binding sites in depressed patients may be related to the presence of these factors.

Differentiating depression from dementia has important therapeutic and prognostic implications. The present study indicates that in elderly depressed patients the density of platelet [³H]-imipramine binding sites is significantly lower than in elderly healthy and Alzheimer's disease subjects. These data suggest that platelet [³H]-imipramine binding may be an important laboratory adjunct in the differential diagnosis of depression and dementia in the elderly. These findings certainly warrant further investigations in depressed and demented populations. For example, comparison of platelet [³H]-imipramine binding in Alzheimer's disease patients with and without depression should further clarify the relationship of altered [³H]-imipramine binding and depressive illness.

References

Ahtee, L., Briley, M., Raisman, R., Lebrec, D., and Langer, S. Z. (1981). Reduced uptake of serotonin but unchanged ³H-imipramine binding in the platelets of cirrhotic patients. Life Sci., 29, 2323–9.

American Psychiatric Association (1980). Diagnostic and Statistical Manual of Mental Disorders (3rd edn.). APA Washington, DC.

Angel, I., and Paul, S. M. (1984). Inhibition of synaptosomal 5-(³H)hydroxytryptamine uptake by endogenous factor(s) in human blood. FEBS Lett., 171, 280–4.

Asarch, B., Shih, J., and Kulcsar, A. (1981). Decreased ³H-imipramine binding in depressed males and females. Commun. Psychopharmac., 4, 425–32.

Barbaccia, M. L., Grandolfi, C., Chuang, D. M., and Costa, E. (1983). Modulation of neuronal serotonin uptake by a putative endogenous ligand of imipramine binding sites. *Proc. Natl. Acad. Sci., USA*, **80**, 5134–8.

Briley, M. S., Raisman, R., and Langer, S. Z. (1979). Human platelets possess high-affinity binding sites for ^{3}H-imipramine. *Eur. J. Pharmacol.*, **58**, 347–48.

Briley, M. S., Langer, S. Z., Raisman, R., Sechter, D., and Zarifian, E. (1980). Tritiated imipramine binding sites are decreased in platelets of untreated depressed patients. *Science*, **209**, 303–5.

Brusov, O. S., Fomenko, A. M., and Katasono, A. B. (1985). Human plasma inhibitors of platelet serotonin uptake and imipramine receptor binding: Extraction and heterogeneity. *Biol. Psychiatry*, **20**, 235–44.

Dumbrille-Ross, A., and Tang, S. W. (1981). Absence of high-affinity [^{3}H]-imipramine binding in platelets and cerebral cortex of Fawn-hooded rats. *Eur. J. Pharmacol.*, **72**, 137–8.

Feighner, J. P., Robins, E., Guze, S. B., Woodruff, R. A., Winokur, G., and Munoz, R. (1972). Diagnostic criteria for use in psychiatric research. *Arch. Gen. Psychiat.*, **26**, 57–62.

Kamal, L. A., Raisman, R., Meyer, P., and Langer, S. Z. (1984). Reduced V_{max} of ^{3}H-serotonin uptake but unchanged ^{3}H-imipramine binding in the platelets of untreated hypertensive subjects. *Life Sci.*, **34**, 2083–8.

Knight, D. L., Krishnan, K. R. R., Blazer, D. G., and Nemeroff, C. B. (1986). Tritiated imipramine binding to platelets is markedly reduced in elderly depressed patients. *Society Neurosci.*, **12**, 1251.

Langer, S. Z., Briley, M. S., Raisman, R., Henry, J.-F., and Morselli, P. L. (1980). Specific ^{3}H-imipramine binding in human platelets: influence of age and sex. *Naunyn-Schmiedeberg's Arch. Pharmacol.*, **313**, 189–94.

Langer, S. Z., Javoy-Agid, F., Raisman, R., Briley, M., and Agid, Yd. (1981a). Distribution of specific high-affinity binding sites for ^{3}H-imipramine in human brain. *J. Neurochem.*, **37**, 267–71.

Langer S. Z., Zarifian, E., Briley, M., Raisman, R., and Sechter, D. (1981b). High affinity binding of ^{3}H-imipramine in brain and platelets and its relevance to the biochemistry of affective disorders. *Life Sci.*, **29**, 211–20.

McAllister, T. W. (1983). Overview: Pseudodementia. *Am. J. Psychiatry*, **140**, 528–33.

Paul, S. M., Rehavi, M., Skolnick, P., and Goodwin, F. K. (1980). Demonstration of specific 'high affinity' binding sites for ^{3}H-imipramine on human platelets. *Life Sci.*, **26**, 953–59.

Paul, S. M., Rehavi, M., Rice, K. C., Ittah, Y., and Skolnick, P. (1981). Does high affinity ^{3}H-imipramine binding label serotonin reuptake sites in brain and platelet? *Life Sci.*, **28**, 2753–60.

Raisman, R., Briley, M., and Langer, S. Z. (1979a). High affinity ^{3}H-imipramine binding in rat cerebral cortex. *Eur. J. Pharmac.*, **54**, 307–8.

Raisman, R., Briley, M., and Langer, S. Z. (1979b). Specific tricyclic antidepressant binding sites in rat brain. *Nature* (Lond.), **281**, 148–50.

Raisman, R., Briley, M., and Langer, S. Z. (1980). Specific tricyclic antidepressant binding sites in rat brain characterized by high-affinity ^{3}H-imipramine binding. *Eur. J. Pharmacol.*, **61**, 373–80.

Rehavi, M., Paul, S. M., Skolnick, P., and Goodwin, F. K. (1980). Demonstration of specific high-affinity binding sites for ^{3}H-imipramine in human brain. *Life Sci.*, **26**, 2273–9.

Rehavi, M., Ventura, I., and Sarne, Y. (1985). Demonstration of endogenous 'imipramine-like' material in rat brain. *Life Sci.*, **36**, 686–93.

Reifler, B. V., Larson, E., and Hanley, R. (1982). Coexistence of cognitive impairment and depression in geriatric outpatients. *Am. J. Psychiatry*, **139**, 623–6.

Sette, M., Raisman, R., Briley, M., and Langer, S. Z. (1981). Localization of tricyclic antidepressant binding sites on serotonin nerve terminals. *J. Neurochem.*, **37**, 40–2.

Sette, M., Briley, M. S., and Langer, S. Z. (1983). Complex inhibition of ^{3}H-imipramine binding by serotonin and non-tricyclic serotonin uptake blockers. *J. Neurochem.*, **40**, 622–8.

Severson, J. A., Marcusson, J. O., Ostenburg, H. H., Finch, E. E., and Winblad, B. (1985). Elevated density of ^{3}H-imipramine binding in aged human brain. *J. Neurochem.*, **45**, 1382–9.

Stanley, M., Virgilio, J., and Gershon, S. (1982). Tritiated imipramine binding sites are decreased in the frontal cortex of suicides. *Science*, 216, 1337–9.

Suranyi-Cadotte, B. E., Wood, P. L., Nair, N. P. V., and Schwartz, G. (1982). Normalization of platelet ^{3}H-imipramine binding in depressed patients during remission. *Eur. J. Pharmacol.*, 85, 357–8.

Suranyi-Cadotte, B. E., Wood, P. L., Schwartz, G., and Nair, N. P. V. (1983). Altered platelet ^{3}H-imipramine binding in schizo-affective and depressive disorders. *Biol. Psychiat.*, 18, 923–7.

Wood, P. L., and Peloquin, H. (1982). Increases in choline levels in rat brain elicited by medofenoxate. *Neuropharmacol.*, 21, 349–54.

Wood, P. L., Suranyi-Cadotte, B. E., Nair, N. P. V., Lafaille, F., and Schwartz, G. (1983a). Lack of association of platelet [^{3}H]imipramine binding sites and serotonin uptake in control, depressed and schizophrenic patients. *Neuropharmacol.*, 22, 1211–14.

Wood, P. L., Suranyi-Cadotte, B. E., Schwartz, G., and Nair, N. P. V. (1983b). Platelet ^{3}H-imipramine binding and red blood cell choline in affective disorders: indications of heterogenous pathogenesis. *Biol. Psychiat.*, 18, 715–19.

11

Lithium Augmentation of Antidepressant Treatments: Evidence for the Involvement of the 5-HT System?

C. de Montigny, Y. Chaput and P. Blier

11.1 Introduction

The use of lithium carbonate addition in treatment-resistant depression is now current practice world-wide. Several approaches had previously been proposed for treatment-resistant depression: reserpine (Poldinger, 1963; Haškovec and Rysánek, 1967; Hopkinson and Kenny, 1975; Zohar *et al.*, 1987), T_3 (Earle, 1969; Ogura *et al.*, 1974; Banki, 1977; Goodwin *et al.*, 1982), psychostimulants (Wharton *et al.*, 1971; Ayd and Zohar, 1987), oestrogen supplementation (Shapira *et al.*, 1985; Zohar *et al.*, 1985; Oppenheim *et al.*, 1987) or combination of a tricyclic antidepressant drug (TCA) with a monoamine oxidase inhibitor (MAOI) (Schuckit *et al.*, 1971; Sethna, 1974; Spiker and Pugh, 1976; Goldberg and Thormson, 1978). However, until recently, electroconvulsive therapy (ECT) remained the treatment of choice for resistant depression (Medical Research Council, 1965; Davidson *et al.*, 1978). British investigators have recently advanced that lithium addition might soon supersede the use of ECT in treatment-resistant depression (Pai *et al.*, 1986).

Amazingly, the *primum movens* of adding lithium in TCA-resistant depression was intended to test the hypothesis that long-term TCA treatment induced in humans, as it does in animals (see below), a sensitisation of postsynaptic neurons to 5-HT (de Montigny *et al.*, 1981b). It was in fact only when lithium addition became widely used that its remarkable therapeutic efficacy was fully realised. The issue of the efficacy of this treatment has largely overshadowed the original heuristic question of the neurobiological substratum of the therapeutic effect of antidepressant treatments.

Thus, it is the aim of the present chapter to examine, in the light of recent pre-clinical and clinical data, whether the original hypothesis of a potentiation of 5-HT neurotransmission is still tenable.

Hence, we first provide an overview of pre-clinical data bearing on the neurobiological effects of antidepressant treatments and of lithium on the 5-HT system, and then confront this data with that obtained from the clinical realm in an attempt to determine if the latter is consistent or not with the notion that the 5-HT system might be involved.

11.2 Effects of Antidepressant Treatments on 5-HT Neurotransmission

11.2.1 Tricyclic Antidepressant Drugs

Despite the ability of most TCA drugs to block the reuptake of monoamines, first demonstrated by Glowinski and Axelrod (1964), several observations have put doubt on the possibility that this property might underly their therapeutic activity. In particular, the fact that some efficacious drugs, such as iprindole and trimipramine (de Montigny, 1982; Cournoyer et al., 1987), are devoid of any monoaminergic reuptake blocking activity (Ross et al., 1971; Hyttel, 1982) constitutes strong evidence against this possibility.

Nevertheless, several early clinical observations indicated that the 5-HT system might be involved in mediating the therapeutic effect of TCA drugs. One of the most striking was a report by Shopsin et al. (1975) who observed that the administration of a 5-HT synthesis inhibitor, p-chlorophenylalanine (PCPA) (Koe and Weissmann, 1966; Jéquier et al., 1967), abolished the therapeutic effect of imipramine in major depression.

Intrigued by this apparent paradox between pre-clinical and clinical data, we studied the effect of long-term administration of TCA drugs on the responsiveness of rat forebrain neurons to microiontophoretically applied 5-HT. It was found that different types of TCA drugs (including iprindole), administered for two weeks at a clinically relevant dosage, induced a sensitisation of dorsal hippocampal pyramidus neurons and of ventral lateral geniculate nucleus neurons to 5-HT (de Montigny and Aghajanian, 1978). Several other studies have confirmed and extended this finding to other brain regions (Gallager and Bunney, 1979; Jones, 1980; Menkes et al., 1980; Wang and Aghajanian, 1980; de Montigny et al., 1981a; Menkes and Aghajanian, 1981; Blier et al., 1984; Gravel and de Montigny, 1987). Consistently with these electrophysiological studies, several behavioural studies have documented an enhanced response to 5-HT precursors or agonists following long-term treatment with these drugs (Friedman and

Dallob, 1979; Mogilnicka and Klimek, 1979; Stolz and Marsden, 1982; Friedman *et al.*, 1983; Stolz *et al.*, 1983).

The demonstration of a sensitisation of postsynaptic neurons to 5-HT was not sufficient to warrant the conclusion that the long-term administration of these drugs resulted in a net enhancement of 5-HT neurotransmission. To this end, two complementary series of experiments were carried out. Firstly, it was shown that long-term treatment with different types of TCA drugs did not alter the firing activity of dorsal raphe 5-HT neurons (Blier and de Montigny, 1980). Secondly, Wang and Aghajanian (1980) have shown that the effect of electrical stimulation of the ascending 5-HT pathway on the firing activity of amygdaloid neurons was enhanced following long-term treatment with different types of TCA drugs. We have recently carried out a similar study in which both the responsiveness of dorsal hippocampal pyramidal neurons to microiontophoretically applied 5-HT and the effectiveness of stimulating the ascending 5-HT pathway were found to be augmented following a three-week treatment with imipramine (Blier *et al.*, 1987a).

11.2.2 Electroconvulsive Treatment

The behavioural response to 5-HT precursors or agonists is markedly enhanced by repeated electroconvulsive treatment (ECT) in the rat, suggesting that this treatment induces a neuronal sensitisation to 5-HT (Evans *et al.*, 1976; Costain *et al.*, 1979; Wielosz, 1985).

In order to verify that forebrain post-synaptic neurons would also exhibit a sensitisation to 5-HT, we determined the responsiveness of dorsal hippocampus pyramidal neurons to microiontophoretically applied 5-HT following six ECTs administered over a two-week period. The responsiveness of these neurons to 5-HT in treated rats was markedly enhanced, whereas those to noradrenaline (NA) and to GABA remained unchanged (de Montigny, 1984). In order to ascertain that this enhanced effectiveness of 5-HT was indeed attributable to a post-synaptic rather than a pre-synaptic modification, we used the 5-HT agonist, 5-methoxydimethyltryptamine, which is not a substrate for the high-affinity 5-HT reuptake process (Horn, 1973). The responsiveness of the same neurons to 5-methoxydimethyltryptamine was increased to an extent similar to that of 5-HT (de Montigny, 1984).

11.2.3 Tetracyclic Antidepressant Drugs and Triazolobenzodiazepines

Representative drugs of the tetracyclic and triazolobenzodiazepine classes of drugs, mianserin and adinazolam, were recently studied. It was found that long-term, but not acute, administration of these drugs enhanced the responsiveness of hippocampal pyramidal neurons to microiontophoretically applied 5-HT without altering their responsiveness to NA and GABA.

It might be recalled here that the antidepressant efficacy of mianserin has been well demonstrated but that the promising preliminary results obtained with adinazolam in major depression remain to be confirmed by double-blind controlled studies.

11.2.4 Serotonin Reuptake Blockers

Six structurally different selective 5-HT reuptake blockers have been studied in major depression. All were found to be efficacious antidepressants (see Asberg et al., 1986, for review).

A two-day treatment with any one of indalpine, zimelidine and citalopram markedly reduced the firing activity of dorsal raphe 5-HT neurons; there was a partial recovery after a 7-day treatment and a complete recovery after a 14-day treatment (Blier and de Montigny, 1983; Blier et al., 1984; Chaput et al., 1986b). The decreased effect of lysergic acid diethylamide (LSD), an agonist of the somato-dendritic 5-HT autoreceptor (Agajanian, 1978), on the firing activity of 5-HT neurons following a 14-day treatment with a 5-HT reuptake blocker suggests that the densensitisation of somato-dendritic autoreceptor underlies the progressive recovery of their firing activity despite the sustained 5-HT reuptake blockade.

None of these treatments altered the responsiveness of hippocampal pyramidal neurons to 5-HT. However, following a 14-day treatment with zimelidine or citalopram, the effectiveness of the stimulation of the ascending 5-HT pathway in depressing the firing activity of the same neurons was markedly enhanced (Blier and de Montigny, 1983; Chaput et al., 1986b). This increased synaptic efficacy appears not to be directly attributable to the blockade of 5-HT reuptake, as the acute administration of citalopram did not increase the efficacy of the stimulation (Chaput et al., 1986b). Using the terminal 5-HT autoreceptor antagonist methiothepin (Moret, 1985; Chaput et al., 1986b), we have provided evidence that a desensitisation of this autoreceptor might underlie the enhanced efficacy of the 5-HT synapse (Chaput et al., 1986a).

11.2.5 Monoamine Oxidase Inhibitors

Serotonin and NA are both deaminated in vivo by the A-form of MAO (Hall et al , 1969; Yang and Neff, 1974). The therapeutic efficacy of MAOI's selective for the A-isoenzyme in major depression (Murphy et al., 1981; Cassachia et al., 1984; Stefanis et al., 1984) suggests that it is the inhibition of this isoenzyme which underlies the antidepressant activity of MAOI.

We have determined in a parallel manner the effect of three MAOI on 5-HT and NA neurotransmission: deprenyl, a selective MAOI-B; clorgyline, a selective MAOI-A; and phenelzine, a non-selective MAOI. As expected from its selectivity for MAO-B, deprenyl affected neither 5-HT nor NA neurotransmission. Hence, we will review here only the effects of clorgyline and phenelzine.

Both MAOIs initially reduced the firing activity of dorsal raphe 5-HT neurons. As was the case with 5-HT reuptake blockers, this was followed by a complete recovery of their firing activity after 21 days of treatment. The use of LSD demonstrated that this recovery is also due to a desensitisation of somato-dendritic 5-HT autoreceptors (Blier and de Montigny, 1985a).

In striking contrast, the initial decrease of the firing of NA neurons in the locus coeruleus was not followed by any recovery, even after 21 days of treatment with either MAOI. Consistent with this finding, the effect of clonidine, an α_2-agonist, on the firing activity of these neurons was unchanged, indicating that somato-dendritic NA autoreceptors are endowed with some immutability (Blier and de Montigny, 1985a).

The effectiveness of the electrical stimulation of the ascending 5-HT pathway, but not that of the dorsal NA bundle, on the firing activity of dorsal hippocampus pyramidal neurons was increased by both MAOIs (Blier et al., 1986).

Hence these results provide a novel argument that the antidepressant efficacy of MAOIs might be related to their effect on 5-HT, rather than NA neurotransmission, since there is a remarkable congruence between the time-course of their effect on 5-HT neuron firing activity and their delayed therapeutic activity.

11.3 Effect of Lithium on 5-HT Neurotransmission

11.3.1 The Effect of Lithium in Behavioural Models

Grahame-Smith and Green (1974) have shown conclusively that the enhancement of 5-HT-mediated hyperactivity in the rat by lithium is attributable to an enhanced efficacy of the 5-HT neurons themselves.

More recently, the same group of investigators (Goodwin et al., 1986) have elegantly shown that the component of the 5-HT syndrome mediated by postsynaptic 5-HT$_{1A}$ receptors in the rat is selectively enhanced by short-term (3 days) as well as by long-term (12 days) treatment with lithium.

11.3.2 The Effect of Lithium in Electrophysiological Paradigms

Strikingly, the electrophysiological investigation of the effect of lithium on 5-HT neurotransmission yielded data which are in complete congruence with both series of behavioural observations mentioned in the previous section.

In a first study, we have shown that short-term lithium administration (plasma levels: 0.4 to 1.1 mEq/l) enhanced the effectiveness of stimulating the ascending 5-HT pathway in depressing the firing activity of postsynaptic dorsal hippocampus pyramidal neurons, without altering their responsiveness to microiontophoretically-applied 5-HT (Blier and de Montigny, 1985b).

In a recent study aimed at determining the properties of dorsal raphe 5-HT neurons following short-term lithium administration, we found that their firing activity and the sensitivity of their somato-dendritic autoreceptor were unaltered. Similarly, the function of the terminal 5-HT autoreceptor appeared to be normal. However, unexpectedly, it was found that the dose–response curve of the effect of the intravenous administration of 8-hydroxy-2-(di-N-propylamino)tetralin (8-OH-DPAT), a selective 5-HT$_{1A}$ receptor agonist, on the firing activity of dorsal raphe 5-HT neurons was shifted to the left (Blier *et al.*, 1987b). Given the direct evidence of an unchanged sensitivity of the somato-dendritic autoreceptor provided by the microiontophoretic applications of 5-HT, LSD and 8-OH-DPAT onto these neurons (Blier *et al.*, 1987b), the enhanced effectiveness of 8-OH-DPAT must then be attributed to a sensitisation of postsynaptic 5-HT$_{1A}$ receptors, presumably located on neurons involved in a negative feedback regulation of 5-HT neuron firing activity.

Hence, these results are fully consistent with those of above-mentioned behavioural studies, as they clearly indicate that short-term lithium administration induces at least two distinct modifications that can affect 5-HT neurotransmission: firstly, lithium enhances the efficacy of 5-HT neurons themselves; secondly, it enhances the response of a subset of 5-HT$_{1A}$ postsynaptic receptors.

11.3.3 Possible Molecular Mechanisms Underlying the Effect of Lithium on 5-HT Neurotransmission

As yet, little is known concerning the substratum for the enhancement of postsynaptic 5-HT$_{1A}$ response by lithium. Although 5-HT$_1$ receptors are not thought to be coupled to phosphatidyl inositol metabolism (Minchin, 1985), it would be premature to rule out the possibility that a subset of postsynaptic 5-HT$_{1A}$ receptor might be. If this were the case then the enhanced effect of 8-OH-DPAT might be explained by the blockade of IP$_1$ degradation by lithium (Berridge *et al.*, 1982).

The molecular mechanism for the increased effectiveness of 5-HT neurons themselves by lithium also remains elusive. However, a number of different mechanisms might be involved. Lithium increases the availability of L-tryptophan in the brain (Perez-Cruet *et al.*, 1971). It also increases the uptake of this amino acid by 5-HT terminals (Knapp and Mandell, 1975). From very low levels (in the range of 0.1 mEq/l) lithium enhances the synthesis of 5-HT (Perez-Cruet *et al.*, 1971; Broderick and Lynch, 1982). Whether the increased synthesis results from an enhanced availability of the precursor or from an increased activity of tryptophan hydroxylase (Knapp and Mandell, 1975) is not entirely clear. Finally, Treiser *et al.* (1981) have shown that lithium increases the basal as well as the K$^+$-stimulated release of 5-HT in the hippocampus.

11.4 Characterisation of the Potentiation of Antidepressant Treatments by Lithium

11.4.1 Antidepressant Treatments Reported to be Potentiated by Lithium Addition

The most striking, and possibly the most interesting, aspect of the effect of lithium addition in resistant depression is that it can potentiate an extremely large spectrum of antidepressant treatments (Table 11.1). To our knowledge, there is not a single type of antidepressant treatment reported not to be potentiated by lithium! However, it must be borne in mind that negative results are less likely to be reported than positive ones.

The percentage of patients reported to be improved by lithium addition is given in Table 11.1 for each type of antidepressant treatment. However, it has to be realised that this estimation of efficacy has only a *relative* value, as, again, it is obvious that successful trials are much more likely to be reported than treatment failures.

Table 11.1 Antidepressant treatments reported to be potentiated by lithium addition

Type of antidepressant	$N(n)^a$	% of patients improved[b]	Reference
Tricyclics	**181 (139)**	**77%**	
	8 (8)		de Montigny et al., 1981b
	42 (33)		de Montigny et al., 1983
	11 (10)		Heninger et al., 1983
	2 (2)[c]		Joyce et al., 1983
	10 (7)		Alvarez et al., 1984
	12 (6)		Cournoyer et al., 1984
	5 (3)		Louie and Meltzer, 1984
	2 (2)[d]		Price et al., 1984
	1 (1)[e]		Rasmussen, 1984
	3 (3)f		Roy and Pickar, 1985
	1 (1)		Schrader and Levien, 1985
	1 (1)[g]		Cournoyer, 1986
	1 (1)[d]		Delisle, 1986
	4 (4)[h]		Garbutt et al., 1986
	4 (1)[i]		Kantor et al., 1986
	3 (3)		Kushnir, 1986
	2 (2)		Madakasira, 1986
	21 (11)[j]		Nelson and Mazure, 1986
	4 (4)		Pai et al., 1986
	35 (24)		Price et al., 1986
	1 (1)[g]		Zohar and Insel, 1987
Tetracyclics	**21 (19)**	**90%**	
Mianserin	4 (4)		Heninger et al., 1983
Mianserin	2 (2)		Joyce et al., 1983
Maprotiline	1 (1)		Weaver, 1983

Maprotiline	1 (1)		Kushnir, 1986
Mianserin	1 (1)		Pai et al., 1986
Mianserin	12 (10)		Price et al., 1986
MAOIs	**20 (18)**	**90%**	
Phenelzine	3 (3)		Nelson and Byck, 1982
Tranylcypromine	2 (2)[c]		Joyce et al., 1983
Phenelzine	2 (1)		Louie and Meltzer, 1984
Tranylcypromine	12 (11)[k]		Price et al., 1985
Phenelzine	1 (1)		Madakasira, 1986
Tranylcypromine	1 (1)		Tariot et al., 1986
5-HT reuptake blockers	**17 (9)**	**53%**	
Zimelidine	6 (4)		Joyce, 1985
Fluvoxamine	11 (5)		Price et al., 1986
Others			
Amoxapine	1 (1)		Louie and Meltzer, 1984
Sleep deprivation	22 (12)[l]		Baxter, 1985
Sleep deprivation	7 (5)[l]		Baxter et al., 1986
Alprazolam	1 (1)		Cerra et al., 1986
Trazodone	1 (1)		Kushnir, 1986
Adinazolam	10 (3)		Price et al., 1986
Bupropion	7 (3)		Price et al., 1986
Trazodone	9 (2)		Price et al., 1986
Carbamazepine	15 (8)		Kramlinger and Post, 1987

[a]N is the number of patients studied and (n) the number reported to be improved.
[b]See text concerning the limited indicative value of this percentage.
[c]One patient was resistant to the combination of amitriptyline and tranylcypromine.
[d]These patients became manic shortly after the addition of lithium.
[e]Presenting a severe obsessive-compulsive disorder.
[f]These patients were resistant to iprindole, a TCA drug which blocks neither 5-HT nor NE reuptake.
[g]Presenting a severe panic disorder.
[h]All four patients had previously failed to respond to the addition of T_3.
[i]The only patient who improved with lithium addition did so only transiently.
[j]These psychotically depressed patients were resistant to the combination of desipramine and a neuroleptic.
[k]These twelve patients had proved to be resistant to the addition of lithium to another type of antidepressant drug.
[l]In these studies the potentiation by lithium consisted in a prolongation of the antidepressant effect of sleep deprivation.

The limited number of patients in each treatment group, and, even more so, the paucity of controlled studies, makes a meaningful comparison of the efficacy of lithium added to different types of antidepressant treatments difficult. Nevertheless, with these limitations in mind, it would appear that, according to the antidepressant treatment pre-administered, the ranking of the efficacy of lithium addition is in the following order: MAOIs = tetracyclic drugs > TCA > 5-HT reuptake blockers ≥ other antidepressant treatments. The apparent superiority of the MAOI-lithium combination, at least over the TCA-lithium one is,

consistent with the impressive data of Price *et al.* (1985) who obtained a favourable effect by combining tranylcypromine and lithium in 11 or 12 patients who
had all failed to respond to the combination of lithium with another antidepressant treatment.

It must be borne in mind that this concerns the *rate* of response to lithium
addition (i.e. the probability of obtaining an improvement by adding lithium)
and not the *degree* of improvement brought about by lithium addition. Concerning this latter aspect, it is clear from the reports available that lithium *can*
produce a dramatic improvement in some patients, whatever the antidepressant
treatment pre-administered.

11.4.2 Clinical Characteristics of the Response to Lithium Addition

The latter point raises the issue of whether or not the response to lithium addition has an 'all or none' feature. In our studies (in which lithium was added only
for 48 or 72 hours) most of the patients fell either into the 'no change' or
'marked improvement' categories, only few showing a 'mild' or a 'moderate'
improvement. This has been the experience of other investigators as well (e.g.
Alvarez *et al.*, 1984). However, in other studies, particularly in those where
lithium was administered for a longer period of time, a full range of improvements was found.

Another important characteristic of lithium addition is that, with the striking
exception of sleep disturbances, the whole range of depressive symptoms are
alleviated simultaneously when a response occurs. This contrasts with the
'sequential' profile of the progressive clinical effect of most, if not all, antidepressant treatments which improve for instance symptoms such as motor
retardation much before they ameliorate other symptoms, such as depressive
mood.

11.4.3 Time-course of the Effect of Lithium Addition

There seems to be some variability as far as the onset of the clinically significant
amelioration brought about by lithium addition is concerned. Purely methodological factors (such as the sensitivity of the scales used, the training of the
evaluators, the frequency of the ratings, the duration of lithium administration,
etc.) most probably contribute to this variability. For instance, in most studies
conducted by our group, lithium was added for either 48 or 72 hours. This
obviously precluded the detection of 'long-latency' responses.

From the reading of the reports listed in Table 11.1, it would appear that
more than two-thirds of treatment-resistant patients show a clinically significant
improvement within a few days, at least during the first week of lithium treatment. However, there are clearly an appreciable number of patients in whom
lithium has to be administered for more than a week in order to produce a
significant improvement. The paucity of systematic studies precludes any definite

conclusion as to the factors determining the onset of the effect of lithium addition. We were however struck by the fact that 'long-latency' responses seem to be more frequent in patients who were treated unsuccessfully, either with several successive antidepressant drugs or for a protracted period with the same antidepressant. If this is true, one possible interpretation could be that lithium addition *accelerates* the therapeutic effect of the antidepressant treatment. Hence, it would mean that the longer the period of pre-treatment, the slower (and probably the shallower) would be the effect of lithium addition.

11.5 Evidence for the Involvement of the 5-HT System in the Potentiation of Antidepressant Treatments by Lithium

11.5.1 Communality

One inescapable conclusion emerging from Table 11.1 is that the potentiation by lithium of different types of antidepressant treatments unveils the *communality* of these treatments. In other words, the fact that this ion can potentiate such a wide spectrum of treatments constitutes strong evidence that these treatments share a common neurobiological substratum upon which lithium might act.

We have reviewed in section 11.2 the evidence that an augmentation of the net efficacy of 5-HT neurotransmission emerges as a possible common denominator of antidepressant treatments. We might add here that sleep deprivation in rats rapidly produces a complete shift in the diurnal rhythm of the responsiveness of hippocampal pyramidal neurons to 5-HT (Brunel and de Montigny, unpublished observation).

We have also reviewed, in section 11.3, the biochemical, behavioural and electrophysiological evidence that lithium potentiates 5-HT neurotransmission. Hence, the least that can be concluded is that there is a remarkable congruence between (a) neurobiological data which point to the 5-HT system as the common target of antidepressant treatments and lithium and (b) clinical data suggesting a communality between antidepressants as unveiled by lithium addition.

11.5.2 Concentration of Lithium

From the very first studies (de Montigny *et al.*, 1981b; de Montigny *et al.*, 1983; Heninger *et al.*, 1983) it was already striking that low plasma levels of lithium (the lowest level being 0.4 mEq/l) were sufficient to induce a potentiation of TCA drugs. In one of our studies, we have failed to detect any significant correlation ($r = 0.2$) between lithium plasma levels and clinical amelioration (de Montigny *et al.*, 1983). This meant that plasma levels greater than 0.4 mEq/l were not likely to produce a greater degree of improvement. Since then, two reports have clearly shown that even lower levels of lithium (ranging from 0.1

to 0.2 mEq/l) were sufficient to potentiate antidepressant treatments (Kushnir, 1986; Madakasira, 1986).

This important aspect of the phenomenon constitutes a valuable indication as to the possible substratum of this effect of lithium. Indeed, biochemical, behavioural and electrophysiological studies have uniformly shown that low plasma levels of lithium are sufficient to enhance 5-HT neurotransmission. For instance, Broderick and Lynch (1982) have detected an increased synthesis of 5-HT in the rat from plasma levels as low as 0.1 mEq/l.

Hence, the fact that very low plasma levels of lithium can potentiate anti-depressant treatments is fully consistent with the hypothesis that an augmentation of 5-HT neurotransmission might underly this phenomenon.

11.5.3 Time-course

As mentioned in the previous section, it appears from available reports that the majority of antidepressant-resistant patients improved by lithium addition do show a significant amelioration within a few days, albeit some patients clearly require a longer treatment. This rapidity of the clinical effect of lithium addition is consistent with the time-constant of its effect on 5-HT neurotransmission. In particular, Grahame-Smith and Green (1974) have determined that, in their behavioural model, the effect of lithium can be detected as soon as thirty-six hours after the initiation of the treatment. Similarly, we have observed that a forty-eight hour treatment with lithium is sufficient to markedly potentiate the electrophysiological effect of stimulating the 5-HT projection (Blier and de Montigny, 1985b).

11.5.4 Effect of Lithium in Humans

It is important to mention that several studies have shown that lithium enhances 5-HT neurotransmission in humans as well as it does in animals. Among the most conclusive data is the neuroendocrinological potentiation by lithium of the effects of 5-hydroxytryptophan and of L-tryptophan on cortisol and prolactin, respectively (Meltzer et al., 1984; Heninger et al., 1985; Glue et al., 1986).

11.5.5 Correlation Between Plasma Prolactin and Clinical Improvement

Since 5-HT stimulates the release of prolactin in humans as well as in animals, we have measured the early-morning prolactin level prior to and after forty-eight hours of lithium administration, in TCA-resistant patients. A significant correlation ($r = 0.62$) was found between the change in prolactin level and the clinical amelioration (Cournoyer et al., 1984). This further militates in favour of an involvement of the 5-HT system in the lithium-induced potentiation of anti-depressant treatments.

11.5.6 The Effect of Lithium Addition is the Mirror Image of that of PCPA

The last point we would like to raise is the striking fact that the potentiation of antidepressant treatments by lithium in resistant depressed patients is the exact mirror image of the reversal by PCPA of the pharmacological improvement of depression brought about by either a TCA or a MAOI treatment (Shopsin *et al.*, 1975; Shopsin *et al.*, 1976).

Given that lithium enhances 5-HT neurotransmission and that PCPA reduces it, this mirror image of the clinical effect of these agents is probably the most convincing evidence that the 5-HT system might be the key to understanding the neurobiology of antidepressant treatments.

Acknowledgements

Supported, in part, by the Canadian Medical Research Council (MRC) grant MA-6444 to C. de M. and by a grant from the Fonds de la recherche en santé du Québec (FRSQ) to the 'Equipe de Recherche sur les Neurotransmetteurs du Cerveau'. C. de M. is in receipt of an MRC Scientist Award, Y. C. of an FRSQ Fellowship and P. B. of an MRC Centennial Fellowship. We thank A. Khan for her secretarial assistance and N. Barton for improving the English of the manuscript.

References

Aghajanian, G. K. (1978). Feedback regulation of central monoaminergic neurons: evidence from single cell recording studies. In Youdim, M. B. J., Lovenberg, W., Sharman, D. F., and Lagnado, J. R. (eds.), *Essays in Neurochemistry and Neuropharmacology*, vol. 3. Wiley, New York, 1-32.

Alvarez, E., Udina, C., Queralto, J. M., Ordoñez, J., Rodriguez, J., and Casas, M. (1984). Factors indicating the favorable response of lithium added to the treatment of resistant depressions. *Coll. Int. Neuropsychopharmacol.*, 14, 75.

Asberg, M., Eriksson, B., Matensson, B., Traskman-Bendz, L., and Wagner, A. (1986). Therapeutic effects of serotonin uptake inhibitors in depression. *J. Clin. Psychiat.*, 47, 23-35.

Ayd, F. J., and Zohar, J. (1987). Psychostimulant therapy for chronic and treatment-resistant depression. In Zohar, J., and Belmaker, R. H. (eds.), *Treating Resistant Depression*. Pergamon, New York, in press.

Banki, C. M. (1977). Cerebrospinal fluid amine metabolites after combined amitriptyline-triodothyronine treatment of depressed women. *Eur. J. Clin. Pharmacol.*, 11, 311-5.

Baxter, L. R. (1985). Can lithium carbonate prolong the antidepressant effect of sleep deprivation? *Arch. Gen. Psychiat.*, 4, 635.

Baxter, L. R., Liston, E. H., Schwartz, J. M., Atlshuler, L. L., Wilkins, J. N., Richeimer, S., and Guze, B. H. (1986). Prolongation of the antidepressant response to partial sleep deprivation by lithium. *Psychiat. Res.*, 19, 17-23.

Berridge, M. J., Downes, C. P., and Hanley, M. R. (1982). Lithium amplifies agonist-dependent phosphatidylinositol response in brain and salivary glands. *Biochem. J.*, 206, 587-95.

Birkhimer, L. J., Alderman, A. A., Schmitt, C. E., and Ednie, K. J. (1983). Combined trazodone-lithium therapy for refractory depression. *Am. J. Psychiat.*, 140, 1382-3.

Blier, P., and de Montigny, C. (1980). Effect of chronic tricyclic antidepressant treatment on the serotoninergic autoreceptor. A microiontophoretic study in the rat. *Naunyn-Schmiedeberg's Arch. Pharmacol.*, **314**, 123–8.

Blier, P., and de Montigny, C. (1983). Electrophysiological investigations on the effect of repeated zimelidine administration on serotonergic neurotransmission in the rat. *J. Neurosci.*, **3**, 1270–8.

Blier, P., and de Montigny, C. (1985a). Serotoninergic but not noradrenergic neurons in rat central nervous system adapt to long-term treatment with monoamine oxidase inhibitors. *Neuroscience*, **16**, 949–55.

Blier, P., and de Montigny, C. (1985b). Short-term lithium administration enhances serotonergic neurotransmission: Electrophysiological evidence in the rat CNS. *Eur. J. Pharmacol.*, **112**, 415–18.

Blier, P., de Montigny, C., and Azzaro, A. J. (1986). Modification of serotonergic and noradrenergic neurotransmission by repeated administration of monoamine oxidase inhibitors: electrophysiological studies in the rat CNS. *J. Pharmacol. Exp. Ther.*, **227**, 987–94.

Blier, P., de Montigny, C., and Chaput, Y. (1987a). Modification of the serotonin system by antidepressant treatments: Implications for their therapeutic effect in major depression. *J. Clin. Psychopharmacol.* (in press).

Blier, P., de Montigny, C., and Tardif, D. (1984). Effects of the two antidepressant drugs mianserin and indalpine on the serotonergic system: Single-cell studies in the rat. *Psychopharmacology*, **84**, 242–9.

Blier, P., de Montigny, C., and Tardif, D. (1987b). Short-term lithium treatment enhances responsiveness of postsynaptic 5-HT$_{1A}$ receptors without altering 5-HT autoreceptor sensitivity: An electrophysiological study in the rat. *Synapse* (in press).

Broderick, P., and Lynch, V. (1982). Behavioral and biochemical changes induced by lithium and L-tryptophan in muricidal rats. *Neuropharmacology*, **21**, 671–9.

Cassachia, M., Carolei, A., Barba, C., and Rossi, A. (1984). Moclobemide (Ro-11-1163) versus placebo: A double-blind study in depressive patients. In Tipton, K. F., Dostert, P., and Strolin Benedetti, M. (eds.), *Monoamine oxidase and disease*. Academic, New York, 607–8.

Cerra, D., Meacham, T., and Coleman, J. (1986). A possible synergistic effect of alprazolam and lithium carbonate. *Am. J. Psychiat.*, **143**, 552.

Chaput, Y., Blier, P., and de Montigny, C. (1986a). In vivo electrophysiological evidence for the regulatory role of autoreceptors on serotonergic terminals. *J. Neurosci.*, **6**, 2796–801.

Chaput, Y., de Montigny, C., and Blier, P. (1986b). Effects of a selective 5-HT reuptake blocker, citalopram, on the sensitivity of 5-HT autoreceptors: electrophysiological studies in the rat. *Naunyn-Schmiedeberg's Arch. Pharmacol.*, **333**, 342–5.

Clemens, J. A., Roush, M. E., and Fuller, R. W. (1978). Evidence that serotonin neurones stimulate secretion of prolactin releasing factor. *Life Sci.*, **22**, 209–21.

Costain, D. W., Green, A. R., and Grahame-Smith, E. G. (1979). Enhanced 5-hydroxytryptamine-mediated behavioral responses in rats following repeated electroconvulsive shock: relevance to the mechanism of the antidepressive effect of electroconvulsive therapy. *Psychopharmacology*, **61**, 167–70.

Cournoyer, G., de Montigny, C., Ouellette, J., Langlois, R., Elie, R., Caillé, G., and Le Morvan, P. (1987). A comparative double-blind controlled study of trimipramine and amitriptyline in major depression: Lack of correlation with 5-HT reuptake blockade. *J. Clin. Psychopharmacol.* (in press).

Cournoyer, G., de Montigny, C., Ouellette, J., Leblanc, G., Langlois, R., and Elie, R. (1984). Lithium addition in tricyclic-resistant unipolar depression: A placebo-controlled study. *Coll. Int. Neuropsychopharmacol.*, **14**, F-177.

Cournoyer, J. (1986). Réponse rapide à l'addition du carbonate de lithium d'un trouble: panique résistant aux antidépresseurs tricycliques. *Can. J. Psychiat.*, **31**, 335–8.

Davidson, J., McLeod, M., Law-Yone, B., and Linnoila, M. (1978). A comparison of electroconvulsive therapy and combined phenelzine-amitriptyline in refractory depression. *Arch. Gen. Psychiat.*, **35**, 639–42.

Delisle, J. D. (1986). Rapid switch in a bipolar patient during lithium-tricyclic therapy. *Am. J. Psychiat.*, **143**, 1326–7.

de Montigny, C. (1982). Iprindole: A cornerstone in the neurobiological investigation of antidepressant treatments. *Mod. Probl. Pharmacopsychiat.*, **18**, 102–16.

de Montigny, C. (1984). Electroconvulsive treatments enhance responsiveness of forebrain neurons to serotonin. *J. Pharmac. Exp. Ther.*, **228**, 230–4.

de Montigny, C., and Aghajanian, G. K. (1977). Preferential action of 5-methoxytryptamine and 5-methoxydimethyltryptamine on presynaptic serotonin receptors: a comparative iontophoretic study with LSD and serotonin. *Neuropharmacology*, **16**, 811–8.

de Montigny, C., and Aghajanian, G. K. (1978). Tricyclic antidepressants: long-term treatment increases responsivity of rat forebrain neurons to serotonin. *Science*, **202**, 1303–6.

de Montigny, C., Blier, P., Caillé, G., and Kouassi, E. (1981a). Pre- and postsynaptic effects of zimelidine and norzimelidine on the serotoninergic system: single cell studies in the rat. *Acta Psychiat. Scand.*, **63**, 79–90.

de Montigny, C., Blier, P., and Chaput, Y. (1984). Electrophysiologically-identified serotonin receptors in the rat CNS. Effect of antidepressant treatment. *Neuropharmacology*, **23**, 1511–20.

de Montigny, C., and Cournoyer, G. (1987). Lithium addition in treatment-resistant major depression. In Zohar, J., and Belmaker, R. H. (eds.), *Special Treatments for Resistant Depression*. Raven, New York (in press).

de Montigny, C., Cournoyer, G., Morissette, R., Langlois, R., and Caillé, G. (1983). Lithium carbonate addition in tricyclic antidepressant-resistant unipolar depression. *Arch. Gen. Psychiat.*, **40**, 1327–34.

de Montigny, C., Elie, R., and Caillé, G. (1985). Rapid response to lithium addition in iprindole-resistant unipolar depression. *Am. J. Psychiat.*, **142**, 220–3.

de Montigny, C., Grunberg, F., Mayer, A., and Deschenes, J. P. (1981b). Lithium induces rapid relief of depression in tricyclic antidepressant drug non-responders. *Br. J. Psychiat.*, **138**, 252–6.

Earle, B. F. (1969). Thyroid hormone and tricyclic antidepressants in resistant depressions. *Am. J. Psychiat.*, **126**, 1667–9.

Evans, J. P. M., Grahame-Smith, D. G., Green, A. R., and Tordoff, A. F. (1976). Electroconvulsive shock increases the behavioral responses of rats to brain 5-hydroxytryptamine stimulation and central nervous system stimulant drugs. *Br. J. Pharmacol.*, **56**, 193–9.

Friedman, E., Cooper, T. B., and Dallob, A. (1983). Effects of chronic antidepressant treatment on serotonin receptor activity in mice. *Eur. J. Pharmacol.*, **89**, 69–76.

Friedman, E., and Dallob, A. (1979). Enhanced serotonin receptor activity after chronic treatment with imipramine and amitriptyline. *Commun. Psychopharmacol.*, **3**, 89–92.

Gallager, D. W., and Bunney, W. E., Jr. (1979). Failure of chronic lithium treatment to block tricyclic antidepressant-induced 5-HT supersensitivity. *Naunyn-Schmiedeberg's Arch. Pharmacol.*, **307**, 129–33.

Garbutt, J. C., Mayo, J. P. Jr, Gillette, G. M., Little, K. Y., and Mason, G. A. (1986). Lithium potentiation of tricyclic antidepressants following lack of T_3 potentiation. *Am. J. Psychiat.*, **143**, 1038–9.

Glowinski, J,, and Axelrod, J. (1964). Inhibition of uptake of tritiated noradrenaline in the intact rat brain by imipramine and structurally related compounds. *Nature*, **204**, 1318–9.

Glue, P. W., Cowen, P. J., Nutt, D. J., Kolakowska, T., and Grahame-Smith, D. G. (1986). The effect of lithium on 5-HT mediated neuroendocrine responses and platelet 5-HT receptors. *Psychopharmacology*, **90**, 398–402.

Goldberg, R. S., and Thormson, W. E. (1978). Combined tricyclic-MAOI therapy for refractory depression: a review with guidelines for appropriate usage. *J. Clin. Pharmacol.*, **18**, 143–7.

Goodwin, F. K., Prange, A. J. Jr, Post, R. M., Muscettola, G., and Lipton, M. A. (1982). Potentiation of antidepressant effects by L-triodothyronine in tricyclic non-responders. *Am. J. Psychiat.*, **139**, 34–8.

Goodwin, G. M., De Souza, R. J., Wood, A. J., and Green, A. R. (1986). The enhancement by lithium of the 5-HT$_{1A}$ mediated serotonin syndrome produced by 8-OH-DPAT in the rat: Evidence for a post-synaptic mechanism. *Psychopharmacology*, **90**, 488–93.

Grahame-Smith, D. G., and Green, A. R. (1974). The role of brain 5-hydroxytryptamine in the hyperactivity produced in rats by lithium and monoamine oxidase inhibition. *Br. J.*

Pharmacol., **52**, 19–26.

Gravel, P., and de Montigny, C. (1987). Noradrenergic denervation prevents sensitization of rat forebrain neurons to serotonin by tricyclic antidepressant treatment. *Synapse* (in press).

Green A. R., and Heal, D. J. (1985). The effects of drugs on serotonin-mediated behavioural models. In Green, A. R. (ed.), *Neuropharmacology of Serotonin*. Oxford University Press, Oxford, 326–65.

Hall, D. W. R., Logan, B. W., and Parsons, G. H. (1969). Further studies on the inhibition of monoamine oxidase by M and B 9302 (Clorgyline). *Biochem. Pharmacol.*, **18**, 1447–54.

Haškovec, L., and Ryšánek, K. (1967). The action of reserpine in imipramine-resistant patients. *Psychopharmacology*, **11**, 18–30.

Heninger, G. R., Charney, D. S., and Price, L. H. (1985). Clinical neurobiologic assessment of 'presynaptic' and 'postsynaptic' serotonergic function in major depression: Effects of antidepressant treatment. *Vth World Congress of Biological Psychiatry*, Philadelphia (PA), 131.

Heninger, G. R., Charney, D. S., and Sternberg, D. E. (1983). Lithium carbonate augmentation of antidepressant treatment. *Arch. Gen. Psychiat.*, **40**, 1335–42.

Hopkinson, G., and Kenny, F. (1975). Treatment with reserpine of patients resistant to tricyclic antidepressants. *Psychiat. Clin.*, **8**, 109–14.

Horn, A. J. (1973). Structure activity relations for the inhibition of 5-HT uptake into rat hypothalamic homogenates by serotonin and tryptamine analogues. *J. Neurochem.*, **21**, 883–8.

Hyttel, J. (1982). Citalopram – pharamacological profile of a specific serotonin uptake inhibitor with antidepressant activity. *Prog. Neuro-Psychopharmacol. Biol. Psychiat.*, **6**, 277–95.

Jéquier, E., Lovenberg, W., and Sjoerdsma, A. (1967). Tryptophan hydroxylase inhibition: The mechanism by which p-chlorophenylalanine depletes rat brain serotonin. *Mol. Pharmacol.*, **3**, 274–8.

Jones, R. S. G. (1980). Long-term administration of atropine, imipramine, and viloxazine alters responsiveness of rat cortical neurones to acetylcholine. *Can. J. Physiol. Pharmacol.*, **58**, 531–5.

Joyce, P. R. (1985). Mood response to methylphenidate and the dexamethasone suppression test as predictors of treatment response to zimelidine and lithium in major depression. *Biol. Psychiat.*, **20**, 598–604.

Joyce, P. R., Hewland, H. R., and Jones, A. V. (1983). Rapid response to lithium in treatment-resistant deperession. *Br. J. Psychiat.*, **142**, 204–6.

Kantor, D., McNevin, S., Leichner, P., Harper, D., and Krenn, M. (1986). The benefit of lithium carbonate adjunct in refractory depression – fact or fiction? *Can. J. Psychiat.*, **31**, 416–18.

Knapp, S., and Mandell, A. J. (1975). Effects of lithium chloride on parameters of biosynthetic capacity for 5-hydroxytryptamine in rat brain. *J. Pharmacol. Exp. Ther.*, **193**, 812–23.

Koe, B. K., and Weissman, A. (1966). p-Chlorophenylalanine: A specific depletor of brain serotonin. *J. Pharmacol. Exp. Ther.*, **154**, 499–516.

Kramlinger, K. G., and Post. R. M. (1987). The addition of lithium carbonate to carbamazepine: Antidepressant efficacy in treatment-resistant depression. *Arch. Gen. Psychiat.* (submitted).

Kushnir, S. L. (1986). Lithium-antidepressant combination of depressed physically ill geriatric patients. *Am. J. Psychiat.*, **143**, 378–9.

Louie, A. K., and Meltzer, H. Y. (1984). Lithium potentiation of antidepressant treatment. *J. Clin. Psychopharmacol.*, **4**, 316–21.

Madakasira, S. (1986). Low dose potency of lithium in antidepressant agumentation. *J. Psychiat. Univ. Ottawa*, **11**, 107–9.

Medical Research Council. (1965). Clinical trial of the treatment of depressive illness. *Br. Med. J.*, 881–6.

Meltzer, H. Y., Lowy, M., Robertson, A., Goodnick, A., and Perline, A. (1984). Effect of 5-hydroxytryptophan on serum cortisol levels in major affective disorders: III. Effect of antidepressants and lithium carbonate. *Arch. Gen. Psychiat.*, **41**, 391–5.

Menkes, D. B., and Aghajanian, G. K. (1981). α_1-Adrenoceptor-mediated responses in the lateral geniculate nucleus are enhanced by chronic antideperessant treatment. *Eur. J. Pharmacol.*, **74**, 27–35.

Menkes, D. B., Aghajanian, G. K., and McCall, R. B. (1980). Chronic antidepressant treatment enhances α-adrenergic and serotonergic responses in the facial nucleus. *Life Sci.*, **27**, 45–55.

Minchin, M. C. W. (1985). Inositol phospholipid breakdown as an index of serotonin receptor function. In Green, A. R. (ed.), *Neuropharmacology of Serotonin*. Oxford University Press, Oxford, 117–30.

Mogilnicka, E., and Klimek, V. (1979). Mianserin, danitracen and amitriptyline withdrawal increases the behavioural responses of rats to L-5-HTP. *J. Pharm. Pharmacol.*, **31**, 704–5.

Moret, C. (1985). Pharmacology of the serotonin autoreceptor. In Green, A. R. (ed.), *Neuropharmacology of Serotonin*. Oxford University Press, Oxford, 21–49.

Murphy, D. L., Lipper, S., Pickar, D., Jimerson, D., Cohen, R. M., Garrick, N. A., Alterman, I. S., and Campbell, I. C. (1981). Selective inhibition of monoamine oxidase type A: clinical antidepressant effects and metabolic changes in man. In Youdim, M. B. H., and Paykel, E. S. (eds.), *Monoamine Oxidase Inhibitors – The State of the Art*. Wiley, New York, 189–205.

Nelson, J. C., and Mazure, C. M. (1986). Lithium augmentation in psychotic depression refractory to combined drug treatment. *Am. J. Psychiat.*, **143**, 363–6.

Nelson, J. C., and Byck, R. (1982). Rapid response to lithium in phenelzine nonresponders. *Br. J. Psychiat.*, **141**, 85–6.

Ogura, C., Okima, T., Uchida, Y., Imai, S., Yogi, H., and Sunami, Y. (1974). Combined thyroid (triodothyronine)-tricyclic antidepressant treatment in depressive states. *Folia Psychiat. Neurol. Jpn.*, **28**, 179–86.

Oppenheim, G., Zohar, J., Shapira, B., and Belmaker, R. H. (1987). The role of estrogen in treating resistant depression. In Zohar, J., and Belmaker, R. H. (eds.), *Treating Resistant Depression*. Pergamon Press, New York (in press).

Pai, M., White, A. C., and Deane, A. G. (1986). Lithium augmentation in the treatment of delusional depression. *Br. J. Psychiat.*, **148**, 736–8.

Perez-Cruet, J., Tagliamonte, A., Tagliamonte, P., and Gessa, G. L. (1971). Stimulation of serotonin synthesis by lithium. *J. Pharmacol. Exp. Ther.*, **178**, 325–30.

Poldinger, W. (1963). Combined administration of desipramine and reserpine or tetrabenazine in depressive patients. *Psychopharmacology*, **4**, 308–10.

Price, L. H., Charney, D. S., and Heninger, G. R. (1984). Manic symptoms following addition of lithium to antidepressant treatment. *J. Clin. Psychopharmacol.*, **4**, 361–2.

Price, L. H., Charney, D. S., and Heninger, G. R. (1985). Efficacy of lithium-tranylcypromine treatment in refractory depression. *Am. J. Psychiat.*, **142**, 619–23.

Price, L. H., Charney, D. S., and Heninger, G. R. (1986). Variability of response to lithium augmentation in refractory depression. *Am. J. Psychiat.*, **143**, 1387–92.

Price, L. H., Conwell, Y., and Nelson, J. C. (1983). Lithium augmentation of combined neuroleptic-tricyclic treatment in delusional depression. *Am. J. Psychiat.*, **140**, 318–22.

Rasmussen, S. A. (1984). Lithium and tryptophan augmentation in clomipramine-resistant obsessive-compulsive disorder. *Am. J. Psychiat.*, **141**, 1283–5.

Richards, G. E., Holland, F. J., and Aubert, M. L. (1980). Regulation of prolactin and growth hormone secretion. *Neuroendocrinology*, **30**, 139–43.

Ross, S. B., Renyi, A. L., and Ogren, S. O. (1971). A comparison of the inhibitory activities of iprindole and imipramine on the uptake of 5-hydroxytyrpamine and noradrenaline in brain slices. *Life Sci.*, **10**, 1267–77.

Roy, A., and Pickar, D. (1985). Lithium potentiation of imipramine in treatment resistant depression. *Br. J. Psychiat.*, **147**, 582–3.

Schrader, G. D., and Levien, H. E. M. (1985). Response to sequential administration of clomipramine and lithium carbonate in treatment-resistant depression. *Br. J. Psychiat.*, **147**, 573–5.

Schuckit, M., Robins, E., and Feighner, J. (1971). Tricyclic antidepressants and monoamine oxidase inhibitors. *Arch. Gen. Psychiat.*, **24**, 509–14.

Sethna, E. R. (1974). A study of refractory cases of depressive illness and their response to combined antidepressant treatment. *Br. J. Psychiat.*, **124**, 265–72.

Shapira, B., Oppenheim, G., Zohar, J., Segal, M., Malach, D., and Belmaker, R. H. (1985). Lack of efficacy of estrogen supplementation to imipramine in resistant female depressives. *Biol. Psychiat.*, **20**, 576-9.

Shopsin, B., Friedman, E., and Gershon, S. (1976). Parachlorophenylalanine reversal of tranylcypromine effects in depressed patients. *Arch. Gen. Psychiat.*, **33**, 811-9.

Shopsin, B., Gershon, S., Goldstein, M., Friedman, E., and Wilk, S. (1975). Use of synthesis inhibitors in defining a role for biogenic amines during imipramine treatment in depressed patients. *Psychopharmacol. Commun.*, **1**, 239-49.

Spiker, D. G., and Pugh, D. D. (1976). Combining tricyclic and monoamine oxidase inhibitor antidepressants. *Arch. Gen. Psychiat.*, **33**, 828-30.

Stefanis, C. N., Alevizos, B., and Papadimitriou, G. N. (1984). Controlled clinical study of moclobemide (Ro-11-1163), a new MAO inhibitor, and desipramine in depressive patients. In Tipton, K. F., Dostert, P., and Strolin Benedetti, M. (eds.), *Monoamine oxidase and disease*. Academic, New York, 377-92.

Stolz, J. F., and Marsden, C. A. (1982). Withdrawal from chronic treatment with metergoline, dl-propranolol and amitriptyline enhances serotonin receptor-mediated behaviour in the rat. *Eur. J. Pharmacol.*, **79**, 17-22.

Stolz, J. F., Marsden, C. A., and Middlemiss, D. N. (1983). Effect of chronic antidepressant treatment and subsequent withdrawal on ^{3}H-5-hydroxytryptamine and ^{3}H-spiperone binding in rat frontal cortex and serotonin receptor-mediated behaviour. *Psychopharmacology*, **84**, 150-5.

Tariot, P. N., Murphy, D. L., Sunderland, T., Mueller, E. A., and Cohen, R. M. (1986). Rapid antidepressant effect of addition of lithium to tranylcypromine. *J. Clin. Psychopharmacol.*, **6**, 165-7.

Treiser, S. L., Cascio, C. S., O'Dohohue, T. L., and Kellar, K. (1981). Lithium increases serotonin release and decreases serotonin receptors in the hippocampus. *Science*, **213**, 1529-31.

Turmel, A., and de Montigny, C. (1984). Sensitization of rat forebrain neurons to serotonin by adinazolam, an antidepressant triazolobenzodiazepine. *Eur. J. Pharmacol.*, **99**, 241-4.

Wang, R. Y., and Aghajanian, G. K. (1980). Enhanced sensitivity of amygdaloid neurons to serotonin and norepinephrine antidepressant treatment. *Commun. Psychopharmacol.*, **4**, 83-90.

Weaver, K. E. C. (1983). Lithium for delusional depression. *Am. J. Psychiat.*, **140**, 962-3.

Wharton, R. N., Perel, J. M., Dayton, P. G., and Malitz, S. (1971). A potential use for methylphenidate with tricyclic antidepressants. *Am. J. Psychiat.*, **127**, 1619-25.

Wielosz, M. (1985). Increased sensitivity to serotonergic agonists after repeated electroconvulsive shock in rats. *Pharmacol. Biochem., Behav.*, **22**, 683-7.

Yang, H. Y. T., and Neff, N. H. (1974). The monoamine oxidase of the brain: Selective inhibition with drugs and the consequences for the mechanism of the biogenic amines. *J. Pharmacol. Exp. Ther.*, **189**, 733-40.

Zohar, J., and Insel, T. R. (1987). Biological approaches to diagnosis and treatment of obsessive compulsive disorder. In Risch, S. C., and Janowsky, D. S. (eds.), *Psychopharmacology Treatment Strategies in Psychiatric Disorders*. Guilford, New York (in press).

Zohar, J., Shapiro, B., Oppenheim, G., Ayd, F. J., and Belmaker, R. H. (1985). Addition of estrogen to imipramine in female resistant depressives. *Psychopharmacol. Bull.*, **21**, 705-6.

Zohar, J., Moscovich, D., and Mester, K. (1987). Addition of reserpine to tricyclic antidepressants in resistant depression. In Zohar, J., and Belmaker, R. H. (eds.), *Treating Resistant Depression*. Pergamon, New York (in press).

12

Is Down-regulation of β-Adrenoceptors Necessary for Antidepressant Activity?

M.-B. Assie, A. Broadhurst and M. Briley

12.1 Introduction

The majority of clinically effective antidepressant drugs are thought to induce, on the basis of *in vitro* neurochemical studies, an increase in the synaptic concentration of noradrenaline and/or serotonin by inhibiting either the metabolism or the neuronal reuptake of these neurotransmitters. Whereas this pharmacological effect is often assumed to be related to the therapeutic effects of these compounds and, indeed, is a commonly used indication of possible antidepressant activity, there exists a poor correlation between the time-course of clinical response to these drugs and their neurochemical effects (Sulser *et al.*, 1978). Thus, despite an immediate manifestation of increased monoamine availability after acute administration, the therapeutic effects of these compounds are not usually seen until after 2 to 3 weeks of continual treatment. Additionally, so-called 'atypical' antidepressants such as mianserin and iprindole appear not to inhibit the metabolism or reuptake of monoamines (see Stone, 1983).

As a result of this temporal discrepancy, numerous workers have investigated the pharmacological consequences of repeated administration of antidepressant compounds to rodents in attempts to uncover a neurochemical link, specific to this mode of administration, with the temporal delay in clinical efficacy.

Whereas subchronic administration of certain antidepressants has been shown to have effects on the density and function of serotonergic (Gandolfi *et al.*, 1984), α-adrenergic (Asakura *et al.*, 1982) and GABAergic receptors (Suzdak and Gianutsos, 1986) in the rodent brain, by far the most consistent change,

seen with the majority of antidepressant treatments, is the 'down-regulation' of
β-adrenoceptors as shown by a decreased density of binding sites (Banerjee *et al.*,
1977) and/or a decreased adenylate cyclase response to noradrenaline (Vetulani
et al., 1976). As such, it has been suggested that the long-term 'down-regulation'
of β-adrenoceptors may be one of the pharmacological mechanisms inherent to
the action of antidepressant therapy, although this has not been shown in man
(Sulser, 1979).

Despite the wide acceptance of this hypothesis it remains a possibility that
'down-regulation' is correlated not to antidepressant efficacy but rather to non-
specific interactions of the drugs tested. This is particularly marked when the
pharmacological profile of archetypal antidepressants such as imipramine and
desipramine is examined. Both these compounds are reported, in addition to
their primary pharmacological effect of uptake blockade, to interact potently
with several neurotransmitter binding sites in the central nervous system (Briley,
1981). Additionally, among other effects, both compounds are reported to
significantly reduce water consumption by rats for periods in excess of 15 days
after start of treatment (Zabik *et al.*, 1977), a physiological effect which might be
expected to result in considerable, stress-related changes in brain biochemistry.

Finally, it has been shown that certain recently developed antidepressants,
such as the selective uptake inhibitors of serotonin (citalopram) (Hyttel, 1982)
and noradrenaline (maprotiline) (Barbaccia *et al.*, 1986), provoke no 'down-
regulation' of β-adrenoceptors upon chronic administration: a feature possibly
related to their more selective acute mode of action.

Thus, considering the importance of, and reliance placed upon, rat β-adreno-
ceptor 'down-regulation' as an indicator of antidepressant activity in man, we
have compared the chronic effects of two antidepressants upon β-adrenoceptor
binding and noradrenaline-stimulated adenylate cyclase activity. The two drugs
chosen were imipramine and midalcipran, a recently developed clinically effective antidepressant drug (Serre *et al.*, 1986) shown to exhibit selective, equipotent inhibition of noradrenaline and serotonin uptake but with no discernable
affinity for any monoamine or other receptors (Moret *et al.*, 1985) and no effect
on water consumption in rodents (unpublished data).

12.2 Methods

12.2.1 Drug Administration

Male Sprague-Dawley rats (220 to 240 g) were maintained at 21 to 23 °C, in
cages of 6 or 7, with food and water *ad libitum* for 6 weeks. Test drugs were
dissolved in the drinking water (approximately 15 mg/kg/day). Three treatment
groups were studied as indicated in Table 12.1. The animals were killed 24 h
after replacement of the drug solution by water. The cerebral cortex was quickly

Table 12.1 [^{3}H]-Dihydroalprenolol binding to rat cortical membranes: effect of chronic antidepressant administration

	Control	Imipramine	Midalcipran
n	10	5	10
K_D	1.50 ± 0.14	1.21 ± 0.21	1.42 ± 0.10
B_{max}	8.53 ± 1.22	5.24 ± 0.33*	7.74 ± 0.71

Results are expressed as mean ± SEM. Units: K_D, nM; B_{max}, pmol/g tissue. *$p < 0.05$ as compared with controls (Student's t-test, two-tailed).

removed: one half was used for the binding assay, the other half for measuring cAMP accumulation.

12.2.2 Binding to β-Adrenoceptors

The cerebral cortex was weighed and homogenised, using an Ultra-Turrax, in ice-cold buffer (mM): NaCl (120), MgCl$_2$ (25), KCl (5), tris-HCl (50), pH 7.4, and centrifuged twice. The final membrane pellet was resuspended with cold buffer and frozen at $-20\,°C$. [^{3}H]-dihydroalprenolol ([^{3}H]-DHA) binding was measured by the method of Bylund and Snyder (1976). Thawed membranes were incubated with six different concentrations of [^{3}H]-DHA (0.25 to 8 nM) in a final volume of 0.5 ml for 30 min at 25 °C. Non-specific binding was measured with (±)propranolol (10 μM). The reaction was terminated by dilution of 100 μl of the medium with 5 ml of cold buffer and immediate filtration through Whatman GF/C filters. Each filter was washed twice before the retained tritium was counted by liquid scintillation spectrometry. The dissociation constant (K_D) and maximal density of binding sites (B_{max}) were determined by Scatchard analysis.

12.2.3 Noradrenaline-stimulated Adenylate Cyclase

Rat cortex was homogenised by hand in 10 vol. homogenising buffer, consisting of (mM): sucrose (250), MgCl$_2$ (5), KCl (25), EGTA (2), isobutylmethylxanthine (IBMX) (0.5) and tris-HCl (50), pH 7.4, and centrifuged at $10\,000g$ for 10 min. The pellet was resuspended in 200 vol and used immediately. The activity of adenylate cyclase was measured in a final volume of 0.5 ml consisting of 0.05 ml tissue suspension and 0.45 ml incubation buffer (mM): ATP (2), GTP (0.01), MgCl$_2$ (3), NaCl (10), KCl (10), EGTA (1), IBMX (0.5) and tris-HCl (50), pH 7.4. The reaction was started by the addition of tissue and was continued for 15 min at 37 °C. The reaction was terminated by heating the tubes at 90 °C for 5 min followed by storage at $-70\,°C$. Measurement of cAMP was performed, after thawing and centrifugation, with a commercially available cAMP analysis kit. Stimulated adenylate cyclase activity was defined as the difference between cAMP accumulation in the absence and presence of 100 μM (−)noradrenaline.

12.2.4 Materials

[^{3}H]-dihydroalprenolol (73 Ci/mmol) was purchased from New England Nuclear, imipramine was kindly provided by Ciba-Geigy and midalcipran was synthesised at Pierre Fabre Medicament. All other materials were obtained from usual commercial sources.

12.3 Results

The effects of chronic imipramine (IMI) and midalcipran upon the binding parameters of [^{3}H]-dihydroalprenolol are shown in Table 12.1 and Figs. 12.1 and 12.2. Whereas neither the K_D nor the B_{max} were significantly different from control values in midalcipran-treated rats, there was a significant reduction (39% $p < 0.05$) in the density of binding sites, but not the K_D, in IMI-treated animals. Table 12.2 shows the effect of subchronic drug administration on the stimulation, by noradrenaline, of adenylate cyclase. In accordance with the binding results, chronic midalcipran had no effect upon noradrenaline-stimulated cAMP accumulation. In contrast, however, IMI administration resulted in a significant attenuation in the response to noradrenaline (13% $p < 0.05$). Basal accumulation was unaffected by either IMI or midalcipran administration.

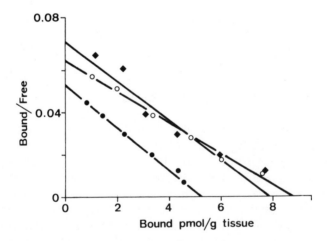

Fig. 12.1 Scatchard analysis of [^{3}H]-dihydroalprenolol binding to rat cortical membranes after chronic administration of imipramine or midalcipran (15 mg/kg/day).

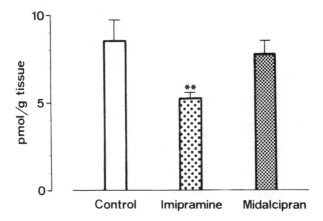

Fig. 12.2 Maximal density of [³H]-dihydroalprenolol binding sites in rat cortex after chronic administration of imipramine or midalcipran (15 mg/kg/day).

Table 12.2 Adenylate cyclase activity in rat cortex: effect of chronic antidepressant administration

	Control	Imipramine	Midalcipran
n	3	3	3
Basal	100	101.9	97.8
Stimulated	177 ± 6.4	152 ± 8.5*	184 ± 25.6

Data are presented in the form of percent control basal activity as mean ± SEM. *$p < 0.05$ as compared with controls (Student's t-test, two-tailed).

12.4 Discussion

As has been previously reported (see section 12.1), IMI, after chronic administration to rats, had a significant effect on both the density and the function of cortical β-adrenoceptors. In contrast, the equipotent noradrenergic and serotonergic antidepressant midalcipran had no effect on either of these parameters. The reasons for this difference are not clear at present, but may relate to the well-characterised secondary pharmacological actions of IMI, a feature absent from the pharmacological profile of midalcipran. These results, therefore, cast further doubt on the role of central β-adrenoceptors in the etiology of depression.

References

Asakura, M., Tsukamoto, T., and Hasegawa, K. (1982). Modulation of rat brain alpha$_2$- and beta-adrenergic receptor sensitivity following long-term treatment with antidepressants. *Brain Res.*, **235**, 192–7.

Banerjee, S. P., Kung, L. S., Riggi, S. J., and Chanda, S. K. (1977). Development of beta-adrenergic receptor subsensitivity by antidepressants. *Nature*, **268**, 455–6.

Barbaccia, M. L., Ravizza, L., and Costa, E. (1986). Maprotiline: an antidepressant with an unusual pharmacological profile. *J. Pharm. Exp. Ther.*, **236**, 307–12.

Briley, M. S. 91981). Alteration in brain receptors in affective disorders. In Hidina, P. D., and Singhol, R. L. (eds.), *Neuroendocrine Regulation and Altered Behaviour*, Croom Helm, London, 299–314.

Bylund, D. B., and Snyder, S. H. (1976). Beta-adrenergic receptor binding in membrane preparations from mammalian brain. *Mol. Pharm.*, **12**, 568–80.

Gandolfi, O., Barbaccia, M. L., and Costa, E. (1984). Comparison of iprindole imipramine and mianserin action on brain serotonergic and beta adrenergic receptors. *J. Pharm. Exp. Ther.*, **229**, 782–6.

Hyttel, J. (1982). Special topic-citalopram: basic and clinical studies. *Progr. Neuro. Psychopharm. Biol. Psychiat.*, **6**, 275–336.

Moret, C., Charveron, M., Finberg, J. P. M., Couzinier, J. P., and Briley, M. (1985). Biochemical profile of Midalcipran (F2207), 1-phenyl-1-diethyl-aminocarbonyl-2-aminomethyl cyclopropane (z) hydrochloride, a potential fourth generation antidepressant drug. *Neuropharm.*, **24**, 1211–19.

Serre, C., Clerc, G., Escande, M., Feline, A., Ginestet, D., Tignol, J., and Van Amerongen, P. (1986). An early clinical trial of midalcipran, 1-phenyl-2-diethylaminocarbonyl-2-aminomethyl cyclopropane (Z) hydrochloride, a potential fourth generation antidepressant. *Curr. Ther. Res.*, **39**, 156–64.

Stone, E. A. (1983). Problems with current catecholamine hypotheses of antidepressant agents: speculations leading to a new hypothesis. *Behav. Brain. Sci.*, **6**, 535–77.

Sudzak, P. D., and Gianutsos, G. (1986). Effect of chronic imipramine or baclofen on GABA$_B$ binding and cyclic AMP production in cerebral cortex. *Eur. J. Pharmac.*, **131**, 129–33.

Sulser, F., Vetulani, J., and Mobley, P. L. (1978). Mode of action of antidepressant drugs. *Bioch. Pharm.*, **27**, 257–61.

Sulser, F. (1979). New perspectives on the mode of action of antidepressant drugs. *Trends Pharm. Sci.*, **1**, 92.

Vetulani, J., Stawarz, R. J., Dingell, J. V., and Sulser, F. (1976). A possible common mechanism of action of tricyclic antidepressant treatments. Reduction in the sensitivity of noradrenergic cyclic AMP generating system in rat limbic forebrain. *Naunyn-Schmiedeberg's Arch. Pharmacol.*, **239**, 109–14.

Zabik, J. E., Levine, R. M., Spaulding, J. H., and Maickel, R. P. (1977). Interactions of tricyclic antidepressant drugs with deprivation-induced fluid consumption by rats. *Neuropharmac.*, **16**, 267–71.

13

BTS 54 524—an Approach to a Rapidly Acting Antidepressant

W. R. Buckett, G. P. Luscombe and P. C. Thomas

13.1 Introduction

Since the tricyclic antidepressant drugs were first introduced into therapy, consistent efforts have been made to improve upon their effects in terms of both increased efficacy and reduced side-effects (Hollister, 1986). In addition, antidepressants having various degrees of selectivity for different monoamine systems (e.g. maprotiline for selective inhibition of noradrenaline reuptake, and fluvoxamine for selective inhibition of serotonin reuptake) have been introduced in the belief that they may treat various subgroups of depressive patients. Overall, however, the wide-spectrum monoamine uptake inhibitors such as dothiepin, imipramine and amitriptyline still remain the most widely used drugs for the treatment of depression, with more recent drugs such as trazodone and mianserin (Ostrow, 1985) also gaining a place on the basis of improvements in tolerability. However, there are still important objectives through which advances in drug therapy of depression can be expected. First, the speed of onset of antidepressant drugs could be increased, and, second, the efficacy could be also improved in the hope of treating, with novel pharmacological agents, those patients currently referred for electroconvulsive therapy.

Preclinical studies with BTS 54 524 (N-1-(1-(4-chlorophenyl)cyclobutyl)-3-methylbutyl-N,N-dimethylamine hydrochloride monohydrate), a novel structural type of putative antidepressant (Fig. 13.1), have suggested that these objectives might be met in clinical practice.

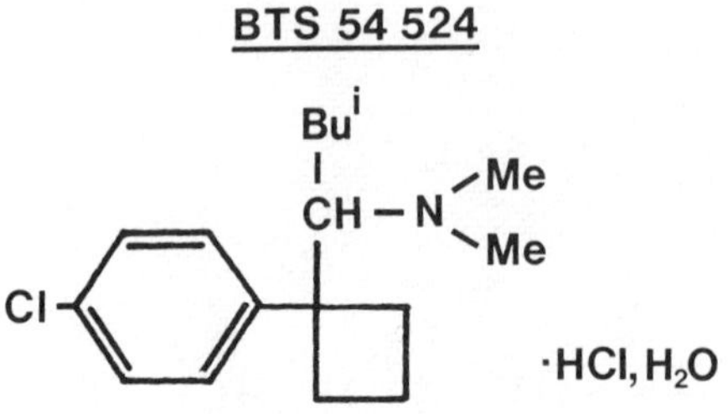

BTS 54 524

Fig. 13.1　The structural formula of BTS 54 524.

13.2 Methods and Results

13.2.1 Tests Indicative of Antidepressant Activity

In reserpine antagonism tests in rodents, BTS 54 524 showed very high potency, with oral ED_{50} values of 1.8 ± 0.3 mg/kg in a reserpine hypothermia reversal test in mice and 0.6 ± 0.2 mg/kg in reserpine ptosis prevention in rats (Buckett *et al.*, 1987a). These values contrast with standard drugs in the rat which had oral ED_{50}s ranging from 1.8 mg/kg for desipramine, through 70 mg/kg for amitriptyline to 160 mg/kg for dothiepin. In the Porsolt test in mice, a putative model of depression (Porsolt, 1981), BTS 54 524 was effective orally, the lowest effective dose ($p < 0.05$) being 10 mg/kg. In this respect BTS 54 524 was equally active with amitriptyline. The potent actions of BTS 54 524, in these acute behavioural tests predictive of antidepressant activity, appear to be largely a consequence of its catecholamine uptake inhibitory properties.

13.2.2 Neurochemical Effects of BTS 54 524

BTS 54 524 inhibits, both *in vitro* and *in vivo*, the neuronal reuptake of noradrenaline, dopamine and serotonin. *In vitro* the inhibition of $[^{14}C]$-noradrenaline uptake into rat cortical slices (IC_{50} 2.2 ± 0.4 μM) and of $[^{14}C]$-dopamine uptake into rat striatal synatosomes (IC_{50} 11.0 ± 4.2 μM) was greater than of $[^{14}C]$-serotonin uptake into rat cortex (IC_{50} 480 ± 110 μM). Catecholamine selectivity is therefore apparent *in vitro*.

In vivo estimates of monoamine uptake inhibition were carried out in the rat using depletion paradigms involving α-methyl-*m*-tyrosine (25 mg/kg i.p.) for noradrenaline and dopamine or *p*-chloroamphetamine (5 mg/kg i.p.) for serotonin, 30 min after oral administration of BTS 54 524, and 4 h before assay of whole brain monoamines by HPLC. Under these conditions BTS 54 524 was similarly active in inhibiting the depletion of noradrenaline (ED_{50} 15 mg/kg), dopamine (ED_{50} 33 mg/kg) and serotonin (ED_{50} 13 mg/kg). BTS 54 524, up to

30 mg/kg orally, did not alter whole-brain monoamine levels. Using the probenecid model of metabolite accumulation (Werdinius, 1967), BTS 54 524 (10 mg/kg orally) reduced DOPAC, HVA and 5-HIAA levels in rat and mouse brains (Table 13.1), suggesting reduced monoamine turnover. Reduced 5-HIAA levels were maintained (34% reduction; $p < 0.05$) in rats dosed over 72 days with BTS 54 524 (3 mg/kg orally), whereas other metabolite or monoamine levels were unchanged. The neurochemical profile exhibited by BTS 54 524 is consistent with some effects of standard antidepressant drugs.

Table 13.1   Effects of BTS 54 524 on monoamine metabolite levels in rat and mouse brain

| Treatment | Species | Whole brain monoamine metabolite levels (ng/g) | | |
		DOPAC	HVA	5-HIAA
Control	Rat	169 ± 3	274 ± 8	800 ± 39
BTS 54 524	Rat	130 ± 9*	194 ± 12†	645 ± 31*
Control	Mouse	116 ± 8	674 ± 31	520 ± 42
BTS 54 524	Mouse	54 ± 3†	467 ± 22†	343 ± 25*

BTS 54 524 (10 mg/kg orally) was administered 30 min prior to probenecid (200 mg/kg i.p.). Ninety minutes later whole brain samples were analysed by HPLC–ECD for dihydroxyphenylacetic acid (DOPAC), homovanillic acid (HVA) and 5-hydroxyindole-3-acetic acid (5-HIAA). *$p < 0.01$ compared with vehicle-dosed controls; †$p < 0.001$.

13.2.3 Tests Predictive of Rate of Onset

The action of antidepressants in reducing the number of β-adrenergic receptors in frontal cortex (B_{max}), without affecting affinity (K_D), has been utilised as a predictive test for anticipated rate of clinical onset (Buckett et al., 1987b). BTS 54 524 (3 mg/kg orally) potently down-regulated the number of [^{3}H]-dihydroalprenolol recognition sites (B_{max}) (29%; $p < 0.01$) without change in affinity (K_D), after only 3 days of treatment. Figure 13.2 illustrates a typical experiment. Significant effects (22% reduction in B_{max}; $p < 0.05$) were also found with BTS 54 524 after 3 days of treatment at 1 mg/kg orally, and no tolerance was observed after 7 days of treatment. Acute dosage with BTS 54 524 (3 to 30 mg/kg orally) did not induce receptor changes and BTS 54 524 (up to 10^{-4} M) did not displace [^{3}H]-dihydroalprenolol binding in vitro. Of standard antidepressants, dothiepin (100 mg/kg orally) and nomifensine (10 mg/kg orally) induced significant ($p < 0.05$) reductions in B_{max} of 15% and 26% respectively after 3 days treatment.

Using a noradrenaline-stimulated adenylate cyclase model of functional β-noradrenergic down-regulation (Mobley and Sulser, 1981), BTS 54 524 (3 mg/kg orally) led to marked and sustained effects after multiple dosing in rats. Thus after 3 days 41% reduction (n.s.) was followed at 7 days by 68% reduction

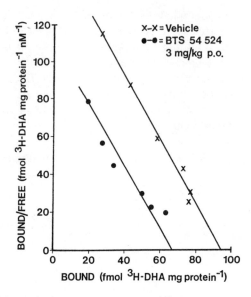

Fig. 13.2   BTS 54 524 induced reduction of β-adrenoceptor binding after 3 days' treatment in rats. The figures shows a Scatchard plot of [³H]-DHA (dihydroalprenolol) binding in rat frontal cortex after oral treatment with BTS 54 524 or vehicle once daily for three days. No change in affinity of [³H]-DHA was observed (K_D vehicle-treated 0.57 nM; K_D BTS 54 524-treated 0.60 nM). B_{max} reduction (28%) was significant ($p < 0.01$).

($p < 0.01$) and at 72 days by 66% reduction ($p < 0.001$) in the sensitivity of the cyclase to generate cyclic-AMP in rat cortical slices in response to noradrenaline (100 μM). 7-day treatments with amitriptyline, iprindole or doxepin (all 25 mg/kg orally) did not down-regulate this response.

In behavioural experiments, repeated treatment with BTS 54 524 (1 to 10 mg/kg, orally or i.p.) generally reduced behavioural responses to clonidine (0.1 mg/kg, i.p.) and to 5-methoxy-N,N-dimethyl-tryptamine (5-MeODMT) (5 mg/kg i.p.) ($p < 0.05$). All changes in behavioural sensitivity were reversible. Acute BTS 54 524 did not alter the serotonergic behaviour induced by 5-MeODMT, but the intensity of the clonidine response was reduced.

13.2.4 Lack of Side-effect Potential

BTS 54 524 was examined in a wide range of conventional receptor binding assays *in vitro*. Up to a concentration of 10 μM no significant displacement of the following tritiated ligands was found:

Ligand   *System*

N-Methylscopolamine   Muscarinic

Prazosin	Noradrenergic-α_1
Dihydroalprenolol	Noradrenergic-β
SCH-23390	Dopaminergic-D1
Sulpiride	Dopaminergic-D2
Serotonin	Serotonergic-5-HT_1
Ketanserin	Serotonergic-5-HT_2

Behavioural observation studies did not reveal sedative or overt stimulation effects in the hole-board or open-field tests. BTS 54 524 was not recognised as amphetamine-like by rats trained to discriminate between dexamphetamine and saline.

An absence of monoamine oxidase (MAO) inhibitory activity was demonstrated in several ways. BTS 54 524 (up to 30 mg/kg orally) did not inhibit rat brain MAO (*ex vivo*), or rat liver MAO (*in vitro* to 100 μM). In addition, BTS 54 524 (30 mg/kg orally) did not potentiate the 1-tryptophan-induced behavioural syndrome in rats.

13.3 Discussion and Conclusions

The experimental results described in this paper strongly suggest that BTS 54 524 would exhibit clinical antidepressant activity. As a monoamine reuptake inhibitor it has the pharmacological and neurochemical properties of a typical antidepressant drug. However, BTS 54 524 does appear to differ from current drugs in several respects. Firstly, BTS 54 524 is a very potent agent and this is typified by the anti-reserpine ED_{50} values of around 1 mg/kg orally. It is possible that this potency contributes to the high degree of noradrenergic down-regulation which is found in the β-adrenoceptor down-regulation models. Although during the past few years data have been generated which cast some doubt on the relevance of β-adrenergic down-regulation to the mode of action of antidepressant drugs (Stone, 1983), the temporal aspect of receptor desensitisation still remains as an adaptive change in animals, which correlates with the onset of clinical antidepressant action in patients. Therefore, within this framework the rapid down-regulation of β-adrenoceptor related phenomena, induced by low doses of BTS 54 524, does suggest that rapid clinical effects may indeed be generated. Secondly, the specificity of BTS 54 524 for monoamine uptake mechanisms, without any binding affinity for ligand binding sites relating to the cholinergic, noradrenergic, dopaminergic or serotonergic systems, whether pre- or postsynaptic, does not predict side-effects common to other antidepressants. Also, the absence of side-effects can be extended to include monoamine oxidase inhibition.

Thus BTS 54 524 has a profile consistent with that of antidepressant drugs as it affects uptake mechanisms for both catecholamines and serotonin. It is clear that both monoaminergic systems are involved in depression (Hollister, 1986), and an interdependence has been established experimentally. However, a noradrenergic mechanism is the final common pathway of effective antidepressants (Sugrue, 1983) and it is evident that BTS 54524 is highly active on β-adrenergic mechanisms. Its action is probably mediated both directly and indirectly, which may be important for the sustained level of reduced noradrenergic subsentivity that has been found.

Acknowledgements

The contributions of Dr D. J. Heal, Dr G. L. Diggory, Dr J. G. Browning, Mr R. H. Hopcroft and Miss P. L. Needham to this research are gratefully acknowledged.

References

Buckett, W. R., Hopcroft, R. H., Luscombe, G. P., and Thomas, P. C. (1987a). BTS 54524, a monoamine uptake inhibitor exhibiting potent actions in models predictive of potential antidepressant activity. *Br. J. Pharmac.*, **90**, in press.

Buckett, W. R., Luscombe, G. P., Thomas, P. C. (1987b). The putative antidepressant BTS 54524 rapidly and potently down-regulates cortical β-adrenoceptors in the rat. *Br. J Pharmac.*, **90**, in press.

Hollister, L. E. (1986). Current antidepressants. *Ann. Rev. Pharmacol. Toxicol.*, **26**, 23–37.

Mobley, P. L., and Sulser, F. (1981). Down-regulation of the central noradrenergic system by antidepressant therapies: biochemical and chemical aspects. In Enna, S. J., Malick, J. B., and Richelson, E. (eds.), *Antidepressants: Neurochemical, Behavioral and Clinical Perspectives*, Raven, New York, 31–45.

Ostrow, D. (1985). The new generation antidepressants: promising innovations or disappointments? *J. Clin. Psychiatry*, **46**, suppl. 2, 6–24.

Porsolt, R. D. (1981). Behavioral despair. In Enna, S. J., Malick, J. B., and Richelson, E. (eds.), *Antidepressants: Neurochemical Behavioral and Clinical Perspectives*, Raven, New York, 121–39.

Stone, E. A. (1983). Problems with current catecholamine hypotheses of antidepressant agents: speculations leading to a new hypothesis. *Behav. Brain Sci.*, **6**, 535–77.

Sugrue, M. F. (1983). Do antidepressants possess a common mechanism of action? *Biochem. Pharmacol.*, **12**, 1811–17.

Werdinius, B. (1967). Effect of probenecid on the levels of monoamine metabolites in the rat brain. *Acta Pharmacol. Toxicol.*, **25**, 18–23.

14

Central and Peripheral Effects of CH-38083: a New α_2-Antagonist

G. T. Somogyi, L. G. Harsing, Jr, and E. S. Vizi

14.1 Introduction

It has long been known that α_2-adrenoceptor agonists decrease the enhanced release of noradrenaline (NA) after subacute administration of clorgyline, a selective antagonist of monoamine oxidase A (MAO-A) (Cohen et al., 1982). Desipramine (DMI) produces a short-lasting decrease in the sedation response to α-agonists (Heal et al., 1983). The functional response of sedation may involve presynaptic α_2-adrenoceptors (see Green and Nutt, 1985): thus DMI exerts its inhibitory effect primarily on presynaptic α_2-adrenoceptors. Since the production of catecholamine metabolites is decreased in the brain of depressed patients (Maas, 1975), this may indicate a primary significance of noradrenergic transmission in depression. Certain tricyclic antidepressants inhibit the neuronal uptake of the monoamines, and, in addition, some also interact directly with α_2-adrenoceptors. Since evidence has been obtained that the release of NA is tonically controlled by a negative-feedback mechanism mediated via presynaptic α-receptors, their antagonists may be effective as antidepressant agents by increasing the release of NA. According to this concept we have developed a potent and selective α_2-adrenoceptor compound, CH-38083 (7,8-(methylenedioxi)-14-alpha-hydroxyalloberbane HCl), which is a berbane derivative (Vizi et al., in press).

14.2 Methods

The experiments were carried out on the following preparations:

Mouse vas deferens The animals were decapitated and vasa deferentia were prepared according to Vizi *et al.* (1985). The preparations were placed into an organ bath (2 ml) in order to incubate them in Krebs containing [^{3}H]-noradrenaline.

Arteria basilaris of rabbit Male albino New Zealand rabbits were killed by injecting air into the marginal vein of the ear. The skull was opened and the brain was removed. Particular care was taken to expose the basilar part of the brain from where the basilar artery was prepared, cut spirally and mounted in an organ bath of 1 ml (Krebs solution).

Frontal cortex and hypothalamus preparation of rat Male CFY rats were decapitated, the skull was opened and the whole brain was removed. Slices weighing about 20 to 30 mg were prepared from the frontal cortex and from the dorsomedian part of the hypothalamus and placed into a 1 ml bath containing Krebs solution.

Incubation The preparations were incubated in Krebs bicarbonate buffer containing 300 μmol/l ascorbic acid, 30 μmol/l Na$_2$EDTA and 10 μCi/ml [^{3}H]-NA (40 Ci/mmol, Amersham) for 60 min at 37 °C. The incubation baths were bubbled with a mixture of 95% O$_2$ and 5% CO$_2$.

Perfusion After incubation with [^{3}H]-NA the tissues were placed in another bath and superfused with Krebs solution at a rate of 1 ml/min. The tissues were washed for 60 min and then the effluents were collected in 3 min fractions by a fraction collector for 60 or 90 min, depending on the experimental protocol. Electrical stimulation (3 min) of supramaximal intensity was applied, via platinium electrodes, at the 69th (S_1) and 99th (S_2) minutes and in the case of the basilar artery and mouse vas deferens also at the 129th (S_3) minute. Drugs were added 15 min before S_2 and S_3. At the end of each experiment the preparations were homogenised in 1 ml 10% trichloroacetic acid. After centrifugation a 0.1 ml aliquot of the supenatant was measured for radioactivity (LKB). The results were expressed as fractional release. The stimulation-induced release of tritium was calculated by subtracting the expected value of the basal outflow from that obtained in response to stimulation. The resulting values were an approximation of the stimulation curve's area and were determined for each stimulation (S_1, S_2, S_3). The change in the release of NA was expressed as a change in the ratio of S_2/S_1 or S_3/S_1.

Statistics One-way analysis of variance was used, and $p < 0.05$ was accepted as significant.

14.3 Results

Neurochemical evidence has been obtained that the three α$_2$-inhibitors studied, yohimbine (YOH), idazoxan (IDAZ) and CH-38083 (CH) increased the release of NA from noradrenergic nerve endings. We chose two peripheral and two central tissues to compare the effect of these three drugs. YOH (0.1 to 1.0 μmol/l) and IDAZ (1.0 μmol/l) were less effective than CH (0.1 μmol/l) from mouse vas deferens in increasing the release of [^{3}H]-NA (Table 14.1). The order of efficacy was YOH < IDAZ < CH. On the basilar artery of the rabbit this order was

Table 14.1   Effect of α_2-antagonists on the release [^{3}H]-NA from the vas deferens of mouse and basilar artery of rabbit

Drugs	μmol/l	% increase (of control)	
		Vas deferens	Basilar artery
Yohimbine	0.1	10.5 ± 6.0	82 ± 12*
	1.0	35.2 ± 8.4	—
Idazoxan	0.1	15.2 ± 3.4	—
CH-38083	0.1	66.0 ± 7.6*	110.0 ± 14*
	1.0	124.0 ± 16.4*	—

*Significantly different from control ($p < 0.05$).

YOH < CH (Table 14.1). CH also proved to be the most effective on rat frontal cortex slices, showing the same order of potency as was described in peripheral tissues (YOH < IDAZ < CH) (Table 14.2). CH doubled the increase of [^{3}H]-NA release from mouse vas deferens, basilar artery and frontal cortex preparations. However, in the hypothalamus of rat the three α_2-adrenoceptor inhibitors were equally effective and the increment was around 50% (Table 14.2).

Xylazine (0.1 to 1 μmol/l) decreased the release of NA from mouse vas deferens and basilar artery of rabbit. Both YOH and CH antagonised the effect of xylazine (Table 14.3).

Table 14.2   Effect of α_2-antagonists on [^{3}H]-NA release from cerebral cortex and hypothalamus of rat

Drugs	μmol/l	% increase (of control)	
		Frontal cortex	Hypothalamus
Yohimbine	0.1	43 ± 5.7*	43 ± 8.1*
Idazoxan	1.0	85 ± 9.3*	54 ± 8.6*
CH-38083	0.1	135 ± 17*	59 ± 8.9*

*Significantly different from control ($p < 0.05$).

Table 14.3   Effect of α_2-antagonists on xylazine-induced inhibition of [^{3}H]-NA release from the vas deferens of mouse and basilar artery of rabbit

Drugs	μmol/l	% decrease (of control) Vas deferens	Basilar artery
Xylazine	1.0	45 ± 7.6*	32 ± 2.6*
Xylazine + yohimbine	1.0 0.1	8 ± 3.6	0
Xylazine + CH-38083	1.0 0.1	0	0

0 indicates that the S_2/S_1 values were over the control level. *Significantly different from control ($p < 0.05$).

14.4 Discussion

Starting from the structure of YOH, a very potent and selective α_2-adrenoceptor antagonist has been synthesised (Vizi *et al.*, in press). This drug was totally ineffective on serotonin or histamine receptors (Vizi *et al.*, 1986), and gave a much better $\alpha_1 : \alpha_2$ ratio than the other two substances.

Since some of the known antidepressant drugs are effective against clonidine-induced depression, possibly via α_2-receptors (Green and Nutt, 1985), the α_2-antagonists might be useful in the treatment of depression. Their selectivity, however, is crucial to this point of view. The berbane derivative CH proved to be the best among the reference drugs applied in three out of four tests used. The relatively reduced efficacy in hypothalamus needs further analysis.

References

Cohen, R. M., Ebstein, R. P., Daly, J. W., and Murphy, D. L. (1982). *J. Neurosci.*, **11**, 1588–95.

Green, A. R., and Nutt, D. J. (1985). In Grahame-Smith, D. G., and Cowen, P. J. (eds.), *Preclinical Psychopharmacology*. Elsevier, Amsterdam, 1–34.

Heal, D. J., Lister, S., Smith, S. L., Davies, C. L., Molyneux, S. G., and Green, A. R. (1983). *Neuropharmacology*, **22**, 983–92.

Maas, J. W. (1975). *Arch. Gen. Psych.*, **32**, 1357–61.

Vizi, E. S., Somogyi, G. T., Harsing, L. G., Jr, and Zimanyi, I. (1985). *Proc. Natl Acad. Sci. USA*, **82**, 8775–9.

Vizi, E. S., Harsing, L. G., Jr, Gaal, J., Kapocsi, J., Bernath, S., and Somogyi, G. T. (1986). *J. Pharmac. Exp. Ther.*, **238**, 701–6.

Vizi, E. S., Toth, I., Harsing, L. G., Jr, Szabo, L., Somogyi, G. T., and Szantay, Cs. (1987). *J. Med. Chem.* (in press).

15

Contributions from Peripheral Autonomic Pharmacology to an Understanding of Antidepressant Drug Action

J. P. M. Finberg, D. Hovevy-Sion and I. J. Kopin

15.1 Introduction

Antidepressant effects in man can be produced by drugs which inhibit noradrenaline or serotonin (5-HT) uptake or deamination, as well as drugs such as iprindole, which are not known to directly affect noradrenergic or serotonergic neurons. The clinical effectiveness of agents such as maprotiline and nisoxetine (Iversen and Mackay, 1979), which selectively inhibit neuronal uptake of noradrenaline, points to the importance of the noradrenergic neurons in antidepressant action. Surprisingly, despite the wealth of information on catecholamine receptors and metabolites following administration of antidepressant drugs in man and laboratory animals, there remains much controversy over the basic effect of these drugs on catecholamine release. This is largely because of the difficulty of determining catecholamine turnover in the presence of drugs such as monoamine oxidase (MAO) inhibitors or tricyclic compounds which markedly alter catecholamine metabolism and overflow.

Study of the action of antidepressant drugs on peripheral sympathetic nerves may contribute much to knowledge of the way these drugs act on central noradrenergic nerves, since the basic processes of amine uptake synthesis, storage, release and metabolism are similar. In addition, studies of amine release and presynaptic or postsynaptic adrenoceptor activation are essentially much easier in the peripheral nervous system. Understanding of the action of antidepressants on sympathetic nerves is also important in relation to clinical effects of these drugs on the cardiovascular system and function of other essential organs, since both tricyclic and MAO inhibitor antidepressants have been reported to cause hypotension, sexual dysfunction and other signs of autonomic disturbance (Berger, 1977; McDaniel, 1986).

Function of sympathetic nerves will naturally differ from those in the central nervous system (CNS) with respect to receptor distribution, synaptic cleft width and amine uptake by extraneuronal tissue. Sympathetic nerve activity will also be controlled by CNS effects of antidepressant drugs.

We have studied the effect of acute and chronic administration of MAO inhibitors and antagonists of neuronal amine uptake on noradrenalin release and presynaptic receptor function in rat vas deferens, anococcygeus muscle and cardiovascular system. We believe that an understanding of the way in which sympathetic nerves adapt to prolonged inhibition of MAO or amine uptake is essential for full appreciation of the mechanism of action of antidepressant drugs.

We used the MAO inhibitors clorgyline (MAO-A selective) and nialamide (MAO-A + −B inhibitor), and the noradrenaline-specific uptake inhibitor desipramine.

15.2 Methods

Rats (200 to 300 g) were injected intraperitoneally (i.p.) acutely (once only) or chronically (once daily for 2 to 3 weeks) with one of the drugs specified or matched saline control, and usually killed 24 h after the last dose of the drug, in order to permit washout of most of the drug from the animal's body. Whole vas deferens and anococcygeus muscle were suspended in organ baths containing oxygenated Krebs solution, and bath fluid changed by draining and refilling the glass chamber containing the tissue. Isometric contraction was measured using Statham transducers and Gould physiological recorders. Electrical field stimulation was applied using lower (hook) and upper (spiral) platinum electrodes delivering square-wave 1 ms pulses at maximal voltage (80 V). In experiments on [^{3}H]-noradrenaline release, tissues were preincubated with [^{3}H]-noradrenaline (0.5 μM) for 30 minutes, rinsed, and efflux determined by collecting and analysing the bath fluid. Release of tritium was determined using electrical field stimulation or veratrine (20 μg/ml), and expressed as fractional release using the formula

$$^3\text{H-FR} = \frac{\begin{array}{c}(^3\text{H release during stimulation period}) \\ - (^3\text{H release in prior control period})\end{array}}{\begin{array}{c}\text{Total } ^3\text{H content of tissue at start of} \\ \text{stimulation period}\end{array}}$$

In pithed rat experiments, the animals were pithed under halothane anesthesia, and electrical stimulation applied either to the whole length of the pithing rod, or in a certain portion only, by coating the steel rod with resistant lacquer, and scraping off the coating in this area only. Arterial blood was collected before and during the fourth minute of electrical stimulation, and catecholamine levels determined using a radioenzymatic assay, as described by Yamaguchi and Kopin (1979). Clorgyline (1 mg/kg) was injected daily for 21 days, and the animals pithed 24 h after the last dose. In these experiments, sympathetic stimulation was applied to the whole spinal cord, and separate experiments carried out with or without yohimbine (1 mg/kg) injected intravenously immediately after pithing. Desimipramine (DMI) was administered by constant infusion using osmotic minipumps (Alzet, 2 ML2) implanted subcutaneously under halothane anesthesia. The concentration of DMI was calculated to yield a daily dose of 10 mg/kg. The pumps were removed under halothane anesthesia 14 days after implantation, and the animals pithed 24 h later. In the experiments with DMI, electrical stimulation (0.1 ms pulses) was applied to the region T6-T9, which produced a well-maintained pressor response without the marked tachycardia which occurs with total sympathetic stimulation. Both DMI-treated and saline-treated controls were injected with DMI (1 mg/kg) immediately after pithing, in order to equalise the degree of inhibition of neuronal uptake. Electrical stimulation was applied at 1 Hz for 4 min followed by 3 Hz for 4 min. The stimulator was then turned off, yohimbine (1 mg/kg) injected, and stimulation repeated 30 min later. Blood samples for plasma catecholamine levels were taken before stimulation, and at the end of each stimulation period.

In separate pithed-rat experiments, total clearance rate of noradrenaline was estimated using a constant infusion method. Noradrenaline was infused at 0.1, 0.3 and 1.0 μg/kg/min for periods of 4 min, and plasma noradrenaline levels measured at the end of each infusion period. The rats were treated chronically with saline, clorgyline or DMI, as above.

In all pithed-rat experiments, gallamine (20 mg/kg) was injected immediately after pithing, to prevent muscular contractions or stimulation.

15.3 Results

15.3.1 Isolated Rat Vas Deferens and Anococcygeus Muscle

When isolated rat vas deferens is stimulated by electrical field stimulation, twitch contractions are produced which are brief in duration in the prostatic end and slower in the epididymal end, resulting in a biphasic contraction in the whole tissue. The rapid, phasic contraction is thought to be non-adrenergic, possibly purinergic, whereas the slower, tonic contraction is thought to be noradrenergic (McGrath, 1978). When the whole vas deferens is stimulated at a rate of 0.1 Hz, only the rapid contraction is seen. Addition of DMI to the preparation stimulated at 0.1 Hz results in an inhibition of the contraction, mediated by an agonist effect at presynaptic inhibitory α_2-adrenoceptors (Brown, et al., 1980; Lotti et al , 1981; Marshall et al., 1977). When DMI (10 mg/kg) was injected and the animals killed 1 h later, no contractile response could be obtained by stimulation of the isolated vas deferens. Animals were therefore killed 24 h after injection of the various antidepressant drugs.

Using the vas deferens preparation stimulated at 0.1 Hz, dose response curves were obtained to the inhibitory effect of clonidine on the contraction. In tissues removed from rats treated chronically with clorgyline or DMI, a reduction in the inhibitory response to clonidine was seen (Finberg and Tal, 1985). This effect has been confirmed by others (Doxey et al., 1985).

Fractional release of total tritium in response to electrical field stimulation (100 pulses at 1 Hz), after prior labelling of the noradrenaline pool with [³H]-noradrenaline, was determined in vas deferens and anococcygeus muscle preparations from rats treated chronically with clorgyline (2 mg/kg for 21 days) or DMI (10 mg/kg for 21 days). As shown in Fig. 15.1, ³H-FR was significantly reduced in both tissues following chronic treatment with clorgyline. Chronic treatment with nialamide (50 mg/kg daily) produced a similar reduction in ³H-FR in vas deferens. Following DMI, a significant increase was seen in anococcygeus muscle, and a non-significant increase in vas deferens. When DMI (0.1 μM) was added directly to the organ bath, no change in ³H-FR in response to stimulation was seen in the anococcygeus muscle, showing that the presynaptic inhibitory effect of DMI on noradrenaline release negated its effect of enhancing [³H]-noradrenaline overflow by inhibition of reuptake (Fig. 15.2). Similarly, application of clorgyline (1 μM) to the vas deferens preparation in vitro did not result in a significant change in ³H-FR following electrical field stimulation.

When the inhibitory effect of clonidine on ³H-FR (electrical stimulation at 1 Hz) was examined in vas deferens, a significant reduction in the clonidine effect was seen in tissues taken from rats treated chronically with either clorgyline or DMI (Table 15.1). This reduction in the clonidine inhibitory effect could be explained by either a reduction in the number of presynaptic α_2-adrenoceptors, or increase in synaptic levels of noradrenaline, which would compete with exogenous clonidine. These possibilities were examined by determining in a similar way the facilitatory effect of yohimbine on ³H-FR in vasa deferentia from rats treated chronically with DMI, nialamide or clorgyline. A significant enhancement in the facilitatory effect of yohimbine was seen following chronic, but not acute, treatment with all three drugs (Horevey-Sion, 1986).

The reduction in ³H-FR elicited by electrical field stimulation following chronic MAO inhibition contrasted with the increased ³H-FR obtained in similarly treated animals when the releasing agent was veratrine (Fig. 15.3). In these experiments, the effluent from the organ bath was fractionated into free ³H-metabolites using the method of Graefe et al. (1973). Following chronic DMI treatment, release by veratrine was not significantly altered.

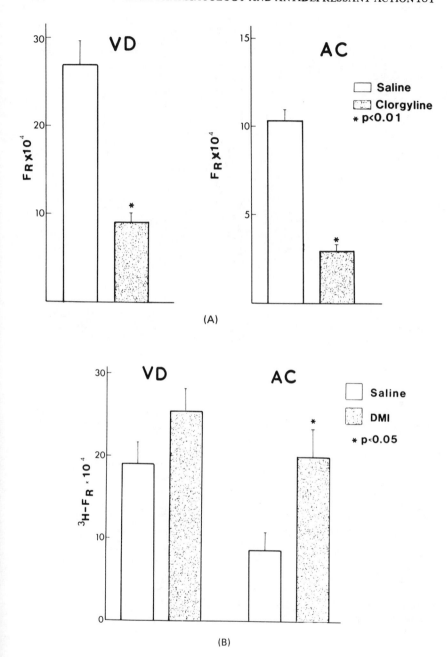

Fig. 15.1 Electrical-field-stimulation-induced release of [³H]-noradrenaline from isolated vas deferens (VD) and anococcygeus muscle (AC) of rats treated chronically with saline, clorgyline (A) or desipramine (B).

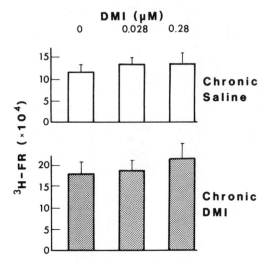

Fig. 15.2 Effect of *in vitro* application of DMI or fractional release of [³H]-noradrenaline (electrical field stimulation) from anococcygeus muscle. The effect of *in vitro* DMI was examined in tissues removed from rats treated chronically with saline or DMI.

Table 15.1 Effect of chronic treatment with clorgyline and DMI on clonidine-induced inhibition of ³H-FR in vas deferens

Fractional release of ³H-FR during electrical field stimulation as a percentage of release in absence of clonidine

Clonidine	(nM)	5.1	12.6	25.2
Saline	(5)	60.7 ± 3.8	37.1 ± 5.3	20.8 ± 1.0
DMI	(5)*	77.0 ± 5.6	53.6 ± 3.4	33.4 ± 5.2
Clonidine	(nM)	1	5	10
Saline	(6)	87.5	73.8	55.5 ± 7.5
Clorgyline	(6)*	106.3 ± 5.6	85.8	77.6 ± 10.0

Number of experiments in brackets. *Significant difference from saline group ($p < 0.05$) by analysis of variance.

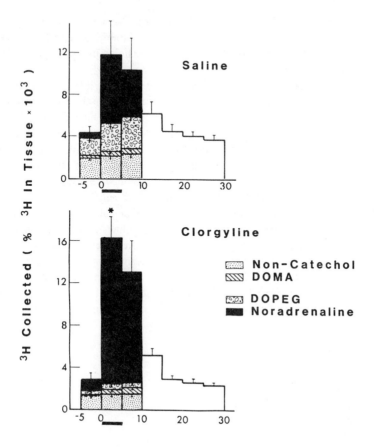

Fig. 15.3 Veratrine-induced release of [³H]-noradrenaline and metabolites from vas deferens of rats treated chronically with saline or clorgyline. The organ bath effluent was fractionated into free [³H]-noradrenaline and [³H]-metabolites, and the release expressed as the percentage of total tritium in the tissue.

The horizontal bar represents the period during which veratrine (20 μg/ml) was present in the organ bath. *Release of free [³H]-noradrenaline significantly greater ($p < 0.05$) than during the corresponding period in the saline-treated control.

15.3.2 Pithed-rat Experiments

Electrical stimulation of the whole sympathetic nervous system in the pithed rat causes a prompt increase in plasma catecholamine concentrations, which achieves a stable level by 4 min (Yamaguchi and Kopin, 1979). Following injection of yohimbine, the plasma catecholamine response to stimulation is potentiated. The dose of yohimbine used in these experiments (1 mg/kg) was maximal for potentiation of the plasma catecholamine response, so that the difference in plasma catecholamine levels in the presence and absence of yohimbine can be taken as an index of α_2-presynaptic adrenoceptor inhibition. This difference can be expressed as the ratio between the plasma catecholamines during stimulation, before and after yohimibine.

In rats treated chronically, but not acutely, with clorgyline (1 mg/kg daily for 21 days), the increments in plasma catecholamine levels during stimulation were significantly greater, both before and after yohimbine injection (Finberg and Kopin, 1986). In these experiments, the acute clorgyline treatment was given 2 h before pithing, and arterial tissue, MAO activity and catecholamine levels were comparable in acute and chronic treatment groups. Ratios of plasma noradrenaline levels in the presence and absence of yohimbine were 1.88 (chronic saline) and 2.09 (chronic clorgyline) and were not significantly different. Systemic clearance of noradrenaline was insignificantly changed by chronic clorgyline treatment, thus the increase in plasma noradrenaline on stimulation was the result of increased release of the neurotransmitter from nerve endings.

Following chronic treatment with DMI, plasma levels of catecholamines showed considerable variability on stimulation, but in the absence of yohimbine were significantly increased in relation to controls, at 3 Hz but not at 1 Hz (Fig. 15.4). The ratio of plasma noradrenaline after yohimbine as against before

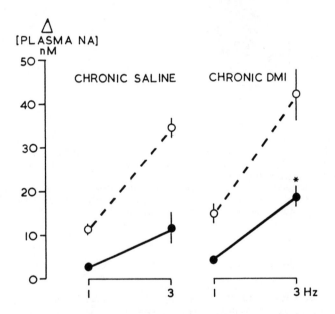

Fig. 15.4 Increment in plasma noradrenaline of pithed rats treated chronically with saline or DMI following stimulation of pressor area of spinal cord. All animals received DMI (1 mg/kg) after pithing. Increment in plasma noradrenaline concentration measured before (continuous line) and after (broken line) injection of yohimbine (1 mg/kg). *$p < 0.05$ for difference from corresponding value in saline-treated control.

yohimbine (3 Hz) was significantly less in chronic-DMI-treated than in saline-treated rats (2.26 ± 0.04 as against 3.05 ± 0.17, $p = < 0.01$), although at 1 Hz the values were not significantly different.

15.4 Discussion

The work described here in both isolated vas deferens and pithed rats can be interpreted in terms of a basic action of the antidepressant drugs to increase noradrenaline release in response to sympathetic stimulation, modulated by a varying degree of presynaptic inhibitory α_2-adrenoceptor stimulation. Blood vessels and vas deferens vary in width of synaptic cleft, and also in the response to neuronal uptake inhibitors. In vas deferens, synaptic cleft width is extremely narrow (20 nm), and the nerve varicosities are embedded within the post-synaptic tissue (Bevan et al., 1984). In the smallest blood vessels, synaptic cleft width is of the order of 60 nm, increasing to much greater values of up to 4000 nm in larger blood vessels such as pulmonary artery (Hume and Bevan, 1984). In nerves with narrow synaptic cleft, the efficiency of reuptake of released noradrenaline is high, whereas in the case of wide synapses much more noradrenaline reaches the circulation by overflow. As a result, most of the plasma noradrenaline following sympathetic stimulation in the pithed rat is believed to orginate from wide blood-vessels, and, therefore, from nerves with wide synapses (Kopin et al., 1978; Hume and Bevan, 1984).

In the isolated, stimulated vas deferens, addition of DMI results in a reduced postsynaptic response to stimulation, whereas in the pithed rat pressor responses to nerve stimulation are potentiated by both cocaine and DMI (Bayorh et al., 1983; Zukowska-Grojec et al., 1983). Contractile responses of the vas deferens of the pithed rat in situ can also be reduced by DMI when repetitive stimulation is given, but if only one pulse is applied then the slow phase of the contractile response is potentiated by cocaine in situ as well as in vitro (McGrath, 1978).

Following chronic MAO inhibition, [^{3}H]-noradrenaline overflow was reduced in vas deferens and anococcygeus muscle, and noradrenaline release from blood vessels was increased. Observation in other tissues, e.g. isolated saphenous vein (Verbeuren and Vanhoutte, 1982; Caramona et al., 1985) and cat spleen (Davey et al., 1963), have also described a reduced noradrenaline release following MAO inhibition. The effect of chronic MAO inhibition appears to be to permit the accumulation of noradrenaline in the cytoplasmic pool of the adrenergic nerve ending (Stefano and Trendelenburg, 1984). This appears to result in enhanced overflow onto presynaptic receptor sites in vas deferens but not blood vessels. This effect is seen only after chronic, not acute, MAO inhibition, possibly because a certain time-period is required for accumulation of a significant amount of noradrenaline in the cytoplasmic pool. As a result, addition of exogenous agonist (clonidine) produces a depressed presynaptic response, but in the presence of yohimibine, enhanced [^{3}H]-noradrenaline efflux can be demonstrated in the vas deferens. In blood-vessels, only the enhanced release of noradrenaline by chronic MAO inhibition is seen. The data show that chronic MAO inhibition produces an increase in the pool of noradrenaline available for release by both exocytotic (nerve stimulation) and trans-membrane efflux (veratrine) processes.

Following chronic MAO inhibition, no proof for down-regulation of pre-synaptic α_2-adrenoceptors was seen, either in vas deferens or in pithed-rat preparations. Indeed, down-regulation of pre-synaptic inhibitory receptors would not be expected after prolonged high agonist levels, since the result (further increase in neurotransmitter release) would not be in keeping with compensatory homeostatic mechanisms. In separate experiments in pithed rats (Finberg and Kopin, 1987), chronic clonidine treatment did not produce any change in release of noradrenaline into the plasma by sympathetic stimulation, either before or after yohimbine injection, and also did not alter the pre-synaptic inhibitory effects of guanabenz on cardioaccelerator stimulation. These experiments, therefore, do not produce any support for the theory (Cohen et al., 1980) that down-regulation of pre-synaptic α_2-adrenoceptors is responsible for increased noradrenaline release by chronic MAO inhibitors.

In the case of DMI, evidence for increased biophase noradrenaline concentrations producing a competition with exogenous α_2-adrenoceptor agonist has been described by others (Pelayo et al., 1980; Enero, 1984; Reichenbacher et al., 1982). The finding of decreased clonidine response and increased yohimbine response in the vas deferens would be compatible with increased biophase noradrenaline levels. The use of veratrine enabled the distinction to be made between the effect of MAO inhibition and DMI on release from the cytoplasmic pool. The increased veratrine-induced release in MAO-inhibited tissues reflected the increased cytoplasmic noradrenaline pool as opposed to the lack of change in veratrine-induced release following DMI. In the case of DMI, therefore, enhanced biophase noradrenaline occurs (as a result of reduced neuronal reuptake) without an increase in the cytoplasmic pool. In the pithed-rat preparation, there was indication for a reduced α_2-adrenoceptor population following chronic DMI treatment. This effect may not necessarily be a compensatory response to increased agonist levels. In fact, DMI possesses the ability to reduce α_2-adrenoceptor number in C6-glioma cells in culture, in the absence of endogenous catecholamines (Fishman and Finberg, 1987), and so could possess a direct effect to reduce α_2-adrenoceptor number too.

The relevance of these data to changes in CNS amine release and adrenoceptors depends on acquisition of further information on pharmacological responses of CNS noradrenergic neurons to antidepressant drugs. Most CNS synapses are probably of the narrow type, and it is interesting that acute injection of DMI in the rat causes inhibition of locus coeruleus spontaneous firing rate (Svensson and Usdin, 1978) in a way similar to the reduction of contractile response in the field-stimulated vas deferens. This reduction in locus coeruleus firing rate is mediated by increased α_2-adrenoceptor activation, since it is reversed by yohimbine. The reduction in locus coeruleus firing rate, if maintained throughout chronic DMI treatment, would be expected to result in reduced noradrenaline turnover in the CNS. Reduced normetanephrine levels have been reported in rat brain during chronic DMI treatment (Racagni et al., 1983), in support of reduced noradrenaline release, but increased turnover and increased levels of brain MOPEG-SO$_4$ have been reported by other workers (Schildkraut et al., 1976; McMillen et al., 1980). At present, therefore, it is impossible to conclude whether CNS neurons respond to chronic antidepressant administration with a decreased noradrenaline release, by analogy with vas deferens, or increased release, as in the blood-vessel type of response.

The data shown here in peripheral systems argue against down-regulation of pre-synaptic α_2-adrenoceptors following chronic antidepressant treatment. Although a number of clonidine-induced CNS responses are decreased by chronic antidepressant drug treatment in rats, and some workers find a reduction in B_{max} of α_2-adrenoceptor selective ligands (Green and Nutt, 1985), at present there is no proof that either of these phenomena represent action at true pre-synaptic receptors, as opposed to post-synaptic or somato-dendritic receptors.

In conclusion, our recent studies of the effects of antidepressant drugs on sympathetic nerves show that both MAO inhibitors and neuronal uptake blockers can produce a basic effect of increased catecholamine release. The net effect on release will depend on modulating factors such as presynaptic receptor control, and the final post-synaptic response will naturally depend on the balance between the amount of amine released and the degree of inhibition of reuptake.

References

Bayorh, M. A., Zukowska-Grojec, Z., and Kopin, I. J. (1983). Effect of desipramine and cocaine on plasma norepinephrine and pressor responses to adrenergic stimulation in pithed rats. J. Clin. Pharmacol., 23, 24–31.

Berger, P. A. (1977). Antidepressant medications and the treatment of depressions. In Barchas, J. D., Berger, P. A., Ciaranello, R. D., and Elliot, G. R. (eds.), Psychopharmacology. Oxford University Press, New York, 174–207.

Bevan, J. A., Tayo, F. M., Rowan, R. A., and Bevan, R. D. (1984). Presynaptic α-receptor control of adrenergic transmitter release in blood vessels. Fed. Proc., 43, 1365–1370.

Brown, J., Doxey, J. C., and Handley, S. (1980). Effects of α-adrenoceptor agonists and antagonists and of antidepressant drugs on pre- and post-synaptic α-adrenoceptors. Eur. J. Pharmacol., 67, 44–40.

Caramona, M. M., Araujo, D., and Brandao, F. (1985). Influence of MAO A and MAO B on the inactivation of noradrenaline in the saphenous vein of the dog. Naunyn-Schmiedeberg's Arch. Pharmacol., 328, 401–6.

Cohen, R. M., Campbell, I. C., Cohen, M. R., Torda, T., Picker, D., Siever, L. J., and Murphy, D. L. (1980). Presynaptic noradrenergic regulation during depression and antidepressant drug treatment. J. Psychiat. Res., 3, 93–105.

Davey, M. J., Farmer, J. B., and Reinert, H. (1963). The effects of nialamide on adrenergic functions. Br. J. Pharmacol., 20, 121–34.

Doxey, J. C., Roach, A. G., and Samuel, J. (1985). Effects of desipramine on stimulation-induced contractions of the vas deferens of rats pretreated either chronically with desipramine or acutely with idazoxan. Clin. Sci., 68 (Suppl. 10), 155–9S.

Enero, M. A. (1984). Influence of neuronal uptake on the presynaptic α-adrenergic modulation of noradrenaline release. *Naunyn-Schmiedeberg's Arch. Pharmacol.*, **328**, 38–40.

Finberg, J. P. M., and Kopin, I. J. (1986). Chronic clorgyline treatment enhances release of norepinephrine following sympathetic stimulation in the rat. *Naunyn-Schmiedeberg's Arch. Pharmacol.*, **332**, 236–42.

Finberg, J. P. M., and Kopin, I. J. (1987). Chronic clonidine treatment produces desensitisation of post- but not pre-synaptic α_2-adrenoceptors. *Eur. J. Pharmacol.* (in press).

Finberg, J. P. M., and Tal, A. (1985). Reduced peripheral presynaptic adrenoceptor sensitivity following chronic antidepressant therapy. *Br. J. Pharmacol.*, **89**, 609–17.

Fishman, P. H., and Finberg, J. P. M. (1987). Effect of the tricyclic antidepressant desipramine on β-adrenergic receptors in cultured rat glioma C6 cells. *J. Neurochem.* (in press).

Graefe, K. H., Stefano, F. J. E., and Langer, S. Z. (1973). Preferential metabolism of $(-)^3$H-noradrenaline through the deaminated glycol in the rat vas deferens. *Biochem. Pharmacol.*, **22**, 1147–60.

Green, A. R., and Nutt, D. J. (1985). Antidepressants. In Grahame-Smith, D. G., and Cowen, P. J. (eds.), *Psychopharmacology 2 – Part 1: Preclinical Psychopharmacology*, Elsevier, Amsterdam, 1–34.

Hovevey-Sion, D. (1986). Effect of acute and chronic treatment with antidepressants on presynaptic alpha$_2$ adrenoceptors and [^{3}H]-noradrenaline release from sympathetic neurons. Ph.D. thesis, Technion, Haifa, Israel.

Hume, W. R., and Bevan, J. A. (1984). The structure of the peripheral adrenergic synapse and its functional implications. In Ziegler, M. G., and Lake, C. R. (eds.), *Norpinephrine*. Williams and Wilkins, Baltimore, 47–54.

Iversen, L. L., and Mackey, A. V. P. (1979). Pharmacodynamics of antidepressants and antimanic drugs. In Paykel, E. S., and Coppen, A. (eds.), *Psychopharmacology of Affective Disorders*, Oxford University Press, Oxford. 60–75.

Kopin, I. J., Lake, R. C., and Ziegler, M. (1978). Plasma levels of norepinephrine. *Annals Int. Med.*, **88**, 671–80.

Lotti, V. J., Chang, R S. L., and Kling, P. (1981). Pre- and postsynaptic adrenergic activation by norepinephrine reuptake inhibitors in the field-stimulated rat vas deferens. *Life Sci.*, **29**, 633–9.

Marshall, I., Nasmyth, P. A., and Shepperson, N. B. (1977). Presynaptic α-adrenoceptors and the inhibition by uptake blocking agents of the twitch response of the mouse vas deferens. *Br. J. Pharmacol.*, **59**, 511.

McDaniel, K. D. (1986). Clinical pharmacology of monoamine oxidase inhibitors. *Clin. Neuropharmacol.*, **9**, 207–34.

McGrath, J. C. (1978). Adrenergic and 'non-adrenergic' components in the contractile response of the vas deferens to a single indirect stimulus. *J. Physiol.*, **283**, 23–39.

McMillen, B. A., Warnack, W., German, D. C., and Shore, P. A. (1980). Effects of chronic desipramine treatment on rat brain noradrenergic responses to α-adrenergic drugs. *Eur. J. Pharmacol.*, **61**, 239–46.

Moret, C., Charveron, M., Finberg, J. P. M., Couzinier, J. P., and Briley, M. (1985). Biochemical profile of midalcipran (F2207), 1-phenyl-1-diethyl-aminocarbonyl-2-amino-methyl-cyclopropane (Z) hydrochloride, a potential fourth generation antidepressant drug. *Neuropharmacol.*, **24**, 1211–19.

Pelayo, F., Dubocovich, M. L., and Langer, S. Z. (1980). Inhibition of neuronal uptake reduces the presynaptic effects of clonidine but not of α-methylnoradrenaline on the stimulation-evoked release of ^{3}H-noradrenaline from rat occipital cortex slices. *Eur. J. Pharmacol.*, **64**, 143–55.

Racagni, G., Mocchetti, I., Calderini, G., Battistella, A., and Brunello, N. (1983). Temporal sequence of changes in central noradrenergic system of rat after prolonged antidepressant treatment: receptor desensitization and neurotransmitter interactions. *Neuropharmacol.*, **22**, 415–24.

Reichenbacher, D., Reimann, W., and Starke, K. (1982). α-Adrenoceptor-mediated inhibition of noradrenaline release in rabbit brain cortex slices. *Naunyn-Schmiedeberg's Arch. Pharmacol.*, **319**, 71–7.

Schildkraut, J. J., Roffman, M., Orsulak, P. J., Schatzberg, A. F., Kling, M. A., and Reigle, T. G. (1976). Effects of short- and long-term administration of tricyclic antidepressants and lithium on norepinephrine turnover in brain. *Pharmakopsych.*, **9**, 193–202.

Stefano, F. J. E., and Trendelenburg, U. (1984). Saturation of monoamine oxidase by intraneuronal noradrenaline accumulation. *Naunyn-Schmiedeberg's Arch. Pharmacol.*, **328**, 135–41.

Svensson, T. H., and Usdin, T. (1978). Feedback inhibition of brain noradrenaline neurons by tricyclic antidepressants: alpha-receptor mediation. *Science*, **202**, 1098–91.

Verbeuren, T. J., and Vanhoutte, P. M. (1982). Deamination of released ^{3}H-noradrenaline in the canine saphenous vein. *Naunyn-Schmiedeberg's Arch. Pharmacol.*, **318**, 148–157.

Yamaguchi, I., and Kopin, I. J. (1979). Plasma catecholamine and blood pressure responses to sympathetic stimulation in pithed rats. *Am. J. Physiol.*, **237**, H305–H310.

Zukowska-Grojec, Z., Bayorh, M. A., and Kopin, I. J. (1983). Effect of desipramine on the effects of α-adrenoceptor inhibitors on pressor responses and release of norepinephrine into plasma of pithed rats. *J. Cardiovasc. Pharmacol.*, **5**, 297–301.

16

Primary Cultures of Monoaminergic Neurons as a Prospective Tool in Neuropharmacology

L. Marlier, F. Finiels-Marlier, P. Poulat, N. Koenig, M.-J. Drian and A. Privat

16.1 Introduction

Primary cultures of central nervous system neurons have been extensively used as a convenient model in the field of developmental neurobiology (Privat *et al.*, 1979). In addition, they provide a simplified model whose environment can be totally controlled and which allows for pharmacological manipulations of living cells.

Beyond the classical primary cultures of neurons our goal was to develop cultures enriched in a particular phenotype, and, at the same time, to elaborate tools for studying the development of this phenotype and for interfering with it (Halgren *et al.*, 1972).

We chose to concentrate on monoaminergic neurons for several reasons. The most obvious one is their implication in several psychiatric disorders (Schildkraut, 1978) of which manic depression is one of the most firmly established (Burney, 1978). In addition, earlier studies have shown the feasibility of such cultures, and the tools for studying them have recently been improved (Privat, 1982).

These models appear to be a good compromise between the '*in-vivo*' situation which most often does not allow an appreciation of the direct effect of a given molecule on a given target, and biochemical studies on synaptosomal preparations which involve only a small segment of a neuron. Moreover, such cultures permit chronic studies since they can be maintained in a steady state for days and even weeks.

One must nevertheless be aware of the main drawbacks of the approach, namely that it is time-consuming and expensive when compared with the classical biochemical approach, and that it constitutes an oversimplified model when compared with the intact animal. Having this in mind, specific questions can be addressed to this model. The purpose of this chapter is to review some of our recent results related to the '*in-vitro*' biology of monoaminergic neurons (Marlier *et al.*, 1986).

16.2 Materials and Methods

Cultures of monoaminergic neurons are performed by microdissection of 14-day-old Sprague-Dawley rat embryos (Fig. 16.1). After removing the foetuses from

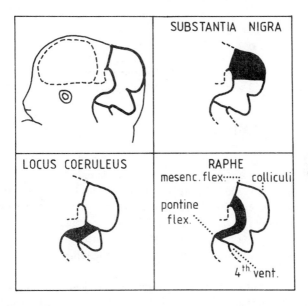

Fig. 16.1 Dissection of the brain of a 14-day embryo.

the pregnant dam, a tissue block which extends from the mesencephalic to the pontine flexure is dissected from the brain. Such a block includes numerous populations of monoaminergic cell bodies:

The rostral half contains the dopaminergic cell bodies situated in the substantia nigra.

The caudal half contains those of noradrenergic phenotype of the locus coeruleus.

The midline is constituted by the serotonergic nuclei of the raphe.

Further dissection according to Fig. 16.1 enables the preparation of cultures enriched in a particular phenotype which will ultimately represent some 2% of all cells.

After a mechanical dissociation in Ca^{2+}-free, Mg^{2+}-free saline buffer (Puck solution), the cells are centrifuged 10 min at $70 \times g$ and the pellet is resuspended in a culture medium made of Hanks BSS 70%, Minimum Eagle Medium 25% and Nu-Serum 5% (collaborative research). Such a medium has been chosen because it minimises the concentration of serum to less than $\frac{1}{100}$.

The cells are plated on 24-well plates coated with poly-D-lysine, in order to yield 700,000 cells per dish, and maintained in an incubator saturated in humidity, at 34 °C with a gas mixture constituted by 95% air, 5% CO_2. Cells were grown under such conditions for three weeks.

16.3 Results

We here describe some general characteristics of the model, centred upon serotonergic cultures, and some pharmacological applications.

16.3.1 Effect of a Target

The aim of this work was to monitor the development of serotonergic neurons co-cultivated with a specific target tissue such as spinal cord.

Co-cultures were made with raphe and spinal cord from 14-day foetuses. The development of these cultures was monitored by immunocytochemistry using a polyclonal antibody directed against 5-HT, and by uptake of tritiated serotonin (Azmitia et al., 1983) (Fig. 16.2). We have shown with double labelling (immunocytochemistry and radioautography) that both phenomena occurred in the same neurons (Fig. 16.3).

Micrographs of cultures processed for immunocytochemistry show a particular orientation of serotonergic neurites that seem to be directed towards the small agglomerates characteristic of spinal neurons in culture (Fig. 16.4). In the same way, the uptake data (Fig. 16.2) showed a stimulated uptake for the co-cultures compared with cultures of raphe alone (Azmitia et al., 1983; Azmitia and Whitaker-Azmitia, 1987). This effect cannot be due to uptake by spinal neurons which do not take up 5-HT when cultured alone. Since it has been well established that uptake is a quantitative and qualitative indicator of neuronal development (Prochiantz et al., 1981), it appears that the development of the serotonergic cells is stimulated by this target. Comparable results have recently been demonstrated by Azmitia and Whitaker-Azmitia (1987) with other targets.

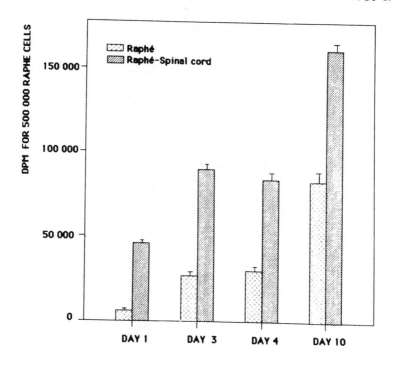

Fig. 16.2 Specific uptake of [³H]-5-HT (5 × 10⁻⁸ M) for 30 min in Hank's buffer in incubator. Non-specific uptake is assessed with addition of 10⁻⁴ M fluoxetine.

16.3.2 Effect of GM1 Gangliosides

Another type of stimulation has been found to occur with GM1 gangliosides that have mainly been implicated in the maturation and the plasticity of the nervous system (Massarelli *et al.*, 1985; Roisen *et al.*, 1981). For the experiments described here, GM1 gangliosides were added at the time of plating and their effect was quantified after two days *in vitro* by digital image analysis of preparations processed for 5-HT immunocytochemistry, and by 5-HT uptake.

Different concentrations between 5 and 20 μg per dish were tested (10 μg/ dish represents 10⁻⁷ M). The uptake data indicate that doses higher than 15 μg completely abolished [³H]-5-HT uptake, while 5 μg stimulates the uptake (Fig. 16.5).

After digitalisation of immunocytochemical preparations, several morphometric parameters were studied (König *et al.*, 1987). We noticed that the distribution of the neuritic field area was shifted to high values for 5 and 10 μg whereas 15 μg produced a shift to lower values. Under the latter condition, many 5-HT immunoreactive neurons were necrotic (Fig. 16.6). A quantitative

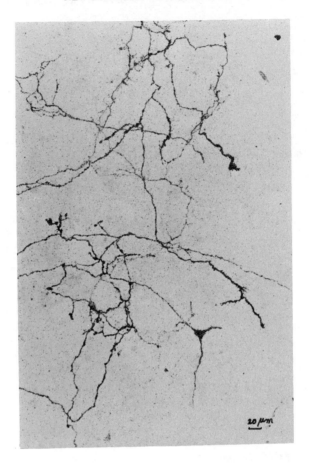

Fig. 16.3 Combined immunocytochemical detection of 5-HT and radioautography after specific uptake of tritiated 5-HT performed on 6 DIV raphe culture.

study disclosed that the neuritic field area was increased by 70 and 85% for, respectively, 5 and 10 μg versus control. In the same way, other parameters were also modified by the treatment (Fig. 16.7):

The total length of all segments for the groups 5 and 10 μg was increased by 32 and 37% respectively versus control.

The mean of the length of all segments were also significantly increased: plus 42% for 5 μg and plus 20% for 10 μg.

This computerised approach of histochemical preparations combined with biochemical data allows one to evaluate precisely the development of cultures treated by GM1, or any other trophic substance.

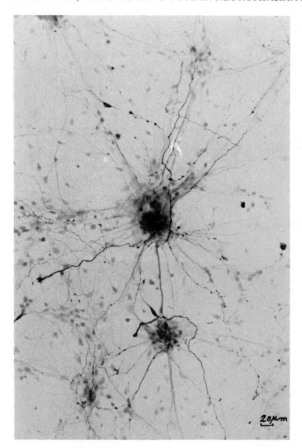

Fig. 16.4   5-HT immunocytochemistry of 13 DIV raphe–spinal cord coculture.

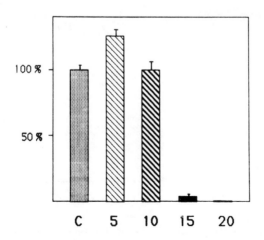

Fig. 16.5   Influence of GM1 gangliosides on the specific uptake of [³H]-5-HT on 2 DIV raphe cultures.

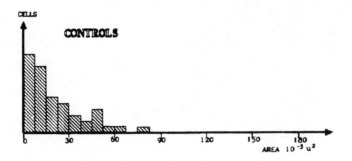

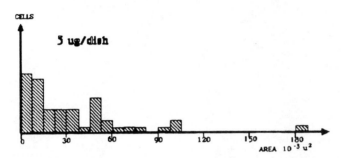

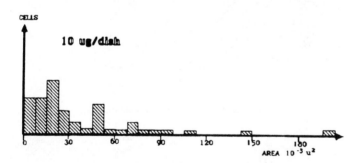

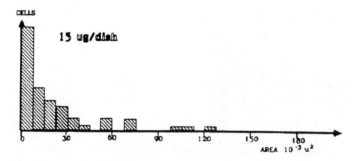

Fig. 16.6 Influence of GM1 gangliosides on the dispersion of the neuritic field area of 2DIV 5-HT immunoreactive neurons. Note for 5 and 10 μg the extension of the distribution towards larger field area.

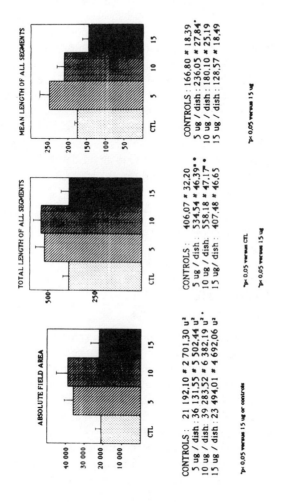

Fig. 16.7 Influence of GM1 gangliosides on three morphometric parameters of 5-HT im-munoreactive neurons, 2 DIV.

16.3.3 Biochemistry of a Second Messenger-related Enzyme: The Protein Kinase C

Protein kinase C is a Ca^{2+}-activated phospholipid dependent enzyme, firmly linked to signal transduction by the demonstration that diacylglycerol, one of the earliest products of signal-induced inositol phospholipid breakdown, greatly increased the affinity of protein kinase C for Ca^{2+}, thereby activating it (Nishizuka, 1986).

This enzyme is widely involved in the proliferation and differentiation of several cell-types (Rovera et al., 1979; Snoek et al., 1986). We hypothesised that it might be the same in the central nervous system. This was, first, because there is a progressive increase in the number of phorbol ester binding sites during the development of rat brain (Murphy et al., 1983). Phorbol esters are exogenous activators of protein kinase C and their binding site seems to be the enzyme itself. Moreover, protein kinase C is involved in long-term potentiation phenomena (Routtenberg, 1986), which is a good example of neuronal plasticity.

To study the effect of protein kinase C in brain development, the culture model described above was used for several reasons:

This model permits a good monitoring of the neuronal development through the immunocytochemistry and the uptake of the corresponding neurotransmitter.
Its ability to make synapses on neurons of target tissues in co-culture is very interesting in a study of neuronal development.
The raphe region is significantly enriched in phorbol ester binding sites during development (Murphy, 1983).

We have been able to measure protein kinase C activity in the serotonergic culture model after partial purification on ion-exchange resin (Fig. 16.8) and it appears that the enzymatic activity is higher during the initial phase of development (first week) than afterwards. But a complete curve of protein kinase C activity evolution has still to be established. If protein kinase C activity increased during the development of the culture, it would be a very good argument to involve the enzyme in neuronal differentiation.

Moreover, we have begun a morphometric study of neurons incubated with a phorbol ester (12-O-tetradecanoyl-phorbol-13-acetate, TPA) during their development. Preliminary results show that TPA modifies neuronal differentiation. Indeed, with 5-HT immunocytochemistry, we observed that neurite outgrowth was increased in cultures treated with TPA as against controls. Axons show a more rigid profile and their terminal parts including growth cones are well developed (Fig. 16.9).

These preliminary results suggest that protein kinase C is involved in neuronal differentiation. But it remains to be shown how it is implicated in this phenomenon and what are the intermediate steps, such as protein phosphorylation, that underline this process.

PURIFICATION AND QUANTIFICATION
OF PROTEIN KINASE C
ON PRIMARY CULTURES OF NEURONES

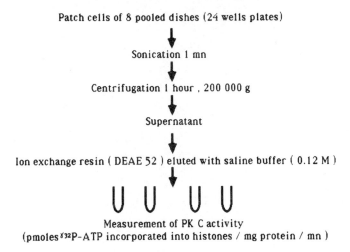

Patch cells of 8 pooled dishes (24 wells plates)

↓

Sonication 1 mn

↓

Centrifugation 1 hour , 200 000 g

↓

Supernatant

↓

Ion exchange resin (DEAE 52) eluted with saline buffer (0.12 M)

↓

U U U U

Measurement of PK C activity
(pmoles ^{32}P-ATP incorporated into histones / mg protein / mn)

Fig. 16.8 Purification and quantification of protein kinase C.

16.3.4 Pharmacology of a New Phencyclidine Derivative: the GK13

Another aspect of the potential interest of our *in vitro* systems is their use in pharmacological studies. Primary cultures of neurons represent an interesting complement to synaptosome preparations, as they preserve the integrity of the neurons.

In this respect, we used this model to determine the capacity for a new PCP derivative to inhibit the uptake of monoamines. So, cultures of each mono-aminergic phenotype (7 to 15 DIV) were used for the uptake procedure, which consisted of increasing the concentration of GK13 or that of a reference inhibitor during the incubation (30 min in incubator):

Fluoxetine for the serotonergic uptake performed with raphe cultures.
Nomifensine for the dopaminergic uptake performed with substantia nigra cultures.
Desipramine for the noradrenergic uptake on locus coeruleus cultures.

Each value represented the mean of at least three dishes and was expressed as a percentage value of the control uptake.

These data are shown in Fig. 16.10. These preliminary results show some differences from those obtained by uptake on synaptosome preparations. Studies are now in progress to see if the uptake site (or sites) involved here could be

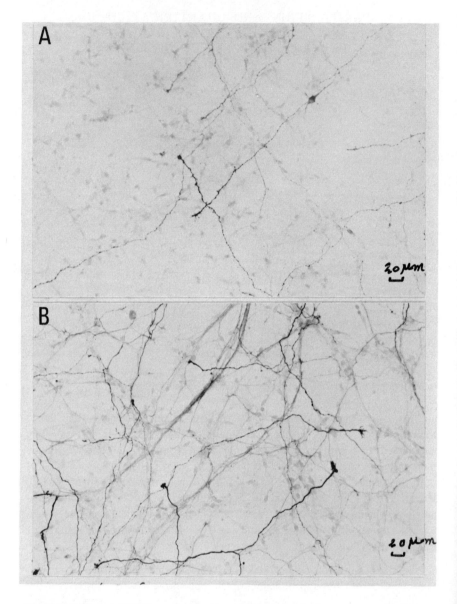

Fig. 16.9 Influence of TPA on the growth of 5-HT immunoreactive neurons. (A) Control 7DIV. (B) Treated with TPA 10^{-9} M at the time of plating and every third day (7 DIV).

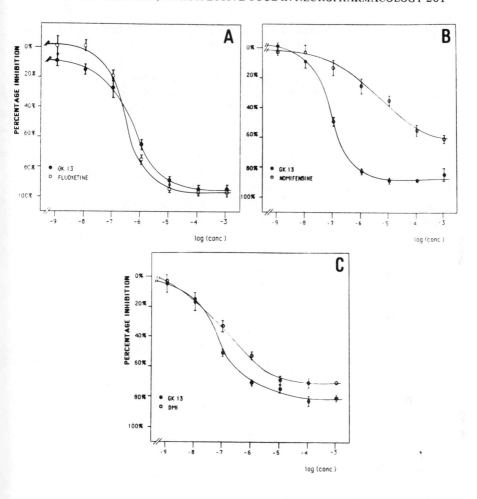

Fig. 16.10 Influence of GK13 on the specific uptake of monoamines. (A) Raphe cultures: uptake of 5×10^{-8} M [^{3}H]-5-HT. (B) Substantia nigra cultures: uptake of [^{3}H]-dopamine 10^{-7} M. (C) Locus coeruleus cultures: uptake of [^{3}H]-norepinephrine 10^{-7} M.

non-synaptic ones. Such results could have a great import for the understanding of pharmacological effects of drugs '*in vivo*'.

16.4 Conclusion

We have attempted here to describe succinctly some applications of primary cultures of nerve cells in various areas of neurobiology. Our goal was not to report in detail on current studies, but rather to illustrate their potential use and how they can complement '*in vivo*' and '*in vitro*' pharmacological approaches. We have shown that the development of identified monoaminergic neurons can be influenced by 'physiological' stimuli such as the presence of a specific target, as well as more artificial ones, such as GM_1 gangliosides. The combination of morphological and biochemical approaches on these models makes it possible to delineate precisely the target of the stimulus. Indeed, GM_1 has a modest influence upon the uptake of neurotransmitter, whereas it shows a pronounced effect upon the initial growth of neurites. Biochemical studies of second-messenger-related enzymes, such as PKC, can be readily performed in such preparations, and yield interesting data in the study of agonist or antagonist molecules. Also more directly relevant to the pharmacology of psychotropic drugs is the assay on specific uptake of monoamines by corresponding neurones, exemplified by the study of GK13. If, indeed, the study of depression is not directly amenable at the cellular level, then the model we have presented here can be of some help to test current hypotheses and to screen relevant drugs.

Acknowledgements

The authors are grateful to Dr J. M. Kamenka for the synthesis and gift of GK13, Dr G. Toffano (Fidia Research, Italy) for the gift of GM_1, Dr C. Le Peuch for help and advice on biochemistry of protein kinase C and Mrs S. Camalon for secretarial help.

This study was supported in part by a grant from IRME.

References

Azmitia, E. C., Whitaker, P. M., Lauder, J., and Privat, A. (1983). Primary culture of dissociated fetal mesencephalic raphe: differential stimulation of serotonergic growth by target tissue. *Abstr. Soc. Neurosc.*, 6–11.

Azmitia, E. C., Whitaker-Azmitia, P. M. (1987). Target cell stimulation of dissociated serotonergic neurons in culture. *Neuroscience*, **20**, 1, 47–64.

Bunney, W. E. (1978). Current status of the catecholamine hypothesis of affective disorders. In Lipton, M. A., Di Mascio, A., and William, K. F. (eds.), *Psychopharmacology: A Generation of Progress*. Raven, New York, 1235–48.

Halgren, E., Varon, S. (1972). Serotonin turnover in cultured raphe nuclei from newborn rat: in-vitro development and drug effects. *Brain Research*, **48**, 438–442.

König, N., Han, V., Lieth, E., and Lauder, J. (1987). Effects of coculture on the morphology of identified raphe and substantia nigra neurons from the embryonic rat brain. *J. Neurosci. Research*, in press.

Marlier, L., Drian, M. J., Kamenka, J. M., Chicheportiche, R., and Privat, A. (1986). Primary cultures of dissociated mesencephalic raphe cells as a pharmacological tool. *Abstr. Soc. Neurosc.*, 86–15.

Massarelli, R., Ferret, B., Gorio, A., Durand, M., and Dreyfus, H. (1985). The effect of exogenous gangliosides on neurons in culture: a morphometric analysis. *Int. J. Devel. Neuroscience*, **3**, 341–8.

Murphy, K. M. M., Oster-Granite, M. L., Gearhart, J. D., and Snyder, S. H. (1983). Phorbol ester receptor: autoradiographic identification in the developing rat. *Science*, **222**, 1036-8.

Nishizuka, Y. (1986). Studies and perspectives of protein kinase C. *Science*, **233**, 305-12.

Privat, A., Marson, A. M., Drian, M. J. (1979). In vitro models of neuronal growth and differentiation. 'Development and chemical specificity of neurons'. In Cuenod, M., Kreutzberg, E. W., Bloom, F. E. (eds.), *Progress in Brain Research, vol. 51*. Elsevier, Amsterdam, 335-6.

Privat, A. (1982). In vitro culture of serotonergic neurons from fetal rat brain. *J. Histochem. Cytochem.*, **30**, 785-7.

Prochiantz, A., Daguet, M. C., Herbert, A., and Glowinski, J. (1981). Specific stimulation of in-vitro maturation of mesencephalic dopaminergic neurons by striatal membranes. *Nature*, **273**, 570-2.

Roisen, F. J., Bartfeld, H., Nagele, L., and Yorke, G. (1981). Gangliosides stimulation of axonal sprouting in vitro. *Science*, **214**, 577-8.

Routtenberg, A. (1986). Phorbolester promotes growth of synaptic plasticity. *Brain Res.*, **378**, 374-8.

Rovera, G., Santoli, D., Damsky, C. (1979). Human promyelocytic leukemia cells in culture differentiate into macrophage like cells when treated with a phorbol ester. *Proc. Natl. Acad. Sci. USA*, **76**, 2779-83.

Schildkraut, J. J. (1978). Current status of the catecholamine hypothesis of affective disorders. In Lipton, M. A., Di Mascio, A., and William, K. F. (eds.), *Psychopharmacology: A Generation of Progress*. Raven, New York, 1223-34.

Snoek, G. T., Mummery, C. E., Van Der Brink, T., Van Der Saag, X. X., and De Laat, S. W. (1986). Protein kinase C and phorbol ester receptor expression related to growth and differentiation of nullipotent and pluripotent embryonal carcinoma cells. *Develop. Biol.*, **115**, 283-92.

17

Effects of the Membrane-active Antidepressant Drugs, Selective 5-HT or NA Uptake Inhibitors, on p-Chloroamphetamine (PCA)-induced Hyperthermia in Heat-adapted Rats

L. Pawłowski

17.1 Introduction

Hyperthermia induced by the 5-hydroxytryptamine (5-HT) releaser parachloro-amphetamine (PCA) in heat-adapted rats is prevented not only by 5-HT receptor blockers or blockers of 5-HT synthesis, but also by membrane-active drugs such as the antidepressants clomipramine, citalopram and zimelidine which are potent 5-HT uptake inhibitors (Frey, 1975; Pawłowski *et al.*, 1980; Pawłowski, 1981). Since clomipramine and citalopram do not prevent the hyperthermia induced by quipazine, a direct 5-HT receptor agonist (Pawłowski, 1984), it may be suggested that the PCA-induced hyperthermia is a good *in-vivo* test for 5-HT uptake inhibitors. It is frequently assumed that the latter drugs block the entrance of 5-HT releasing agents (e.g. PCA) into 5-HT neurons by inactivation of the specific carrier system for 5-HT which — at the same time — operates also for these agents (Fuller, 1980).

However, it may be argued that the PCA-induced hyperthermia is a universal test for all the membrane-active antidepressants, including drugs which are highly selective noradrenaline (NA) uptake inhibitors. Indeed, it has been suggested (Valdman and Avdulov, 1984) that all antidepressants are able to change the fluidity characteristics of neuronal membranes; such an effect could also modify (inhibit) the PCA transport into 5-HT neurons, obviously in a non-specific way (Overath et al., 1970; Valdman and Avdulov, 1984). To test the latter possibility the present paper compared the effects of antidepressant drugs which are selective 5-HT or NA uptake inhibitors on PCA-induced hyperthermia in heat-adapted rats. Desmethyl metabolites of the 5-HT uptake inhibitors were also tested. It is reported here that the PCA-induced hyperthermia in rats should be regarded as a sensitive and specific (obviously relatively) test for 5-HT uptake inhibitors.

17.2 Methods

The experiments were carried out according to the method described previously (Pawłowski, 1981) at an ambient temperature of $28 \pm 1\,^{\circ}C$. Oesophageal body temperature was recorded every 30 min for 120 min, starting 30 min after intraperitoneal (i.p.) injection with the hyperthermising agent (PCA, quipazine, clenbuterol), using an Ellab-T3 thermometer. The investigated compounds were given i.p. (monoamine uptake inhibitors) or subcutaneously (s.c.) (pirenperone) 60 min before the hyperthermising drugs. The results are expressed as a change in body temperature (Δt) with respect to the basal body temperature, measured at the beginning of the experiment. The statistical significance of results was assessed by Student's t-test (two-tailed). Each experimental group consisted of 6 to 18 rats.

17.3 Results and Discussion

Of all the antidepressant drugs used in this study (including the tested metabolites), none (when given alone) decreased the body temperature in rats kept at $28\,^{\circ}C$, whereas some (imipramine, clomipramine, cianopramine, fluoxetine, protriptyline, talsupram and oxaprotiline) (in a dose of 30 mg/kg) even increased the body temperature (data not shown).

Imipramine, a classical membrane-active antidepressant drug which is a non-specific 5-HT and NA uptake inhibitor, and the antidepressants that are selective 5-HT uptake inhibitors (clomipramine, cianopramine, citalopram, femoxetine, fluoxetine and zimelidine) antagonised hyperthermia induced by PCA (6.5 mg/kg), as a rule in a dose-dependent manner (see Table 17.1). The only exception was fluoxetine, whose action was slightly weaker when the drug was used in the highest dose (Table 17.1); however, this finding can easily be explained by the fact that high doses of fluoxetine may inhibit catabolism of PCA in the rat (Ricaurte et al., 1983). The membrane-active antidepressant drugs that are extremely selective and potent NA uptake inhibitors, i.e. protriptyline, oxaprotiline and talsupram (for comparison with other drugs of this type see: Hyttel,

Table 17.1 Effects of imipramine, a non-selective monoamine uptake inhibitor, and selective inhibitors of the uptake of 5-HT (clomipramine, cianopramine, citalopram, femoxetine, fluoxetine, zimelidine) or NA (protriptyline, oxaproti-line, talsupram) upon PCA-induced hyperthermia in rats kept at the ambient temperature of $28 \pm 1\,^{\circ}C$

Treatment (mg/kg)		Change from baseline oesophageal temperature at x min after challenge ($^{\circ}C \pm$ SEM)			
		$x = 30$	60	90	120
PCA 6.5		2.2 ± 0.16	3.2 ± 0.21	2.9 ± 0.24	3.0 ± 0.29
IMI	3 + PCA 6.5	1.9 ± 0.23	2.7 ± 0.33	2.7 ± 0.24	2.6 ± 0.22
IMI	10 + PCA 6.5	1.1 ± 0.35†	1.9 ± 0.43†	2.4 ± 0.52	2.6 ± 0.49
IMI	30 + PCA 6.5	0.7 ± 0.20†	1.3 ± 0.33‡	1.7 ± 0.24*	1.9 ± 0.20*
CLOMI	3 + PCA 6.5	1.9 ± 0.38	2.5 ± 0.26	2.6 ± 0.18	2.6 ± 0.26
CLOMI	10 + PCA 6.5	1.2 ± 0.22‡	2.1 ± 0.14*	2.4 ± 0.15	2.3 ± 0.20
CLOMI	30 + PCA 6.5	0.5 ± 0.15‡	1.0 ± 0.20‡	1.4 ± 0.13†	1.5 ± 0.18†
CIANO	1 + PCA 6.5	2.1 ± 0.17	2.5 ± 0.21	2.6 ± 0.20	2.6 ± 0.19
CIANO	3 + PCA 6.5	1.6 ± 0.12*	2.3 ± 0.19*	2.3 ± 0.10	2.3 ± 0.26
CIANO	10 + PCA 6.5	1.4 ± 0.17*	1.6 ± 0.14‡	2.0 ± 0.15	2.1 ± 0.11
CIT	3 + PCA 6.5	1.9 ± 0.07	2.9 ± 0.22	3.0 ± 0.23	3.0 ± 0.31
CIT	10 + PCA 6.5	2.2 ± 0.23	2.3 ± 0.28*	2.3 ± 0.34	2.5 ± 0.44
CIT	30 + PCA 6.5	1 1 ± 0.19†	1.5 ± 0.17‡	1.6 ± 0.10†	1.8 ± 0.10*
FEM	3 + PCA 6.5	1.3 ± 0.15†	2.4 ± 0.10	2.7 ± 0.17	2.9 ± 0.15
FEM	10 + PCA 6.5	1.1 ± 0.18†	1.7 ± 0.21†	2.1 ± 0.18	2.2 ± 0.15
FEM	30 + PCA 6.5	0.6 ± 0.21‡	1.2 ± 0.16‡	1.3 ± 0.26†	1.5 ± 0.19†
FLUOX	3 + PCA 6.5	1.6 ± 0.14*	2.1 ± 0.14†	2.1 ± 0.25	2.5 ± 0.27
FLUOX	10 + PCA 6.5	1.0 ± 0.19‡	1.8 ± 0.18†	1.8 ± 0.19*	1.9 ± 0.16
FLUOX	30 + PCA 6.5	1.1 ± 0.36†	1.9 ± 0.27†	2.1 ± 0.30	2.2 ± 0.32
ZIM	3 + PCA 6.5	1.4 ± 0.13†	2.3 ± 0.11*	2.7 ± 0.27	2.6 ± 0.21
ZIM	10 + PCA 6.5	1.7 ± 0.14*	2.0 ± 0.19†	2.0 ± 0.15†	2.0 ± 0.13†
ZIM	30 + PCA 6.5	1.5 ± 0.27*	1.7 ± 0.17‡	1.7 ± 0.15†	1.8 ± 0.16*
PROTR	15 + PCA 6.5	1.5 ± 0.41	3.2 ± 0.51	3.6 ± 0.48	3.4 ± 0.53
PROTR	30 + PCA 6.5	2.3 ± 0.41	4.3 ± 0.25*	D	D
OXAPR	15 + PCA 6.5	2.1 ± 0.21	3.3 ± 0.22	2.6 ± 0.45	2.8 ± 0.51
OXAPR	30 + PCA 6.5	2.9 ± 0.26	4.2 ± 0.15*	D	D
TALS	15 + PCA 6.5	2.2 ± 0.21	3.1 ± 0.18	2.9 ± 0.14	3.1 ± 0.28
TALS	30 + PCA 6.5	2.3 ± 0.43	3.7 ± 0.20	D	D

*$p < 0.05$; †$p < 0.01$; ‡$p < 0.001$ (difference from group receiving PCA alonge; Student's t-test).

D: death of some animals in the group. IMI = imipramine, CLOMI = clomipramine, CIANO = cianopramine, CIT = citalopram, FEM = femoxetine, FLUOX = fluoxetine, ZIM = zimelidine, PROTR = protriptyline, OXAPR = oxeprotiline, TALS = talsupram.

1982), used in doses of 15 to 30 mg/kg, either did not affect hyperthermia induced by PCA or even potentiated it (Table 17.1).

Desmethyl metabolites of the selective 5-HT uptake inhibitors (desmethyl-clomipramine, desmethylcianopramine, desmethylcitalopram, norfemoxetine, norfluoxetine, norzimelidine) antagonised the PCA hyperthermia in a manner similar to that of their parent compounds, though the action of desmethyl-clomipramine and desmethylcianopramine, which have recently been recognised as very potent NA uptake inhibitors with a rather poor inhibitory effect on the uptake of 5-HT (Maj *et al.*, 1982; Pawłowski *et al.*, 1985a), was apparently weaker than that of clomipramine and cianopramine, respectively (see the data in Tables 17.1 and 17.2). Desipramine, a desmethyl metabolite of imipramine frequently regarded as a fairly selective NA uptake inhibitor, was (surprisingly, though) also active in the PCA hyperthermia test (Table 17.2). However, the antagonistic action of desipramine against the PCA-induced hyperthermia appeared to be quite specific and related with a presynaptic mechanism, as the drug did not antagonise the hyperthermia induced by the direct agonist of 5-HT receptors quipazine (Table 17.3). This finding is consistent with the fact that

Table 17.2   Effects of desipramine, a mono N-desmethyl metabolite of imipramine, and mono N-desmethyl metabolites of the selective 5-HT uptake inhibitors (desmethylclomipramine, desmethylcianopramine, desmethylcitalopram, norfemoxetine, norfluoxetine, norzimelidine) upon PCA-induced hyperthermia in rats kept at the ambient temperature of $28 \pm 1\,^{\circ}C$

Treatment (mg/kg)		Change from baseline oesophageal temperature at x min after challenge ($^{\circ}C \pm$ SEM)			
		$x = 30$	60	90	120
PCA 6.5		2.1 ± 0.11	3.0 ± 0.12	2.9 ± 0.15	3.2 ± 0.18
DMI	15 + PCA 6.5	1.0 ± 0.18‡	1.9 ± 0.27‡	3.0 ± 0.33	2.9 ± 0.28
DCLOMI	15 + PCA 6.5	2.2 ± 0.21	3.3 ± 0.24	3.4 ± 0.26	3.5 ± 0.18
DCLOMI	30 + PCA 6.5	1.0 ± 0.17‡	2.0 ± 0.21‡	2.5 ± 0.29	2.6 ± 0.25
DCIANO	15 + PCA 6.5	2.3 ± 0.21	2.8 ± 0.24	3.4 ± 0.29	3.1 ± 0.23
DCIANO	30 + PCA 6.5	0.6 ± 0.09‡	1.7 ± 0.15‡	2.2 ± 0.24*	2.5 ± 0.28
DCIT	15 + PCA 6.5	1.7 ± 0.28	2.4 ± 0.30*	2.8 ± 0.30	2.8 ± 0.30
DCIT	30 + PCA 6.5	0.7 ± 0.30‡	1.6 ± 0.41‡	2.1 ± 0.48	2.4 ± 0.52
NORFEM	15 + PCA 6.5	0.9 ± 0.29‡	2.0 ± 0.22‡	1.9 ± 0.16†	2.1 ± 0.19†
NOR-FLUOX	15 + PCA 6.5	0.8 ± 0.11‡	2.1 ± 0.09‡	2.2 ± 0.20*	2.4 ± 0.17*
NORZIM	15 + PCA 6.5	1.8 ± 0.27	2.0 ± 0.12‡	2.0 ± 0.13†	2.1 ± 0.21†

*$p < 0.05$; †$p < 0.01$; ‡$p < 0.001$ (difference from group receiving PCA alone; Students t-test). DMI = desipramine, DCLOMI = desmethylclomipramine, DCIANO = desmethylcianopramine, DCIT = desmethylcitalopram, NORFEM = norfemoxetine, NORFLUOX = norfluoxetine, NORZIM = norzimelidine.

Table 17.3 Effects of the monoamine uptake inhibitor desipramine (DMI) and the 5-HT receptor antagonist pirenperone on hyperthermia induced by PCA, quipazine or the beta-adrenoceptor agonist clenbuterol in heat-adapted rats

Treatment (mg/kg)	Change from baseline oesophageal temperature at x min after challenge ($^\circ$C ± SEM)			
	$x = 30$	60	90	120
PCA 6.5 (PCA)	2.1 ± 0.11	3.0 ± 0.12	2.9 ± 0.15	3.2 ± 0.18
DMI 15 + PCA	1.0 ± 0.18‡	1.9 ± 0.27‡	3.0 ± 0.33	2.9 ± 0.28
Pirenperone 0.1 + PCA	0.4 ± 0.07‡	0.7 ± 0.15‡	0.9 ± 0.15‡	1.2 ± 0.25‡
Qipazine 5 (QUIP)	1.8 ± 0.17	1.9 ± 0.16	1.7 ± 0.21	1.6 ± 0.18
DMI 15 + QUIP	1.6 ± 0.19	1.9 ± 0.19	1.7 ± 0.14	1.6 ± 0.15
Pirenperone 0.1 + QUIP	0.2 ± 0.20‡	0.3 ± 0.19‡	0.2 ± 0.19‡	0.1 ± 0.20‡
Clenbuterol 2 (CLEN)	1.1 ± 0.08	1.7 ± 0.16	1.8 ± 0.10	2.0 ± 0.09
DMI 15 + CLEN	1.5 ± 0.14*	1.8 ± 0.20	2.0 ± 0.13	2.1 ± 0.15
Pirenperone 0.1 + CLEN	1.0 ± 0.13	1.6 ± 0.21	1.6 ± 0.26	1.9 ± 0.21

*$p < 0.05$; ‡$p < 0.001$ (difference from group receiving PCA, quipazine or clenbuterol alone; Student's t-test).

desipramine can protect the rat brain against the 5-HT depletion produced by PCA (Wong and Bymaster, 1976), and the rat and mouse brain against the 5-HT depletion produced by the tyramine derivative H 75/12 (Carlsson et al., 1969; Maître et al., 1980, 1982). As shown in Table 17.3, pirenperone, which is a potent 5-HT receptor antagonist (Pawłowski et al., 1985b), antagonised both the PCA- and the quipazine-induced hyperthermia, but did not affect the hyperthermia induced by the β-adrenoceptor agonist clenbuterol, evoked by a non-5-HT mechanism (Mogilnicka et al., 1985). In comparison with pirenperone, desipramine slightly potentiated the clenbuterol-induced hyperthermia (Table 17.3).

17.4 Conclusions

(a) The obtained results exclude the possibility that all antidepressant drugs can inhibit the PCA-induced hyperthermia in heat-adapted rats: protriptyline, oxaprotiline and talsupram, i.e. antidepressants which are highly potent and selective NA uptake inhibitors, without any effect on the 5-HT uptake, do not antagonise the hyperthermia.

(b) Furthermore, these results suggest that PCA-induced hyperthermia in heat-adapted rats may be regarded as a sensitive in-vivo test for 5-HT uptake inhibitors; it was found that all the tested 5-HT uptake inhibitors (imipramine, clomipramine, desmethylclomipramine, cianopramine, desmethylcianopramine, citalopram, desmethylcitalopram, femoxetine, norfemoxetine, fluoxetine, norfluoxetine, zimelidine and norzimelidine) do antagonise the hyperthermia, and, at least for some drugs, the direct proportion between the dose and the effect was demonstrated. Moreover, using the PCA hyperthermia test it was possible to demonstrate the weak inhibitory effect of desipramine on the uptake of 5-HT *in vivo*; desipramine is frequently incorrectly regarded as a wholly selective NA uptake inhibitor.

Acknowledgements

The author's thanks are due to A/S Ferrosan for femoxetine and norfemoxetine, to Astra for zimelidine and norzimelidine, to Ciba-Geigy for clomipramine, desmethylclomipramine, desipramine and oxaprotiline, to Dr K. Thomae for clenbuterol, to Eli Lilly & Co. for fluoxetine and norfluoxetine, to H. Lundbeck & Co. for citalopram, desmethylcitalopram and talsupram, to Hoffmann La Roche for cianopramine and desmethylcianopramine, to Janssen Pharmaceutica for pirenperone, to Miles Laboratories for quipazine and to Polfa for imipramine.

References

Carlsson, A , Corrodi, H., Fuxe, K., and Hökfelt, T. (1969). Effect of antidepressant drugs on the depletion of intra-neuronal brain 5-hydroxytryptamine stores caused by 4-methyl-α-ethyl-meta-tyramine. *Eur. J. Pharmacol.*, **5**, 357-66.

Frey, H. H. (1975). Hyperthermia induced by amphetamine, p-chloro-amphetamine and fenfluramine in the rat. *Pharmacology*, **13**, 163-76.

Fuller, R. W. (1980). Mechanism by which uptake inhibitors antagonize p-chloroamphetamine-induced depletion of brain serotonin. *Neurochem. Res.*, **5**, 241-5.

Hyttel, J. (1982). Citalopram – pharmacological profile of a specific serotonin uptake inhibitor with antidepressant activity. *Proc. Neuro-Psychopharmacol. Biol. Psychiat.*, **6**, 277-95.

Maître, L., Baumann, P. A., Jaekel, J., and Waldmeier, P. C. (1982). 5-HT uptake inhibitors: psychopharmcological and neurobiochemical criteria of selectivity. *Adv. Biochem. Psychopharm.*, **34** (Serotonin in Biological Psychiatry), 229-46.

Maître, L., Moser, P., Baumann P. A., and Waldmeier, P. C. (1980). Amine uptake inhibitors: Criteria of selectivity. *Acta Psychiat. Scand.*, **61** (suppl. 280), 97-110.

Maj, J. Stala, L., Górka, Z., and Adamus, A. (1982). Comparison of the pharmacological actions of desmethylclomipramine and clomipramine. *Psychopharmacol.*, **78**, 165-9.

Mogilnicka, E., Klimek, V., Nowak, G., and Czyrak, A. (1985). Clonidine and β-agonists induce hyperthermia in rats at high ambient temperature. *J. Neural Transm.*, **63**, 223-5.

Overath, P., Schairer, H. U., and Stoffel, W. (1970). Correlation of in vivo and in vitro phase transitions of membrane lipids in Escherichia coli. *Proc. Nat. Acad. Sci. USA*, **67**, 606-12.

Pawłowski, L. (1981). Different action of 5-hydroxytryptamine (5-HT) uptake inhibitors on fenfluramine- but not p-chloro-amphetamine-induced hyperthermia in rats. *J. Pharm. Pharmacol.*, **33**, 538-40.

Pawłowski, L. (1984). Amitriptyline and femoxetine, but not clomipramine or citalopram, antagonize hyperthermia induced by directly acting 5-hydroxytryptamine-like drugs in heat adapted rats. *J. Pharm. Pharmacol.*, **36**, 197-9.

Pawłowski, L., Nowak, G., Górka, Z., and Mazela, H. (1985a). Ro 11-2465 (cyan-imipramine), citalopram and their N-desmethyl metabolites: Effects on the uptake of 5-hydroxytryptamine and noradrenaline in vivo and related pharmacological activities. *Psychopharmacol.*, **86**, 156–63.

Pawłowski, L., Ruczyńska, J., and Maj, J. (1980). Zimeldine and clomipramine: different influence on fenfluramine– but not p-chloroamphetamine-induced pharmacological effects. *Neurosci. Lett.*, **16**, 203–7.

Pawłowski, L., Siwanowicz, J., Bigajska, K., and Przegaliński, E. (1985b). Central antiserotonergic and antidopaminergic action of pirenperone, a putative 5-HT$_2$ receptor antagonist. *Pol. J. Pharmacol. Pharm.*, **37**, 179–96.

Ricaurte, G. A., Fuller, R. W., Perry, K. W., Seiden, L. S., and Schuster, C. R. (1983). Fluoxetine increases long-lasting neostriatal dopamine depletion after administration of d-methamphetamine and d-amphetamine. *Neuropharmacol.*, **22**, 1165–9.

Valdman, A. V., and Avdulov, N. A. (1984). Membrane-related effects of atypical antidepressants. *Ann. Inst. Super. Sanita*, **20**, 65–72.

Wong, D. T., and Bymaster, F. P. (1976). The comparison of fluoxetine and nisoxetine with tricyclic antidepressants in blocking the neurotoxicity of p-chloroamphetamine and 6-hydroxydopamine in the rat brain. *Res. Comm. Chem. Pathol. Pharmacol.*, **15**, 221–31.

18

Involvement of both α₁- and β-Adrenoceptors in the Antagonism of Tetrabenazine-induced Effects by Antidepressants

J. Laval, A. Stenger and M. Briley

18.1 Introduction

Antagonism of tetrabenazine-induced depressant effects in rodents is a widely used model to screen for antidepressant drugs (Howard *et al.*, 1981). Like reserpine, tetrabenazine acts by depleting catecholamines and serotonin from their presynaptic storage sites. In contrast to the irreversible action of reserpine, however, tetrabenazine blocks the storage mechanism reversibly and has a rapid onset of action. Experimental data indicate that catecholamines play a more important role than serotonin. Unlike reserpine, tetrabenazine blocks pre-synaptic and post-synaptic dopamine receptors (Reches *et al.*, 1983). The observed signs in mice are most frequently ptosis and hypothermia. The involvement of β-adrenoceptors in the mechanism of action of tricyclic antidepressants has been suggested (Frances *et al.*, 1983; Souto *et al.*, 1979) and β-adrenoceptor blockade shown to prevent the antagonist action of imipramine in reserpine-induced hypothermia. The present study was designed to examine which neuromediators, and, in particular, which adrenoceptor component, are involved in the anti-tetrabenazine effect of the noradrenaline uptake inhibitors desipramine and midalcipran. This latter drug, which also inhibits serotonin uptake, is devoid of any acute post-synaptic effects (Moret *et al.*, 1985; Stenger *et al.*, 1987).

18.2 Materials and Methods

Experiments were conducted on male Swiss mice (20 to 26 g) housed at 22 ± 2 °C with free access to tap water and fed a standard laboratory rodent diet. Drugs tested were tetrabenazine hydrochloride, scopolamine bromo-hydrate, methysergide bimaleate, idazoxan, piperoxane, propranolol ((D-, L- and DL-forms) and prazosin hydrochloride. Midalcipran was synthesised by the Pierre Fabre Research Centre, desipramine hydrochloride was kindly provided by Ciba-Geigy.

Antagonism of tetrabenazine-induced ptosis and hypothermia in mice was measured as described by Howard *et al*. (1981). Antidepressants were administered orally 30 min. before the injection of 40 mg/kg i.p. tetrabenazine. The mice were then isolated and 30 min later each mouse was scored for eyelid opening (0 to 2). The observer was unaware of the experimental groups being tested. Ptosis antagonism fifty per cent inhibiting dose (ID_{50}) values were calculated by log-probit analysis for desipramine and midalcipran. Rectal temperatures were then recorded with the aid of an electric thermometer (Ellab Instruments Co), type TE_3, using a probe RM_6. Neurotransmitter antagonists were injected s.c. 60 min prior to administration of the median doses of desipramine or midalcipran.

18.3 Results

Experimental data are expressed in Fig. 18.1 for desipramine and in Fig. 18.2 for midalcipran.

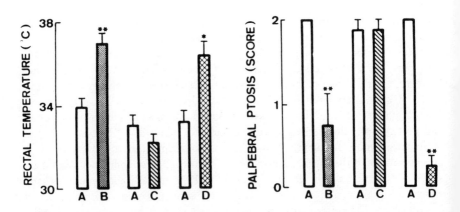

Fig. 18.1 Effects of prazosin and propranolol on the inhibition of tetrabenazine-induced hypothermia and ptosis by desipramine. (A) Mice receiving tetrabenazine. (B) Mice receiving desipramine and tetrabenazine. (C) Mice receiving prazosin in addition to desipramine and tetrabenazine. (D) Mice receiving propranolol in addition to desipramine and tetrabenazine. *$p < 0.05$; **$p < 0.01$ by Student's *t*-test compared with mice receiving tetrabenazine.

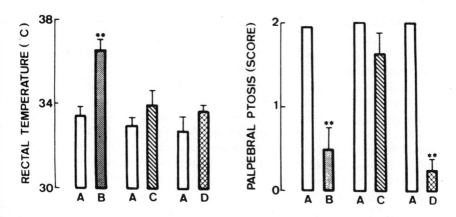

Fig 18.2 Effects of prazosin and propranolol on the inhibition of tetrabenazine-induced hypothermia and ptosis by midalcipran. (A) Mice receiving tetrabenazine. (B) Mice receiving midalcipran and tetrabenazine. (C) mice receiving prazosin in addition to midalcipran and tetrabenazine. (D) mice receiving propranolol in addition to midalcipran and tetrabenazine. $*p < 0.05; **p < 0.01$ by Student's t-test compared with mice receiving tetrabenazine.

In vehicle-treated mice, the ID_{50} values for the antagonism of tetrabenazine-induced ptosis were 2.4 ± 1.1 mg/kg for desipramine and 1.0 ± 0.5 mg/kg for midalcipran. Pretreatment by the α_1-adrenoceptor antagonist prazosin (Cambridge *et al.*, 1977) attenuated the effect of the antidepressants. The ID_{50} values for this attenuation by prazosin of 1 mg/kg of midalcipran, or 2.5 mg/kg of desipramine, were respectively 0.09 mg/kg and 0.37 mg/kg for the ptosis response. The minimal significant doses of prazosin to inhibit the antihypothermia effect of both antidepressants was 0.1 mg/kg.

Alone, up to 3 mg/kg s.c. prazosin had no hypothermic effect and only marginally potentiated the hypothermia induced by tetrabenazine.

The effects of propranolol were less clear. The L- and DL-forms opposed hypothermia significantly in mice receiving midalcipran, whereas the effect of desipramine was only partially opposed. Given alone up to 3 mg/kg s.c., L-propranolol was devoid of any effect on ptosis. As prazosin, propranolol alone only mildly potentiated tetrabenazine-induced hypothermia.

The other neurotransmitter antagonists (piperoxane, idazoxan, haloperidol, methysergide, scopolamine, naloxone and D-propranolol) were devoid of any effect.

18.4 Discussion

The results show that α_1-adrenoceptors seem to be involved in the antagonism of tetrabenazine effects. Whereas prazosin opposed the inhibition of both ptosis and hypothermia, L- or DL-propranolol only opposed significantly the antagonism of hypothermia when midalcipran but not desipramine was used as antidepressant. Propranolol, DL or L, like prazosin, opposed the antiptosis effects of both antidepressants. These experimental data suggest that the pharmacological effects of these antidepressants may be, at least partially, mediated through stimulation of α_1- and β-adrenoceptors.

The role of β-adrenoceptors has been previously suggested by the demonstration that β-adrenoceptor blockade prevented the antagonist action of antidepressants in the apomorphine hypothermia test (Frances et al., 1983; Lecrubier et al., 1980). Similarly, Lapin (1980) has shown that pretreatment with the inhibitor of tyrosine hydroxylase, α-methyl tyrosine, or with the β-adrenoceptor blocker, pindolol, decreased yohimbine-induced mortality in mice treated with a combination of desipramine and yohimbine. Our results complement those obtained on the antagonism of reserpine-induced hypothermia by some tricyclic antidepressants and β-adrenoceptor antagonists, such as salbutamol (Souto et al., 1979; Ross, 1980).

The involvement of the α_2-adrenoceptor appears to be excluded, since the selective blockers, piperoxane and idazoxan, were inactive. Similarly, serotonergic, dopaminergic, cholinergic and opioid receptor mechanisms are excluded since their antagonists methysergide, haloperidol, scopolamine and naloxone were devoid of any significant effect.

In conclusion, the present results add support to earlier data obtained in other tests predictive of antidepressant activity that the acute action of some antidepressants depends on activation of α_1- and β-adrenoceptors.

Acknowledgements

We thank H. Calmel, L. Carlier and M. Tranier for their help with the preparation and the typing of the manuscript.

References

Cambridge, D., Davey, M. J., and Massingham, R. (1977). Prazosin, a selective antagonist of postsynaptic alpha-adrenoceptors. Br. J. Pharmacol., 59, 514–17.

Frances, H., Puech, A. J., Danti, S., and Simon, P. (1983). Attempt at pharmacological differentiation of central beta-adrenergic receptors. Europ. J. Pharmacol., 92, 223–30.

Howard, J. L., Soroko, F. E., and Cooper, B. R. (1981). Empirical behavioral models of depression, with emphasis on tetrabenazine antagonism. In Enna, S. J., Malick, J. B., and Richelson, E. Antidepressants, Neurochemical Behavioral and Clinical Perspectives. Raven, New York, 107–20.

Lapin, I. P. (1980). Adrenergic non specific potentiation of yohimbine toxicity in mice by antidepressant and related drugs and antiyohimbine action of antiadrenergic and serotoninergic drugs. Psychopharmacology, 70, 179–85.

Lecrubier, Y., Puech, A. J., Jouvent, R., Simon, P., and Widlöcher, D. (1980). A β-adrenergic stimulant salbutamol versus clomipramine in depression: a controlled study. *Br. J. Psychiatry*., **136**, 354–8.

Moret, C., Charveron, M., Finberg, J. P. M., Couzinier, J. P. and Briley, M. (1985). Biochemical profile of Midalcipran (F2207) (1-phenyl-1-diethylaminocarbonyl-2-aminomethyl-cyclopropane), a potential fourth generation antidepressant drug. *Neuropharmacology*, **24**, 1211–19.

Reches, A., Burke, R. E., Kuhn, C. M., Hassan, M. N., Jackson, U. R., and Fahns, S. (1983). Tetrabenazine, an amine depleting drug, also blocks dopamine receptors in rat brain. *J. Pharm. Exp. Therap*., **225**, 515–21.

Ross, S. B. (1980). Antagonism of reserpine-induced hypothermia in mice by some beta-adrenoceptor agonists. *Acta Pharmacol. Toxicol*., **47**, 347.

Souto, M., Frances, H., Lecrubier, Y., Puech, A. J., and Simon, P. (1979). Antagonism by d, l-propranolol of imipramine effects in mice. *Europ. J. Pharm*., **60**, 105–8.

Stenger, A., Couzinier, J. P., and Briley, M. (1987). Psychopharmacology of midalcipran, 1-phenyl-1-dethylamino-carbonyl-2-amino-methyl cyclopropane, hydrochloride (F2207), a new potential antidepressant. *Psychophramacology*, **91**, 147-153.

19

Pretreatment by DSP$_4$ Fails to Reduce the Effectiveness of Desipramine in Blocking Tetrabenazine-induced Ptosis or Hypothermia

A. Stenger, C. Palmier and M. Briley

19.1 Introduction

The involvement of the noradrenergic system in the mechanism of some tricyclic antidepressants, such as desipramine, is well documented. Desipramine strongly inhibits neuronal uptake of noradrenaline (Carlsson *et al.*, 1969) and increases brain 3-methoxy-4-hydroxy-phenylglycol (MHPG), an important metabolite of noradrenaline (Przegalinsky *et al.*, 1981). Souto *et al.* (1979) have shown a partial antagonism of the effects of imipramine by propranolol, and salbutamol, a specific β-adrenergic stimulant, has been suggested to possess antidepressant effects in animals and man (Simon *et al.*, 1978). Recently, both α_1- and β-adrenoceptors have been shown to be involved in the antagonism, by desipramine, of apomorphine-induced hypothermia (Pawłowski and Mazela, 1986) and tetrabenazine-induced effects (Laval *et al.*, 1988).

Electrophysiological data have demonstrated the involvement of noradrenergic neurones, belonging to the dorsal bundle from the locus coeruleus, in the action of antidepressants, since acute and repeated administration of tricyclic antidepressants reduces the firing rate of these neurones (Svensson and Usdin, 1978). Similarly, noradrenergic neurones belonging to the ventral bundle have been shown to play an important role in the mechanism of affective disorders (Kostowski, 1981).

Contradictory results have, however, been obtained in mice pretreated by the selective noradrenergic neurotoxin N-chloroethyl-N-ethyl-2-bromobenzylamine hydrochloride (DSP_4) (Jonsson et al., 1981). DSP_4 is reported to be a selective noradrenergic toxin more effective at destroying the terminals of neurons that originate in locus coeruleus than those of neurons that originate in subcoeruleus nuclei (Hallman et al., 1984).

Menon et al. (1984) reported that DSP_4 failed to prevent the antagonist action of desipramine on apomorphine-induced hypothermia. This effect results from stimulation of dopamine receptors in the preoptic anterior hypothalamus (Cox et al., 1978). The neurochemical mechanism by which this hypothermia is inhibited by antidepressants is, however, not well understood. Menon et al. (1984) have suggested that desipramine might antagonise a dopaminergic receptor, whereas other authors have shown that the noradrenergic system is implicated (Maj et al., 1974; Puech et al., 1978; Pawlowski and Mazela, 1986).

The present study investigates the effect of pretreatment with DSP_4 on the antagonism by desipramine of tetrabenazine-induced ptosis and hypothermia.

19.2 Methodological Aspects

Experiments were performed on male Swiss mice, weighing 23 to 28 g, kept at $22 \pm 1\,°C$. Noradrenergic degeneration was induced by DSP_4 (2×50 mg/kg i.p.) associated with zimelidine (5 mg/kg i,p.). This protocol was repeated 7 days later (Heal et al., 1985). Co-administration of DSP_4 and the selective 5-HT uptake inhibitor preferentially destroys the noradrenergic system. Two days after the second treatment, desipramine was given orally 30 min before tetrabenazine (40 mg/kg i.p.) and 60 min before rectal temperature and palpebral ptosis measurements (Howard et al., 1981).

The effect of DSP_4 pretreatment on noradrenaline uptake in the mice hypothalamus was measured two days after the second administration of the neurotoxin, in comparison with controls receiving zimelidine alone, as described by Ross and Renyi (1975).

19.3 Results

The behavioural results are expressed in Table 19.1. Mean rectal temperatures ($\pm$ SEM) induced by tetrabenazine alone (40 mg/kg i.p.) were $33.6\,°C \pm 0.3$ in control and $32.1\,°C \pm 0.6$ in DSP_4-pretreated animals. The palpebral ptosis scores were maximal in both groups.

Desipramine antagonised the tetrabenazine-induced ptosis and hypothermia and no significant differences were seen between DSP_4-treated and vehicle-treated mice. The ID_{50} (ptosis) value for desipramine (mean with 95% confidence

Table 19.1 Antagonism of tetrabenazine-induced ptosis and hypothermia by desipramine on mice pretreated by DSP_4 or vehicle

| | Control | | DSP_4 | |
	Ptosis	Rectal temp.	Ptosis	Rectal temp.
Vehicle	2.0	33.6 ± 0.3	1.9 ± 0.2	32.1 ± 0.6
Desipramine 2 mg/kg	1.2* ± 0.2	35.1† ± 0.3	1.3* ± 0.2	34.8† ± 0.5
Vehicle	2.0	33.7 ± 0.5	2.0	34.1 ± 0.3
Desipramine 10 mg/kg	0.3† ± 0.1	37.1† ± 0.1	0.3† ± 0.1	37.1† ± 0.2

Results are expressed as the median score (± SEM) of ptosis scored 0 to 2 and the median rectal temperature (± SEM). 10 mice were used per dose. *$p < 0.01$ (Wilcoxon test). †$p < 0.001$ (Wilcoxon test).

limits) was 4 mg/kg p.o. (1 to 17) in controls and 3 mg/kg p.o. (0.5 to 16) in DSP_4-treated mice.

Noradrenaline uptake in the hypothalamus was 512 ± 27 (pmol/min/10 mg tissue) for control and 109 ± 20 (pmol/min/10 mg tissue) for DSP_4-treated mice, a reduction of 78% of the noradrenaline uptake ($p < 0.001$).

19.4 Discussion

In this study where DSP_4 treatment is associated with a serotonin uptake inhibitor (zimelidine) we obtained a decrease of 78% of the noradrenaline uptake in the hypothalamus. In the study, we investigated the antagonism by desipramine, a strong noradrenaline uptake inhibitor, on tetrabenazine-induced ptosis and hypothermia in animals pretreated by DSP_4 versus vehicle-pretreated mice. The experimental data show no significant difference between the two groups.

The failure of DSP_4 pretreatment to reduce the effectiveness of desipramine has also been found in the antagonism of apomorphine-induced hypothermia (Menon et al., 1984). These authors suggested that desipramine may have a selective blocking effect at hypothalamic dopaminergic receptors stimulated by apomorphine. Pawlowski and Mazela (1986), however, have shown that α_1- and β-adrenoceptors are involved in this action of desipramine and they excluded any involvement of 5-HT or dopamine receptors.

Tetrabenazine, like reserpine, is thought to deplete cerebral catecholamines and antagonism of the induced ptosis and hypothermia is widely used as an antidepressant screening test (Bourin et al., 1983). In addition, tetrabenazine is claimed to possess dopamine-blocking activity (Reches *et al.*, 1983) which should exclude any dopaminergic component of the mechanism. We have also excluded 5-HT receptor involvement in that methysergide does not antagonise the effect of desipramine on tetrabenazine-induced ptosis and hypothermia (Laval *et al.*, 1988). Both α_1- and β-adrenoceptors do however appear to be involved (Laval *et al.*, 1988).

The reason for the lack of effect of DSP_4 is unclear. DSP_4 has, however, been shown to produce supersensitivity of post-synaptic adrenergic receptors (Mogilnicka, 1986), which may compensate sufficiently for the partial reduction of the functional pool of noradrenaline. On the other hand, the effects of DSP_4 on noradrenaline levels differ among brain regions, the greatest reduction occurring in the cortex and the hippocampus. It is thus possible that the neurotoxicity affects essentially the locus coeruleus noradrenergic system and that this system is not directly implicated in the behavioural changes measured here.

Acknowledgements

We are grateful to E. Couret, J. Laval and M. Tranier for their technical assistance and for L. Carlier and H. Calmel for typing the manuscript.

References

Bourin, M., Poncelet, M., Chermat, R., and Simon, P. (1983). The value of the reserpine test in psychopharmacology. *Arzneim. Forsh.*, **33**, 1173-6.

Carlsson, A., Corrodi, H., Fuxe, K., and Hokfelt, T. (1960). Effects of some antidepressant drugs on the depletion of intraneuronal brain catecholamines stores caused by 4-alpha-dimethylmetatyramine. *Eur. J. Pharmac.*, **5**, 367-73.

Cox, B., Kerwin, R., and Lee, T. F. (1978). Dopamine receptors in the central thermo-regulatory pathway of the rat. *J. Physiol.*, **282**, 471-83.

Hallman, H., Sundstrom, E., and Jonsson, S. (1984). Effects of the noradrenaline neuro-toxin DSP_4 on monoamine neurones and their transmitter turnover in rat CNS. *J. Neural Transm.*, **60**, 89-102.

Heal, D. J., Davies, C. L., and Goodwin, G. M. (1985). DSP_4 lesioning prevents the enhance-ment of dopamine and 5-hydroxytryptamine mediated behavioural changes by repeated electroconvulsive shock. *Eur. J. Pharmac.*, **115**, 117-21.

Howard, J. L., Soroko, F. E., and Cooper, B. R. (1981). Empirical behavioral models of depression with emphasis on tetrabenazine antagonism. In Enna, S. J., Malick, J. R., and Richelson, E. (eds.), *Antidepressants, Neurochemical Behavioral and Clinical Perspectives*. Raven, New York, 107-20.

Jonsson, G. H., Hallman, H., Ponzio, F., and Ross, S. (1981). DSP_4 (N-(2-chloroethyl)-N-ethyl-2-bromobenzylamine), a useful denervation tool for central noradrenaline neurons. *Eur. J. Pharmac.*, **72**, 173-88.

Kostowski, W. (1981). Brain noradrenaline, depression and antidepressant drugs. Facts and hypothesis. *Trend in Pharm. Sci.*, **2**, 314-17.

Laval, J., Stenger, A., and Briley, M. (1988). Involvement of both α_1- and β-adrenoreceptors in the antagonism of tetrabenazine-induced effects by antidepressants in mice. In Briley, M., and Fillion, G. (eds.), *New Concepts in Depression*. Macmillan, Basingstoke, 211-15.

Maj, J., Pawlowski, L., and Wiszniowska, G. (1974). The effect of tricyclic antidepressants on apomorphine-induced hypothermia in mice. *Pol. J. Pharmac. Pharm.*, **26**, 329–36.

Menon, M. K., Vivonia, C. A., and Kling, A. S. (1984). Pharmacological studies on the antagonism by antidepressants of the hypothermia induced by apomorphine. *Neuropharmacol.*, **23**, 121–7.

Mogilnicka, E. (1986). Increase in β and α_1-adrenoceptor binding sites in the rat brain and in the α_1-adrenoceptor functional sensitivity after the DSP_4-induced noradrenergic denervation. *Pharmacol. Biochem. Behav.*, **25**, 743–6.

Pawlowski, L., and Mazela, H. (1986). Effects of antidepressants drugs, selective noradrenaline or 5-hydroxytryptamine uptake inhibitors, on apomorphine-induced hypothermia in mice. *Psychopharmacol.*, **88**, 240–6.

Przegalinsky, E., Kordecka-Magiera, A., Mogilnicka, E., and Maj, J. (1981). Chronic treatment with some atypical antidepressants increase the brain levels of 3-methoxy-4-hydroxyphenylglycol. *Psychopharmacol.*, **74**, 187–90.

Puech, A. J., Frances, H., and Simon, P. (1978). Imipramine antagonism of apomorphine-induced hypothermia. *Eur. J. Pharmac.*, **47**, 125–7.

Reches, A., Burke, R. E., Kuhn, C. M., Hassan, M. N., Jackson, U. R., and Fahn, S. (1983). Tetrabenazine, an amine depleting drug, also blocks dopamine receptors in rat brain. *J. Pharm. Exp. Ther.*, **225**, 515–21.

Ross, S. B., and Renyi, A. L. (1975). Tricyclic antidepressant agents. Comparison of the inhibition of the uptake of ^{3}H-noradrenaline and ^{14}C-5-hydroxytryptamine in slices and crude synaptosome preparations from the midbrain-hypothalamus region of the rat brain. *Acta Pharmacol. Toxicol.*, **36**, 382–94.

Simon, P., Lecrubier, Y., Jouvent, R., Puech, A. J., Allilaire, J. F., and Widlöcher, D. (1978). Experimental and clinical evidence of the antidepressant effect of a beta-adrenergic stimulant. *Psycho. Med.*, **8**, 335–8.

Souto, M., Frances, H., Lecrubier, Y., Puech, A. J., and Simon, P. (1979). Antagonism by d,l-propranolol of imipramine effects in mice. *Eur. J. Pharmac.*, **60**, 105–8.

Svensson, Th., and Usdin, T. (1978). Feedback inhibition of brain noradrenaline neurons by tricyclic antidepressants: alpha receptor mediation. *Science*, **202**, 1089–91.

20

In-vivo Study of the Effect of TRH on Dopamine and Serotonin in the Rat Nucleus Accumbens

F. Crespi and P. E. Keane

20.1 Introduction

Thyrotropin-releasing hormone (TRH) has a neuroendocrinological function in the hypothalamus, but is also present in numerous other brain areas, particularly in the forebrain (Brownstein *et al.*, 1974). A neuromodulator or neurotransmitter role of TRH has been supported by its localisation in synaptosomes (Barnea *et al.*, 1978), the existence of calcium-dependent release of the peptide from neuronal preparations (Bennett, 1981) and the discovery of specific TRH binding sites in the brain (Burt and Taylor, 1980).

TRH produces marked stimulatory effects on behaviour, and this has been attributed by some authors to the release of dopamine from the nucleus accumbens (Miyamoto and Nagawa, 1977, Heal and Green, 1979). Studies *in vitro* have indicated that high concentrations of TRH or analogues (10 to 1000 μM) can release dopamine from nerve endings in this brain area (Sharp *et al.*, 1982; Kerwin and Pycock, 1979). However, in view of the high concentrations necessary to produce this release, the relevance of this phenomenon to the activity of TRH *in vivo* has been questioned (Metcalf, 1982). In addition, some studies indicate a close relationship between TRH and serotonin (5-HT) in the brain. For example, both substances have been co-localised in some medullary neurones (Johansson *et al.*, 1981). Lighton *et al.* (1984) have found a significant correlation between TRH and 5-HT content in the nucleus accumbens. Furthermore, specific lesions of serotonergic neurones produced by 5,7-dihydroxytryptamine significantly reduce TRH levels in this nucleus (Lighton *et al.*, 1984). In view of these observations, we have used differential pulse voltammetry in order to examine the effects of TRH on dopaminergic and serotonergic synaptic activity in the nucleus accumbens of the rat *in vivo*.

20.2 Methods

20.2.1 Experimental Procedure

Male Sprague-Dawley rats (CD, Charles River, France) weighing 250 g were anaesthetised with nembutal (5%, 1 ml/kg i.p.), held in a stereotaxic frame, and implanted with one working electrode in the nucleus accumbens (co-ordinates A 3.4, L 1.4, V 7.0) (Pellegrino *et al.*, 1967). Auxiliary (silver wire) and reference (Ag/AgCl) electrodes were placed on the dura surface of the parietal area of the cortical bone (Crespi *et al.*, 1983). In all experiments, a Tacussel PRG5 pulse voltammetric apparatus was used. The working electrode received a new electrical pretreatment in order to detect simultaneously ascorbic acid, catechols and 5-hydroxyindoles. Monopyrolytic carbon fibre electrodes were first pretreated as described for the recording of peak 3 (Crespi *et al.*, 1983). Then two successive continuous potentials were applied to the electrode (+ 2 V for 10 s, then − 1 V for 10 s). This process enabled the detection of three separate peaks *in vitro* in a solution of ascorbate (5 mM, DOPAC (50 μM) and 5-HIAA (25 μM)) (Fig. 20.1(a)) (Crespi *et al.*, 1984).

20.2.2 Drugs

TRH (L-pyroglutamyl-L-histidyl-L-prolineamide) (obtained from Bachem Ltd), dissolved in physiological saline was injected intraperitoneally (i.p.) in a volume of 2 ml/kg.

20.2.3 Histology

At the end of each experiment, the position of the electrode tip in each nucleus was verified. An electrolytic lesion (5 mA, 5 s) was made using the working electrode, then the brain was rapidly removed for standard histological processing (using cresyl violet dye).

20.2.4 Analysis of Data

A peak current value (nA) was determined by constructing a tangent to the shoulders of the peak and measuring the perpendicular height between the tangent and the centre of the peak. Preliminary experiments showed that injections of saline (600 μl NaCl 0.9% i.p., $n = 5$) did not alter any of the three peaks over

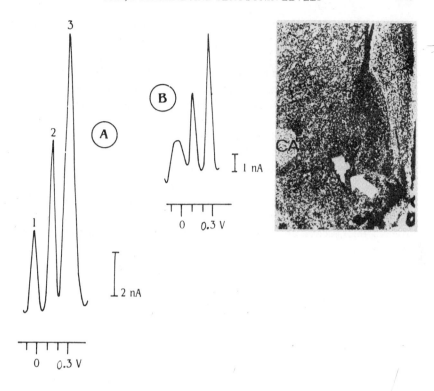

Fig. 20.1 (A) Response of the working electrodes *in vitro* to ascorbic acid (5 mM, peak 1 at −50 mV), DOPAC (50 μM, peak 2 at +100 mV) and 5-HIAA (25 μM, peak 3 at +280 mV). (B) A typical *in-vivo* recording and electrode placement in the nucleus accumbens.

a 5-hour recording period (maximum variation was about 10% of the mean peak height). Thus data were subjected to an analysis of variance, and comparisons between experimental points and their respective pre-injection controls were performed using the Dunnet test.

20.3 Results

20.3.1 Voltammetric Analysis of Extracellular DOPAC and 5-HIAA with a Single Electrode

Fig. 20.1(A) shows the *in vitro* response of the working electrodes to ascorbic acid (5 mM, peak 1 at −50 mV), DOPAC (50 μM, peak 2 at +100 mV) and 5-HIAA (25 μM, peak 3 at +280 mV). The same electrode enables the detection of both the catechol and the indole. Fig. 20.1(B) shows typical *in vivo* recordings and electrode emplacements in the nucleus accumbens. In untreated rats, values of peaks 1, 2 and 3 were stable for over three hours. In agreement with previous studies, pharmacological analysis indicates that the peaks recorded *in vivo* correspond to the acidic metabolites DOPAC and 5-HIAA (Crespi *et al.*, 1984). No statistically significant alterations in peak 1 have been observed in these experiments, and the data concerning this peak are therefore not presented.

20.3.2 Effects of TRH on Extracellular DOPAC in the Nucleus Accumbens

Although 5 mg/kg TRH did not alter peak 2 height in the nucleus accumbens (results not shown), both 10 and 20 mg/kg produced significant increases, to a maximum of 147% of controls after the lower dose, and 215% of controls after the higher dose (Fig. 20.2). The maximum increase was observed 60 minutes after 20 mg/kg TRH, and peak 2 height was still significantly elevated 2 hours after this treatment.

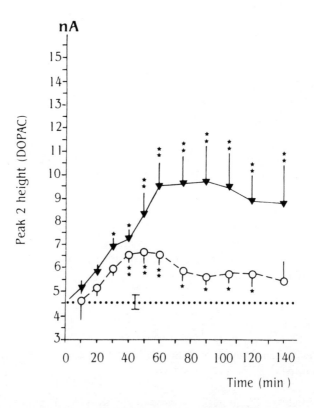

Fig. 20.2   Effects of 10 mg/kg (○) and 10 mg/kg (▲) TRH on peak 2 height in the nucleus accumbens. Values are mean ± SD of values (nA) in 5 rats. Control data, calculated as the signal height in each rat over a period of 30 minutes immediately prior to injection of TRH, are shown by the dotted line and its error bar. *$p < 0.05$; **$p < 0.01$.

20.3.3 Effects of TRH on Extracellular 5-HIAA in the Nucleus Accumbens

The lowest dose of TRH (5 mg/kg i.p.) was inactive, but the doses of 10 and 20 mg/kg TRH increased peak 3 height to a maximum of 164 to 170% of control values, about 2 hours after injection (Fig. 20.3). In contrast to the effect on peak 2 in this nucleus, no difference was seen between the 2 doses concerning peak 3 height. The maximum rise in peak 3 was delayed compared with that of peak 2.

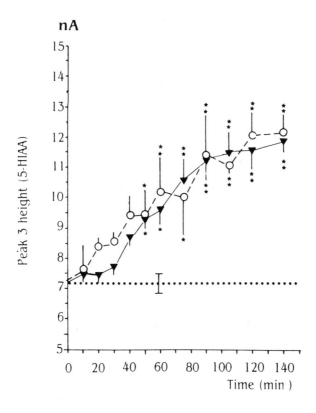

Fig. 20.3   Effects of 10 mg/kg (○) and 20 mg/kg (▲) TRH on peak 3 height in the nucleus accumbens. Values are mean ± SD of values (nA) in 5 rats. Control data, calculated as the signal height in each rat over a period of 30 min immediately prior to injection of TRH, are shown by the dotted line and its error bar. *$p < 0.05$; **$p < 0.01$.

20.4 Discussion

The present results show that TRH produces a dose-dependent increase in extracellular levels of DOPAC in the nucleus accumbens. This may indicate an increased release of dopamine by TRH in this nucleus. Our observations in the nucleus accumbens are in agreement with the findings of Kerwin and Pycock (1979) *in vitro*, and confirm the conclusions of pharmacological studies performed by Miyamoto and Nagawa (1977) and Heal and Green (1979). Furthermore, Sharp *et al.* (1984) studied the effects of local injections of TRH and its analogue CG 3509 on peaks 1 and 2, and peak 3 in the nucleus accumbens and striatum, using a voltammetric technique. These authors observed an increase in peaks 1 and 2 in the nucleus accumbens, but not in the striatum after CG 3509.

TRH also produces a marked increase in peak 3 height in the nucleus accumbens. The delayed time-course of this effect on 5-HIAA suggested that the action of TRH on serotonergic neurones might be a secondary phenomenon, produced as a result of the peptide's effect on dopaminergic neurones, although further experiments will be required to confirm this suggestion. No previous studies have examine the effects of TRH on serotonin in this brain area. However, Agarwal *et al.* (1977) have shown that chronic administration of TRH increases 5-HIAA in the cerebral cortex. Furthermore, the TRH analogue MK-771 increased 5-HIAA levels in a number of brain regions (Rastogi *et al.*, 1981).

An action of TRH on serotonergic transmission in the nucleus accumbens may have implications for some behavioural effects of the peptide. Heal and Green (1979) observed that after systemic administration of the monoamine oxidase inhibitor tranylcypromine, TRH reduced locomotor activity, and introduced head-jerking and padding behaviour. Numerous studies have shown that increased serotonergic neuronal activity produces head-twitching and padding (Jacobs, 1976; Sloviter *et al.*, 1978). Furthermore, TRH produces wet-dog shakes (Wei *et al.*, 1975), a behaviour which is mediated by the stimulation of 5-HT receptors (Bedard and Pycock, 1977).

In conclusion, systemically administered TRH increases the release of both dopamine and 5-HT in the nucleus accumbens of the rat. Both these effects of TRH appear to contribute to the behavioural effects of the peptide.

Acknowledgements

We greatly appreciate the technical assistance provided by J. Paret and the histological and photographic assistance provided by R. Gilardi.

References

Agarwal, R. A., Rastogi, R. B., and Singhal, R. L. (1977). Enhancement of locomotor activity and catecholamine and 5-hydroxy-tryptamine metabolism by thyrotropin releasing hormone. *Neuroendocrinology*, 23, 236–47.
Barnea, A., Neaves, W. B., Cho, G., and Porter, J. C. (1978). A subcellular pool of hypoosmotically resistant particles containing thyrotropin-releasing hormone, alpha-melanocyte stimulating hormone and luteinising hormone releasing hormone in the rat hypothalamus. *J. Neurochem.*, 30, 937–48.

Bedard, P., and Pycock, C. J. (1977). 'Wet-dog' shake behaviour in the rat: a possible quantitative model of central 5-hydroxytryptamine activity. *Neuropharmacol.*, **16**, 663–8.

Bennett, G. W. (1981). Release of neuropeptide hormones from synaptosomes: response to depolarization and neurotransmitters. In Millar, R. P. (ed.), *Neuropeptides*. Churchill Livingston, New York, 61–77.

Brownstein, M., Palkovits, M., Saavedra, J. M., Bassiri, R. M., and Utiger, R. D. (1974). Thyrotropin-releasing hormone in specific nuclei of rat brain. *Science*, **183**, 267–9.

Burt, D. R., and Taylor, R. L. (1980). Binding sites for thyrotropin-relasing hormone in sheep nucleus accumbens resemble pituitary receptors. *Endocrinology*, **106**, 1415–23.

Crespi, F., Cespuglio, R., and Jouvet, M. (1983). Differential pulse voltammetry in brain tissue: mapping of the rat serotoninergic raphe nuclei by electrochemical detection of 5-HIAA. *Brain Res.*, **270**, 45–54.

Crespi, F., Paret, J., Keane, P. E., and Morre, M. (1984). An improved differential pulse voltammetry technique allows the simultaneous analysis of dopaminergic and serotonergic activities in vivo with a single carbon fibre electrode. *Neurosci. Lett.*, **52**, 159–64.

Heal, D. J., and Green, A. R. (1979). Administration of thyrotropin releasing hormone (TRH) to rats releases dopamine in n. accumbens but not in n. caudatus. *Neuropharmacol.*, **18**, 23–31.

Jacobs, B. L. (1976). An animal behaviour model for studying central serotoninergic synapses. *Life Sci.*, **19**, 777–83.

Johansson, O., Hokfelt, R., Pernow, B., Jeffcoate, S. L., White, N., Steinbusch, H. W. M., Verhofstad, A. A. J., Emson, P. C., and Spindel, E. (1981). Immunohistochemical support for three putative transmitters in one neurone: coexistence of 5-HT, substance P and TRH-like immunoreactivity in medullary neurons projecting to the spinal cord. *Neuroscience*, **6**, 1857–81.

Kerwin, R. W., and Pycock, C. J. (1979). Thyrotropin releasing hormone stimulates release of (^{3}H)-dopamine from slices of rat nucleus accumbens in vitro. *Br. J. Pharmacol.*, **67**, 323–6.

Lighton, C., Marsden, C. A., and Bennett, G. W. (1984). The effects of 5,7-dihydroxytryptamine and p-chlorophenylalanine on thyrotropin-releasing hormone in regions of the brain and spinal cord of the rat. *Neuropharmacol.*, **23**, 55–60.

Metcalf, G. (1982). Regulatory peptides as a source of new drugs – the clinical prospects for analogues of TRH which are resistant to metabolic degradation. *Brain Res. Rev.*, **4**, 389–408.

Miyamoto, M., and Nagawa, Y. (1977). Mesolimbic involvement in the locomotor stimulant action of thyrotropin-releasing hormone (TRH) in rats. *Eur. J. Pharmacol.*, **44**, 143–52.

Pellegrino, L. J., Pellegrino, A. S., and Cushman, A. J. (1967). *A Stereotaxic Atlas of the Rat Brain*. Appleton-Century-Crofts, New York.

Rastogi, R. B., Singhal, R. L., and Lapierre, Y. D. (1981). Effects of MK-771, a novel TRH analog, on brain dopaminergic and serotonergic systems. *Eur. J. Pharmacol.*, **73**, 307–12.

Sharp, T., Bennett, G. W., and Marsden, C. A. (1982). Thyrotropin-releasing hormone analogues increase dopamine release from slices of rat brain. *J. Neurochem.*, **39**, 1763–6.

Sharp, T., Brazell, M. P., Bennett, G. W., and Marsden, C. A. (1984). The TRH analogue CG 3509 increases in vivo catechol/ascorbate oxidation in the n. accumbens but not in the striatum of the rat. *Neuropharmacol.*, **23**, 617–23.

Sloviter, R. S., Drust, E. G., and Connor, J. D. (1978). Specificity of a rat behaviour model for serotonin receptor activation. *J. Pharmacol. Exp. Ther.*, **206**, 339–47.

Wei, E., Siegel, S., Loh, H., and Way, E. L. (1975). Thyrotropin-releasing hormone and shaking behaviour in rat. *Nature* (London), **253**, 739–40.

21

Sleep Polygraphic Recordings as a Probe for Central Dopamine Deficiency: Polygraphic and Clinical Criteria of Dopamine-dependent Depressions

J. Mouret, P. Lemoine, M.-P. Minuit and S. Lacroze

21.1 Introduction

In the biological approach to depressive disorders, sleep recordings are most often looked upon as one of the best tools of non-clinical investigations. However, one must also accept that they are of little, if any, help in orienting pharmacological therapeutics. Among the sleep modifications specific to depressive patients, a shortened REM sleep latency together with reduced slow wave sleep (SWS) amounts and increased wakefulness, especially in the last part of the night, are the best accepted (Kupfer, 1976; Kupfer et al., 1986).

As for the biological theories, it is obvious that dopamine has been most often neglected in contrast with the other amines, serotonin (Coppen, 1967) and noradrenaline (Schildkraut, 1965), even though a number of data (Willner, 1983a, b) favour the role of this neglected amine in the pathogenesis or aetiophenomenology of depression.

In spite of our increasing knowledge on depression, it is generally accepted that one-third of depressive patients do not react to classical antidepressant treatments and constitute the 'refractory depression group'. Once patients with sleep apnoeas or cardiac arythmias during sleep have been diagnosed, there remains however a group of 'true' refractory depressive patients which raises serious therapeutic problems.

We will report here the sleep polygraphic criteria allowing the precise diagnosis of dopamine-dependent depression, together with their clinical counterpart. This study consists of several steps, from diagnosis to therapeutic tests.

21.2 Methods

All the patients referred to our board for non-reactive depression were first withdrawn from their treatment, if any, during a period of at least three weeks. At the end of this period, they were recorded during two or three consecutive nights, following two nights of habituation to the recording conditions.

The records, taken at a paper speed of 5 mm/s, were visually scored to the nearest minute according to Rechtschaffen and Kales international criteria in order to provide the quantitative criteria listed in Table 21.1.

Table 21.1

TST	Total sleep time (expressed in minutes)
ST. I	Stage one sleep (in minutes)
ST. II	Stage two sleep (in minutes)
DELTA	Sum of stages three and four sleep (i.d.)
REM	Rapid eye movements sleep (i.d.)
AV. DUR	Average duration, in minutes, of REM sleep within REM sleep episodes*
RSI	REM sleep stability index: percentage of effective REM sleep within REM episodes*
SLEEP LAT	Sleep latency: time from light out to the beginning of the first episode of stage II sleep
REM LAT	REM sleep latency: time from the beginning of the first episode of stage II sleep to the beginning of the first REM sleep episode minus wake time
W./H	Intrasleep wake time per hour of sleep
N. W./H	Number of intrasleep wake episodes per hour of sleep
SHIFTS/H	Number of shifts from one sleep stage to another one or from a sleep stage to wakefulness and vice versa
SL. EFFIC.	Sleep efficiency index: sleep time versus time in bed (from the lights off to the morning awakening limited to 10 minutes)

*REM sleep episodes are looked upon as different when separated by more than 20 minutes.

The interesting point is that some distinctive *qualitative* patterns were observed on the records of some of these patients which were quite similar to those already described (Mouret, 1975) in parkinsonian patients. Among these qualitative signs, blepharospasms, which represent a distinctive feature of all recorded parkinsonian patients, were obvious in the records of some depressive patients.

Given that some technical tricks are necessary in order to record these spasms and that one has to be trained in order to recognise them, it was of interest to try to find some quantitative counterparts to these qualitative polygraphic symptoms.

In order to do so, the quantitative sleep data of 12 patients with these qualitative signs were compared with those of 12 paired depressive patients whose records were qualitatively normal. Needless to say, patients with sleep apnoeas or sleep-linked cardiac arythmias were not included in this study.

All the patients were recorded under the previously described conditions and were major depressives according to DSM III, MADRS, Hamilton depressive scale, and clinical interviews.

As shown in Fig. 21.1 and Table 21.2, while there is no statistical difference between groups on non-REM sleep parameters, the two groups are different at a

Table 21.2 Comparison between polygraphic data obtained from twelve depressed patients without qualitative signs of dopamine deficiency (depressed) and twelve paired depressive patients with *qualitative* signs of dopamine deficiency (DA-depressed), recorded during two to three nights after habituation to the recording conditions

	Depressed ($n = 12$)	p	DA-depressed ($n = 12$)
TST	380	ns	350
ST. I	34	ns	37
ST. II	225	ns	231
DELTA	26	ns	21
TST-ST. I	346	ns	313
REM	93	0.001	58
AV. DUR. REM	23	0.041	16
RSI	77.96	0.001	64.01
SLEEP LAT	45	0.017	25
REM LAT	51	ns	67
W./H	6.7	0.009	19.8
NW./H	1.5	0.003	2.7
SL.EFFIC	82.18	0.015	70.01

TST: total sleep time expressed in minutes.
St. I and St. II: respectively stage I and II sleep expressed in minutes.
Delta: sum of stages III and IV sleep (in minutes).
TST-ST. I: total sleep time minus stage I sleep (in minutes).
REM: rapid eye movement sleep expressed in minutes.
Av. dur. REM: average duration of REM episodes, given that two REM sleep episodes are looked upon as different when separated by more than 20 minutes.
RSI: REM sleep stability index: percentage of REM sleep episodes corresponding to effective REM sleep.
Sleep lat: time, in minutes, between the moment when the lights are switched off and the occurrence of the first episode of stage II sleep.
REM lat: latency between the beginning of the first episode of stage II sleep and the begin-

ning of the first REM sleep episode minus interoccurring wakefulness (in minutes).

W/H: intra-sleep wakefulness per hour of sleep (in minutes).

NW/H: number of intra-sleep wake episodes per hour of sleep.

Sl. effic: sleep efficiency index: percentage of time spent asleep versus time in bed, the morning awakening duration being limited to 10 minutes.

Statistical tests were performed on the average values from each patient during the two to three control sleep recordings (t-tests).

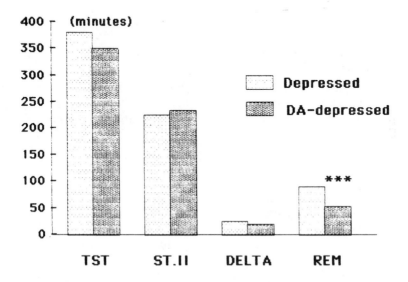

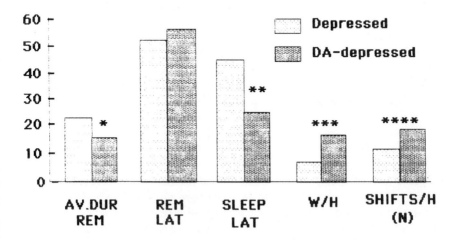

Fig. 21.1 Graphic representation of the data in Table 21.2.

highly significant level on all items directly related to REM sleep, except for its latency. The same applies to those items related to sleep stability, namely wake time per hour, number of wake episodes per hour of sleep, and sleep efficiency index. The combined use of these parameters allowed a 99% differentiation between the two groups of patients.

21.3 Therapeutic Test of Dopamine Deficiency

On the assumption that the qualitative signs allowing such a quantitative differentiation were linked to dopamine deficiency, these patients were given a dopamine agonist (Piribedil), which led, *within two to three days* to a complete disappearance of depressive symptoms and to a completely normal mood. Such a therapeutic test did not improve the mood of the patients in the other group.

21.4 Clinical Counterpart

Given that the onset of depression may, in some cases, precede the onset of neurological symptoms (Asnis, 1977; Vogel, 1982; Mayeux *et al.*, 1984; Mindham, 1970), the patients were carefully tested for the latter and in one patient only was it possible to detect a minor rigidity after the patient had been submitted to rather strenuous physical exercise.

As compared with the other group of patients, neither bradykinesia nor psychomotor retardation were noticed. The main clinical differences are found in the interviews, since in this dopamine-deficient group an important stress, whether chronic or limited in time, was reported. Another easily recognisable point, which confirms the data from the polygraphic recordings, is that these patients have a very agitated sleep and a particularly disturbed bed in the morning.

We are currently establishing a simple interview checklist to allow the diagnosis of these dopamine-dependent depressions.

21.5 Discussion

Our results, even though they are based on a different approach, are in keeping with a number of data in the literature. It has been consistently shown that there is a decreased accumulation of HVA in the CSF after probenecid in some or all depressed patients (Berger *et al.*, 1980; Sjostrom and Roos, 1972; Subramanyam, 1975; Takahashi *et al.*, 1974), especially in those with marked psychomotor retardation (van Praag and Korf, 1971; Papeschi and McClure, 1971; van Praag *et al.*, 1973; Banki, 1977; Banki *et al.*, 1981). The latter data raise the question as to whether dopamine dysfunction is the cause or simply the result of psycho-motor retardation.

In order to understand the discrepancy between these data and most currently accepted theories one must however consider the fact that depressive patients referred to specialised clinical units are most often non-reactive depressives, a group among which dopamine-dependent depressives are most likely found.

Our data also raise the question of dopamine involvement in some aspects of REM sleep. Besides the data from our sleep studies in parkinsonian patients, showing a decrease in the average duration of REM episodes, such a correlation also stems from studies performed in patients with specific sleep disorders who show an impressive correlation between HVA accumulation in CSF after pro-benecid and the average duration of REM episodes (Mouret *et al.*, 1976, 1978) and from a number of pharmacological and experimental studies (see review by Stock, 1984).

21.6 Conclusion

The interest of this study is that all the patients diagnosed according to these polygraphic criteria improved after receiving a dopamine agonist and that, based on the clinical interview, clinicians in our board are now able to diagnose and treat in this way non-reactive dopamine-deficient depressive patients, thus show-ing for the first time, with non-invasive techniques, the existence of a dopamine-dependent type of depression.

References

Asnis, G. (1977). Parkinson's disease, depression and ECT: a review and case study. *Am. J. Psychiat.*, **134**, 191-5.

Banki, C. M. (1977). Correlation between CSF metabolites and psychomotor activity in affective disorders. *J. Neurochem.*, **28**, 255-7.

Banki, C. M., Molnar, G., and Vojnik, M. (1981). Cerebrospinal fluid amine metabolites, tryptophan and clinical parameters in depression. *J. Affect. Disord.*, **3**, 91-9.

Berger, P. A., Faull, K. F., Kilkowski, J., Anderson, P. J., Kraemer, H., Davis, K. L., and Barchas, J. D. (1980). CSF monoamine metabolites in depression and schizophrenia. *Am. J. Psychiat.*, **137**, 174-9.

Coppen, A. (1967). The biochemistry of Affective Disorders. *Br. J. Psychol.*, **113**, 1237-64.

Kupfer, D. J. (1976). REM latency: A psychobiological marker for primary depressive disease. *Biological Psychiatry*, **11**, 159-64.

Kupfer, D. J., Reynolds, C. F., Grochocinski, Y. J., Ulrich, R. F., and McEachran, A. (1986). Aspects of Short REM Latency in Affective States: A Review. *Psychiat. Res.*, **17**, 49-59.

Mayeux, R., Williams, J. B. W., Stern, Y., and Côté, L. (1984). Depression and Parkinson's disease. In Hassler, R. G., and Christ, J. F. (eds.), *Adv. in Neurol.*, **40**. Raven, New York, 241-50.

Mindham, R. H. S. (1970). Psychiatric symptoms in parkinsonism. *J. Neurol. Neurosurg. Psychiat.*, **33**, 188-205.

Mouret, J. (1975). Differences in sleep in patients with Parkinson's disease. *EEG Clin. Neurophysiol.*, **38**, 653-7.

Mouret, J., Debilly, G., Renaud, B., and Blois, R. (1976). Narcolepsy and hypersomnia: diseases or symptoms? Polygraphic and pharmacological studies. In Weitzman, E. D. (ed.), *Narcolepsy, Adv. in Sleep Res.*, Spectrum, New York, 571-84.

Mouret, J., Renaud, B., and Blois, R. (1978). Central dopamine metabolism in human paradoxical sleep disorders. In Usdin, E., Kopin, I. J., and Barchas, J. (eds.), *Catecholamines: Basic and Clinical Frontiers*, vol. 2. Pergamon, New York, 1581-3.

Papeschi, R., and McClure, D. J. (1971). Homovanillic acid and 5-hydroxyindoleacetic acid in cerebrospinal fluid in depressed patients. *Arch. gen. Psychiat.*, 25, 354-8.

Schildkraut, J. J. (1965). The catecholamine hypothesis of affective disorders: a review supporting evidence. *Am. J. Psychiat.*, 122, 509-22.

Sjostrom, R., and Roos, B. E. (1972). 5-hydroxyindoleacetic acid and homovanillic acid in cerebrospinal fluid in manic-depressive psychosis. *Europ. J. Clin. Pharmacol.*, 4, 170-6.

Stock, G. (1984). Neurobiology of REM sleep: a possible role for dopamine. In Ganten, D., and Pfaff, D. (eds.), *Sleep. Clinical and Experimental Aspects. Current Topics in Neuroendocrinology*. Springer, Berlin, 1-36.

Subramanyam, S. (1975). Role of biogenic amines in certain pathological conditions. *Brain Res.*, 87, 335-62.

Takahashi, S., Yamane, H., Kondo, H., Tani, N., and Kato, N. (1974). CSF monoamine metabolites in alcoholism: a comparative study with depression. *Folia Psychiat. Neurol. Jap.*, 28, 347-54.

Van Praag, H. M., and Korf, J. (1971). Retarded depression and dopamine metabolism. *Psychopharmacology*, 18, 199-203.

Van Praag, H. M., Korf, J., and Schut, T. (1973). Cerebral monoamines and depression. An investigation with the probenecid techniques. *Arch. gen. Psychiat.*, 28, 827-31.

Vogel, H. P. (1982). Symptoms of depression in Parkinson's disease. *Pharmacopsychiat.*, 15, 192-6.

Willner, P. (1983a). Dopamine and depression: a review of recent evidence. I. Empirical studies. *Brain Res. Rev.*, 6, 211-24.

Willner, P. (1983b). Dopamine and depression: a review of recent evidence. III. The effects of antidepressant treatments. *Brain Res. Rev.*, 6, 237-46.

22

Hypothalamo-hypophyseal Mechanisms Involved in the Regulation of Hormones and Behaviour

C. Kordon

Appropriate endocrine parameters have been proposed as 'markers' of coping or non-coping situations. This is due to the fact that hormonal profiles can be concomitant with, or influenced by, discrete behavioural situations. Those changes are functional and adaptive, in the sense that they participate in the adaptation of metabolic parameters to environmental challenges. In that case, they are readily reversible. A temporary imbalance tends to become chronic only when the challenge leads to a non-coping response; in that case it is accompanied by lasting changes in the endocrine regulation of central and peripheral functions. Such prolonged deviations from 'normal' hormonal profiles are sometimes considered as 'vectors of somatisation', and their assessment has thus been proposed as predictive indices of peripheral pathologies associated with coping impairment.

Measurement of hormone profiles has also been proposed as a diagnostic complement of certain psychiatric disorders. Examples of this are presented in Figs. 22.1 and 22.2. Discrete changes in cortisol levels can be recorded in patients with psychiatric disorders. They are detectable only at certain periods of the circadian cycle (Fig. 22.1),[1] as well as under strict methodological conditions. For instance, the pulsatile nature of pituitary secretion (Fig. 2? 4) makes it necessary to rely on several sequential blood samples in order to obtain a valid evaluation of actual secretion rates. Measurement of hormone receptors in peripheral tissue, as shown in Fig. 22.2 for glucocorticoid receptors in lymphocytes,[2] can also be used as a marker of the 'recent history' of hormone circulating levels. In that case, a discrete decrease of binding is observed during endogenous

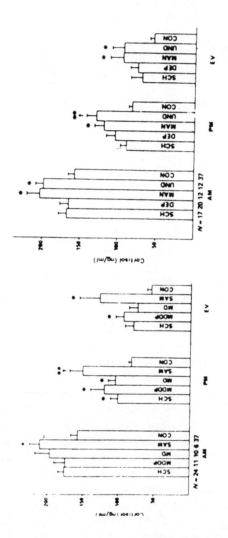

Fig. 22.1 Plasma cortisol concentrations from three sequential samples taken at various times of the day (AM, 07.00 to 08.00; PM, 15.00 to 16.00; EV, 23.00 to 24.00) in control (CON), schizophrenic (SCH), major psychotic depressive (MDDP), manic (MD or MAN), schizoaffective manic (SAM), depressed (DEP) or undiagnosed psychotic (UND) patients. From Christie et al.[1]

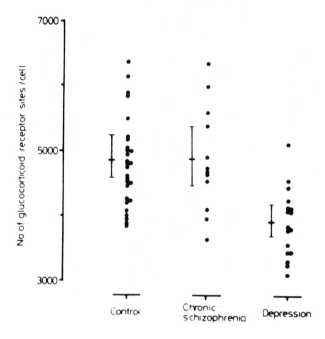

Fig. 22.2 Mean number of lymphocyte glucocorticoid receptors (with 95% confidence limits) in 29 controls, 12 chronic schizophrenes and 17 depressed patients. From Whalley et al.[2]

depression, while a pathological condition could not be discriminated by monitoring only cortisol levels. This decrease is statistically significant, but shows a large overlap of individual values; it is thus uneasy to apply for purposes of individual diagnostic. That statement also applies to so-called 'reactivity' tests (dexamethasone suppression of cortisol- or thyrotropin-releasing-hormone-induced responses of growth hormone for instance).

In this chapter, we deal mainly with processes involved in the common regulation of neuroendocrine and behavioural parameters, and discuss relevance of hormonal levels as 'markers' in psychiatry or in clinical research.

22.1 Mechanisms of Neuroendocrine Control

Our representation of neuroendocrine control mechanisms has undergone important changes over the last years. Until recently, it was thought that a small number of central transmitters was enough to control the pituitary: dopamine and thyrotropin releasing hormone (TRH) for prolactin, corticotrophin releasing factor (CRF) for adrenocorticotrophic hormone (ACTH), or growth hormone releasing factor (GHRF) and somatostatin (SRIF) for growth hormone. In fact, we now know over thirty transmitters and neuropeptides which are all released from the hypothalamus and active on pituitary functions. Most of them act on more than one of the five major pituitary cell types, all of which express receptors for several of those transmitters.

At the hypothalamic level, the organisation of neuroendocrine structures in charge of hormonal control also looks much more complex than previously believed. The hypothalamo-infundibular tract is organised as a consistent pathway, in the sense that its neuronal projections, as diverse in origin (four major structures in the hypothalamus) or in transmitter content as they may be, all converge as one final common pathway innervating the median eminence. Figure 22.3 exemplifies this common architectonic pattern for a few neurons involved in hormonal control. But all those neurons have also been shown to exhibit a very large number of collateral axons, innervating a wild variety of brain structures. For instance (not shown in the figure), SRIF neurons from the preoptic area (APO) send numerous projections to the locus coeruleus;[3] paraventricular (PV) neurons innervate many structures involved in autonomous control.[4] In addition, a few fibres from extrahypothalamic systems, as dopamine fibres from the nigrostriatal tract, also send a few branches to the median eminence.[5]

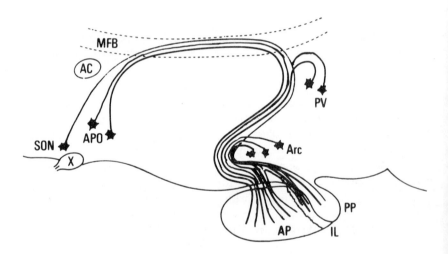

Fig. 22.3 Schematic representation of some hypothalamic inputs to the median eminence and the posterior pituitary in the rat. Supraoptic (SON) and paraventricular (PV) nuclei supply vasopressin and oxytocin; the paraventricular also elaborates other important peptides, such as CRF, TRH and cholecystokinin (CCK). The preoptic area (APO) is the source of luteinising hormone releasing hormone (LHRH) and somatostatin, while the arcuate nucleus (Arc) elaborates dopamine, β-endorphin and GABA. AC, anterior commissure; MFB, medial forebrain bundle; AP, IL, PP anterior, intermediate and posterior lobe of the pituitary; X, optic chiasma. In man, corresponding neurons appear less scattered, owing to the more funnel-shaped infundibular region, but the basic distribution pattern of the neurons is the same. From Kordon et al.[6]

Consequently, hypothalamic neurons form an exceptionally interconnective network with brain structures involved in non-hormonal functions. Co-ordination of behavioural and neuronal parameters can no longer be assumed to depend upon the simple fact that a few transmitters participate in both sets of functions, or upon a simple anatomical connection between structures involved in their respective regulation. It is instead integrated in densely interconnected circuits, activation of which results from a complex coding of neuronal communication (see review in reference 6). Opiate peptides, for instance, induce a pre-synaptic inhibition over the release of most hypothalamic neuropeptides;[7] this results in a partial uncoupling of the pituitary from its driving hypothalamic information. Most hormonal changes recorded after treatment with opiate peptides or morphine are consistent with that hypothesis. In view of the stress-induced changes in central and peripheral opiate activity, this class of transmitters is now considered as playing an important role in inducing hormonal changes during non-coping behaviour; all these changes testify to a decreased hypothalamic 'tone' on pituitary functions under those conditions.

Interference of neurotransmitters or hormones on the hypothalamic 'oscillators' responsible for episodic release of pituitary hormones also account for more discrete behaviour-linked changes. The ultradian pattern now recognised for secretion of gonadotropins (Fig. 22.4),[8] growth hormone, and also ACTH shows characteristic frequencies; those frequencies are sensitive to the physiological condition of the animal, and their fluctuations can induce important changes in peripheral hormone output. Mechanisms regulating ultradian frequency are entirely located within the hypothalamus; they involve complex redundant loops, with an important dopaminergic, opioidergic and noradrenergic component (Fig. 22.5).[9] Those components exhibit receptors for pituitary or peripheral hormones (as shown in the figure for the prolactin interaction with dopamine activity and the estrogen sensitivity of dopamine, opiate and GABA neurons). Discrete changes in the levels of those hormones or in the noradrenaline or the opiate 'tone' on such loops can result in dramatic changes in the characteristic frequency of those oscillators and, hence, in plasma levels of the corresponding peripheral hormones such as sex or adrenal steroids.

22.3 Pituitary Message Integration

As we have seen, each pituitary cell type expresses a large number of transmitters or neuropeptide receptors and is thus submitted to a complex, multi-factorial environment of signals (Fig. 22.6). Many documented examples indicate that the secretory response to this complex signal environment differs from the arithmetic sum of responses to individual signals, a statement which can be represented as

$$M \neq \Sigma s$$

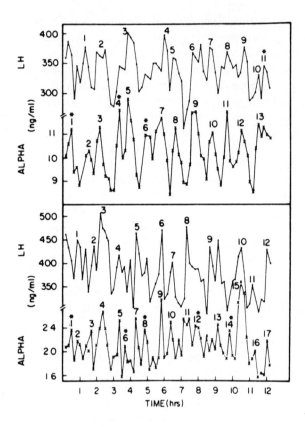

Fig. 22.4 Pulsatile patterns of LH and its subunit in two normal men. Pulses are numbered after separation from background fluctuations by computer. Frequencies of such pulses appear characteristic of the endocrine condition of the subject. From Winter and Troen.[8]

where M is being the overall message received by the cell

and Σs is the arithmetic sum of individual signals.

For instance, opiates can block the dopamine inhibition of prolactin secretion, without exhibiting any activity by themselves; this effect does not involve competition at the receptor level.[10] Vasoactive intestinal peptide (VIP) is also able to potentiate, in a dose-dependent manner, the ACTH response to CRF, without influencing this response in the absence of CRF (Léonard and Bluet-Pajot, unpublished data). An interesting VIP-TRH interaction has also been shown to to exert converse effects on two pituitary cell types which respond identically to each of them applied alone. When applied in combination, VIP potentiates the action of TRH on lactotrophs whereas both effects antagonise each other on thyreotrophs (Fig. 22.7). Similar mechanisms are presumably involved in moni-

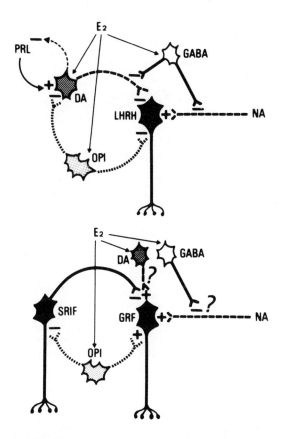

Fig. 22.5 Schematic representation of hypothalamic neuronal loops involved in the control of LH (above) and GH (below) pulsatility. Although oscillating frequencies for the two hormones are quite different, both loops present several common features: opiate (presumably β-endorphin) neurons innervate more than one component of the loops; an important extrinsic noradrenergic, GABA-sensitive component is present in both cases; several oestrogen-sensitive neurons are included in the network (and account for the effect of that hormone on the control of oscillating frequency). From Rotten and Kordon.[9]

toring the selectivity of differential responses by different cell types to combinations of neuropeptides.

How can cells decode differentially messages that they receive over common sets of receptors? Recent data suggest that this property does not depend upon characteristics of the receptors themselves, since those appear universely coupled in the same manner on any tissue; that means that a given subset of receptors, for instance the D2 dopamine receptors, the α_1-noradrenaline receptor, the δ-opiate receptor, etc., can be characterised both by its binding kinetics and by a constant coupling mechanism. Differential decoding depends instead upon cell-specific interactions between coupling chains. As shown in Fig. 22.8 for two

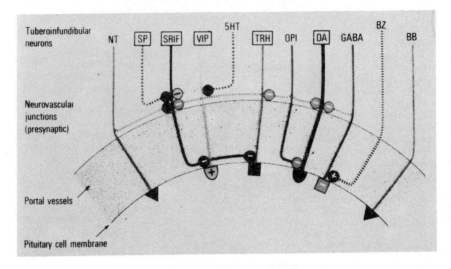

Fig. 22.6 Representation of the multifactorial regulation of prolactin secretion. Several neurohormones are recognised by the lactotroph membrane (inner circle), where they either affect synthesis and release of prolactin (full symbols) or alter the responsiveness of the cell to other factors (modulatory effects, open circles). Some of those factors are also able to interfere with each other's release from the median eminence (outer circle). VIP, vasoactive intestinal peptide; NT, neurotensin; SP, substance P; 5-HT, serotonin; OPI, opiates; DA, dopamine; BZ, benzodiazepines; BB, bonbesin.

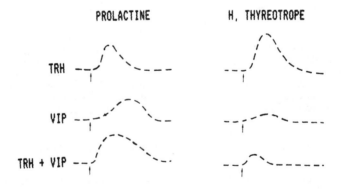

Fig. 22.7 Differential effect of VIP and TRH on prolactin and thyreotropin secretion. In a perifusion system, each peptide induces a comparable stimulation of both hormones when added separately; administered alone, they act synergistically on prolactin and antagonistically on TSH. (Bluet-Pajot, unpublished data.)

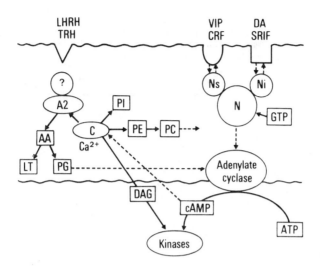

Fig. 22.8 Interactions between adenylate cyclase and phospholipase dependent coupling chains. Depending upon the cell type, activation of the latter can induce prostaglandin (PG) synthesis, and, indirectly, drive the adenylate cyclase independently of a cyclase-coupled receptor. In other cases, cAMP can feed back on phospholipase-C and turn it off; AA, arachidonic acid; AC, adenylate cyclase; LT, leukotrienes; A2, phospholipase A_2; PI, phosphatidil-inositol; PE, phosphatidilethanolamine; PC, phosphatidil-choline; DAG, diacylglycerol; N, regulatory subunit (Ns, stimulating subunit; Ni, inhibitory subunit). From Kordon et al.[6]

theoretical receptors, one coupled to phospholipase-C and the other to adenylate cyclase, activation of one of those enzymes can secondarily affect the other. cAMP, the reaction product of cyclase activation, can inhibit phospholipase-C; conversely, secondary products of phospholipase-C activation, like prostaglandins, can directly stimulate the cyclase independently from the receptor-mediated modulation of that enzyme. Those interferences occur in some cell types and not in others, thus accounting for a *latent programme* which permits the cell to exhibit selective decoding processes beyond an initial, non-cell-specific transduction event. Other cell-specific receptor modulations can involve homologous or heterologous changes in receptor or coupling properties, induced by phosphorylation of the corresponding proteins.

This permits a considerable flexibility in the cellular decoding of complex signals. Processes related to the latent programme can be modulated by peripheral hormones. Estrogens, for instance, decrease the efficacy of negative adenylate cyclase coupling; as shown in Fig. 22.9, the capacity of dopamine to inhibit adenylate cyclase over D2 dopamine receptors (and, in parallel, to decrease prolactin secretion) is considerably attenuated after pretreatment of the cell with estradiol.[11] Interestingly, the same mechanism is observed in the brain; after blockade of D1 striatal receptors in order to unmask the response to D2

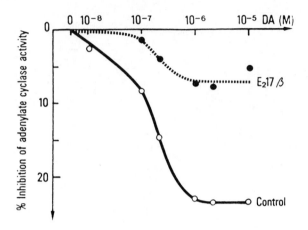

Fig. 22.9 Pretreatment of pituitary cells with estradiol (10^{-9} M) for 24 hours strongly decreases the capacity of dopamine D2 receptors to inhibit adenylate cyclase. From Enjalbert et al.[11]

stimulation, the D2 adenylate cyclase response to dopamine disappears almost completely after pretreatment with estrogen.[12] Similar mechanisms may account for estrogen-dependent fluctuations of behavioural parameters, like those involved in the modified occurrence of depressive episodes at given stages of the menstrual cycle.

22.4 Relevance of Hormonal Parameters for Psychiatric Research

Whatever the mechanisms involved, we thus see that neuroendocrine control systems are quite sensitive to discrete neurotransmitter changes which can also affect, or be affected by, behavioural changes.

As mentioned before, hormonal profiles can be useful to monitor biological responses connected with coping strategies or with patterns of professional challenges. The rationale for this stems from the high probability of observing discrete hormonal changes as a function of the efficacy of coping strategies. However, and in spite of the statistical significance of those changes in different groups, dispersion of individual values within groups does not really permit individual prediction.

It has recently been proposed that diagnostic prediction could be possible in the case of a few neurological diseases, for instance by monitoring neurophysin or growth hormone levels in Alzheimer patients compared with an age-matched population of non-Alzheimer demented patients.[13] Markers may prove useful in that case. They also can have predictive value as to the outcome of drug treatments, since they may provide an evaluation of the drug efficiency on receptors involved both in behavioural and in hormonal control. They can also be used successfully as a screening procedure for drug research. In contrast, it now seems that use of endocrine markers as a complement to the clinical diagnosis of psychiatric disorders should be considered with great caution. In spite of extensive research since Bleuler first raised the question of the possible relevance, almost forty years ago, the viability of such markers in terms of diagnostics cannot yet be considered as formally established. In addition, most changes in pituitary sensitivity connected with pathological states are indicative of global changes in the signal environment of the gland, rather than of a specific disturbance in one particular signal. This might call for a reassessment of the extensive and expensive hormone assay procedures currently used in psychiatric research.

References

[1] Christie, J. E., Whalley, L. D., Dick, H., Blackwood, D. H. R., Blackburn, I. M., and Fink, G. (1986). Raised plasma cortisol concentrations a feature of drug-free psychotics and not specific for depression. *Br. J. Psychiatry*, **1438**, 58-65.

[2] Whalley, L. J., Barthwick, N., Copolou, D., Dick, H., Christie, J. E., and Fink, G. (1986). Glucocorticoid receptors and depression. *Br. Med. J.*, **292**, 859-61.

[3] Palkovits, M., Epelbaum, J., Tapia-Arancibia, L., and Kordon, C. (1982). Somatostatin in catecholamine rich nuclei of the brain stem. *Neuropeptides*, **3**, 139-44.

[4] Palkovits, M. (1987). Organisation of the stress response at the anatomical level. In de Kloet, E. R., Wiegant, V. M., and de Wied, D. (eds.), *Progress in Brain Research*. Elsevier, Amsterdam, **72** (in press).

[5] Renaud, L. P. (1981). A neurophysiological approach to the identification, connections and pharmacology of the hypothalamic tubero-infundibular system. *Neuroendocrinology*, **33**, 186-91.

[6] Kordon, C., Bluet-Pajot, M. T., Clauser, H., Drouva, S., Enjalbert, A., Epelbaum, J., Leblanc, P., and Rotten, D. (1987). Brain modulatory neuroendocrine peptides and the pituitary. In De Groot, H. (ed.), *Endocrinology*. Plenum, New York (in press).

[7] Drouva, S. V., Epelbaum, J., Tapia-Arancibia, L., Laplante, E., and Kordon, C. (1981). Opitate receptors modulate LHRH and SRIF release from mediobasal hypothalamic neurons. *Neuroendocrinology*, **32**, 163-7.

[8] Winter, S. J., and Troen, P. H. (1985). Pulsatile secretion of immunoreactive α subunit in man. *J. Clin. Endocrinol. Metab.*, **60**, 344-8.

[9] Rotten, D., Durand, D., Bluet-Pajot, M. T., and Kordon, C. (1987). Neuroendocrine control of episodic hormone secretion. In Wagner, R., and Silicori, M. (eds.), *Episodic Hormone Secretions: from Basic Signs to Clinical Applications*. Springer, Halemn, 25-36.

[10] Enjalbert, A., Ruberg, M., Arancibia, S., Priam, M., Kordon, C. (1979). Endogenous opiates block dopamine inhibition of prolactin secretion in vitro. *Nature*, **280**, 595-7.

[11] Enjalbert, A., Drouva, S. V., Bertrand, P., Krantic, S., Epelbaum, J., Laplante, E., Rerat, E., and Kordon, C. (1986). Effects of estradiol on receptors coupled to adenylate cyclase and on phospholipid methylation of anterior pituitary cells. *Neuroendocrinology*, abstract of the First International Congress of Endocrinology, San Francisco, 75.

[12] Enjalbert, A., Bertrand, P., Drouva, S., Kordon, C., Maus, M., Chneiweiss, H., and Prémont, J. (1986). Estradiol modulation of coupling of D2 dopamine receptors to adenylate cyclase in anterior pituitary and striatal neurons in primary culture. In *Society for Neuroscience, 16th annual meeting*, abstract 11, 273.

[13] Christie, J. E., Whalley, L., Bennie, D., Blackburn, I. M., Blackwood, D. H. R., and Fink, G. (1987). Characteristic plasma hormone changes in Alzheimer areas. *Br. J. Psychiatry*, in press.

23

Endogenous Enkephalins, Depression and Antidepressants

J.-C. Schwartz, J. van Amsterdam, C. Llorens-Cortes and J. Costentin

A series of clinical and experimental observations support the notion that cerebral opioid peptides may play a role in mood regulation and could be involved in the pathophysiology of affective disorders and the action of antimanic and antidepressant treatments. The oldest evidence for this hypothesis is that for many years, before the advent of tricyclic antidepressants, the 'opium cure' was used with some beneficial effect in the treatment of depressed patients in spite of obvious side-effects. Indeed, the three families of opioid peptides and their receptors are particularly abundant in several limbic structures believed to be involved in mood regulation (Cuello, 1983). Stimulation of these receptors by opiates has been known for centuries to have hedonic actions in humans, eliciting a dream-like euphoria, for which presumably they have been self-administered. It has even been hypothesised that opiate-dependent individuals become addicted because opiates relieve their depressive symptoms (McLellan *et al.*, 1982). A slight antidepressant activity of morphine has been reported (Extein *et al.*, 1981). Also, buprenorphine, a partial agonist at opiate receptors, was recently shown to ameliorate symptoms in depressed patients (Emrich *et al.*, 1982). Similar observations were made following the intravenous administration of β-endorphin (Kline *et al.*, 1977; Angst *et al.*, 1977; Gerner *et al.*, 1980) but could not be replicated in another study (Pickar *et al.*, 1981).

These various observations have prompted studies aimed at identifying a defect in the metabolism of endogenous opioid peptides in depressive or manic-depressive patients. Lindström (1978) reported that a fraction of the opiate activity evaluated by opiate receptor binding in the cerebrospinal fluid of manic-depressive patients was higher during mania than during depression. This observation was partly confirmed by others, although the total opioid activity and β-endorphin immunoreactivity did not significantly differ in the cerebrospinal fluid of depressed patients as compared with normal volunteers (Naber *et al.*, 1981; Pickar *et al.*, 1982).

Regarding the modes of actions of effective antidepressant and antimanic treatments, much less is known about the possible involvement of cerebral neuropeptides than that of monoamines. However, several tricyclic antidepressants display naloxone-reversible antinociceptive activity in animal tests, suggesting a possible involvement of endogenous opioid peptides in their activity (Lee and Spencer, 1977). In addition, chronic treatments with tricyclic antidepressants (De Felipe *et al.*, 1985), electroconvulsive shocks and lithium chloride (LiCl) (Gillin *et al.*, 1978; Staunton *et al.*, 1982) significantly increased the steady-state levels of enkephalins in various regions of rat brain, but these changes were not easily interpretable because of the lack of suitable methods to evaluate the turnover rate of these peptides.

Hence, taken together, these various observations suggest that endogenous opioid peptides may be involved in mood disorders as well as in the mode of actions of treatments used to alleviate their symptoms. In the present work we have attempted to further investigate the implications of endogenous enkephalins, starting from the knowledge accumulated during recent years regarding their modes of inactivation. It has been pregressively established that inactivation occurs via operation of two pathways both involving membrane-bound peptidases: the first occurs through cleavage of the Tyr^1-Gly^2 amide bond by aminopeptidase-M (EC 3.4.11.2) (Gros *et al.*, 1985), the second through cleavage of the Gly^3-Phe^4 amide bond by enkephalinase (EC 3.4.24.11) (Malfroy *et al.*, 1978). Inhibition of these two pathways by compounds such as bestatin and thiorphan results in the protection of endogenous enkephalins and in a variety of opioid-like, naloxone-reversible effects presumably elicited by the neuropeptides (Schwartz *et al.*, 1981, 1982, 1985). These agents were presently used to evaluate the participation of endogenous enkephalins in (a) the control of monoaminergic neurons in brain for which an extensive literature suggests their participation in mood disorders, (b) an animal test of antidepressant activity.

In addition it progressively appears that the steady-state level of the tripeptide Tyr-Gly-Gly (YGG), an extracellular metabolite of enkephalins, reflects the activity of enkephalin neurons in brain (Llorens-Cortes *et al.*, 1986). The effects of acute and subchronic treatments with a tricyclic antidepressant as well as with LiCl, an antimanic agent, were therefore evaluated.

23.1 Effects of Inhibitors of Enkephalin-degrading Peptidases on Turnover of Cerebral Monoamines

Simultaneous inhibition of enkephalinase by thiorphan and aminopeptidase-M by bestatin provides a complete protection of endogenous enkephalins released by depolarisation of brain slices (De la Baume *et al.*, 1983; Giros *et al.*, 1986a, b). A similar effect of the inhibitors is observed *in vivo* as shown by the progressive accumulation of (Met^5)enkephalin in an extrasynaptosomal fraction from mouse striatum (Llorens-Cortes *et al.*, 1986). Hence the various naloxone-reversible changes in monoamine turnover which followed the co-administration of the two peptidase inhibitors seem attributable to overstimulation of opiate receptors by their endogenous ligands. The present studies indicate that the turnover of the monoamines noradrenaline, dopamine and serotonin in mouse brain was significantly modified following inhibition of the two peptidase activities responsible for the inactivation of endogenous enkephalins e.g. enkephalinase and the bestatin-sensitive aminopeptidase-M activity.

In the case of cortical noradrenaline the α-methyl-p-tyrosine (α-MPT)-induced depletion was reduced by about 50% following administration of thiorphan and bestatin (Table 23.1). The effect was completely prevented by naloxone pre-

Table 23.1   Effects of thiorphan and bestatin on the α-methyl-p-tyrosine-induced decline in noradrenaline in cerebral cortex and dopamine in striatum of mice

	α-Methyl-tyrosine-induced changes (%) in	
	Cortical noradrenaline	Striatal dopamine
Vehicle	-38 ± 2	-23 ± 3
Thiorphan + bestatin	-20 ± 3**	-39 ± 5*
Naloxone	-44 ± 6^{NS}	-28 ± 3^{NS}
Thiorphan + bestatin + naloxone	-46 ± 3^{NS}	-24 ± 5^{NS}

Groups of 9 to 33 mice received vehicle or thiorphan (25 μg) and bestatin (50 μg) by the intracerebroventricular route and naloxone (10 mg/kg, i.p.) 70 min prior to sacrifice. α-methyl-p-tyrosine (200 mg/kg, i.p.) was administered 60 min prior to sacrifice. Monoamines were evaluated spectrofluorometrically after isolation by ion-exchange chromatography. Values are expressed as percentage changes ($\pm$ SEM) as compared to controls i.e. 246 $\pm$ 7 ng/g for cortical noradrenaline and 9.3 $\pm$ 0.4 μg/g for striatal dopamine. *$p < 0.05$; **$p < 0.001$; NS: non-significant as compared with vehicle-treated mice.

treatment, indicating that it resulted from the stimulation of opiate receptors, presumably induced by endogenous opioid peptides when the latter were protected from degradation. The naloxone dose (10 mg/kg) was selected in order to ensure a persistent and non-selective blockade of the various subclasses of opioid receptors. Acetorphan, a parenterally active enkephalinase inhibitor, also reduced significantly and in a naloxone-reversible manner the turnover of cortical noradrenaline (Lecomte *et al.*, 1986). Synthetic opiates and opioid peptides have been shown previously to inhibit the firing of noradrenergic neurons in the locus coeruleus (Korf *et al.*, 1974; Bird and Kuhar, 1977; Young *et al.*, 1977) and to inhibit the depolarisation-induced release of noradrenaline from slices of cerebral cortex (Montel *et al.*, 1975; Arbilla and Langer, 1978). Both actions are consistent with the presence of enkephalin neurons surrounding noradrenergic cells in the locus coeruleus (Cuello, 1983) and of opiate receptors in this structure (Pert et al., 1976) as well as on noradrenergic terminals (Llorens et al., 1978). However, the effect of exogenous opiates on cerebral noradrenaline turnover is more controversial. A decrease (particularly following morphine in low dosage) has been reported from some studies (Tanaka et al., 1982; Attila and Ahtee, 1983) and an increase from others (Smith et al., 1972; Bloom et al., 1976). These discrepancies might arise, among other reasons, from the involvement of various subtypes of opiate receptors and/or from indirect effects of exogenous opiates administered in pharmacological dosages. In contrast, our results suggest that endogenous opioids (most probably enkephalins since the metabolism of other endogenous opioid peptides is less readily affected by thiorphan and bestatin) inhibit the activity of noradrenergic neurons.

In the case of striatal dopamine, thiorphan and bestatin increased by about 50% the rate of α-MPT-induced decline, an effect which was completely prevented with naloxone (Table 23.1). Thiorphan, as well as another enkephalinase inhibitor phosphoryl-Phe-Leu, was previously shown to increase DOPAC levels in rat striatum (Algeri et al., 1981; Wood, 1982). Thiorphan microinjections into the ventral tegmental area was also shown to increase dopamine metabolism in the nucleus accumbens, prefrontal cortex and septum (Kalivas and Richardson-Carlson, 1986). These effects are consistent with numerous observations of enkephalin neurons interacting in a complex manner with nigrostriatal dopaminergic neurons (Cuello, 1983), opiate receptors being present on the latter (Pollard et al., 1977; Carenzi et al., 1978; Reisine et al., 1979) and exogenous opiates or opioid peptides increasing their activity as well as the turnover of the catecholamines through several mechanisms (Pert, 1978).

Finally, the two peptidase inhibitors elicited, again in a naloxone-reversible manner, a significant increase in cortical 5-hydroxyindolacetic acid (5-HIAA) levels and the ratio of 5-HIAA to serotonin (5-HT) levels, taken as an index of the indoleamine turnover, was elevated by about 50% (Table 23.2). A similar effect was recently observed following parenteral administration of acetorphan (Lecomte et al., 1986). Again these data are consistent with the presence of enkephalin neurons in the raphe complex (Cuello, 1983) and the elevation of 5-HT turnover rate by exogenous opiates and opioid peptides (Yarbrough et al., 1973; Algeri et al., 1978). Interestingly, whereas naloxone prevented all the modifications of monoamine turnover elicited by the two peptidase inhibitors, the opiate receptor antagonist had no significant effect on its own. This suggests that the endogenous opioid peptides do not exert marked tonic control on the activity of cerebral monoaminergic neurons, at least under basal conditions, and that their normal inactivation processes have to be blocked to reveal their action.

To what extent do these observations suggest that inhibition of enkephalin-degrading peptidases may constitute a novel approach to the treatment of depressed patients? A large number of monoamine oxidase inhibitors and tri-

Table 23.2 Effects of thiophan and bestatin on serotonin metabolism in mouse cerebral cortex

	5-HIAA/5-HT
Controls	0.76 ± 0.04
Thiorphan + bestatin	$1.12 \pm 0.08^*$
Naloxone	0.83 ± 0.05^{NS}
Thiorphan + bestatin + naloxone	0.82 ± 0.04^{NS}

Groups of 11 to 21 mice received thiorphan (25 μg, i.c.v.) and bestatin (50 μg, i.c.v.) 20 min before and/or naloxone (10 mg/kg, i.p.) 40 min before sacrifice. The levels of 5-hydroxyindolacetic acid (5-HIAA) and serotonin (5-HT) were measured spectrofluorometrically after ion-exchange and Sephadex G-10 chromatography and their ratios calculated for each animal. Control values were 240 ± 12 and 331 ± 17 ng/g for 5-HIAA and 5-HT respectively. $^*p < 0.001$; NS: non-significant as compared with controls.

cyclic antidepressants presently used in therapeutics are known to increase serotonin (5-HT) availability while some of them also increase dopamine availability. Whereas both acute effects could be expected to occur with the peptidase inhibitors, the latter decreased noradrenaline turnover and this contrasts with a large number of tricyclic antidepressants which have opposite effects.

23.2 Effects of a Chronic Treatment with Acetorphan, an Enkephalinase Inhibitor, on Cerebral β-Adrenoreceptor Sensitivity

Evidence has accumulated for the contribution of a post-synaptic regulatory mechanism involving the cerebral β-adrenergic receptors-coupled adenylate cyclase system in the action of antidepressants. Following the administration of a large variety of antidepressant drugs on a clinically relevant time basis, decreased responsiveness of the cyclic AMP generating system to noradrenaline progressively develops (Sulser, 1978). Subsensitivity develops following chronic administration not only of compounds which acutely affect noradrenergic transmission but also of compounds like the 'atypical' antidepressants which do not have this acute action. This process, which seems at least partly mediated by a decreased number of β-adrenoreceptors, has been largely studied in the hope that it might constitute an index allowing the detection of antidepressant activity of new compounds in rodents. It was therefore of interest to ascertain the effect of chronic enkephalinase inhibition on this test system. This could be performed following the design of acetorphan, a potent and parenterally active inhibitor of the cerebral enzyme (Lecomte et al., 1986).

Following chronic administration of acetorphan to rats, the noradrenaline-induced accumulation of cyclic AMP in slices of cerebral cortex was significantly increased (Table 23.3). This hypersensitivity typically consisted in an elevated maximal response without significant modification of the ED_{50} of the amine and was accompanied by an increased number of [^{3}H]-dihydroalprenolol binding sites (not shown). Such changes, the opposite of those triggered by antidepres-

Table 23.3 Noradrenaline-induced accumulation of cyclic AMP in slices of rat cerebral cortex: effects of chronic acetorphan

	Stimulation by noradrenaline	
	ED_{50} (μM)	Maximal stimulation (% of controls)
Vehicle	2.4 ± 0.1	271 ± 16
Acetorphan	2.1 ± 0.3	390 ± 38*

Groups of 10 rats received two injections (50 mg/kg, i.p.) of acetorphan each day during the first week then four injections (50 mg/kg, i.p., and 25 mg/kg, s.c.) during the second week and were killed 17 h after the last injection. Slices of cerebral cortex were prepared and the noradrenaline-induced stimulation of cyclic AMP measured as described (Llorens-Cortes et al., 1978). Basal cyclic AMP levels (pmol/mg protein) were 6.0 ± 0.6 and 5.5 ± 0.7 in vehicle- and acetorphan-treated animals respectively. The body weights of the two groups did not differ significantly at the end of treatment and no overt sign of withdrawal was noted. *$p < 0.01$.

sants, are reminiscent of those occurring in rats chronically treated with morphine (Llorens-Cortes et al., 1978). As in the latter case, it can be attributed to the development of a process of disuse-hypersensitivity following a sustained impairment of noradrenergic stimulation of target cells in the cerebral cortex. In the case of morphine it has been proposed that this process of disuse-hypersensitivity may underline the development of tolerance and dependence (Llorens-Cortes et al., 1978). In fact, this view is challenged by the observation that chronic treatments with acetorphan does not lead to a diminished antinociceptive activity of the drug nor to the appearance of any withdrawal symptom following naloxone (Lecomte et al., 1986).

23.3 Effects of Acetorphan in the Mouse Behavioural Despair Test

Naloxone inhibits the effects of clomipramine in the 'forced swimming' or 'behavioural despair' test (Porsolt et al., 1977), suggesting that endogenous opioids might mediate the effects of antidepressants in this test (Devoize et al.,

1982). In addition, opiate receptor agonists including $(DA1A^2, Met^5)$enkephalin shorten the immobility time, as do the clinically active antidepressants in the same test (Ben Natan et al., 1984).

Acetorphan elicited a similar behavioural response in this test, as shown by the significant reduction of the immobility time (Table 23.4). This effect was completely reversed by naloxone, suggesting that it was mediated by protection of endogenous enkephalins. One may wonder whether this effect is connected with a potential antidepressant activity of enkephalinase inhibitors. Although the 'behavioural despair' test is positive for various antidepressant compounds,

Table 24.4   Effects of acetorphan in the mouse 'behavioural despair test'

	Immobility time (s)
Vehicle	188 ± 7
Acetorphan	$145 \pm 12*$
Vehicle + naloxone	201 ± 5
Acetorphan + naloxone	98 ± 5

Groups of 24 mice received vehicle, acetorphan (50 mg/kg, i.p.) and/or naloxone (1 mg/kg, s.c.) 6 min before being introduced into a swimming bath (Porsolt et al., 1977). After a 2 min time lag, the time that the animal spent motionless during the following 4 min period was measured. $*p < 0.01$.

i.e. tricyclics, monoamine oxidase inhibitors and atypical antidepressants, as well as for electroconvulsive shocks, its selectivity seems questionable (Schechter and Chance, 1979). In particular, drugs eliciting a motor stimulation are known to also reduce the immobility time and enkephalinase inhibitors were recently shown to increase spontaneous motor activity, presumably by activating dopaminergic neurons ending in the nucleus accumbens (Kalivas et al., 1986; Costentin et al., submitted). Nevertheless, in the case of thiorphan and bestatin the locomotor activation and reduction in immobility time could be clearly separated (Ben Natan et al., 1984). In any event, the present data further support the view that endogenous enkephalins are involved in the 'behavioural despair' test.

23.4 Effects of Desipramine and Lithium Chloride on (Met^5)Enkephalin and Tyr-Gly-Gly Levels in Rat Brain

The effects of psychotropic drugs on peptidergic systems in brain is still poorly understood, mainly because of lack of suitable methods to evaluate neuropeptide turnover rates. Regarding enkephalins, we have recently shown that the tripeptide YGG is an extracellular metabolite produced by their cleavage through the action of enkephalinase (Llorens-Cortes *et al.*, 1985a b; Giros *et al.*, 1986b). This metabolite is in a highly dynamic state, its half-life being about 10 min in mouse striatum, and its steady-state level appears to constitute a reliable index of enkephalin release (Llorens-Cortes *et al.*, 1986). It was therefore of interest to evaluate the effects of treatments with antidepressants or LiCl on YGG contents in cerebral regions in order to explore the hypothesis that the actions of these agents were mediated by changes in the activity of enkephalin neurons.

In rats receiving a single administration of desipramine no significant change in the levels of either (Met^5)enkephalin or YGG could be detected in three brain areas after 2 h (Table 23.5).

In contrast, LiCl elicited after the same tissue a slight but significant decrease in hypothalamic (Met^5)enkephalin Tyr-Gly-Gly-Phe-Met (YGGFM) accompanied by a nearly 50% increase in YGG. Both changes are consistent with an increased activity of enkephalin neurons in hypothalamus. The unmodified levels of YGGFM in striatum and globus pallidus after a single administration of LiCl is in agreement with previous reports (Gillin *et al.*, 1978; Sabol *et al.*, 1983; Sivam *et al.*, 1986).

Following a 7-day treatment with desipramine, no significant change in either YGGFM or YGG contents were found (Table 23.6). With LiCl, the 7-day treatment at a dosage compatible with serum Li^+ concentrations effective in mania (Gillin *et al.*, 1978) resulted in an elevation (by about 50%) of YGGFM contents in both globus pallidus and striatum (but not hypothalamus). Similar changes were previously reported (Gillin *et al.*, 1978; Staunton *et al.*, 1982; Sivam *et al.*, 1986) and found in the last report to be accompanied by a rise in the levels of the proenkephalin A precursor and its mRNA. They are therefore likely to reflect an increased rate of the enkephalin precursor synthesis. However, interestingly, the level of YGG was not significantly modified (Table 23.6), suggesting that the treatment with the antimanic agent did not result in any increase in the rate of enkephalin release. At this step the mechanism by which LiCl modifies the steady-state level of enkephalins is not easily interpretable. Because this change is transient (Gillin *et al.*, 1978) it may reflect a compensatory mechanism affecting enkephalin neurons indirectly without marked changes in enkephalinergic transmissions.

23.5 Conclusions

Studies with enkephalinase inhibitors indicate that this novel class of pharmacological agents displays an original spectrum of neurochemical and behavioural actions in rodents. They acutely affect monoaminergic systems in brain in the same manner as opiates, by activating serotonin and dopamine systems and decreasing the activity of noradrenaline systems. Like those of opiates their actions are prevented by naloxone and, when administered subchronically, they

Table 23.5 (Met^5)Enkephalin and Tyr-Gly-Gly contents in cerebral regions of rats treated with desipramine or LiCl (single administration)

	Peptide levels (pmol/mg protein)							
	Hypothalamus		Globus pallidus		Striatum			
	YGGFM	YGG	YGGFM	YGG	YGGFM	YGG		
Controls	6.5 ± 0.3	0.62 ± 0.02	17 ± 1	2.6 ± 0.2	13 ± 1	0.80 ± 0.08		
Desimipramine	7.2 ± 0.3	0.68 ± 0.06	19 ± 1	2.3 ± 0.2	12 ± 1	0.80 ± 0.08		
LiCl	5.7 ± 0.2*	0.89 ± 0.06**	20 ± 2	3.1 ± 0.2	13 ± 1	0.76 ± 0.07		

Male rats received saline, desipramine (10 mg/kg, i.p.) or LiCl (3 mEq/kg, i.p.) and were killed 2 h later. Means ± SEM of 15–33 experiments. *$p < 0.05$; **$p < 0.001$ as compared to controls. LiCl = lithium chloride. YGG = Tyr-Gly-Gly. YGGFM = Tyr-Gly-Gly-Phe-Met.

Table 23.6 (Met^5)Enkephalin and Tyr-Gly-Gly contents in cerebral regions with rats treated with desipramine or LiCl (7-day treatment)

	Peptide levels (pmol/mg protein)					
	Hypothalamus		Globus pallidus		Striatum	
	YGGFM	YGG	YGGFM	YGG	YGGFM	YGG
Controls	6.6 ± 0.3	0.49 ± 0.04	16 ± 2	2.1 ± 0.1	14 ± 1	0.95 ± 0.06
Desimipramine	6.9 ± 0.5	0.45 ± 0.03	19 ± 1	2.1 ± 0.3	15 ± 1	1.0 ± 0.1
LiCl	7.1 ± 0.4	0.48 ± 0.04	26 ± 1*	2.2 ± 0.2	19 ± 1*	0.96 ± 0.07

Male rats received saline, desipramine (10 mg/kg, i.p.) or LiCl (3 mEq/kg, i.p.) once daily for 7 days and were killed 17 h after the last injection. Means ± SEM of 15 to 20 experiments. *$p < 0.01$ as compared to controls.

give rise to β-adrenoreceptor supersensitivity. However, in contrast to opiates, they fail to induce respiratory depression as well as the development of withdrawal symptoms, indicating that their use in therapeutics might be much less risky.

As compared with antidepressants presently used in therapeutics, they display some common effects (activation of serotonin and dopamine pathways, effects in the 'mouse despair' test) but also a major difference: they do not trigger β-adrenoreceptor subsensitivity.

The hypothesis that tricyclic antidepressants modify enkephalinergic transmission in brain has not been substantiated in the present studies with desipramine, which did not significantly change the steady-state level of the metabolite YGG in three cerebral areas. At this step it cannot entirely be ruled out that this index of enkephalin release might be modified in other discrete brain areas and/or upon treatment with other antidepressant agents. However, it seems unlikely that a direct and general action of antidepressants on enkephalinergic neurons represents their primary mode of action.

Finally, it appears that LiCl affects enkephalin neurons in the brain but the exact mode of action of this ion remains to be clarified, since the enhanced steady-state levels of the transmitter are not accompanied by an apparent change in its rate of release.

References

Algeri, S., Altstein, M., De Simone, M., and Guardabasso, G. M. (1981). *Eur. J. Pharmacol.*, 74, 207-9.

Algeri, S., Brunello, N., Calderini, G., and Consolazione, A. (1978). In Costa, E., and Trabucchi, M. (eds.), *Advances in Biochemical Psychopharmacology*, vol. 18. Raven, New York, 199-210.

Angst, J., Autenrieth, V., Brem, F., Kokkou, M., Meyer, H., Stassen, H. H., and Storck, U. (1979). In Usdin, E., and Bunney, W. E. (eds.), *Endorphins in Neutral Health Research*. Macmillan, London, 518-28.

Arbilla, S., and Langer, S. Z. (1978). *Nature*, 271, 559-60.

Attila, L. M. J., and Ahtee, L. (1983). Supplement to *Progress in Neuropsychopharmacology and Biological Psychiatry*, 25, 74.

Ben Natan, L., Chaillet, P., Lecomte, J.-M., Marcais, H., Uchida, G., and Costentin, J. (1984). *Eur. J. Pharmacol.*, 97, 301-4.

Bird, S. J., and Kuhar, M. J. (1977). *Brain Res.*, 122, 523-33.

Bloom, A. S., Dewey, W. L., Harris, L. S., and Brosius, K. K. (1976). *J. Pharmacol. Exp. Ther.*, 198, 33-41.

Carenzi, A., Frigeni, V., and Della Bella, D. (1978). In Costa, E., and Trabucchi, M. (eds.), *The Endorphins*, vol. 3. Raven, New York, 265-70.

Cuello, A. C. (1983). *Brit. Med. Bull.*, 39, 11-16.

De Felipe, M. C., De Ceballos, M. L., Gie, C., and Fueutes, J. A. (1985). *Eur. J. Pharmacol.*, 112, 119-22.

De La Baume, S., Yi, C. C., Schwartz, J.-C., Chaillet, P., Marcais-Collado, H., and Costentin, J. (1983). *Neuroscience*, 8, 143-51.

Devoize, J. L., Rigal, A., Eschalier, A., and Trolese, J. F. (1982). *Eur. J. Pharmacol.*, **78**, 229-32.
Emrich, H. M., Vogt, P., and Herz, A. (1982). *Ann. N.Y. Acad. Sci.*, **398**, 108-12.
Extein, I., Pickar, D., Gold, M. S., Gold, P. W., Pottash, A. L. C., Sweeney, D. R., Ross, R. J., Rebard, R., Martin, D., and Goodwin, F. K. (1981). *Pharmacol. Bull.*, **17**, 29-33.
Gerner, R. H., Catlin, D. H., Gorelick, D. A., Huie, K. K., and Li, C. H. (1980). *Arch. Gen. Psychiatry*, **37**, 642-7.
Gillin, J.-C., Hong, J. S., Yang, H. Y. T., and Costa, E. (1978). *Proc. Natl Acad. Sci. USA*, **75**, 1991-3.
Giros, B., Gros, C., Solhonne, B., and Schwartz, J.-C. (1986a). *Mol. Pharmacol.*, **29**, 281-7.
Giros, B., Llorens-Cortes, C., Gros, C., and Schwartz, J.-C. (1986b). *Peptides*, **7**, 669-78.
Gros, C., Giros, B., and Schwartz, J.-C. (1985). *Biochemistry*, **24**, 2179-85.
Kalivas, P. W., and Richardson-Carlson, R. (1986). *Am. J. Physiol.*, **251**, R243-9.
Kline, N. S., Li, C. H., Lehmann, H. E., Lajtha, A., Laski, E., and Cooper, T. B. (1977). *Arch. Gen. Psych.*, **34**, 1111-3.
Kotf, J., Bunney, B. S., and Aghajanian, G. K. (1974). *Eur. J. Pharmacol.*, **25**, 165-9.
Lecomte, J.-M., Costentin, J., Vlaiculescu, A., Chaillet, P., Marcais-Collado, H., Llorens-Cortes, C., Leboyer, M. and Schwartz, J.-C. (1986). *J. Pharmacol. Exp. Ther.*, **237**, 937-44.
Lee, R., and Spencer, P. S. J. (1977). *J. Int. Med. Res.*, **5**, 146-56.
Lindström, L. H., Widerlof, E., Gunne, L. M., Wahlstrom, A., and Terenius, L. (1978). *Acta Psychiatr. Scand.*, **57**, 153-64.
Llorens-Cortes, C., Gros, C., and Schwartz, J.-C. (1985b). *Eur. J. Pharmacol.*, **119**, 183-91.
Llorens-Cortes, C., Gros, C., and Schwartz, J.-C. (1986). *Proc. Natl Acad. Sci. USA*, **83**, 6226-30.
Llorens, C., Martres, M. P., Baudry, M., and Schwartz, J.-C. (1978). *Nature*, **274**, 603-5.
Llorens-Cortes, C., Schwartz, J.-C., and Gros, C. (1985a). *FEBS Lett.*, **189**, 325-8.
Malfroy, B., Swerts, J. P., Guyon, A., Roques, B. P., and Schwartz, J.-C. (1978). *Nature*, **276**, 523-6.
McLellan, A. T., Woody, G. E., Evans, B. D., and O'Brien, C. P. (1982). *Ann. N.Y. Acad. Sci.*, **398**, 65-78.
Montel, H., Starke, K., and Taube, H. D. (1975). *Naunyn Schmiedelberg's Arch. Pharmacol.*, **288**, 427.
Naber, D., Pickar, D., Post, R. M., Van Kammen, D. P., Waters, R. N., Ballinger, J. C., Goodwin, F. K., and Bunney, W. E. J. (1981). *Am. J. Psychiatry*, **138**, 1457-62.
Pert, A. (1978). In Van Ree, J. M., and Terenius, L. (eds.), *Characteristics and Functions of Opioids*. Elsevier, Amsterdam, 389-99.
Pert, C. B., Kuhar, M. J., and Snyder, S. H. (1976). *Proc. Natl Acad. Sci., USA*, **73**, 3729-33.
Pickar, D., Davis, G. C., Schulz, S. C., Extein, I., Wagner, R., Naber, D., Gold, P. W., Van Kammen, D. P., Goodwin, F. K., Wyatt, R. J., Li, Ch., and Bunney, W. E. (1981). *Am. J. Psychiatry*, **138**, 160-6.
Pickar, D., Vartanian, F., Bunney, W. E., Maier, H. D., Gastpar, M. T., Prakash, R., Setthi, B. B., Belgaer, B., Tsultulkausa, M., Junghunz, G., Nedopil, T. N., Verhoeven, W., and Van Praag, H. (1982). *Arch. Gen. Psychiatry*, **39**, 313-9.
Pollard, H., Llorens-Cortes, C., and Schwartz, J.-C. (1977). *Nature*, **268**, 745-7.
Porsolt, R. D., Bertin, A., and Jalfre, M. (1977). *Arch. Int. Pharmacodyn. Ther.*, **229**, 327-35.
Reisine, T. D., Nagy, A. L., Beaumont, K., Fibiger, H. I., and Yamamura, H. I. (1979). *Brain Res.*, **177**, 241-5.
Sabol, S. L., Yoshikawa, K., and Hong, J. S. (1983). *Biochem. Biophys. Res. Commun.*, **113**, 391-9.
Schechter, M. D., and Chance, W. T. (1979). *Eur. J. Pharmacol.*, **60**, 139-43.
Schwartz, J.-C., Costentin, J., and Lecomte, J.-M. (1985). *Trends Pharmacol. Sci.*, **6**, 472-6.
Schwartz, J.-C., De La Baume, S., Yi, C. C., Chaillet, P., Marcais-Collado, H., and Costentin, J. (1982). *Prog. Neuro. Psych.*, **6**, 665-71.
Schwartz, J.-C., Malfroy, B., and De La Baume, S. (1981). *Life Sci.*, **29**, 1715-40.
Sivam, S. P., Strunk, C., Smith, D. R., and Hong, J. S. (1986). *Mol. Pharmacol.*, **30**, 186-91.
Smith, C. B., Sheldon, M. I., Bednarczyk, J. H., and Villarreal, J. E. (1972). *J. Pharmacol. Exp. Ther.*, **180**, 547-57.

Staunton, D. A., Deyo, S. N., Shoemaker, W. J., Etterberg, A., and Bloom, F. E. (1982). *Life Sci.*, **39**, 1837–40.

Sulser, F., Ventulani, J., and Mobly, P. L. (1978). *Biochem. Pharmacol.*, **27**, 257–61.

Tanaka, M., Kohno, Y., Nakagawa, R., Ida, Y., Imori, K., Hoaki, Y., Tsuda, A., and Nagakai, N. (1982). *Life Sci.*, **30**, 1663–9.

Wood, P. L. (1982). *Eur. J. Pharmacol.*, **82**, 119–20.

Yarbrough, G. G., Buxbaum, D. M., and Sander-Bush, E. (1973). *J. Pharmacol. Exp. Ther.*, **185**, 328–35.

Young, W. S., Bird, S. J., and Kuhar, M. J. (1977). *Brain Res.*, **129**, 366–70.

24

Neuroendocrine Responses in Major Depression

P. Rogue, J. P. Macher, R. Minot, F. Duval, M. A. Crocq and F. Fleck

Various neuroendocrine abnormalities have been reported in depressives as a group (see for review Kalin and Dawson, 1986). The way they relate to the aetiology of depression remains unknown. Yet there must be some form of association between these alterations. The use of a battery of neuroendocrine tests, whereby multiple hormonal responses to a series of challenges are measured in the same patients, allows the study of these interrelationships. Through this strategy an increased variability in neuroendocrine responsiveness (Amsterdam *et al.*, 1983), and the presence of more abnormalities in patients with a positive familial history (Rogue *et al.*, 1985), have been evidenced in major depression.

The use of several pharmacological agents known to have selective effects on specific receptors not only can help identify possible patterns of hormonal dysfunction, but also provides an integrative approach to physiopathology. Attention here has particularly focused on central noradrenergic and serotoninergic systems. The secretion of pituitary hormones in response to specific challenges can be considered as a window open upon these pathways. A blunting of the growth hormone secretion after administration of the α_2-selection agonist clonidine is a consistent finding (Matussek *et al.*, 1980; Siever *et al.*, 1982). Though less well replicated, an enhanced cortisol response to 5-hydroxytryptophan has also been reported (Meltzer *et al.*, 1984 and 1986). Recent evidence suggests a very close link between noradrenergic and serotoninergic systems. Selective lesioning of the forebrain serotoninergic system results in an increase in the number of adrenergic receptors in the frontal cortex and hippocampus of rats (Stockmeier *et al.*, 1985). β-adrenergic receptors are involved in the mechanism of action of antidepressant treatments which desensitise and often down-regulate them, and this phenomenon is prevented by specific lesions of central serotoninergic axons (Janowsky et al., 1982). α_2-adrenergic receptors also influence β-adrenergic receptors. α_2-adrenergic agonists, though having alone little effect on cyclicAMP production in brain slices, amplify the response to the β-adrenergic agonists isoproterenol, and this potentiating effect is diminished after chronic administration of antidepressants (Pilc and Enna, 1986).

These interactions may be of importance in the physiopathology of depression, and they can be studied in patients using a neuroendocrine test battery with suitable challenges. We here report preliminary results obtained with such a strategy. We administered on following days 5-hydroxytryptophan (5-HTP) and clonidine, and measured the growth hormone (GH), prolactin, cortisol and adrenocorticotropic hormone (ACTH) responses of subjects with major depression as compared with patients with schizoaffective disorder and schizophrenia. Insensitivity to dexamethasone suppression of cortisol secretion, though of unclear significance, is the most widely documented endocrine abnormality in depression. The dexamethasone suppression test (DST) was therefore also practised. Other endocrine parameters were monitored, but they are not considered in this chapter.

24.1 Subjects and Methods

We studied 25 recently admitted patients who met DSM III criteria for either major depressive episode (MDE, 8 women and 4 men), schizophrenia (1 woman and 7 men) or schizoaffective disorder (SzAD, 3 women and 2 men). Normal controls (4 women and 1 man) were also included for certain tests; they consisted of drug-free hospital personnel and were studied as outpatients. All subjects were determined to be free of serious medical illness on the basis of a complete physical, neurologic and biological evaluation. Before testing they were evaluated using the Brief Psychiatric Rating Scale (BPRS) and the 24-item Hamilton Rating Scale (HRS) for depression. The demographic features for the sample are described in Table 24.1.

Tests were performed in a sequential fashion at the end of a minimum 1 week in-hospital washout period. On day 1, the DST was performed according to the protocol described by Carroll et al. (1981). Serum cortisol was assayed at 08.00, 16.00 and 23.00 hours after the ingestion of 1 mg of dexamethasone at 23.00 hours the previous day. At 08.00 hours on day 4, following an overnight fast, an i.v. line was inserted into a forearm vein and kept open by a slow infusion of a 0.9% saline solution. Subjects remained recumbent for the duration of the test. 5-HTP (200 mg) was given orally (Meltzer et al., 1984) at 08.30 hours. Blood for plasma GH, prolactin, cortisol and ACTH determination was drawn 30 minutes, 15 minutes and immediately prior to 5-HTP ingestion, and 15, 30, 60, 90, 120 and 150 minutes after. Blood pressure was monitored at each sampling time-

Table 24.1 Demographic and clinical data for patient groups and controls*

	Major depressive episode	DSM III diagnostic categories schizoaffective disorder	Schizophrenia	Controls
Age, years	39.9 (12.4)	37.6 (16.4)	27.1 (6.8)	26.3 (5.1)
Sex, M/F	4/8	2/3	7/1	1/4
Weight, kg	65.6 (8.4)	59.5 (5.8)	67.3 (1.2)	
Height, cm	161 (6)	165 (11)	168 (8)	
BPRS NS	46 (4)	55 (20)	54 (4)	
HRS † NS	29 (11)	29 (14)	25 (12)	

*(Standard deviation.) †24-item Hamilton Rating Scale for depression.

point. A similar protocol was followed on day 7 for the clonidine test (5 µg/kg given orally) (Charney et al., 1982).

The blood aliquots were drawn in chilled tubes; EDTA was added for ACTH sampling. Plasma was separated by centrifugation at $4\,^{\circ}C$ within 2 hours of drawing and stored at $-20\,^{\circ}C$ until the time of assay. Hormone levels were determined by radioimmunoassay. Intra- and interassay coefficients of variation were respectively: 5.2% and 8.3% (GH); 7.7% and 9.0% (prolactin); 3.2% and 5.0% (cortisol); 6.2 and 8.3% (ACTH).

Data from time-points -15 and 0 minutes were averaged to obtain a single baseline value for each hormone. Maximum increment of hormonal release (delta) above the baseline was then calculated by subtracting this basal value from the peak concentration (Table 24.2). The criterion for non-suppression following DST was failure to suppress the serum cortisol concentration below 193 nmol/l (laboratory norm) in any one of the three samples. A blunted GH response to clonidine was arbitrarily defined as a delta-GH less than 8 ng/ml; this corresponds approximately to one standard deviation below the mean value for controls. Differences between subject groups were compared using analysis of variance for continuous data and chi-squared tests for categorical data. The relationships between hormonal delta-values and diagnosis, anthropometric features and rating scale scores, were analysed by multiple linear regression and Pearson correlation coefficients.

24.2 Results

Table 24.1 shows the demographic and clinical ratings of the patients and normal subjects. The proportion of males was significantly higher among schizophrenics than in the other patients categories ($\chi^2 = 6.003$, $df = 2$, $p < 0.05$). Schizophrenics tended to be younger than the other patients but this trend was not significant ($F2, 24 = 2.903$, $p < 0.10$).

GH response to clonidine stimulation was significantly blunted in MDE and SzAD patients as compared with schizophrenics ($F2, 21 = 4.176$, $p < 0.05$) (Fig. 24.1) and controls. However there was a significant negative correlation between delta-GH values and age ($r = -0.478$, $df = 21$, $p < 0.025$) (Fig. 24.2). Though diagnosis was significant, multiple linear regression using delta-GH as the dependent variable confirmed that age also significantly explained part of the variance ($r^2 = 0.228$). There were no significant intergroup differences for the other hormonal parameters measured after clonidine. In particular, we could not reproduce the greater cortisol decrease reported in depressives as compared with controls (Siever et al., 1984a) ($F2, 22 = 0.737$, $p > 0.25$). Neither did the blood pressure fall differ.

Similarly, neuroendocrine responses to 5-HTP did not differ significantly across subject groups. An enhanced 5-HTP-induced plasma cortisol rise has been reported in depressives as compared with controls (Meltzer et al., 1984, 1986).

Table 24.2　Maximum hormonal responses of patients*

	Major depressive episode	DSM III diagnostic categories schizoaffective disorder	Schizophrenia
Clonidine challenge			
delta-GH (ng/ml)	5.3 (7.7)	2.4 (1.9)	16.1 (13.1)
delta-prolactin (ng/ml)	4.6 (3.8)	2.3 (1.2)	4.3 (2.4)
delta-cortisol (nmol/l)	267 (137)	189 (55)	242 (119)
delta-ACTH (pg/ml)	9 (9)	2.3 (1.5)	13.2 (9.3)
5-HTP challenge			
delta-GH (ng/ml)	2 (1.7)	4.3 (5.8)	1
delta-prolactin (ng/ml)	3.4 (1.5)	4.3 (2.1)	4.4 (3.6)
delta-cortisol (nmol/l)	260 (130)	211 (107)	226 (92)
delta-ACTH (pg/ml)	10.9 (8)	9.2 (10)	10.9 (10.4)

*(Standard deviation.) Delta: maximum increment of hormonal release.

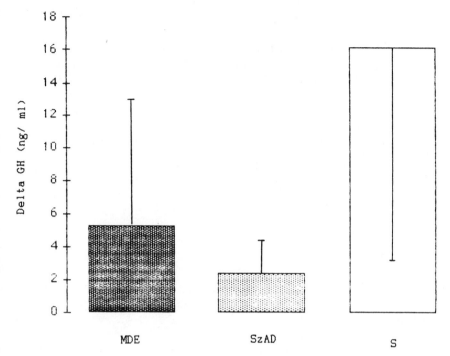

Fig. 24.1 GH response to clonidine across diagnostic categories (MDE, major depressive episode; SzAD, schizoaffective disorder; S, schizophrenia) (mean ± SD).

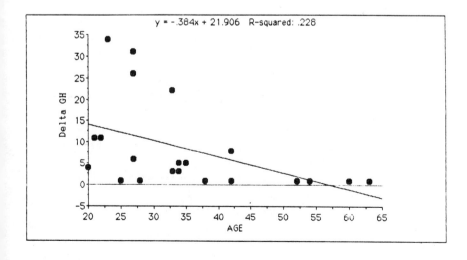

Fig. 24.2 Correlation between delta-GH and age.

In our sample there was a trend for greater delta-cortisol values in MDE cases than in controls, but it was seen in all patient categories and was not significant ($F2, 27 = 2.604, 0.05 < p < 0.10$). The plasma prolactin rise induced by another serotoninergic agonist, fenfluramine, has been found to be blunted in depressed patients (Siever et al., 1984b). Again, we could not reproduce this finding ($F2, 15 = 0.184, p > 0.25$).

Finally, dexamethasone non-suppression was unevenly distributed, with a tendency to be more frequent in MDE cases than in other patient categories ($\chi^2 = 4.977$, $df = 2$, $0.05 < p < 0.10$). Subjects with major depression also had significantly more endocrine abnormalities than other patients ($\chi^2 = 13.075$, $df = 4, p < 0.02$).

24.3 Comment

The MDE and SzAD patients in this study show a blunted GH secretion in responses to clonidine, even after allowing for age. Such a blunting is well documented in depression (Matussek et al., 1980; Siever et al., 1982) and reveals hyporesponsiveness of central postsynaptic α_2-adrenergic receptors. For MDE cases, it is associated with dexamethasone non-suppression, itself indicative of hyporeactive central glucocorticoid receptors.

No relationship was found with results from the 5-HTP test. Meltzer et al. (1984, 1986) have reported an enhanced cortisol secretion in response to this challenge, and taken this as evidence for supersensitive 5-HT receptors in depressive patients. Our negative results could be the consequence of the limited sample-size, especially with regard to controls. However, the regulation of cortisol secretion is complex, and 5-HTP may not be a specific serotoninergic agonist (van Praag, 1986). Furthermore, overall evidence seems more in favour of the original 'indoleamine hypothesis of depression' rather than with the 'hypersensitive serotonin receptor' theory (Willner, 1985).

An increased clonidine-induced plasma cortisol fall in major depression has been found by Siever et al. (1984a). However, studies of α_2-adrenergic receptors in depression show somewhat divergent results. Thus the cortisol responses to the α_2-adrenergic antagonist yohimbine has also been reported to be significantly greater in depressed patients than in controls (Price et al., 1986). Results from radioligand binding techniques are also discrepant (Piletz et al., 1986). The dysregulation hypothesis of depression (Siever and Davis, 1985) is a model which could account for this discrepancy. It supposes that persistant impairment in one or more neurotransmitter homeostatic mechanism is implicated in the physiolpathology of affective disorders. It is compatible with the increased variability in hormonal responses seen using a neuroendocrine test battery (Amsterdam et al., 1983) as well as with the present results.

This impairment of neurotransmitter homeostasis could be linked to a dysfunction of the transduction mechanisms which generate second messengers, that is cyclic AMP or phosphatydylinositoldiphosphate cleavage products. An abnormality at this level could account both for the multiplicity of receptor changes encountered in depression and for the possible existence of a predisposing single gene defect. Better knowledge of these complex systems will no doubt help further our understanding of the neuroendocrine alterations encountered in affective disorders.

Bibliography

Amsterdam, J. D., Winokur, A., Lucki, I., Caroff, S., Snyder, P., and Rickels, K. (1983). A neuroendocrine test battery in bipolar patients and healthy controls. *Archives of General Psychiatry*, **40**, 515-21.

Carroll, B. J., Feinberg, M., Greden, J. F., Tarika, J., Albala, A. A., Haskett, R. F., James, N., Kronfol, Z., Lohr, N., Steiner, M., de Vigne, J. P., and Young, E. (1981). A specific laboratory test for the diagnosis of melancholia. Standardization, validation and clinical utility. *Arch. Gen. Psychiatry*, **38**, 15-22.

Charney, D. S., Heninger, G. R., Steinberg, D. E., Hafstad, K. M., Giddings, S., and Landis, D. H., (1982). Adrenergic receptor sensitivity in depression. Effects of clonidine in depressed patients and healthy subjects. *Arch. Gen. Psychiatry*, **39**, 290-4.

Janowsky, A., Okada, F., Manier, D. H., Applegate, C. L., Sulzer, F. E., and Steranka, L. R. (1982). Role of serotoninergic input in the regulation of the adrenergic receptor-coupled adenylate cyclase system. *Science*, **218**, 900-1.

Kalin, N. H., Dawson, G. (1986). Neuroendocrine dysfunction in depression: hypothalamic-anterior pituitary systems. *Trends in Neuroscience*, **9**, 261-6.

Matussek, N., Ackenheil, M., Hippius, H., Muller, F., Schroder, H. T. H., Schultes, H., and Wasilewski, B. (1980). Effects of clonidine on growth hormone release in psychiatric patients and controls. *Psychiatry Res.*, **2**, 25-36.

Meltzer, H. Y., Umberkoman-Witta, B., Robertson, A., Tricou, B. J., and Perline, R. (1984). Effects of 5-hydroxytryptophan on serum cortisol levels in major affective disorders. *Arch. Gen. Psychiatry*, **41**, 366-74.

Meltzer, H. Y., Umberkoman-Witta, B., Robertson, A., Tricou, B. J., and Perline, R. (1986). Correction and amplification: cortisol responses to 5-HTP. *Arch. Gen. Psychiatry*, **43**, 815.

Piletz, J. E., Schubert, D. S., and Halaris, A. (1986). Evaluation of studies on platelet alpha 2-adrenoreceptors in depressive illness. *Life Sciences*, **39**, 1589-1616.

Price, L. H., Charney, D. S., Rubin, A. L., and Heninger, G. R. (1986). α2-adrenergic receptor function in depression. The cortisol response to yohimbine. *Arch. Gen. Psychiatry*, **43**, 849-58.

Pilc, A., Enna, S. J. (1986). Antidepressant administration has a differential effect on rat brain $α_2$-adrenoreceptor sensitivity to agonists and antagonists. *Eur. J. of Pharmacol.*, **132**, 277-82. *Science*, **230**, 323-5.

Rogue, P., Duval, F., Crocq, M. A., Minot, R., Macher, J. P., Gindein, J., and Fleck, F. (1985). Genetic aspects of the responses to a neuroendocrine test battery in affective illness. In *Abstr. Assn Européenne de Psychiatrie*, 2nd Annual Meeting, Strasburg, 1985.

Siever, L. J., Uhde, T. W., Silberman, E. K., Jimerson, D. C., Aloi, J. A., Post, R. M., and Murphy, D. L. (1982). The growth hormone response as a probe of noradrenergic responsiveness in affective disorder patients and controls. *Psychiatry Res.*, **6**, 171-183.

Siever, L. J., Uhde, T. W., Jimerson, D. C., Post, R. M., Lake, R., and Murphy, D. L. (1984a). Plasma cortisol responses to clonidine in depressed patients and controls. *Arch. Gen. Psychiatry*, **41**, 63-8.

Siever, L. J., Murphy, D. L., Slater, S., de la Vega, E., Lipper, E. (1984b). Plasma prolactin changes following fenfluramine in depressed patients compared to controls: an evaluation of central serotoninergic responsivity in depression. *Life Sciences*, **34**, 1029–39.

Siever, L. J., Davis, K. L. (1985). Overview: toward a dysregulation hypothesis of depression. *Am. J. Psychiatry*, **142**, 1017–31.

Stockmeier, C. A., Martino, A. M., and Kellar, K. J. (1985). A strong influence of serotonin axons on β-adrenergic receptors in rat brain. *Science*, **230**, 393–5.

Van Praag, H. M. (1987). Measuring central serotoninergic function via the 'neuroendocrine window'. *Actualities Psychiatriques* (in press).

Willner, P. (1985). Antidepressants and serotonergic neurotransmission: an integrative review. *Psychopharmacol.*, **85**, 387–404.

25

Prediction of Treatment Response to Selective Antidepressants from Clonidine and Apomorphine Neuroendocrine Challenges

M. Ansseau, R. von Frenckell, D. Maassen, J.-L. Cerfontaine, P. Papart,
M. Timsit-Berthier, J. -J. Legros and G. Franck

25.1 Introduction

Classically, the biochemical pathophysiology of depression is based on central disturbances in catecholaminergic and serotonergic neurotransmission (van Praag, 1980a, b). However, antidepressants are only effective in 60 to 75% of depressive disorders and their success rates are very similar in double-blind studies (Davis, 1985). Recent 'second-generation' antidepressants are characterised by their selective activity on neurotransmitter systems. Compounds like zimeldine, fluoxetine, or fluvoxamine selectively inhibit serotonin reuptake, while compounds like nomifensine, maprotiline, or amineptine selectively inhibit catecholamine reuptake. However, it remains quite difficult to define either by clinical or biological parameters which patients would preferentially benefit from one or the other type of antidepressants.

The growth hormone (GH) response to pharmacologic agents may provide an indirect index of the functional state of neurotransmitter systems, which could help to define individual biochemical patterns of depression that could facilitate more specific treatment (Ansseau et al., 1984). A blunted GH response to clonidine might be an argument favouring noradrenergic deficit and therefore orientate to 'noradrenergic' antidepressants (Matussek et al., 1980; Checkley et al., 1981; Ansseau et al., 1987 and submitted), while a blunted GH response to apomorphine might represent an argument favouring dopaminergic deficit and therefore orientate to 'dopaminergic' antidepressants (Ansseau *et al.*, 1986, 1987 and submitted). A normal GH response to both challenges could reflect normal catecholaminergic neurotransmission and orientate to 'serotonergic' antidepressants.

In this context, the purpose of our study was to investigate possible differences in treatment outcome following selective antidepressants in major depressive outpatients according to their normal or blunted GH response following clonidine and apomorphine challenges. Two antidepressants were compared: zimeldine, which selectively inhibits serotonin reuptake (Heel *et al.*, 1982), and nomifensine, which selectively inhibits noradrenaline and dopamine reuptake (Hoffmann, 1982).

25.2 Methods

25.2.1 Subjects

A total of 62 major depressive inpatients defined according to Research Diagnostic Criteria (Spitzer *et al.*, 1978) were included in the study. This sample comprised 32 male and 30 female patients, with age ranging from 19 to 66 years (mean age = 42.0 ± 11.9 years). All patients were free of medical illness and tested after a drug-free period of at least two weeks. They were informed of the purpose of the study and gave their consent.

25.2.2 Neuroendocrine Test Procedures

Clonidine and apomorphine challenge tests were performed in this order according to the same procedure with at least a 2-day interval between the tests. At 7 a.m., after an overnight fast, an indwelling catheter was inserted in a forearm vein. Blood samples of 10 ml were collected every 20 minutes for 40 minutes before and 120 minutes after injection at 8 a.m. of either clonidine 0.15 mg, diluted in saline to obtain 20 ml intravenously in 10 minutes, or apomorphine 0.5 mg, diluted in saline to obtain 0.5 ml subcutaneously.

The neuroendocrine tests were performed between the third and the twelfth day of the menstrual cycle in premenopausal women. Patients with a basal systolic blood pressure less than 100 mlHg were excluded from the study. Moreover, in order to be included, patients should present basal (t_0) GH level less than 5 ng/ml before both pharmacologic challenges (Ansseau *et al.*, 1984). Normal GH response to both pharmacologic agents was defined by a GH peak following injection higher than 5 ng/ml (Ansseau *et al.*, 1984).

GH was measured with a double antibody radioimmunoassay, with intra- and inter-assay coefficients of variation of respectively $13.3 \pm 4.7\%$ and $14.8 \pm 9.6\%$ and a detection limit of 0.2 ng/ml (Franchimont, 1968).

25.2.3 Treatment Procedure

After completion of neuroendocrine tests, patients were randomly assigned to treatment by either nomifensine or zimeldine: 100 mg during 3 days then 200 mg during the remaining of a three-week period. All clinical evaluations were made without knowledge of endocrine data. Clinical results following the three weeks of therapy were assessed by means of the second part of the Clinical Global Impression (CGI-2) (Guy, 1976), with scores ranging from 1 to 7 according to the following meaning: 1 = very much improved, 2 = much improved, 3 = minimally improved, 4 = no change, 5 = minimally worse, 6 = much worse, 7 = very much worse. In case of treatment failure (CGI-2 $\geqslant$ 3), the patients were then switched to the other antidepressant for 3 more weeks and reassessed with CGI-2.

25.2.4 Data Analysis

For clonidine as well as apomorphine challenges, treatment response as measured by CGI-2 was assessed by variance analysis (ANOVA), including three factors: GH response (blunted v. normal), antidepressant (zimeldine v. nomifensine), and the interaction between GH response and antidepressant.

25.3 Results

25.3.1 Clonidine Test

Following clonidine, 30 patients exhibited a blunted GH response and 23 patients a normal GH stimulation. Their assignment to nomifensine or zimeldine, their mean final CGI-2 scores as well as the number of patients who had to be switched to the other compound and their final CGI-2 scores are displayed in Table 25.1. The ANOVA was statistically significant ($F = 6.8$, df = 3, $p = 0.0006$). Patients with blunted GH response exhibited a trend toward better treatment outcome as compared with patients with normal GH response ($2.57 \, v. \, 3.33, f = 2.9, p = 0.10$) and zimeldine was more active than nomifensine ($2.31 \, v. \, 3.33, \, f = 8.4, \, p = 0.006$). However, the maximal statistical difference came from the interaction between GH response and antidepressant ($f = 9.1; \, p = 0.004$): patients with normal GH response responded much better to zimeldine than to nomifensine. Supporting these results is the finding that 92% of nomifensine-treated patients had to be switched to zimeldine while only 11% of zimeldine-treated patients had to be switched to nomifensine.

Table 25.1 CGI-2 mean scores ± SD following treatment by nomifensine (nom) or zimeldine (zim) among patients with blunted or normal GH response to clonidine

	First antidepressant	Switch in case of failure
Blunted GH response (n = 30)	nom (n = 15) = 2.60 ± 1.24 →	zim (n = 8) = 2.13 ± 0.64
	zim (n = 15) = 2.53 ± 1.36 →	nom (n = 6) = 1.83 ± 0.75
Normal GH response (n = 23)	nom (n = 12) = 4.25 ± 1.60 →	zim (n = 11) = 1.82 ± 0.87
	zim (n = 11) = 2.00 ± 0.77 →	nom (n = 1) = 1.00 ± 0.0

Table 25.2 CGI-2 mean scores ± SD following treatment by nomifensine (nom) or zimeldine (zim) among patients with blunted or normal GH response to apomorphine

	First antidepressant	Switch in case of failure
Blunted GH response (n = 15)	nom (n = 7) = 1.43 ± 0.79 ⟶	zim (n = 1) = 1.00 ± 0.00
	zim (n = 8) = 3.13 ± 1.36 ⟶	nom (n = 6) = 2.00 ± 1.10
Normal GH response (n = 39)	nom (n = 21) = 4.38 ± 1.12 ⟶	zim (n = 21) = 2.10 ± 0.83
	zim (n = 18) = 2.11 ± 0.96 ⟶	nom (n = 2) = 2.00 ± 1.40

25.3.2 Apomorphine Test

Following apomorphine, 15 patients exhibited a blunted GH response and 39 patients a normal GH stimulation. The assignment of patient to nomifensine or zimeldine, their mean final CGI-2 scores as well as the number of patients who had to be switched to the other compound and their final CGI-2 scores are displayed in Table 25.2. The ANOVA was statistically significant ($F = 20.8$, $df = 3$, $p = 0.0001$). Patients with blunted GH response responded better than patients with normal GH response ($F = 9.4$, $p = 0.003$). Zimeldine was more effective than nomifensine ($F = 17.5$, $p = 0.0001$) and the interaction between GH response and antidepressant was also very significant ($F = 35.4$, $p = 0.0001$). While patients with blunted GH response responded better to nomifensine than to zimeldine, the opposite was true for patients who exhibited normal GH response. These results are confirmed by the proportion of patients who had to be switched to the other compound: among patients with blunted GH response, 14% of nomifensine-treated subjects as compared with 75% of zimeldine-treated subjects and among patients with normal GH stimulation, 100% of nomifensine-treated subjects as compared with 11% of zimeldine-treated subjects.

25.4 Discussion

The results of this study suggest that GH response to clonidine or apomorphine may be helpful in predicting treatment outcome following selective antidepressants. Schematically, a normal GH response to clonidine is indicative of a good outcome following a 'serotonergic' antidepressant such as zimeldine; however, a blunted GH response following clonidine is not associated with a preferential response to a selective antidepressant of any type. Following apomorphine, a normal GH response indicates favouring a better outcome with zimeldine, a blunted GH response a preferential response to a 'catecholaminergic' antidepressant such as nomifensine.

These results are in agreement with the proposed interpretation of blunted response to catecholaminergic challenges. A blunted response to clonidine could correspond to a central noradrenergic hyposensitivity and therefore orientate to drugs which increase noradrenergic neurotransmission. A blunted GH response to apomorphine could correspond to a decreased sensitivity in central dopaminergic receptors and therefore is consistent with the better treatment outcome following antidepressants which increase dopaminergic neurotransmission. The only discrepant finding in our study is the lack of better response to nomifensine among patients with blunted response to clonidine. According to recent studies, a blunted GH response to clonidine may represent a 'trait marker' for depressive disorders (Hoehe et al., 1986; Siever et al., 1986; Ansseau et al., 1987). Indeed, depressive patients tested after complete remission of their depressive episode still exhibited blunted GH response to clonidine. Our results suggest that those patients may be treated by 'catecholaminergic' as well as 'serotonergic' antidepressants. In contrast, major depressives which do not exhibit this 'trait marker' would suffer from a 'serotonergic' depression.

Unfortunately, both nomifensine and zimeldine have been withdrawn from the market because of side-effects. However, the conclusions of this study may probably be applicable to antidepressants exhibiting similar biochemical profiles.

In conclusion, the GH response to pharmacologic agents seems to present considerable interest for the orientation to selective antidepressants. In comparison with clinical symptoms which lack specific association with biochemical mechanisms and to plasma, urinary, or cerebrospinal fluid levels of neurotransmitter metabolites, such as 3-methoxy-4-hydroxyphenylglycol (MHPG) and 5-hydroxy-indolacetic acid (5-HIAA), which yield controversial interest (Zarifian and Lôo, 1982), the GH response to clonidine and apomorphine may represent an actual advance towards a more selective and more active antidepressant therapy.

References

Ansseau, M., Scheyvaerts, M., Doumont, A., Poirrier, R., Legros, J. J., and Franck, G. (1984). Concurrent use of REM latency, dexamethasone suppression, clonidine, and apomorphine tests as biological markers of endogenous depression: a pilot study. *Psychiat. Res.*, **12**, 261–72.

Ansseau, M., von Frenckell, R., Cerfontaine, J. L., Papart, P., Franck, G., Timsit-Berthier, M., Geenen, V., and Legros, J. J. (1987). Neuroendocrine evaluation of catecholaminergic neurotransmission in mania. *Psychiat. Res.*, in press.

Ansseau, M., von Frenckell, R., Cerfontaine, J. L., Papart, P., Franck, G., Timsit-Berthier, M., Geenen, V., and Legros, J. J. (subm.). Neuroendocrine evidence for noradrenergic and dopaminergic disturbance in endogenous depression. *Br. J. Psychiat.*

Ansseau, M., von Frenckell, R., Franck, G., Timsit-Berthier, M., Geenen, V., and Legros, J. J. (1986). Blunted growth hormone responses to clonidine and apomorphine challenges in endogenous depression. In Shagass, C., Josiassen, R. C., Bridger, W. H., Weiss, K. S., Stoff, D., Simpson, G. M. (eds.), *Biological Psychiatry 1985*, Elsevier, New York, 793–5.

Checkley, S. A., Slade, A. P., and Shur, E. (1981). Growth hormone and other responses to clonidine in patients with endogenous depression. *Br. J. Psychiat.*, **138**, 51–5.

Davis, J. M. (1985). 'Antidepressants'. In Sadock, B. J., and Kaplan, H. I. (eds.), *Comprehensive Textbook of Psychiatry IV*. Williams & Wilkins, Baltimore, 1513–37.

Franchimont, P. (1968). Le dosage radio-immunologique de l'hormone de croissance humaine. *Cah. Méd. Lyonnais*, **44**, 887–98.

Guy, W. (ed.) (1976). *ECDEU Assessment Manual for Psychopharmacology*. National Institute of Mental Health, Psychopharmacology Research Branch, Rockville, Md.

Heel, R. C., Morley, P. A., Brogden, R. N., Carmine, A. A., Speight, T. M., and Avery, G. S. (1982). Zimeldine: A review of its pharmacological properties and therapeutic efficacy in depressive illness. *Drugs*, **24**, 169–206.

Hoehe, M., Valido, G., and Matussek, N. (1986). Growth hormone response to clonidine in endogenous depressive patients: Evidence for a trait marker in depression. In Shagass, C., Josiassen, R. C., Bridger, W. H., Weiss, K. S., Stoff, D., and Simpson, G. M. (eds.), *Biological Psychiatry 1985*. Elsevier, New York, 862–4.

Hoffmann, I. (1982). Pharmacology of nomifensine. *Int. Pharmacopsychiat.*, **17**, 4–20.

Matussek, N., Hippius, H., Muller, H., Schroder, F., Schultes, H.Th., Wasilewski, B. (1980). Effect of clonidine on growth hormone release in psychiatric patients and controls. *Psychiat. Res.*, **2**, 25–36.

Siever, L. J., Coccaro, E. F., Adan, F., Benjamin, E., and Davis, K. L. (1986). The growth hormone response to clonidine in acute and remitted affective disorder patients. In Shagass, C., Josiassen, R. C., Bridger, W. H., Weiss, K. S., Stoff, D., and Simpson, G. M. (eds.), *Biological Psychiatry 1985*, Elsevier, New York, 791-2.

Spitzer, R. L., Endicott, J., and Robins, E. (1978). Research Diagnostic Criteria: Rationale and reliability. *Arch. Gen. Psychiat.*, **35**, 773-82.

van Praag, H. M. (1980a). Central monoamine metabolism in depressions. I. Serotonin and related compounds. *Compreh. Psychiat.*, **21**, 30-43.

van Praag, H. M. (1980b). Central monoamine metabolism in depressions. II. Catecholamines and related compounds. *Compreh. Psychiat.*, **21**, 44-54.

Zarifian, E., Lôo, H. (1982). *Les Antidépresseurs. Aspects Biologiques, Cliniques et Thérapeutiques*, Roche, Paris.

26

Defective Second-messenger Function in the Etiology of Endogenous Depression: Novel Therapeutic Approaches

H. Wachtel

26.1 Introduction

The discovery of the antidepressant activity of iproniazid (Crane, 1957; Loomer et al., 1957) and of imipramine (Kuhn, 1957) strongly stimulated the formulation of hypotheses on the physical basis of endogenous depression. It soon became clear that both types of drugs accomplished a similar effect: an increase of the concentration of the monoamines noradrenaline (NA), dopamine (DA) or serotonin (5-HT) in the synaptic cleft with a consequent greater stimulation of postsynaptic receptors. This effect is achieved by iproniazid by blockade of the metabolism of monoamines within presynaptic nerve terminals via inhibition of monoamine oxidase (MAO) (Spector et al., 1958) and by the tricyclic agent imipramine by inhibition of the reuptake of monoamines into the nerve endings from which they were released (Axelrod et al., 1961). These pharmacological findings provided a foundation for a now widely accepted hypothesis that a deficient monoaminergic transmission in the central nervous system (CNS) plays an important role in the etiology of endogenous depression (Schildkraut, 1965; Coppen, 1967; Lapin and Oxenkrug, 1969; Horn et al., 1971). Since the discovery of MAO inhibition and reuptake blockade, another mechanism of antidepressant drug action has emerged with mianserin which blocks central presynaptic α_2-receptors, thereby causing enhanced release of NA into the synaptic cleft (Baumann and Maitre, 1977).

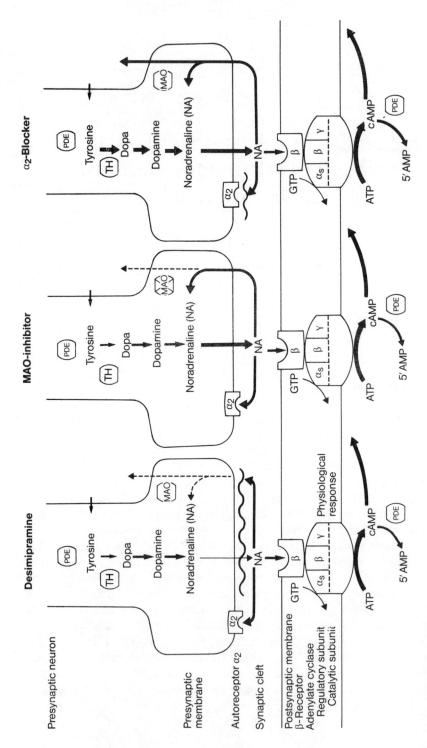

Fig. 26.1 (*caption opposite*)

MAO: Monoaminooxidase
PDE: Phosphodiesterase
TH: Tyrosinhydroxylase

Thus, all somatic treatments currently used in the therapy of endogenous depression have in common the ability to intensify acutely in animal experiments the monoamine (MA) availability at central synapses. This is achieved by three mechanisms of action: (1) inhibition of monoamine reuptake, (2) inhibition of intraneuronal monoamine catabolism and (3) increase of monoamine release. They all rely upon interactions with neuronal target sites located *presynaptically* to increase monoamine concentrations in the synaptic cleft with a consequent greater stimulus to post-synaptic receptors (Fig. 26.1). The newer antidepressants developed during the last 30 years represent perpetuations and refinements of the established principles which have resulted in more selective drugs with fewer side-effects but no clear-cut improvement of antidepressant activity.

The present work is aimed at showing up alternatives for the development of novel, more reliably effective antidepressants. Whereas research on antidepressants up to now has concentrated on influencing the neurotransmission via the first messengers (monoamines) and therefore acting extracellularly, in this chapter some aspects of the neuronal signal transduction process *beyond the receptor level* are considered as potential target sites for the development of novel antidepressants. In pursuit of this approach, rolipram, a stereospecific inhibitor of a neuronal calmodulin-independent cyclic adenosine $3',5'$-monophosphate (cAMP) phosphodiesterase (PDE) isoenzyme, was predicted to exert antidepressant activity at 10 to 100 times lower dosages than conventional antidepressants (Wachtel, 1982a; 1983a; Przegalinski and Bigajska, 1983). The antidepressant activity of rolipram was confirmed in open and controlled clinical trials in patients with endogenous depression (Zeller *et al.*, 1984; Horowski and Sastre-y-Hernandez, 1985; Bobon *et al.*, 1986; Bertolino *et al.*, unpublished

---

Fig. 26.1 (opposite) Influence of classic antidepressants on monoaminergic neurotransmission shown on a noradrenaline (NA) synapse. Tricyclic antidepressants like desipramine prevent the reuptake of released NA into the presynaptic neuron and thereby increase the availability of NA in the synaptic cleft. NA binds to presynaptic β-receptors to stimulate, via adenylate cyclase, the formation of the intracellular second-messenger cAMP which mediates the cullular response of the postsynaptic neuron upon the first-messenger stimulus. Part of the synaptic NA activates presynaptic α_2-receptors which inhibit further NA release. MAO inhibitors increase NA availability in the synaptic cleft by inhibiting the metabolism of recaptured NA by MAO within the presynaptic neuron. Thus, on depolarisation more NA is released which acts on β- and α_2-receptors as described above. α_2-blockers, by preventing inhibitory effects on NA release mediated by presynaptic α_2-receptors, enhance NA release and synthesis and thus increase NA availability in the synaptic cleft. NA acts on β-receptors as described above and is taken up by the presynaptic neuron to be metabolised in part by MAO. Thus, the classic antidepressants advance the first-messenger component of neurotransmission by interacting with target sites located *presynaptically*. CaM-kinases, protein kinases calmodulin dependent; cAMP-kinases, protein kinases cAMP dependent; C-kinases, protein kinases C; DG, 1,2-diacylglycerol; IP_3, inositol-1,4,5-triphosphate; M, muscarinic effect; MA_i, monoamine inhibition; MA_s, monoamine stimulation; MAO, monoamine oxidase; PDE, phosphodiesterase; PIP_2, phosphatidyl inositol-4,5-biphosphate; R_i, inhibited protein receptor; R_s, stimulated protein receptor; TH, thyrosine hydroxylase.

results). These findings are of considerable heuristic value and disclose the possibility of gaining further insight into the pathobiochemistry of affective disorders. A conceptual framework will be presented indicating that defective CNS second-messenger function might be causally linked to endogenous depression.

26.2 Signal Transduction Beyond the Receptor Level

The classic neurotransmitters (first messengers) utilise intracellular mediators (second messengers) for signal transduction to the effector cells. Two major second-messenger systems known to amplify extracellular signals are adenylate cyclase (AC) and phospholipase C (PLC). The following considerations should be seen against the background of the assumption of a functionally deficient monoaminergic transmission (Schildkraut, 1965; Coppen, 1967; Lapin and Oxenkrug, 1969; Horn *et al.*, 1971) and/or a monoaminergic-cholinergic dysbalance (Janowsky *et al.*, 1972) in the etiology of endogenous depression.

According to the latter hypothesis, a given affective state may represent a balance between central monoamine-mediated and acetylcholine (ACh)-mediated neurotransmitter activity, with depression being a disease of functionally insufficient monoaminergic neurotransmission associated with cholinergic dominance and mania being the converse (Janowsky *et al.*, 1972). In the following I will focus on post-receptor effects of ACh and of NA.

26.3 Adenylate Cyclase System

Neurotransmitter-sensitive membrane-bound adenylate cyclase catalyses the formation of the second messenger cAMP from adenosine 5'-triphosphate (ATP). Adenylate cyclase is a multicomponent system made up of several heterologous subunits that reversibly interact with each other by means of association–dissociation reactions (Fig. 26.2). The regulatory subunit (N) acts as a transducer between receptor (R) occupancy and expression of the catalytic activation of adenylate cyclase. It is a guanosine 5'-triphosphate (GTP) binding protein consisting of α-' β- and γ-subunits. The regulatory subunit is coupled either positively (N_s) or negatively (N_i) to adenylate cyclase activity; NA receptors linked stimulatorily to adenylate cyclase are β-adrenoceptors, whereas α_2-adrenoceptors are coupled inhibitorily to adenylate cyclase. The two regulatory subunits (N_s and N_i) apparently differ only in their α-subunit (α_s, α_i). Occupancy of the α subunit by GTP destabilises its interaction with the receptor and enhances its association with the catalytic subunit (C) of adenylate cyclase. Activation or inhibition of adenylate cyclase persists until GTP is hydrolysed to guanosine 5'-diphosphate (GDP) by a GTPase function of the α- and catalytic subunit complexes (for review see Codina *et al.*, 1984).

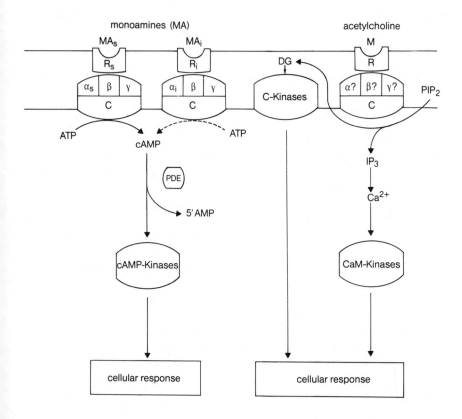

Normal

Fig. 26.2   Under normal conditions there is a well-balanced ratio of the function of the two major second-messenger systems, cAMP (left) and inositol-1,4,5-triphosphate/1,2-diacyl-glycerol (right), on cellular responses of the postsynaptic neuron reflecting the co-ordinated influence of the monoaminergic and cholinergic transmission on the effector cell. CaM-kinases, protein kinases calmodulin dependent; cAMP-kinases, protein kinases cAMP dependent; C-kinases, protein kinases C; DG, 1,2-diacylglycerol; IP_3, inositol-1,4,5-triphosphate; M, muscarinic effect; MA_i, monoamine inhibition; MA_s, monoamine stimulation; MAO, mono-amine oxidase; PDE, phosphodiesterase; PIP_2, phosphatidyl inositol-4,5-biphosphate; R_i, inhibited protein receptor; R_s, stimulated protein receptor; TH, thyrosine hydroxylase.

Some of the second messenger cAMP produced by NA via stimulation of β-adrenoceptors activates cAMP-dependent protein kinases (cAMP kinases) which, by phosphorylating enzymes or proteins of the membrane or of ion channels, regulate the cellular response of the effector cell to the first messenger stimulus (Krebs and Beavo, 1979; Levitan *et al.*, 1983). Conversion of cAMP to adenosine 5′-monophosphate (5′-AMP) by cyclic nucleotide phosphodiesterases is the only known enzymatic mechanism for terminating the actions of the second messenger; thus, phosphodiesterase plays a crucial role in determining the intensity and duration of the effector cell response to the intracellular signal (Strada *et al.*, 1984).

26.4 The Phospholipase C System

There is increasing evidence that phospholipase C (PLC) (Fig. 26.2), similar to adenylate cyclase, represents a multicomponent system consisting of a receptor protein, a GTP-binding regulatory subunit (α, β, γ) and a catalytic subunit (for review see Taylor and Merrit, 1986). Binding of acetylcholine (ACh) to muscarinic (M) receptors, or of NA to α_1-adrenoceptors, leads to the phosphodiesteratic cleavage of a small, metabolically highly active membrane pool of phosphatidylinositol-4,5-biphosphate (PIP_2) by phospholipase C to release the second messenger inositol-1,4,5-triphosphate (IP_3) and 1,2-diacylglycerol (DG). The inositol-1,4,5-triphosphate, a strong polyanionic compound, mobilises Ca^{2+} from intracellular compartments. The released Ca^{2+} binds to the intracellular calcium receptor protein calmodulin (CaM). Calmodulin activates calmodulin-dependent protein kinases (CaM kinases), whereas 1,2-diacylglycerol activates protein kinase C (C kinase), which, by phosphorylating substrate proteins, regulate the cellular response of the effector cell to the first messenger signal (Berridge, 1984; Nishizuka, 1984). Thus, as with the cAMP second-messenger system, the inositol-1,4,5 triphosphate/1,2-diacylglycerol system acts through protein phosphorylation as a final common pathway. Normally, these two second-messenger systems participate jointly in the regulation of neuronal function.

26.5 The Second-messenger Dysbalance Hypothesis

It is proposed that affective disorders arise from the dysbalance of the two major intraneuronal signal amplification systems, the adenylate cyclase–cAMP kinases system and the phospholipase C-calmoduline kinase C system with depression resulting from reduced function of the adenylate cyclase–cAMP kinase pathway (Fig. 26.3) and mania resulting from the converse. This hypothesis unites the classic monoamine hypotheses (Schildkraut, 1965; Coppen, 1967; Lapin and Oxenkrug, 1969; Horn *et al.*, 1971), the monoaminergic/cholinergic dysbalance hypothesis (Janowsky *et al.*, 1972), and the output deficiency hypothesis (Stone, 1983) and explains the therapeutic and prophylactic effect of lithium in bipolar depression. Lithium's therapeutic effect, in case of mania, would result from dampening the overactive adenylate cyclase system by means of its adenylate cyclase inhibitory action (Dousa and Hechter, 1970; Newman *et al.*, 1983) and its prophylactic effect, in case of depression,

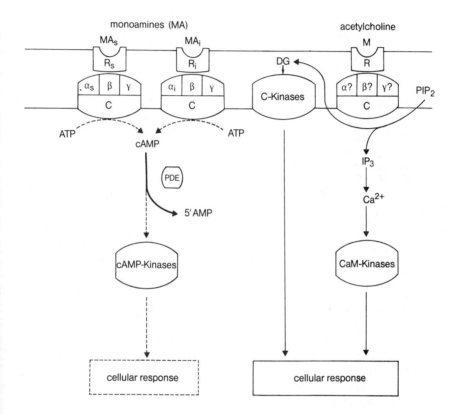

Fig. 26.3 In depression the ratio of the functions of the cAMP system (left) and the inositol-1,4,5-triphosphate/1,2-diacylglycerol system (right) on cellular responses of the postsynaptic neuron is unbalanced. There is a functional deficiency of the cAMP system compared with the inositol 1,4,5-triphosphate/1,2-diacylglycerol system reflecting the disturbed influences of the monoaminergic and cholinergic transmission on the effector cell. The functional cAMP deficiency may result from defects at the levels of (a) the presynaptic neuron, (b) the postsynaptic monoamine receptors, (c) adenylate cyclase and (d) cAMP phosphodiesterase. CaM-kinases, protein kinases calmodulin dependent; cAMP-kinases, protein kinases cAMP dependent; C-kinases, protein kinases C; DG, 1,2-diacylglycerol; IP$_3$, inositol-1,4,5-triphosphate; M, muscarinic effect; MA$_i$, monoamine inhibition; MA$_s$, monoamine stimulation; MAO, monoamine oxidase; PDE, phosphodiesterase; PIP$_2$, phosphatidyl inositol-4,5 biphosphate; R$_i$, inhibited protein receptor; R$_s$, stimulated protein receptor; TH, thyrosine hydroxylase.

from preventing over-activity of the phospholipase C system through attenuation of phosphatidyl inositol 4,5-biphosphate resynthesis by inhibition of inositol-1-phosphatase (Hallcher and Sherman, 1980; Sherman et al., 1981).

26.6 Conceivable Target Sites of Novel Antidepressants Manipulating Second-messenger Functions Beyond Transmitter Receptors

According to the second-messenger dysbalance hypothesis, the core disturbance in depression lies in the decreased functional availability of cAMP for adequate cellular responses of the effector cell. As stated above, cyclic nucleotide phosphodiesterases are the only enzymes terminating the action of cAMP. Therefore, the selective inhibition of a neuronal, low-K_m, high-affinity cAMP phosphodiesterase isoenzyme should increase cAMP availability and exert antidepressant activity (Fig. 26.4). Whichever component of the adenylate cyclase signal propagation cascade might be affected in depression (e.g. disturbance of presynaptic transmission, decreased affinity of NA to the β-receptor, decreased β-receptor density, impaired coupling between receptor and adenylate cyclase, decreased activity of the regulatory subunit or catalytic subunit or increased cAMP phosphodiesterase activity), this approach would ensure increased availability of cAMP to counterbalance the abnormal cellular response.

Alternatively, selective neurotropic phospholipase C inhibitors should be of potential usefulness for the treatment of depression. Recently we have provided evidence for antidepressant properties of forskolin, an activator of the catalytic subunit of adenylate cyclase (Wachtel and Löschmann, 1986). Theoretically also, calmodulin antagonism or protein kinase C inhibition are conceivable mechanisms. Although there is no concrete evidence, these approaches are worth pursuing.

It has previously been suggested that intracellular cAMP deficiency is related to depressive illness and that an excess leads to mania (Abdulla and Hamadah, 1970). The unexpectedly high coincidence of depression and atopic disorder, an inherited disposition to allergy, provoked Ossofsky (1976) to speculate on the basis of the β-adrenergic subsensitivity theory of atopic disease (Szentivanyi, 1968) that 'cAMP abnormality defines an *intracellular* etiology for depression'. There are some recent reports indicating decreased responsiveness or loss of responsiveness to β-agonist-stimulated cAMP accumulation in lymphocytes or leucocytes of depressed patients (Extein et al., 1979; Pandey et al., 1979). As the incidence of depression prevails in the elderly, the recently summarised evidence of an age-associated decline in β-adrenergic cAMP responsiveness in man is of particular interest (Ebstein et al., 1986); the authors suggest a deficit at two levels of the adenylate cyclase complex, namely an impaired receptor-stimulated/regulatory-subunit-stimulated and regulatory subunit stimulated/catalytic subunit coupling, respectively.

Rolipram in Depression

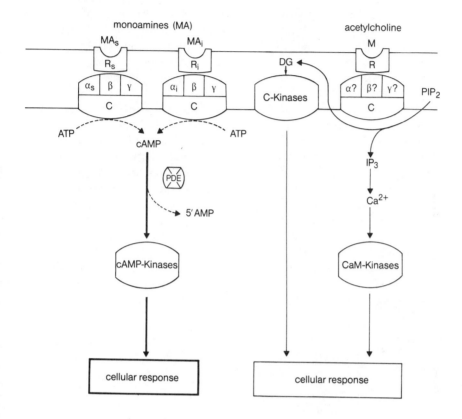

Fig. 26.4 By selectively inhibiting a neuronal low-K_m, high-affinity cAMP phosphodiesterase isoenzyme, i.e. a key enzymatic mechanism for terminating intraneuronal cAMP action, rolipram and related neurotropic cAMP-selective phosphodiesterase inhibitors increase cAMP availability to counterbalance the disturbed ratio of the cAMP and the inositol-1,4,5-triphosphate/1,2-diacylglycerol second-messenger function on the cellular response of the post-synaptic effector cell in depression. CaM-kinases, protein kinases calmodulin dependent; cAMP-kinases, protein kinases cAMP dependent; C-kinases, protein kinases C; DG, 1,2-diacylglycerol; IP_3, inositol-1,4,5-triphosphate; M, muscarinic effect; MA_i, monoamine inhibition; MA_s, monoamine stimulation; MAO, monoamine oxidase. PDE, phosphodiesterase; PIP_2, phosphatidyl inositol-4,5 biphosphate; R_i, inhibited protein receptor; R_s, stimulated protein receptor; TH, thyrosine hydroxylase.

26.7 Neurotropic cAMP-selective Phosphodiesterase Inhibitors – a Novel Approach for the Treatment of Depression

The highest cAMP phosphodiesterase activity, in comparison with other organs, is found in the brain of various mammalian species including man (Williams *et al.*, 1971); regional analysis revealed particularly high cAMP phosphodiesterase activity in cerebral cortex, limbic system and striatum (Weiss and Costa, 1968). The finding that there exist several distinct molecular forms of phosphodiesterase (for review see Strada and Thompson, 1978) which vary according to substrate specificity, intracellular location, kinetic behaviour, molecular size and sensitivities to activators, has renewed interest in inhibitors of cyclic nucleotide phosphodiesterases as potential therapeutic agents (Weishaar *et al.*, 1985) because of their key role in cyclic nucleotide inactivation.

According to the second-messenger dysbalance hypothesis the selective inhibition of a neuronal low-K_m, high-affinity cAMP phosphodiesterase should ensure a sufficient increase of intraneuronal cAMP availability to counterbalance the functional deficiency of the cAMP compared inositol-1,4,5 triphosphate/ 1,2-diacylglycerol second messenger on neuronal activity in depression. The cAMP phosphodiesterase inhibitory activity of such a compound should be confined to the CNS and it should exert antidepressant activity independently of the presynaptic release of first messengers.

Rolipram, one of the most potent derivatives of the novel class of neuroactive dialkoxyphenyl-2-pyrrolidones synthesised by Schmiechen in 1974 (Fig. 26.5), does fulfill these criteria; other neurotropic cAMP-selective phosphodiesterase inhibitors like Ro 20-1724, ICI 63 197 or TV 2706 (Wachtel, 1982b, 1983a; Wachtel and Schneider, 1986) are further potential candidates.

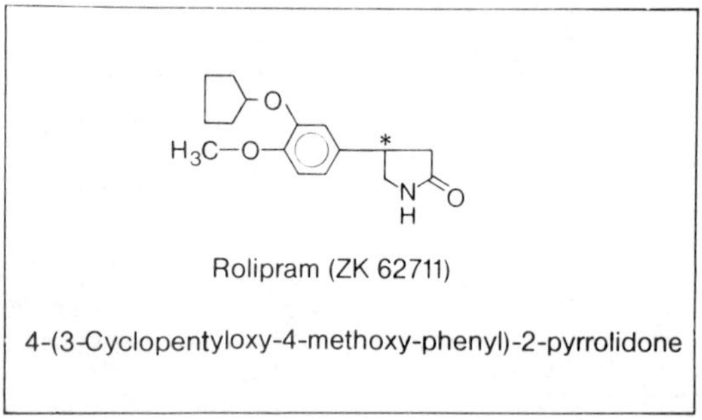

Rolipram (ZK 62711)

4-(3-Cyclopentyloxy-4-methoxy-phenyl)-2-pyrrolidone

Fig. 26.5 Chemical structure of rolipram. The asterisk marks the asymmetric carbon atom.

Rolipram and other cAMP-selective phosphodiesterase inhibitors induce a characteristic behavioural syndrome in rats characterised by locomotor inhibition, hypothermia and increased maintenance activity (forepaw shaking, grooming, head twitches) which is not shared with classic phosphodiesterase inhibitors (Wachtel, 1982b). Behavioural studies and measurements of brain cAMP levels *in vivo* revealed that the (−)-enantiomer of rolipram is only slightly more potent than the racemate whereas the (+)-enantiomer is much less active, suggesting a highly stereoselective interaction of rolipram with a brain cAMP phosphodiesterase isoenzyme (Wachtel, 1983b; Schneider, 1984a). Partially purified calmodulin-independent phosphodiesterase from rat brain was inhibited exclusively by the (−)-enantiomer with an IC_{50} of 1.25 μM whereas the (+)-enantiomer possessed little potency (Schultz and Schmidt, 1986). Rolipram displayed a marked substrate specificity for the inhibitor of calcium-independent phosphodiesterase of rat brain, with IC_{50} values for cAMP hydrolysis and cGMP hydrolysis being 1 μM and much more than 100 μM, respectively (Davis, 1984). After the isoelectric fractionation of rat brain phosphodiesterases, the cytosolic pI 5.6 form was shown to be strongly inhibited by rolipram (IC_{50} : 0.3 μM); this partially purified enzyme form (preferentially) hydrolyses cAMP, is insensitive to calmodulin effects, exhibits non-Michaelis, negatively co-operative kinetics and could represent the pharmacological target of rolipram (Nemoz et al., 1985). Thus, within the bulk of the predominantly calcium-dependent brain phosphodiesterases the rolipram-sensitive cAMP phosphodiesterase isoenzyme represents only a minor portion, which, however, seems to play an important role in brain function as judged from the impressive neurotropic effects following its inhibition by rolipram (Wachtel, 1982b). Finally, there exist stereospecific, high-affinity binding sites for rolipram in the brain which are associated with cAMP phosphodiesterase activity (Schneider, 1984b). Binding is detected both to membrane-bound and soluble sites of rat forebrain, with dissociation constants K_d of 1.2 and 2.4 nM, respectively. [^{3}H]-Rolipram binds to brain tissue of all mammalian species tested, including man, while tissue from bird and fish shows less binding. Organs other than brain exhibit only negligible binding. Only cAMP-selective neurotropic phosphodiesterase inhibitors like ICI 63 197 and Ro 20–1724 are potent competitors, while rolipram itself is inactive in a variety of receptor binding assays of neuroactive ligands (Schneider et al., 1986). These findings strongly suggest that the effect of rolipram is confined to the CNS.

Rolipram is devoid of MAO inhibitory action, does not inhibit reuptake of monoamines, but increases brain NA turnover by stimulation of tyrosine hydroxylase and NA release (Kehr et al., 1985). A direct stimulation of neurotransmitter receptors by rolipram can be excluded in view of the finding that the compound did not compete with the binding of a variety of ligands for neurotransmitter receptors on brain membranes (Schneider et al., 1986). The potential usefulness of rolipram and other cAMP-selective phosphodiesterase inhibitors as antidepressants was suggested on the basis of their pronounced efficacy in classic animal tests being predictive of antidepressant action (Wachtel, 1982a, 1983a; Przegalinski and Bigajska, 1983). It was assumed that their antidepressant effect is based on an enhancement of central NA transmission (Fig. 26.6) which is achieved by their ability to increase the turnover of NA and concomitantly to enhance the postsynaptic cAMP-generating effect of NA via their intrinsic cAMP phosphodiesterase inhibitory action (Wachtel, 1982, 1983a). Thus, unlike conventional antidepressants (Fig. 26.1), which rely upon interactions with target sites located *presynaptically* to increase monomaine concentrations in the synaptic cleft (with consequent greater stimulation of postsynaptic receptors),

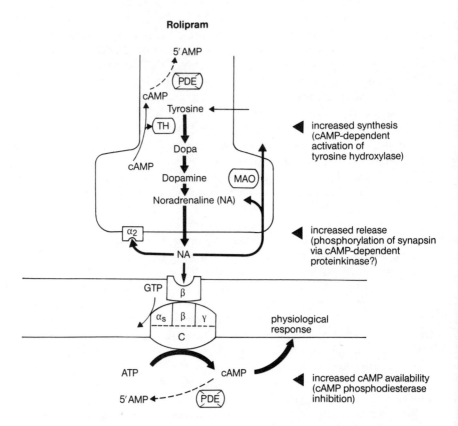

Fig. 26.6 Influence of rolipram and related neurotropic cAMP-selective phosphodiesterase inhibitors on monoaminergic neurotransmission shown on a noradrenaline (NA) synapse. In contrast with classic antidepressants (see Fig. 26.1), rolipram influences neurotransmissions *pre-synaptically and post-synaptically* by a direct, transmitter receptor-independent intra-neuronal mechanism: the enhancement of cAMP availability due to stereospecific inhibition of a neuronal cAMP phosphodiesterase isoenzyme. *Presynaptically*, rolipram thus (a) enhances NA synthesis due to cAMP-dependent activation of tyrosine hydroxylase (TH) and increases NA release, conceivably via cAMP-dependent phosphorylation of synapsin I, a synaptic vesicle-associated nerve-terminal-specific protein. *Postsynaptically*, rolipram, by inhibiting cAMP PDE, favours those receptor functions of physiological first messengers on cellular response which utilise cAMP as a second messenger. CaM-kinases, protein kinases calmodulin dependent; cAMP-kinases, protein kinases cAMP dependent; C-kinases, protein kinases C; DG, 1,2-diacylglycerol; IP_3, inositol-1,4,5-triphosphate; M, muscarinic effect; MA_i, mono-amine inhibition; MA_s, monoamine stimulation; MAO, monoamine oxidase; PDE, phospho-diesterase; PIP_2, phosphatidyl inositol-4,5 biphosphate; R_i, inhibited protein receptor; R_s, stimulated protein receptor; TH, thyrosine hydroxylase.

rolipram and other cAMP-selective phosphodiesterase inhibitors stimulate both the *presynaptic* as well as the *postsynaptic* component of monoaminergic transmission. It is assumed that their presynaptic action is due to an increase of intracellular cAMP availability following cAMP phosphodiesterase inhibition. There is good evidence for activation of tyrosine hydroxylase by cAMP kinase (Morgenroth *et al.*, 1975). Phosphorylation by cAMP kinase of the head region of synapsin I, a synaptic vesicle-associated nerve terminal protein, has been suggested to be involved in neurotransmitter release (for review see de Camilli and Greengard, 1986). A cAMP overload of the effector cell following inhibition of the rolipram-sensitive cAMP phosphodiesterase is unlikely to occur because the activity of the other phosphodiesterase isoenzymes, which are present in the neuron in abundance and which are especially effective at high cAMP concentrations (Strada *et al.*, 1984), is not affected by rolipram.

Evidence in support of the preponderance of the post-synaptic mechanism of antidepressant action of rolipram and related compounds has recently been demonstrated by the finding that the cAMP-selective phosphodiesterase inhibitors, unlike the reuptake blocker imipramine or the MAO inhibitor pargyline, reversed the hypothermia and hypokinesia of mice depleted of endogenous brain monoamines by pretreament with reserpine together with the monoamine synthesis inhibitors α-methyl-p-tyrosine and p-chlorophenylalanine; the antagonistic effects of rolipram were not prevented by DA or β-receptor blockade (Wachtel and Schneider, 1986). These data indicate that rolipram and related compounds exert their antidepressant activity via a postsynaptic mechanism of action beyond the receptor level, independent of the availability of endogenous presynaptically released monomaines, and therefore differ fundamentally from conventional antidepressants.

Most neurotransmitters assumed to be of importance in affective disorders utilise both second-messenger systems. For instance, physiologically released NA will act on β-receptors stimulating cAMP generation, on α_2-receptors inhibiting adenylate cyclase and on α_1-receptors activating inositol-1,4,5 triphosphate/ 1,2-diacylglycerol formation. At the level of the NA effector cell both signal amplification systems are interrelated to allow tuning of the physiological response and adaptive changes to subsequent stimulation. Rolipram, due to its potent cAMP phosphodiesterase inhibitory action, will favour those functions of physiological neurotransmitters which are mediated by cAMP and thereby should outweigh the relative preponderance of the inositol-1,4,5 triphosphate/ 1,2-diacylglycerol system on neuronal response in depression. Thus, in contrast to classic antidepressants, which, necessarily less directly, stimulate the various pre- and post-synaptic receptor subgroups of physiological neurotransmitters wih their often counteracting functions, rolipram and related compounds favour the immediate and continuous cAMP-mediated signal flow directed towards the effector cell. These unique properties of rolipram should enable more efficient transduction of postsynaptic signals by circumventing presynaptic inhibitory feedback mechanisms, responsible for the delay of the optimal therapeutic efficacy of classic antidepressants.

Because of its novel mechanism of action, rolipram is anticipated (a) to be a potent antidepressant, being effective at dosages 10 to 100 times lower than agents currently used, (b) to have a less delayed onset of the antidepressant activity and (c) to be a safe, reliably effective and well-tolerated antidepressant lacking anticholinergic activity (Wachtel, 1982a, 1983a; Wachtel and Schneider, 1986).

Open clinical phase I/II studies conducted on nearly 200 depressed patients (predominantly endogenous or chronic depression, often resistant to conventional drugs) at 20 separate and independent testing centres, confirmed the predicted antidepressant activity of rolipram (Zeller *et al.*, 1984; Horowski and Sastre-y-Hernandez, 1985). Rolipram was administered in increasing dosages up to 3 x 1.0 mg/d. Until now, in nearly 150 patients, a good to very good antidepressant effect has been observed in about two-thirds of the cases, even though these patients represented a negative selection. The effect began within the first 12 hours to 10 days. The tolerance was generally judged to be good to very good. Double-blind controlled studies of rolipram versus desipramine (Bobon *et al.*, 1986), amitriptyline (Eckman *et al.*, unpublished results) and imipramine (Bertolino *et al.*, unpublished results) in patients with endogenous depression confirm the results obtained in open trials.

26.8 Outlook

Hypotheses on the pathophysiology of endogenous depression were always intimately linked to the knowledge and interpretation of the mechanism of action of antidepressant drugs. In this respect the discovery of the antidepressant activity of neurotropic cAMP-selective phosphodiesterase inhibitors like rolipram is of theoretical and practical interest. With rolipram, for the first time, a mechanism of antidepressant action completely different from known agents emerged: the direct and specific manipulation of intraneuronal cAMP-mediated signal propagation beyond first-messenger receptors located on the surface of the neuronal membrane. Consequently this discovery has created the conceptual framework of the unifying hypothesis on the etiology of affective disorders. In future the growing knowledge concerning the regulation of intraneuronal reactions by second messengers will open up new insights for the elucidation of the pathoneurobiochemistry of affective disorders to test the validity of the second-messenger dysbalance hypothesis. It is my impression that with the current antidepressants we have tried, by simply manipulating the keys of a piano, to generate a harmonious melody without realising that the strings behind the keys were out of tune; however, this may always be the case when we are listening to new sounds on a classic instrument.

Acknowledgements

I thank P.-A. Löschmann for discussions and his assistance in designing the illustrations and B. Fogel and E. Weber for typing the manuscript. I am grateful to Dr M. Briley and Dr G. Fillion for inviting me to the International Symposium on New Concepts in Depression.

References

Abdulla, Y. H., and Hamadah, K. (1970). 3',5' cyclic adenosine monophosphate in depression and mania. *Lancet*, i, 378-81.

Axelrod, J., Withby, L. G., and Hertting, G. (1961). Effect of psychotropic drugs on uptake of ³H-norepinephrine by tissue. *Science*, 133, 383-4.

Baumann, P. A., and Maitre, L. (1977). Blockade of presynaptic receptors and of amine uptake in the rat brain by the antidepressant mianserin. *Naunyn-Schmiedeberg's Arch. Pharmacol.*, 300, 31-7.

Berridge, M. J. (1984). Inositol triphosphate and diacylglycerol as second messengers. *Biochem. J.*, 220, 345-60.

Bobon, D., Breulet, M., Gerard, M.-A., Guit, B., and Troisfontaines, B. (1986). Double dummy study of rolipram and desipramine in hospitalized major depressives: An interim analysis. *Abstr. 15th CINP Congress*, San Juan, Puerto Rico, 254.

Codina, J., Hildebrandt, J., Sunyer, T., Sekura, R. D., Manclark, C. R., Iyengar, R., and Birnbaumer, L. (1984). Mechanisms in the vectorial receptor–adenylate cyclase signal transduction. In Greengard, P., Robison, G. A., Paoletti, R., and Nicosia, S. (eds.), *Advances in Cyclic Neucleotide and Protein Phosphorylation Research*, Raven, New York, vol. 17, 111-25.

Coppen, A. (1967). The biochemistry of affective disorders. *Br. J. Psychiat.*, 113, 1237-64.

Crane, G. E. (1957). Iproniazid (Marsilid) phosphate, a therapeutic agent for mental disorders and debilitating diseases. *Psychiat. Res. Rep. Amer. Psychiat. Ass.*, 8, 142-52.

Davis, C. W. (1984). Assessment of selective inhibition of rat cerebral cortical calcium-independent and calcium-dependent phosphodiesterases in crude extracts using deoxy-cyclic AMP and potassium ions. *Biochim. Biophys. Acta*, 797, 354-62.

de Camilli, P. and Greengard, P. (1986). Synapsin I: A synaptic vesicle-associated neuronal phosphoprotein. *Biochem. Pharmacol.*, 24, 4249-57.

Dousa, T., and Hechter, O. (1970). Lithium and brain adenyle cyclase. *Lancet*, i, 834-5.

Ebstein, R. P., Oppenheim, G., Ebstein, B. S., Amiri, Z., and Stessman, J. (1986). The cyclic AMP second messenger system in man: the effects of heredity, hormones, drugs, aluminium, age and disease on signal amplification. *Progr. Neuropsychopharmacol. Biol. Psychiat.*, 10, 323-53.

Extein, I., Tallman, J., Smith, C. C., and Goodwin, F. K. (1979). Changes in lympocyte beta-adrenergic receptors in depression and mania. *Psychiat. Res.*, 1, 191-7.

Hallcher, L. M., and Sherman, W. R. (1980). The effects of lithium ion and other agents on the activity of myo-inositol-1-phosphatase from bovine brain. *J. Biol. Chem.*, 225, 10896-901.

Horn, A. S., Coyle, J. T., and Snyder, S. H. (1971). Catecholamine uptake by synaptosomes from rat brain. Structure activity relationships of drugs with differential effects on dopamine and norepinephrine neurons. *Mol. Pharmacol.*, 7, 66-80.

Horowski, R., and Sastre-y-Hernandez, M. (1985). Clinical effects of the neurotropic selective cAMP phosphodiesterase inhibitor rolipram in depressed patients: Global evaluation of the preliminary reports. *Current Ther. Res.*, 38, 23-9.

Janowsky, D. S., El-Yousef, M. K., Davis, J. M., and Sekerke, H. J. (1972). A cholinergic-adrenergic hypothesis of mania and depression. *Lancet*, ii, 632-5.

Kehr, W., Debus, G., and Neumeister, R. (1985). Effects of rolipram, a novel antidepressant, on monoamine metabolism in rat brain. *J. Neural Transm.*, 63, 1-12.

Krebs, E. G., and Beavo, J. A. (1979). Phosphorylation-dephosphorylation of enzymes.

Ann. Rev. Biochem., **48**, 923–59.

Kuhn, R. (1957). Ueber die behandlung depressive zustaende mit einen iminodibenzyl-derivat (G 22 455). *Schweiz. Med. Wschr.*, 35/36, 1135–40.

Lapin, I. P., and Oxenkrug, G. F. (1969). Intensification of central serotoninergic processes as a possible determinant of the thymoleptic effect. *Lancet*, i, 132–6.

Levitan, I. B., Lemos, J. R., and Novak-Hofer, I. (1983). Protein phosphorylation and the regulation of ion channels. *TINS*, 6, 496–9.

Loomer, H. P., Saunders, J. C., and Kline, N. S. (1957). A clinical and pharmacodynamic evaluation of iproniazid as a psychic energizer. *Psychiat. Res. Rep. Amer. Psychiat. Ass.*, 8, 129–41.

Morgenroth, V. H., Hegstrand, L. R., Roth, R. H., and Greengard, P. (1975). Evidence for involvement of proteinkinase in the activation by adenosine 3'5'-monophosphate of brain tyrosine 3-monooxygenase. *J. Biol. Chem.*, 250, 1946–8.

Nemoz, G., Prigent, A.-F., Moueqqit, M., Fougier, S., Macovschi, O., and Pacheoco, H. (1985). Selective inhibition of one of the cyclic AMP phosphodiesterases from rat brain by the neurotropic compound rolipram, *Biochem. Pharmacol.*, 34, 2997–3000.

Newman, M., Klein, E., Birmaher, B., Feinsod, M., and Belmaker, R. H. (1983). Lithium at therapeutic concentrations inhibits human brain noradrenaline-sensitive cyclic AMP accumulation. *Brain Res.*, 278, 380–1.

Nishizuka, Y. (1984). The role of protein kinase C in cell surface signal transduction and tumour promotion. *Nature*, 308, 693–8.

Ossofsky, H. J. (1976). Affective and atopic disorders and cyclic AMP. *Compre. Psychiat.*, 17, 335–46.

Pandey, G., Dysken, M. W., and Garver, D. L. (1979). Beta-adrenergic receptor function in affective illness. *Amer. J. Psychiat.*, 136, 675–78.

Przegalinski, E., and Bigajska, K. (1983). Antidepressant properties of some phosphodi-esterase inhibitors. *Polish J. Pharmacol. Pharm.*, 35, 233–40.

Schildkraut, J. J. (1965). The catecholamine hypothesis of affective disorders: A review of supporting evidence. *Amer. J. Psychiat.*, 122, 509–22.

Schneider, H. H. (1984a). Brain cAMP response to phosphodiesterase inhibitors in rats killed by microwave irradiation or decapitation, *Biochem. Pharmacol.*, 33, 1690–3.

Schneider, H. H. (1984b). High affinity binding of the selective adenosine monophosphate (cAMP) phosphodiesterase (PDE) inhibitor rolipram to an isolated soluble PDE from rat brain. In Strada, S. J., and Thompson, W. J. (eds.), *Advances in Cyclic Nucleotide and Protein Phosphorylation Research*. Raven, New York, vol. 17, 426–51.

Schneider, H. H., Schmiechen, R., Brezinski, M., and Seidler, J. (1986). Stereospecific binding of the antidepressant rolipram to brain protein structures. *Eur. J. Pharmacol.*, 127, 105–15.

Schultz, J. E., and Schmidt, B. H. (1986). Rolipram, a stereospecific inhibitor of calmodulin-independent phosphodiesterase, causes β-adrenoceptor subsensitivity in rat cerebral cortex. *Naunyn-Schmiedeberg's Arch. Pharmacol.*, 333, 23–30.

Sherman, W. R., Leavitt, A. L., Honchar, M. P., Hallcher, L. M., and Phillips, B. E. (1981). Evidence that lithium alters phosphoinositide metabolism: Chronic administration elevates primarily D-myoinositol-1-phosphate in cerebral cortex of the rat. *J. Neuro-chem.*, 36, 1947–51.

Spector, S., Prockop, D., Shore, P. A., and Brodie, B. B. (1958). Effect of iproniazid on brain levels of norepinephrine and serotonin. *Science*, 127, 704.

Stone, E. A. (1983). Problems with current catecholamine hypotheses of antidepressant agents: Speculations leading to a new hypothesis. *Behav. Brain Sci.*, 6, 535–77.

Strada, S. J., and Thompson, W. J. (1978). Multiple forms of cyclic nucleotide phospho-diesterases: anomalies or biologic regulators? In George, W. J., and Ignarro, L. J. (eds.), *Advances in Cyclic Nucleotide Research*. Raven, New York, vol. 9, 265–83.

Strada, S. J., Martin, M. W., and Thompson, W. J. (1984). General properties of multiple molecular forms of cyclic nucleotide phosphodiesterase in the nervous system. In Strada, S. J., and Thompson, W. J. (eds.), *Advances in Cyclic Nucleotide and Protein Phos-phorylation Research*, Raven, New York, vol. 16, 13–29.

Szentivanyi, A. (1968). The beta adrenergic theory of the atopic abnormality in bronchial asthma. *J. Allergy*, 42, 203–32.

Taylor, C. W., and Merritt, J. E. (1986). Receptor coupling to polyphosphoinoside turnover: A parallel with the adenylate cyclase system. *TIPS*, 7, 238-42.

Wachtel, H. (1982a). Selective cyclic adenosine 3',5'-monophosphate phosphodiesterase inhibitors – a novel class of antidepressants? *Abstr. 13th C.I.N.P. Congress*, Jerusalem, 740.

Wachtel, H. (1982b). Characteristic behavioral alterations in rats induced by rolipram and other selective adenosine cyclic 3'5'-monophosphate phosphodiesterase inhibitors. *Psychopharmacology*, 77, 309-16.

Wachtel, H. (1983a). Potential antidepressant activity of rolipram and other selective cyclic adenosine 3',5'-monophosphate phosphodiesterase inhibitors. *Neuropharmacology*, 22, 367-72.

Wachtel, H. (1983b). Neurotropic effects of the optical isomers of the selective adenosine cyclic 3'5'-monophosphate phosphodiesterase inhibitor rolipram in rats in vivo. *J. Pharm. Pharmacol.*, 35, 440-4.

Wachtel, H., and Löschmann, P.-A. (1986). Effects of forskolin and cyclic nucleotides in animal models predictive of antidepressant activity: Interactions with rolipram. *Psychopharmacology*, 90, 430-5.

Wachtel, H., and Schneider, H. H. (1986). Rolipram, a novel antidepressant drug, reverses the hypothermia and hypokinesia of monoamine-depleted mice by an action beyond postsynaptic monoamine receptors. *Neuropharmacology*, 25, 1119-26.

Weishaar, R. E., Cain, M. H., and Bristol, J. A. (1985). A new generation of phosphodiesterase inhibitors: Multiple molecular forms of phosphodiesterase and the potential for drug selectivity. *J. Med. Chem.*, 28, 537-45.

Weiss, B., and Costa, E. (1968). Regional and subcellular distribution of adenyl cyclase and 3'5'-cyclic nucleotide phosphodiesterase in brain and pineal gland. *Biochem. Pharmacol.*, 17, 2107-16.

Williams, R. H., Little, S. A., Beug, A. G., and Ensinck, J. W. (1971). Cyclic nucleotide phosphodiesterase activity in man, monkey, and rat. *Metabolism*, 20, 743-8.

Zeller, E., Stief, J.-J., Pflug, B. and Sastre-y-Hernandez, M. (1984). Results of a phase II study of the antidepressant effect of rolipram. *Pharmacopsychiatry*, 17, 188-90.

27

Differential Scanning Calorimetry Studies of the Interaction of Antidepressant Drugs, Noradrenaline and Serotonin with a Membrane Model

M. Bauer, C. Megret, A. Lamure and C. Lacabanne

27.1 Introduction

The idea of protein receptors plays an important role in biochemistry. The concept of 'structural complementarity' between an exogenous or endogenous molecule and the protein binding site(s) is now well established. This requirement will be designated by 'structural specificity'. We will develop here a complementary point of view, based on the existence of 'thermodynamic specificity'. It may be explained by considering the example of noradrenaline (NA), serotonin (5-HT) and four antidepressant drugs (midalcipran, citalopram, indalpine, and imipramine), blockers of the uptake of the above endogenous neuromediators.

27.1.1 Hypothesis of Thermodynamic Specificity

For over ten years, the role of the physical state of the phospholipids constituting the biological membrane (Sandermann, 1978; Chapman et al., 1982) on the activity of the membrane proteins has been widely investigated. On the other hand, biological membranes constitute a double interface system separating domains of different polarity in which molecules will be preferentially localised according to their chemical potential.

In the case of the presynaptic neuronal membrane, the uptake proteins orientate their uptake site(s) towards the hydrophilic domain (Fig. 27.1). Nor-

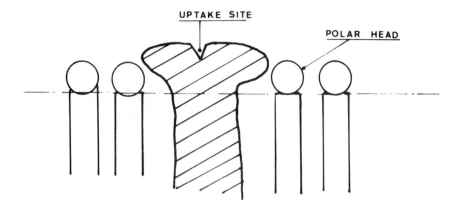

Fig. 27.1   Scheme of the phospholipid–uptake protein complex.

adrenaline and serotonin probably have hydrophilic/lipophilic partition coefficients which statistically favour their localisation in the hydrophilic domain. Thus, uptake efficiency has been assumed to be maximum (assuming that the requirements of structural specificity have been fulfilled). This condition has been designated as 'thermodynamic specificity'.

Let us consider now the antidepressant drugs which inhibit 5-HT and NA uptake. From the point of view of uptake efficiency, they must have the same approach as endogenous neuromediators they mimic. Thus they need to satisfy the structural and thermodynamic specificities and to be localised in the domain corresponding to the uptake zone of the protein.

To test this hypothesis experimentally, a study of the interactions of a membrane model and the endogenous neuromediators on the one hand and drugs known as neuromediator uptake inhibitors on the other hand (Moret et al., 1985) has been undertaken using differential scanning calorimetry. Four drugs have been investigated, imipramine, citalopram, indalpine and midalcipran.

Dipalmitoyl phosphatidyl choline (DPPC) was chosen as the synthetic model of the membrane. This phospholipid autoassembles into large multilamellar liposomes (Chapman et al., 1967; Knight, 1981; Puisieux and Delattre, 1985). Such a liposomal structure shows an endothermic phase transition from gel to liquid crystal. A pretransitional endotherm is also exhibited by DPPC but this is not discussed here. We focus our attention on the main endotherm corresponding to the primary phase change. Figure 27.2 shows the DPPC thermogram with the phase transition observed at about 42 °C.

Analysis of the endothermic peak gives an activation enthalpy of 30 kJ mol^{-1}. The interaction of the liposome with a molecule may be characterised from the modification of this transition.

The perturbation will, of course, be strongly related to the drug's position inside the bilayer. A classification based on this criterion has been proposed by

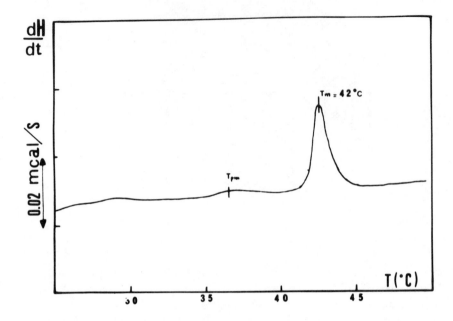

Fig. 27.2   DSC thermogram of a pure DPPC liposome.

Jain and Wu (1977). Figure 27.3 illustrates the four domains they have designated A, B, C and D. Without going further into details presented elsewhere (Bauer, 1987), we will just mention here that the D-domain is characterised by the presence of a new endothermic peak: for the D↓-profile, the peak is shifted towards lower temperatures: for the D↑-profile, towards higher temperatures. This terminology is used later on.

27.2 Material and Methods

27.2.1 Materials

The L-α-DPPC (99% purity), serotonin and noradrenaline were purchased from Sigma. Indalpine was provided by Pharmuka, imipramine by Rhône-Poulenc, citalopram by Lundbeck Labs, Denmark, and midalcipran (F 2207) by Pierre Fabre Medicament.

The buffer consisting of $CaCl_2$ (10 mM)-TRIS (100 mM) was adjusted to pH 7.2 with hydrochloric acid. Phospholipid bilayer vesicles were prepared as follows. Chloroform (5 ml) containing 50 mg of DPPC was evaporated to dryness. Buffer solution (1 ml) was added and a homogeneous solution was obtained by mixing on a Vortex shaker. The suspension was left to incubate for 30 min

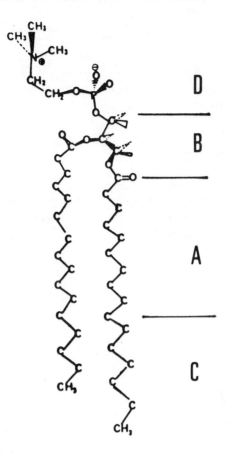

Fig. 27.3   Definition of the various zones of localisation of a drug within the bilayer according to Jain and Wu (1977).

at 50 °C and finally shaken again for several minutes. The sample was then allowed to equilibrate for 30 min at room temperature.

   The additions were then made by one of the following methods. If the drug was soluble in chloroform (midalcipran, indalpine and citalopram) an appropriate solution in chloroform was evaporated to dryness. The liposomes were then prepared as described above. If the additive was insoluble in chloroform then the compound was mixed with the buffer (serotonin, noradrenaline and imipramine).

   10 to 40 mg of the multilamellar liposomes were used for differential scanning calorimetry.

27.2.2 Method

The calorimetric scan was performed on Perkin Elmer DSC II apparatus using a heating rate of $5°/$min. The first run was performed in the temperature range 20 to $50°C$. Then the sample was cooled at a rate of $10°/$min and kept a few minutes at $20°C$ before the second run.

27.3 Results and Discussion

Figures 27.4a to f show the various thermograms obtained for increasing molar ratios, R, of the different drugs in the DPPC liposome. R is defined as $C_{drug}/(C_{drug} + C_{DPPC})$ where C_{drug} is the molar concentration of the drug and C_{DPPC} the molar concentration of DPPC.

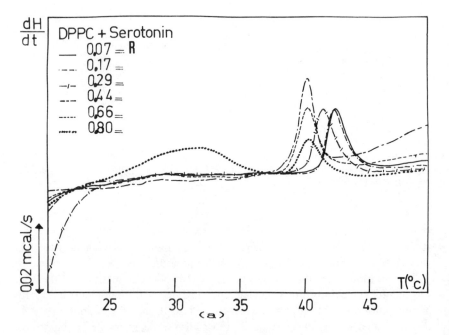

Fig. 27.4 Thermograms of DPPC liposome for various increasing molar ratios: (a) 5-HT; (b) NA; (c) imipramine.

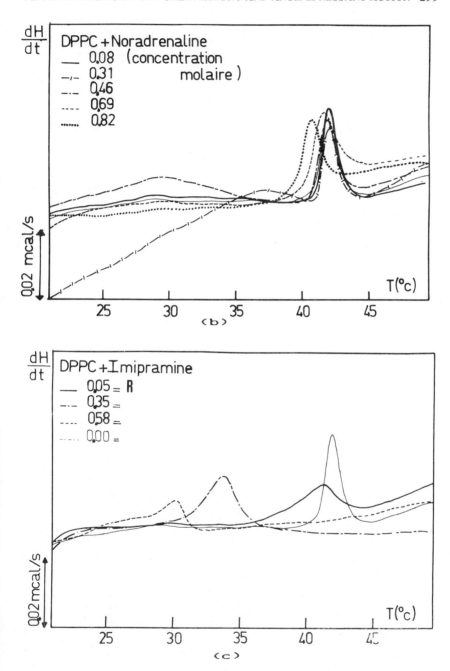

Fig. 27.4 (*also continued overleaf*)

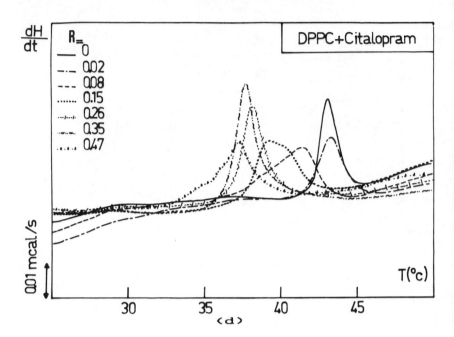

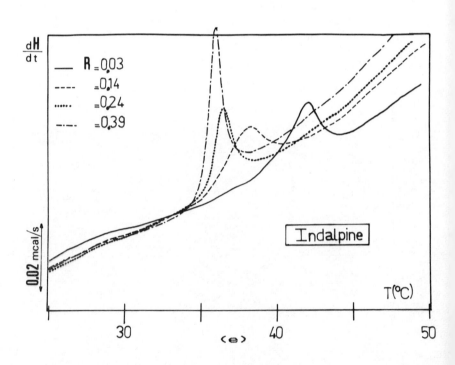

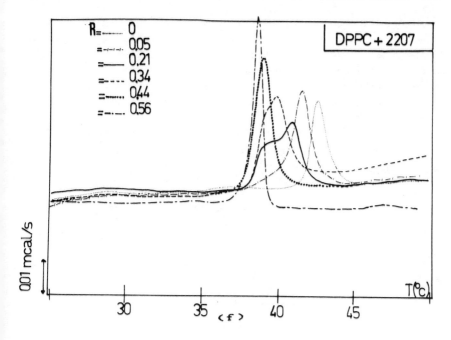

Fig 27.4 Thermograms of DPPC liposome for various increasing molar ratios (cont.): (d) citalopram; (e) indalpine; (f) midalcipran (2207).

The examination of the thermograms shows the existence of two types of behaviour:

(a) The interactions with serotonin and noradrenaline are characterised respectively by a weak and very weak perturbation of the initial liposome transition and of its associated thermotropic behaviour. Consequently, those molecules appear to be essentially localised in the aqueous phase and are thus fully available for the uptake mechanism. The observed hydrophilicity of noradrenaline and serotonin and their lack of localisation inside the bilayer explains why they do not cross the blood–brain barrier after exogenous injection (Borgmann et al., 1973).

(b) On the other hand, the interactions of midalcipran, citalopram, indalpine and imipramine are clearly characterised by the formation of a new phase, with a lower transition temperature. As indicated above, those molecules clearly induce D↓-type profiles, suggesting a position between the hydrophilic and lipophilic domains of the bilayer.

According to Jain and Wu (1977), this behaviour is characteristic of cationic molecules, which corresponds to the ionic state of the four drugs at the pH used.

It has been postulated that electrostatic interactions exist between the (R_1, R_2, R_3N^+-H) group of the molecules and the (R_4-O-PO_2-O-R_5) phosphate group of the liposome. Thus, the four products have the required thermodynamic specificity to allow them to interact on the side of the interface near the protein receptors.

Despite similar thermodynamic behaviour, the various molecules also show significant differences in their thermograms. This includes in particular the ΔT_t parameter, which is measured as described in Fig. 27.5.

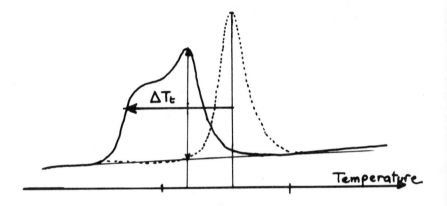

Fig. 27.5 Method of ΔT_t determination. Broken line, pure liposome; unbroken line, liposome + drug (for a given R).

The parameter, ΔT_t, takes into account the broadening of the peak and the decreasing of the maximum temperature of the transition. It directly reflects the penetration of the drug inside the bilayer.

Thus the ΔT_t parameter varies in a manner similar to that of molecule lipophilicity (Jain and Wu, 1977) and is directly related to the partition coefficient of the drug (Bauer, 1987). Figure 27.6 represents the ΔT_t variation versus R for the various investigated molecules.

It appears clearly that midalcipran has a behaviour closer to that of neuromediators, noradrenaline and serotonin, as concerns their thermodynamic specificity. More generally, a classification of molecules based on their increasing lipophilicity can be proposed: noradrenaline $<$ serotonin $<$ midalcipran $<$ citalopram $\leqslant$ indalpine $<$ imipramine. Such a classification is confirmed by considering the more classical values of the octanol/buffer partition coefficient (Bauer, 1987). Figure 27.7 (p. 304) summarises schematically our concept of thermodynamic specificity as applied to molecules of various lipophilicity–hydrophilicity.

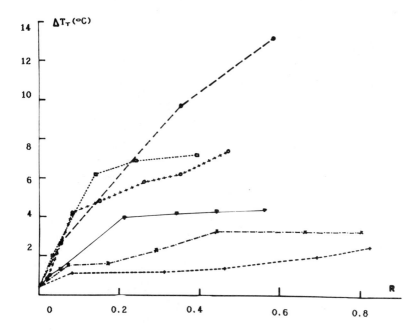

Fig. 27.6   Variation of the ΔT_t parameter with R for different drugs (+-- noradrenaline, X --- serotonin, ▼ – midalcipran, ○+++ citalopram, □···· indalpine, ● - - imipramine).

The higher hydrophilicity of midalcipran, as compared with the other three antidepressant drugs, is unfavourable to the crossing of the blood–brain barrier (Briley, 1987). However, once this has been crossed, this hydrophilicity confers on midalcipran a better thermodynamic specificity in its interaction with the membrane, which can explain the lack of certain side-effects such as local anaesthesia. Lee (1976) has suggested that the mechanism of action of local anaesthetics is based on their ability to penetrate, more or less deeply, within the lipid bilayer. That interaction of midalcipran with the phospholipids takes place essentially at the surface of the membrane may explain why this drug is devoid of local anaesthetic effects (Stenger, 1987).

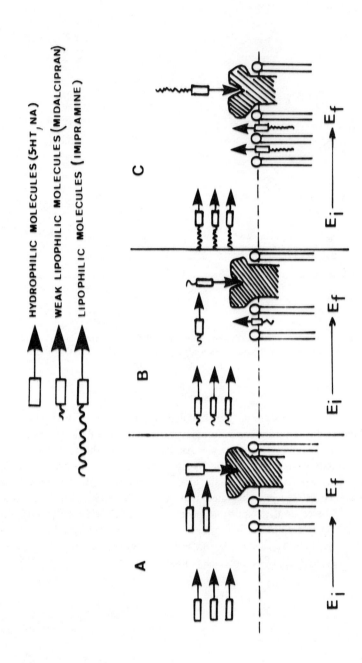

References

Bauer, M. (1987). Étude par analyse enthalpique différentielle de l'interaction de drogues inhibitrices de l'activité de la phospholipase A$_2$ et de drogues antidepressives avec le liposome DPPC pris comme modèle de la membrane biologique. *Diplôme universitaire de recherche*, Université Paul Sabatier, Toulouse, France.

Borgmann, R. J., McPhillips, J. J., Stitzel, R. E., and Goodman, I. J., (1973). Centrally acting dopamines derivatives, *J. Med. Chem.*, **16**, 630-3.

Briley, M. (1987), personnal communication.

Chapman, D., Williams, R. M., and Ladbrooke, B. O. (1967). Physical studies of phospholipids. VI thermotropic and lipotropic mesomorphism of some 1,2-diacyl-phosphatidyl-cholines, *Chem. Phys. Lipids*, **1**, 445-75.

Chapman, D., Gomez-Fernandez, J. C., and Goni, F. M. (1982). The interaction of intrinsic proteins and lipids in biomembranes, *TIBS*, Feb., 67-70.

Jain, M. R., and Wu, N. M. (1977). Effect of small molecules on the dipalmitoyl lecithin liposomal bilayer: phase transition in lipid bilayer, *J. Membrane Biol.*, **34**, 157-201.

Lee, A. G. (1976). Model for action of local anaesthetics. *Nature*, **262**, 545-8.

Moret, C., Charveron, M., Finberg, J. P. M., Couzinier, J. P., and Briley, M. (1985). Biochemical profile on midalcipran, a potential fourth generation antidepressant drug. *Neuropharm.*, **24**, 1211-19.

Puisieux, F., and Delattre, J. (1985). *Les Liposomes, Techniques et Documentation.* Lavoisier, Paris.

Sandermann, H. (1978). Regulation of membrane enzymes by lipids. *Biochim. Biophys. Acta*, **515**, 209-37.

Stenger, A. (1987). Personnal communication.

Szoka, F., and Papahadjopoulous, D. (1981). Liposomes: preparation and characterization. In Knight, C. R. (ed.), *Liposomes: From Physical Structure to Therapeutic Applications.* Elsevier/North Holland Biomedical Press, Amsterdam, 51-77.

Fig. 27.7 Hypothetical scheme describing the situation of the membrane–protein–drug complex in relation to the hydrophilic–lipophilic balance of the molecules (thermodynamical specificity). Imagine three molecules, initially present in the aqueous synaptic gap (initial state E_i), which remains in the final state (E_f).: (A) Three molecules of neuromediators in the aqueous phase, zero in the lipophilic phase. (B) Two weak lipophilic molecules in the aqueous phase, one in the lipophilic phase. (C) One lipophilic molecule in the aqueous phase, two in the lipophilic phase.

28

Immunopharmacological Aspects of Mental Disorders

K. Mašek

In recent years there have been more and more data available suggesting the existence of links between mental disorders, including depression, and an abnormality in the immune response. In general, however, it is not completely clear how these disorders are linked together and what might be their biochemical background.

In patients with depression the frequency of antinuclear antibodies which might reflect an autoimmune process has been reported to be increased (von Brauchitsch, 1972; Deberdt et al., 1976), but real evidence for an autoimmune character of this disease has never been presented. More recently, several workers, investigating the lymphocyte function in depressed patients, concluded that the lymphocyte stimulation to three tested mitogens, phytohaemagglutinin (PHA), concanavalin A (Con A) and pokeweed mitogen (PWM), was significantly lower in the group of depressed patients examined. The total number of T- and B-cells was also lower in the depressed patients but the percentage of the cell types did not differ (Schleifer et al., 1985). Beside the lymphocytes, however, some phagocytic cells may also be affected in depressive illness (Gottschalk et al., 1983). The above-mentioned studies, of course, need to be extended and more immunological parameters measured to elucidate how depressive states may be associated with immunological abnormalities.

If an association between depression and altered immune function exists, as suggested by some recent reports, then common factors, in immune disturbances as well as in depressive illness, might be involved. One can, of course, find a number of possible candidates for such a role, including glucocorticoids and neurotransmitters. Both are known to have effects on the immune response as well as on mental functions.

In the light of the possible role which an abnormality of amine functions might play in depressed patients, our finding that muramyl peptide, a unit of a bacterial cell wall which possesses immunomodulatory activity, interacts with amine, in particular serotonin, receptors, with resultant changes in receptor sensitivity, might open new aspects in this field.

We have been studying the role of serotonin and catecholamines in behavioural changes as well as in the immune response for several years. In the present chapter I review some of our data regarding the effect of muramyl peptides on some neurotransmitters and immune and central nervous system functions.

The synthesis of muramyl peptides was the outcome of a longtime effort for a better adjuvant, a compound which enhances the immune response (Ellouz *et al.*, 1974). The chemical structure of muramyl peptide (MDP) is depicted in Fig. 28.1; as can be seen, *N*-acetylmuramic acid is linked to L-alanine and D-isoglutamine. The compound, as well as a number of analogs which are now available, possesses many interesting immunological activities and these are summarised in Table 28.1. It has to be stressed, however, that the overall effect on

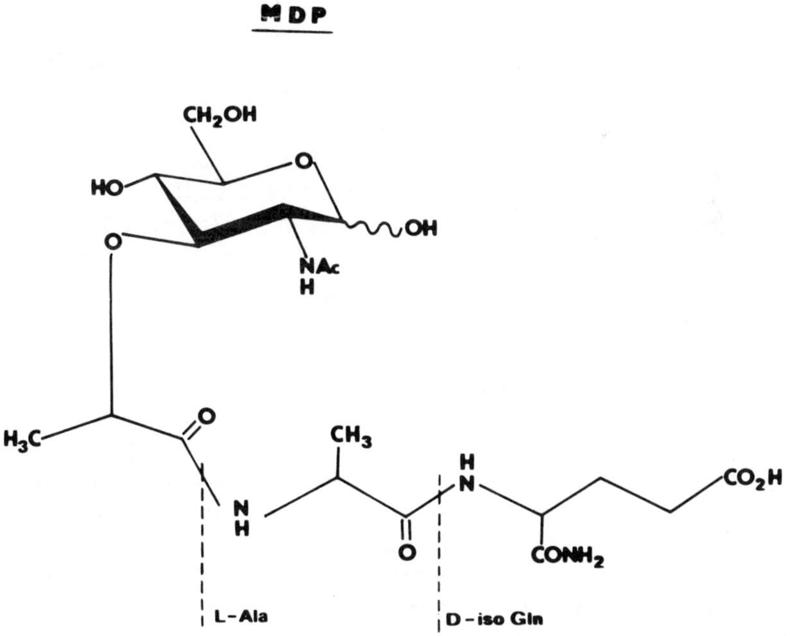

Fig. 28.1 Structure of *N*-acetyl-muramyl-L-alanyl-D-isoglutamine/muramyl dipeptide (MDP).

Table 28.1   Biological activities of muramyl peptides

Potentiation or inhibition of antibody-mediated immune response
Potentiation or inhibition of cell-mediated immune response
Stimulation of reticuloendothelial system
Effect on leukocyte and trombocyte counts
Stimulation of myelopoiesic
Increase of natural resistance to microbial and viral infections
Increase of natural resistance to tumour development
Induction or inhibition of autoimmune diseases
Pro-inflammatory or anti-inflammatory effects
Immunogenicity
Pyrogenicity
Effect on sleep
Effect on pain threshold

---

the immune system always depends on the administered dose. At lower doses the effect is generally immunostimulatory and at higher doses it is immunosuppressive. The exact mechanisms by which MDP exerts its immunomodulatory effect are not fully understood. T-cells are of paramount importance for the mediation of the immunostimulatory as well as immunosuppressive effect, but apparently other cells, like macrophages, are also involved (Löwy *et al.*, 1977; Fevrier *et al.*, 1978; Schindler *et al.*, 1986).

Under certain experimental conditions MDP can induce autoimmune diseases like encephalomyelitis. In this case, however, besides MDP, tryptophan-containing nonapeptide is also needed (Nagai *et al.*, 1978a, b). The other autoimmune diseases reported from experimental studies are adjuvant arthritis, orchitis and uveoretinitis (Adam, 1985). In guinea-pigs MDP can induce, under certain conditions, a demyelinating disease which resembles multiple sclerosis (Colover, 1980).

It has been fifteen years since we started to investigate the effects of muramyl peptides, at that time, of course, of bacterial origin, on the central nervous system and we have reported a number of effects including changes in behaviour, temperature and sleep (Mašek *et al.*, 1973). We have also observed with bacterial peptidoglycans an interaction with the serotonergic system. When synthetic products became available we reinvestigated the observed phenomena and concluded that the effects on behaviour, temperature control and sleep were present even after the administration of synthetic MDP. More recently, we have also observed an effect on pain threshold (Horák and Mašek, 1985).

While investigating possible links between the effect of MDP on temperature, sleep and immunostimulation, we have been able to demonstrate that the central nervous system is involved in the effect of MDP on the immune system. Electrolytic lesions placed in different areas of the brain stem influence markedly the effect of MDP. So far the obtained results suggest particularly the involvement of the serotonergic groups $B_{6,7,8}$, with serotonergic pathways in the upper region of the reticular formation, and catecholaminergic groups $A_{1,3,5,7}$ in the caudal part of the reticular formation with participation of the corresponding pathways. A summary of our findings is presented in Fig. 28.2. The methods have been reported previously (Mašek *et al.*, 1985). Lesions in the rostral part of the reticular formation (raphe dorsalis, linearis caudalis, intermedius and rostralis) markedly

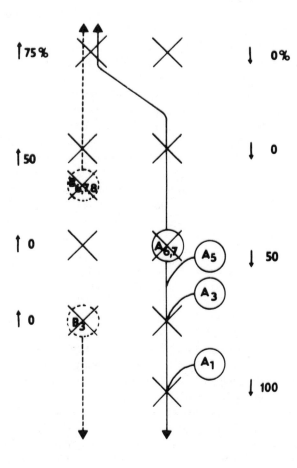

Fig. 28.2 Diagram of lesions placed in different areas of the brain stem from medulla oblongata to the mesencephalon with their effect on the adjuvant activity of MDP measured by the method of delayed hypersensitivity. B = serotonergic cell groups, A = catecholaminergic cell groups, X = lesions, O = nucleus, ↑↓ % of adjuvant activity expressed in percentage of sham operated animals.

increased the adjuvant activity of MDP. Lesions in these areas also influenced the MDP effects on temperature and sleep. On the contrary, lesions placed in the raphe region, caudal to the mesencephalo-pontine regions, had no effect. As far as the catecholaminergic structures are concerned, the most pronounced effect was at the level of the lower pons and in the medulla oblongata, especially in the region where $A_{1,3,5,7}$ cell groups are localised. The efferent projections from these cells are directed mainly caudally to the vegetative spinal centers. In their vicinity are also located direct hypothalamo-spinal connections that terminate in the gray matter in the spinal cord. It is possible that the effects which we have observed could also have been a result of the destruction of the hypothalamo-spinal pathways, but this is less probable since the lesions in the upper pons and mesencephalon which destroyed the hypothalamo-spinal pathways had no effect. Thus our results suggest that the effect of MDP on the immune system is, at least, partly regulated by the brain stem mechanisms with a participation of serotonergic and catecholaminergic structures. Although the exact mechanism is not yet completely clear, the results suggest that the role of serotonin in the immune response might be inhibitory and that of catecholamines, stimulatory. Such a conclusion is supported by previous investigators, who evaluated the effect of pharmacological manipulation of the levels of serotonin or catecholamines on the immune response and also by *in-vitro* studies where different neurotransmitters have been added to immunocompetent cells in tissue culture (Devoino *et al.*, 1968a, b; Cross *et al.*, 1986; Sanders and Munson, 1984). However, it has to be added that the interpretation of results obtained with lesions is complicated by the fact that serotonergic or catecholaminergic groups probably contain other neurotransmitters. The whole concept of possible immuno-neuroendocrine interactions has been discussed recently by Besedovsky *et al.* (1985). The involvement of central serotonergic and catecholaminergic pathways in MDP-induced modulation of immunity is further supported by our biochemical experiments in which we have measured the turnover of these amines in different areas of the brain. The results of these experiments are summarised in Table 28.2. The method for the measurement of the turnover rates of amines has been reported previously (Mašek *et al.*, 1980). From the results it is evident that only the dose which is immunoadjuvant increases the turnover rate of serotonin in all investigated regions, but particularly in the upper part of the brain stem. The results of experiments in which we have measured the turnover rate of noradrenaline, are not so clear. As can be seen from the results depicted in Fig. 28.3, the administration of the central serotonin receptor antagonist methiothepin (1-/10,11-dihydro-8-(methylthio)dibenzo-/b,f/thiepin-10-yl/-4-methylpiperazine maleate) had an effect similar to that of the lesion since the delayed hypersensitivity response induced by MDP was increased.

Another CNS-mediated effect of muramyl peptides is the effect on sleep. 15 years ago we reported that bacterial peptidoglycans, which have the muramyl dipeptide subunits in their structure, markedly influenced sleep pattern in rats. The effect was not due to a simultaneous increase of body temperature since the

Table 28.2

Treatment	Turnover rate of serotonin (μg/g/h[†])		
	Hypothalamus	Midbrain	Medulla oblongata + Pons
Control	0.75 ±		
Control	0.75 ± 0.15	0.45 ± 0.08	0.52 ± 0.15
MDP 25 μg/kg	0.87 ± 0.19	0.65 ± 0.16	0.95 ± 0.20*
MDP 250 μg/kg	1.65 ± 0.42*	0.97 ± 0.24*	1.05 ± 0.30*

*Statistically significant results. $p < 0.05$
†Values are means ± SEM

Turnover rate of noradrenaline

Treatment	Tissue	Steady state level (μg/g[†])	Rate constant of amine loss/h	Turnover rate (μg/g/h)
Control	Hypothalamus	1.64 ± 0.32	0.20	0.33
MDP 250 μg/kg		1.69 ± 0.38	0.29	0.49
Control	Midbrain	0.42 ± 0.04	0.16	0.07
MDP 250 μg/kg		0.38 ± 0.03	0.15	0.06
Control	Medulla oblongata + Pons	0.55 ± 0.06	0.16	0.10
MDP 250 μg/kg		0.52 ± 0.05	0.28	0.15

†Values are means ± SEM.

Delayed hypersensitivity

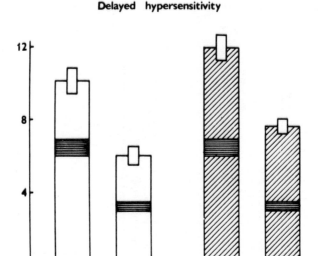

Fig. 28.3 The effect of central serotonin receptor antagonist methiothepin on MDP adjuvant activity measured by the method of delayed skin hypersensitivity to ovalbumin. Horizontal hatching: control animals injected by Freund incomplete adjuvant (FIA). Unhatched: animals injected with 100 μg of MDP + FIA. Diagonal hatching: animals injected with 100 μg of MDP + FIA and 5 mg/kg of methiothepin.

administration of salicylates, which abolish fever, did not influence the effect on sleep (Masek *et al.*, 1973). Working with the synthetic MDP, we have been able to show that the effect on sleep is evidently dose-dependent. Very small doses of MDP (25 μg/kg), which are neither pyrogenic nor immunogenic, enhanced both the slow wave sleep (SWS) and the rapid eye movement (REM) sleep. On the other hand, high doses, such as 1000 μg/kg, had the opposite effect and caused a pronounced inhibition of REM sleep. The results of experiments on rats where sleep cycles were evaluated by means of bipolar stainless electrodes bilaterally implanted in frontal cortex and dorsal hippocampus have been reported previously (Kadlecová and Mašek, 1986), and are summarised in Table 28.3. The administration of an inhibitor of serotonin synthesis, para-chlorophenylalanine (PCPA), twice in a dose of 300 mg/kg, resulted in the inhibition of both types of sleep, SWS and REM. This, of course, is not surprising since such an effect has been noted previously by several authors in different animal species (Koella *et al.*, 1968). However, if MDP was administered to such animals in a sleep-promoting dose (25 μg/kg), the effect was antagonised and the sleep patterns in this groups of animals was the same as in the control group injected only with saline. The involvement of serotonergic structures in the MDP-evoked

Table 28.3   Effect of PCPA and MDP on sleep in rat

Treatment	% SWS*	% REM†
Control	49.96 ± 2.25	6.2 ± 1.98
PCPA 300 mg/kg × 2	36.4‡ ± 6.59	1.5‡ ± 1.19
MDP 25 μg/kg	53.7 ± 1.77	14.9‡ ± 0.99
PCPA + MDP	50.8 ± 3.84	6.6 ± 0.4

*% SWS values are means ± SEM for 1 to 4 h. †% REM values are means ± SEM for 1 to 4 h. ‡Significantly different $p < 0.05$. PCPA: para-chlorophenylalanine.

effect on sleep is supported also by biochemical experiments where the turnover of serotonin was measured. In a sleep-promoting dose of MDP turnover was increased in medulla oblongata and pons (Mašek, 1986).

As far as the pyrogenicity of muramyl peptide is concerned, we have reported previously that not only central serotonergic neurons but also the prostaglandin system is involved (Masek, 1986). It is important, however, to point out that the pyrogenic effect of MDP might be dissociated from the effect on sleep and immune response. The administration of compounds like indomethacin, which is a prostaglandin synthetase inhibitor, at a dose of 3 mg/kg, can abolish the effect of MDP on temperature, but does not affect the MDP-induced sleep changes or immune response. The measurement of the turnover rate of serotonin in different regions of the brain reflected these changes (Masek, 1986).

Changes in body temperature as well as changes in the sleep–waking cycle are frequently reflected not only by changes in the immune response but also by changes in the pain threshold. Recently we have, therefore, investigated the effect of MDP on the pain threshold using two methods, the hot plate method, a test that involves measurement of the time it takes the animal to perceive an uncomfortable warming, and the writhing test – where acetic acid is injected intraperitoneally and the writhing of animals registered. We have observed a dose-dependent antinociceptive effect of MDP in both tests. A link with the serotonergic system is again evident, since the effect of PCPA, which significantly decreases the threshold of pain, can be antagonised by the administration of MDP. The results of these experiments are summarised in Fig. 28.4.

While the relationship of the temperature increase to the immune response seems clear, that of sleep is less so. In-vivo, as well as in-vitro, experiments suggest that the mild increase of temperature enhances the immune response and increases T- and B-cell function (Duff, 1986). On the other hand, evidence for a beneficial effect of sleep is more indirect in that sleep deprivation may decrease cell-mediated immune reactions, and thus host defence (Palmblad et al., 1979).

Since, on the basis that muramyl peptide possesses, in addition to immunological activity, also neuropharmacological effects mediated via serotonergic structures, we have started to investigate a possible interaction of muramyl

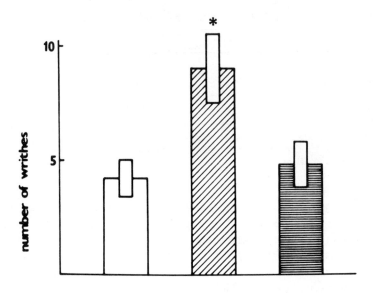

Fig. 28.4 The effect of administration of 25 μg/kg of MDP i.v. on hyperalgesia in mice induced by i.v. administration of an inhibitor of tryptophan hydroxylase para-chlorophenylalanine in two doses 400 mg/kg. Pain thresholds were assessed by acetic acid writhing test. Unhatched: control animals; diagonal hatching: PCPA-treated animals; horizontal hatching: PCPA-treated animals injected with MDP.

peptides with serotonin receptors. Simple and rapid methods to study central and peripheral serotonin binding sites are at present available, but such radio-ligand binding studies are prone to many artefacts, and functional correlates are not easy to find. In addition, recent evidence suggests that there might be multiple types of [³H]-5-HT binding sites in the CNS (Blurton and Wood, 1986).

We therefore decided to approach this problem by classical pharmacological methods using different isolated tissues. We have used the guinea-pig ileum, rat stomach strip, rat colon ascendens and the guinea-pig and mouse vas deferens to analyse possible effects of MDP on different types of receptors. The results obtained suggest that MDP has an affinity for serotonin receptors in both guinea-pig ileum and rat stomach strip. The contractions caused by MDP are specific since the isomer of muramyl dipeptide, MDP-D, which is biologically inactive, did not evoke contractions. Additionally, the MDP effect could be specifically antagonised by the serotonin antagonists lisuride, methysergide and methiothepin. Antagonists of other neurotransmitters had no effect. Moreover, the preparation desensitised to the effect of serotonin did not react by an increase in the twitch peak tension or by contraction upon the addition of MDP. A summary of these results is presented in Fig. 28.5. Details of the method and results have been published previously (Kadlec *et al.*, 1984). In addition, we have noted

Guinea-pig ileum twitches

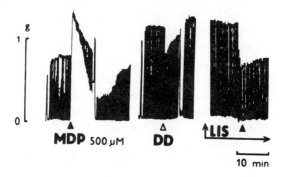

Rat stomach strip d-rc

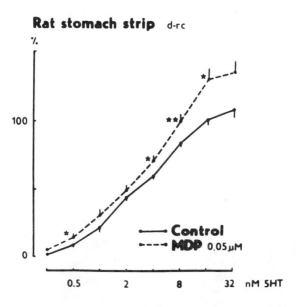

Fig. 28.5 Top: The effect of MDP (Muramyl L-Ala, D-iGlu) and or DD (Muramyl D-Ala, D-iGlu) on twitch contractions of the strip preparation from the guinea-pig ileum. The twitches were evoked by electrical neurogenic stimulation (0.1 Hz). MDP or DD were added in a concentration of 500 μmol/l. Lisuride (LIS, 1 μmol/l) prevented the contractile effect of MDP. Bottom: The effect of MDP (0.05 μmol/l) on the dose–response curve (d–r c) of 5-HT in rat stomach strip preparations. Means ± SEM of 20 control or 15 determinations in the presence of MDP are given. Asterisks denote a significant increase (t-test for paired data) in the tension reached in the presence of MDP compared with the control situation.

that a very low concentration of MDP (50 nmol/l) increases the sensitivity of the rat stomach strip to serotonin in *in-vitro* experiments, as well as *in-vivo* situations when MDP is administered in a dose of 1 µg/h for 10 days by Alzet osmotic pumps. Large doses of MDP or longer times of application have the opposite effect, i.e. a desensitisation (Kadlec *et al.*, 1985).

More recently, we have been able to show that MDP has an effect on the rate of disappearance of [³H]-serotonin from different areas of the brain. In these experiments MDP was injected in the dose of 250 µg/kg intravenously 10 min after [³H]-serotonin (specific activity 30.0 Ci/mmol; NEN)) was injected in the dose of 5 µCi in 20 µl of Merlis solution into the cerebral ventricles of rats. The group of animals were killed by decapitation 1, 2 and 3 hours after the administration of the labelled compound and the brains removed, rapidly rinsed 3 times, chilled and the hypothalamus, midbrain and medulla oblongata plus pons dissected, as described by Glowinski and Iversen (1966). The radioactive serotonin in tissue samples was determined, after separation on a Dowex-50 column with a Beckman scintillation counter (Schildkraut *et al.*, 1969). The results are summarised in Fig. 28.6. It can be seen that, particularly in the midbrain, the level of [³H]-serotonin was decreased in the animals treated with muramyl dipeptide.

Similar results have been obtained in experiments where MDP was injected *in vivo*, at the same dose of 250 µg/kg, and the release of serotonin measured *in*

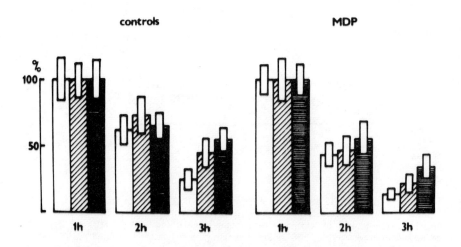

Fig. 28.6   The effect of *in-vivo* administration of 250 µg/kg of MDP on release of [³H]-5-HT from different areas of rat brain after i.c.v. administration. Unhatched, hypothalamus; diagonal hatching, midbrain; horizontal hatching, medulla oblongata + pons. Columns represent the mean ± SEM.

vitro from brain tissue sliced and incubated as described by Bineau-Thurotte *et al.* (1984). As can be seen from Fig. 28.7, MDP increased both spontaneous release and release stimulated by depolarisation (25 mmol/1 K^+). Details of the method and results have been reported previously (Horák, in press).

So, a common set of receptors in different tissues for serotonin and MDP seems to exist since these have also been demonstrated by radioligand binding studies on macrophages (Silverman *et al.*, 1985). The identification and characterisation of serotonin binding sites for muramyl peptide in the central nervous system is the subject of our present effort. It is certainly of interest that the tryptophan region of myelin basic protein has been suggested to be one of the possible binding sites for serotonin and muramyl peptides (Root-Bernstein and Westall, 1983).

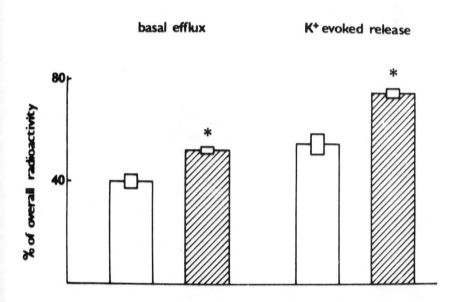

Fig. 28.7   The effect of *in-vivo* administration of 250 μg/kg of MDP on basal and potassium evoked release of [^{3}H]-5-HT from rat brain subcortical prisms. Prisms previously preloaded with [^{3}H]-5-HT were incubated in medium with low (3 mmol/l) or high (25 mmol/l) concentration of K^+ to obtain basal efflux and K^+-evoked release. Each column represents the mean ± SEM. Unhatched: control animals; hatched: MDP-treated animals. *Statistical significance, $p < 0.05$.

A number of neurophysiological and mental disorders, including depression, are known to involve disturbance of serotonergic systems. Even more specifically, 5-HT_2 sites have also been suggested to have a role in the etiology of some depressive illnesses, on the basis that they are apparently down-regulated (Peroutka and Snyder, 1980).

Muramyl peptides have been found in mammalian tissues such as the liver, kidney or the brain, but also in fluids (Zhai and Karnovsky, 1984). If these compounds bind to serotonergic binding sites in the CNS, as we have suggested, such a binding might, of course, have important consequences. It might result in the discovery of receptors of a new subtype and it also might, for instance, influence the binding ability and reactivity of the serotonin receptor. It might even influence, by a feedback mechanism, the release and synthesis of the neurotransmitter itself. One can even consider the possibility of formation of antibodies against such a receptor which might offer an explanation for the role of MDP in some autoimmune diseases.

That MDP binds to serotonin receptors might help us to explain at least some of the effects of muramyl peptide which we have observed, including the effects on temperature, sleep, pain reception and the immune response. Moreover, having in mind the possible role of serotonin in depressive illness, the binding of muramyl peptide to serotonin receptor might even offer new aspects in the search for the biochemical background of this disease.

I believe that immunopharmacological approaches in the research of mental disorders, including the depression illness, are worthy of further research. They can bring not only new data for better understanding of these widespread diseases but they can also improve our understanding of the possible relationship between depression and altered immunity. Immunopharmacological approaches might even lead to the development of new compounds for the treatment of patients suffering from this disease.

References

Adam, A. (1985). *Synthetic Adjuvants (Modern Concepts in Immunology, VI)*. Wiley-Interscience, New York, 23–6.

Besedovsky, H. O., del Rey, A. E., and Sorkin, E. (1985). *J. Immunol.*, **135**, 750–4.

Bineau-Thurotte, M., Godefroy, F., Weil-Fugazza, J., and Bessan, J. M. (1984). *Brain Res.*, **291**, 293–9.

Blurton, P. A., and Wood, M. D. (1986). *J. Neurochem.*, **46**, 1392–8.

von Brauchitsch, H. (1972). *Am. J. Psychiatry*, **129**, 1552–3.

Colover, J. (1980). *Br. J. Exp. Pathol.*, **61**, 390–400.

Cross, R. J., Jackson, J. C., Brooks, W. H., Sparks, D. L., Markesbery, W. R., and Rozsman, T. L. (1986). *Immunology*, 57, 145–52.

Deberdt, R., van Hooren, J., Biesbrouck, M., and Amery, W. (1976). *Biol. Psychiatry*, **11**, 69–74.

Devoino, L. V., and Ilyutchenok, R. Y. (1968a). *Eur. J. Pharmacol.*, **4**, 449–56.

Devoino, L. V., Korovina, L. S., and Ilyutchenok, R. Y. (1968b). *Eur. J. Pharmacol.*, **4**, 441–8.

Duff, W. G. (1986). *Yale J. Biol. Med.*, **59**, 125–130.

Ellouz, F., Adam, A., Ciorbaru, R., and Lederer, E. (1974). *Biochem. Biophys. Res. Commun.*, **59**, 1317–25.

Fevrier, M., Birrien, J. L., Leclerc, C., Chedid, L., and Liacopoulos, P. (1978). *Eur. J. Immunol.*, **8**, 558–62.

Glowinski, J., and Iversen, L. L. (1966). *J. Neurochem.*, **13**, 655–69.
Gottschalk, L. A., Welch, W. D., and Weiss, J. (1983). *Psychother. Psychosom.*, **39**, 23–35.
Horák, P., and Mašek, K. (1985). *Abstracts*, Symposium Current Problems in Testing and Evaluation of Experimental and Clinical Effects of Immunomodulators, Prague, May 12–14, 100.
Horák, P. (in press). *Meth. Find. Exptl Clin. Pharmacol.*
Kadlec, O., Mašek, K., Gulda, O., Růžička, V., Parant, M., and Chedid, L. (1984). *Pharmacology*, **29**, 31–9.
Kadlec, O., Mašek, K., Zídek, Z., and Leclerc, C. (1985). *Abstracts*, Symposium Current Problems in Testing and Evaluation of Experimental and Clinical Effects of Immunomodulators, Prague, May 12–14, 109.
Kadlecová, O., and Mašek, K. (1986). *Meth. and Find. Exptl Clin. Pharmacol.*, **8**, 111–15.
Koella, W. P., Feldstein, A., and Czicman, J. S. (1968). *Electroenceph. Clin. Neurophysiol.*, **25**, 481–84.
Löwy, I., Bona, C., and Chedid, L. (1977). *Cell. Immunol.*, **29**, 195–9.
Mašek, K. (1986). *Federation Proc.*, **45**, 2549–51.
Masek, K., Kadlecová, O., and Petrovický, P. (1980). In J. M. Lipton (ed.), *Fever*. Raven, New York, 123–30.
Mašek, K., Kadlecová, O., and Petrovický, P. (1985). *Brain Research Bull.*, **15**, 443–6.
Mašek, K., Kadlecová, O., and Rašková, H. (1973). *Neuropharmacology*, **12**, 1039–47.
Nagai, Y., Akiyama, K., Kotani, S., Watanabe, Y., Shimono, T., Shiba, T., and Kusumoto, S. (1978a). *Cell. Immunol.*, **35**, 168–72.
Nagai, Y., Akiyama, K., Suzuki, K., Kotani, S., Watanabe, Y., Shimono, T., Shiba, T., Kusumoto, K., Ikuta, F., and Takeda, S. (1978b). *Cell. Immunol.*, **35**, 158–67.
Palmblad, J., Petrini, B., Wasserman, J., and Åkersted, T. (1979). *Psychosom. Med.*, **41**, 273–8.
Peroutka, S. J., and Snyder, S. H. (1980). *J. Pharmac. Exp. Ther.*, **215**, 582–7.
Root-Bernstein, R. S., and Westall, F. C. (1983). *Lancet*, i, /8325/, 653.
Sanders, V. M., and Munson, A. E. (1984). *J. Pharmacol. Exp. Ther.*, **231**, 527–31.
Schildkraut, J. J., Schanberg, S. M., Breese, R. G., and Kopin, I. J. (1969). *Biochem. Pharmac.*, **18**, 1971–8.
Schindler, T. E., Coffey, R. G., and Hadden, J. W. (1986). *Int. J. Immunopharmac.*, **8**, 487–98.
Schleifer, S. J., Keller, S. E., Siris, S. G., Davis, K. L., and Stein, M. (1985). *Arch. Gen. Psychiatry*, **42**, 129–33.
Sen, Z., and Karnovsky, M. L. (1984). *Infec. Immun.*, **43**, 937–41.
Silverman, D. H. S., Wu, H., and Karnovsky, M. L. (1985). *BBRC*, **131**, 1160–7.
Zhai, S., Karnovsky, M. L. (1984). *Infect. Immun.*, **43**, 937–41.

29

New Concepts in the Action of Mood Stabilisers and Antidepressants

H. M. Emrich, C. Schmauss, M. Dose, M. Lonati-Galligani, K. M. Pirke and M. Weber

29.1 Introduction

Psychotropic compounds, which exert an immediate effect on mood, may be subdivided into three groups of drugs, namely the 'unidirectional antimanics', the 'unidirectionally operating, activating, "high"-producing compounds', and the 'mood stabilisers'. If a 'mood balance' is regarded as representing a relevant model of the biological features of affective disorders then these three groups of drugs may qualitatively be described as depicted in Fig. 29.1. Unidirectional antimanics are the neuroleptics and the cholinergic drugs like physostigmine (Janowsky et al., 1973) and RS 86 (Berger et al., 1986). Undirectionally operating, 'high'-producing compounds appear to be the MAO-inhibitor tranylcypromine which has an amphetamine-like side-effect (A. Delini-Stula, personal communication), the amphetamines, cocaine, and, probably, the opiates, at least if they are presented in a galenic formulation allowing for a rapid transport across the blood–brain barrier (e.g. heroin i.v.). (The classical tri- and tetracyclic antidepressants are not discussed here, since they require a longer latency-period for psychomotor and mood activation.) Within the group of mood stabilisers, besides lithium, the anticonvulsants carbamazepine and valproate are listed. The calcium antagonists possibly also have to be classified as 'mood stabilisers', since they apparently exert antimanic as well as antidepressant effects. However, a clear decision in this regard cannot be made at present. One problem in Fig. 29.1 is the possible position of the 'mood stabilisers' in relation to the 'mood balance', since they apparently act therapeutically on both mania and depression, though

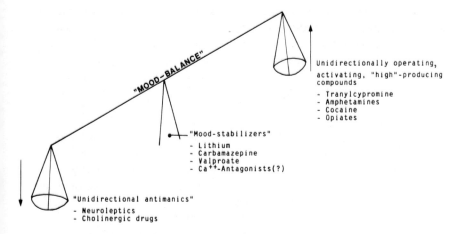

Fig. 29.1 Schematic representation of psychopharmacological influences on the regulation of mood, modified after Post (1984).

the acute antidepressant effects of these compounds are less pronounced and take longer to occur than the antimanic actions (Post *et al.*, 1984). This problem of 'bifunctionality' of mood stabilisers will be discussed at the end of this paper in relation to a speculative model of the neurobiological basis of the regulation of mood.

29.2 Endorphin Research and Depression

The discovery of the endorphins and the speculation about a possible abnormality of these opioids in endogenous depression has readdressed an old question, namely whether opiates represent a relevant contribution to the arsenal of antidepressants and, if they do so, whether they are active by compensating an endogenous opioid-system deficiency or whether they act at only a symptomatic level.

29.2.1 History of the Use of Opiates in Depression

Historically, opiates have apparently been used as antidepressants at least since the time of Hippocrates. Though this is generally known (for review see Herz and Emrich, 1983) it is often overlooked that opiates played a major role in pharmacotherapy of psychotic disorders, especially of depression, in the nineteenth century in Germany and in England.

Homer's *Odyssey* already describes a substance named 'nepenthes' with anti-depressant effects, 'a remedy against grief and grudge', that probably contained opium. Other ancient and medieval medical authors, e.g. Dioskurides and Hildegard Bingensis, or Avicenna, observed not only the hypnotic or sedative but also the undesired effects of opium. However, antidepressant impacts and concepts regarding drug-dependency were not specified. One of the earliest reliable references as to a therapeutic use of opium for depressive disorders can be found in medieval German pharmacopoeias.

Theophrastus Paracelsus is often considered as the Renaissance authority who caused the reintroduction of opium into European medicine, although his well-known 'laudanum' may not have been identical to the opium-containing tincture propagated by some of his later disciples like Oscar Croll. Thomas Sydenham recommended opium for different diseases, including 'mania', and initiated the general acceptance of opium in the medicine of modern times.

Sources of the seventeenth and eighteenth centuries delivered both unsystematic reports and more elaborate theories about opium use for psychic disorders. Balthasar Tralles, Hermann Boerhaave and Gerhard van Swieten mentioned a method of gradual increase and reduction of the opium doses prescribed for the treatment of mania and depression. Albrecht von Haller exactly described the development of an opium-dependency he acquired after having started an opium therapy for cystopyelitis.

During the Romantic era of German psychiatry the practical value of opium in psychiatry was vehemently discussed. Supporters and opponents of the method could neither prove their clinical results nor clarify contemporary pharmacological theories and the concepts were dominated by idealistic philosophical ideas or very early physiological and biochemical experiments. Interestingly, at about 1840 opium was, nevertheless, a fundamental but also a questioned part of psychiatric pharmacotherapy.

Hermann and Friedrich Engelken from Lower Saxonia and Bremen (Northern Germany), members of the Engelken family of psychiatrists, who had developed a systematic variant of the opium therapy in affective disorders, alcoholic and puerperal psychoses since 1800, prompted an international debate about opium in psychiatry with their articles (Engelken, 1851) and lectures. They denied an iatrogenic dependence if the indications (e.g. severe 'major' depressive disorders) were recognised. As had been the case fifty years earlier, the problems of the theoretical background and clinical efficacy of opium therapy remained unsolved.

However, the Engelken method of systematic and gradual increase and decrease of opium doses in relation to the psychopathological status of the depressed patient remained the only rational psychopharmacological therapy for affective disorders until 1940. In particular, the new galenic form of morphine injections gained importance in clinical psychiatry. There are no verified historic reports about opiate dependency induced by the classic *Opiumkur* of severely depressed patients. Psychiatric textbooks written before 1950 generally recommend the *Opiumkur*.

Since the introduction of tricyclic antidepressants and owing also to the development of heroin dependency, the opiate therapy of depression completely disappeared in clinical practice. However, the search for alternative therapeutic strategies and the discovery of opiate receptors and endorphins have been responsible for the new interest in opium derivatives, an interesting re-establishment of a discussion which is as old as occidental medicine.

29.2.2 Electroconvulsion and Endorphins

Regarding the mode of action of electroconvulsion (ECT), a number of different mechanisms have been suggested, ranging from psychological mechanisms to the effects on the molecular biology of the brain (Fink, 1979; Palmer, 1981). The impact of ECT on the operation of brain monoamines is the focus of neurobiological research as to the clinical mode of action of ECT. According to these findings, ECT increases the response to brain monoamines (Grahame-Smith et al., 1978), is effective via a noradrenergic mechanism of action in potentiating sero-tonin- and dopamine-mediated behaviours (Green and Deakin, 1980) and induces a down-regulation of β-adrenergic receptors (Pandey et al., 1979). These findings may explain some of the antidepressant and anticatatonic effects of ECT. On the other hand, as reviewed by Fink (1979), the neurohormonal effects of ECT also demand consideration. Neuropeptides especially may play an important role in the mediation of the beneficial effects of ECT.

Owing to the parallelism in the secretion of β-endorphin and ACTH (Guillemin et al., 1977) and the finding that ECT induces an elevation of plasma ACTH Allen et al., 1974), an activating effect of ECT on plasma β-endorphin immuno-reactivity may be anticipated. In line with this, Emrich et al. (1979a) observed an elevation of β-endorphin immunoreactivity in the plasma of patients suffering from endogenous depression 10 min subsequent to ECT. The determinations were performed by the use of a radioimmunoassay exhibiting a detection limit for β-endorphin of 35 pg/ml (Höllt et al., 1978). 10 min after ECT, β-endorphin immunoreactivity increased from about 40 to more than 60 pg/ml. These findings have been confirmed by Inturrisi et al. (1982), who found a rise of plasma β-endorphin immunoreactivity from about 30 to 80 to 90 pg/ml. These findings are also in line with the animal work of Holaday and co-workers (1981), pointing to an ECT-induced activation of central endorphinergic systems.

Emrich and co-workers (1979a) hypothesised that (at least some part of) the therapeutic action of ECT may be mediated via an endophinergic type of mechanism. Evidence obtained from a comparison of the clinical profiles of ECT and of opioids is, at present, not sufficiently comprehensive to be really convincing. In this context, it should be pointed out that ACTH is, apparently, not the relevant therapeutic factor, since, as summarised by Fink (1979), it has no real antidepressant activity.

29.2.3 Opioid Therapy in Depression, using Buprenorphine

The finding that the opiate mixed agonist/antagonist buprenorphine (Lewis, 1980) had mood-improving effects in post-operative patients (Harcus *et al.*, 1980) and, most importantly, that this strong analgesic substance is devoid of psychotomimetic effects and has a very low abuse potential (Jasinksi *et al.*, 1978; Mello *et al.*, 1981) suggested the performance of a clinical trial in resistant depression. Furthermore, it had been shown by Mello and Mendelson (1980) that buprenorphine exerts extremely positive subjective effects in opiate addicts. The aim of the investigation was to develop a new opioid substance with a strong antidepressant potency and a high degree of drug safety.

The study was performed by use of double-blind $A_1/B/A_2$ design ($A_{1/2}$ = placebo, B = buprenorphine). 13 patients who met the research diagnostic criteria (Spitzer *et al.*, 1978) for major depressive disorders gave their informed consent to participate in the study. The duration of the three therapeutic phases varied between: A_1, 1 and 7 days; B, 5 and 8 days; and A_2, 0 and 4 days. The patients were free of conventional thymoleptic drugs. Before commencement of the trial, a wash-out period of 4 days was performed. During the buprenorphine treatment phase, two sublingual tablets (0.2 mg per day) were given at 8.30 and 16.30 h. Psychopathological evaluation was performed by a trained psychiatrist every two days in the afternoon by use of the Inpatient Multidimensional Psychiatric Scale (IMPS) (Lorr *et al.*, 1962) and the Hamilton Scale for depression (Hamilton, 1960). Additionally, the global impression of depression and, as a screening of side effects, the symptoms 'nausea', 'vomiting', 'dizziness' and 'euphoria' were evaluated by use of the VBS (Verlaufs-Beurteilungs-Skala; Emrich *et al.*, 1977).

The mean results of the Hamilton scores before (A_1), during (B_1), (B_2) and (B_3) and after (A_2) buprenorphine treatment are depicted in Fig. 29.2. The data from B_1 to B_3 represent the average values of the Hamilton score at the beginning of the blind buprenorphine treatment (B_1), in the middle of buprenorphine treatment phase (B_2), and at the end of the buprenorphine treatment (B_3). A_2 represents the average data of the Hamilton scores at the end of the second placebo treatment period. As can be seen in Fig. 29.2, there is a strong reduction in the Hamilton scores during phases B_1 to B_3 in comparison with the placebo phases A_1, and, to a lesser degree, also in comparison with the second placebo phase A_2. These differences are highly significant ($p < 0.02$, Wilcoxon test).

An evaluation of the single data of individual patients reveals that about 50% of the patients responded very strongly to buprenorphine, whereas the other 50% were, apparently, non-responders. Since practically all the patients included in the study were non-responders to conventional thymoleptic therapy, this is a significant result. Most of the patients experienced some degree of slight nausea, dizziness and sedation (vomiting in one case) in the course of the study, but these side-effects, with the exception of the one case of vomiting, never became a problem during therapy.

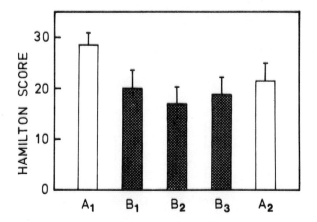

Fig. 29.2   Average Hamilton scores of 10 depressed patients before (A$_1$), during (B$_1$ to B$_3$) and after (A$_2$) buprenorphine treatment. Bars, SEM; for details see text.

29.2.4 Neuroendocrine Research Using Buprenorphine in Depression

The finding of Judd *et al.* (1983) that plasma prolactin responded to opiate challenge represented an important contribution to the biological psychiatry of depression, since it supported the assumption of an abnormal opioid function in depression, possibly at the opiate receptor level or at the level of secondary transmission. Therefore a replication of these findings was tried using buprenorphine as the opioid stimulant. The investigation was performed in $n = 12$ patients with endogenous depression in comparison with $n = 10$ normal probands. The prolactin increase after 0.2 mg buprenorphine (sublingual application) was identical in the two groups (Fig. 29.3). The conclusion to be drawn from the failure of replication of the findings of a blunted opioid-induced prolactin response is that, apparently, no decision can presently be made whether opioids are active by compensating an endogenous opioid deficiency (on the level of opioid release) or simply by a symptomatic effect on mood. However, apparently, the opiate receptor/secondary transmitter system is undisturbed in endogenous depression.

29.3 Clinical Psychopharmacology of 'Mood Stabilisers'

29.3.1 Lithium

The clinical pharmacology of mood stabilisers began with the introduction of lithium into the arsenal of psychoactive compounds in psychiatry in 1949 by

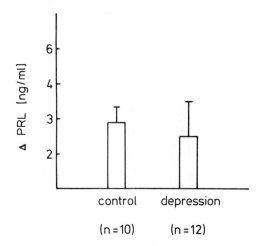

Fig. 29.3 Prolactin-increase after 0.2 mg buprenorphine (sublingual application) in 10 control subjects and 12 patients with endogenous depression.

John Cade, and, later on, by Baastrup and Schou (1967). Interestingly, Cade, in his classical work, had already described the most important features of the action (profile) of lithium, namely the acute antimanic effect, the prophylactic effect against mania, and the weakness of efficacy against schizophrenia. However, the prophylactic effect regarding depression and also the weak acute antidepressant effect of lithium was discovered later on by Baastrup and Schou (1967).

29.3.1.1 Prediction of Response

One serious problem in lithium therapy is the question as to whether the patient will respond to the therapy or not. Since about one-third of the patients, during long-lasting treatment, turn out to be non-responders, a prediction regarding the prospective individual responsiveness of the patient to lithium is of great clinical importance: an insufficient therapy could be avoided by such a procedure and an alternative drug could be prescribed earlier. In present research two different attempts have been initiated to solve this problem: registration of dark adaptation under lithium in comparison with pre-lithium conditions and measurement of lithium-impairment of cAMP synthesis in lymphocytes upon β-receptor stimulation with isoproterenol. Dark adaptation research regarding lithium has been established using two techniques: the 'Arden ratio', which is measured using electro-oculographic (EOG) recordings, reflects the corneo-fundal potential in retinal illumination and dark adaptation and is influenced by the state of dark adaptation; and direct measurement of dark adaptation using the 'Tübingen perimeter' (Ullrich *et al.*, 1985). Each variable demonstrates a strong reduction under lithium treatment in healthy volunteers as well as in patients with affective disorders. The data, accumulated up to now, are in line with the hypothesis that patients not properly responding to lithium also exhibit a blunted reduction of dark adaptation under lithium. However, the present data are not sufficient for a decisive conclusion in this regard.

The isoproterenol-induced cAMP-synthesis in human lymphocytes was measured in two groups of subjects:

(a) a group of normal subjects ($n = 10$) before and after lithium treatment (mean lithium plasma levels 0.7 mEq/l);

(b) a group of manic-depressive patients ($n = 7$) during lithium monotherapy (mean lithium plasma levels 0.75 mEq/l).

In the control subjects, the cAMP-levels after lithium treatment were reduced in comparison with the cAMP-levels before lithium treatment. The cAMP-levels of lithium-treated patients with affective disorders were decreased in a similar fashion as in the lithium-treated controls. The question whether cAMP-synthesis impairment during lithium treatment is a predictor of clinical response is at present being investigated in a similar fashion as for using dark adaptation for this purpose.

29.3.2 Anticonvulsants

Although the introduction of lithium into the therapy of affective disorders represented a real breakthrough, since it was possible for the first time to perform a prophylaxis of a psychosis, lithium therapy is burdened by a number of unresolved problems. One is the fact that, as stated above, a sizable number of patients do not properly respond to the treatment (lithium 'non-responders'). The other problem is the observation that many patients complain about a greater number of side-effects (e.g. weight gain, thyroid and kidney problems, tremor, etc.), often leading to non-compliance. This is a toxicity problem, which apparently is related to the low therapeutic range of the compound, also leading to the necessity of a continuous careful observation of the blood lithium levels. Alternatives as well as adjuncts, allowing for the adjustment of lower lithium levels, have been developed in the past, all of them representing anticonvulsants, namely valproate, dipropylacetamide, carbamazepine and oxcarbazepine (for review see Emrich *et al.*, 1984).

29.3.2.1 Valproate and Dipropylacetamide

The rationale for the investigation of the possible therapeutic effects of valproate in affective disorders was based on two observations. First, research as to the possible antimanic action of high dosages of the β-receptor blocker propranolol revealed that also the D-stereoisomer, dexpropranolol, exerted antimanic effects, leading to speculation that a type of mode of action unrelated to β-receptors is responsible for the effect (Emrich *et al.*, 1979b). Delini-Stula and Meier (1976) and Bernasconi (1982) demonstrated a GABAergic component within the action of high-dosage propranolol, leading to the idea of trying antimanic therapy using a GABAergic compound. Since valproate at that time was the only clinically introduced GABAergic drug, it was chosen for these trials (Emrich *et al.*, 1983). The other basis for this evaluation was found in the findings of Lambert *et al.* (1975), demonstrating therapeutic effects of the amidation product of valproate (dipropylacetamide) in affective disorders, though no operationalization of the clinical observations had been performed. Using a placebo-controlled ABA design, it could be demonstrated that sodium valproate exerts an acute anti-manic effect (Emrich *et al.*, 1980). Furthermore, a long-term prophylactic therapy with valproate (in one case with dipropylacetamide) was performed in 12 lithium nonresponders. In 11 of these cases the prophylaxis was performed in combination with low doses of lithium (serum levels 0.4 to 0.8 mEq/l). Over the five years preceding the valproate treatment, the average interval between phases ranged from 3 to 19 months (mean 10 months), whereas the relapse-free time during the prophylactic treatment ranged from 18 to 78 months (mean 41 months). Figure 29.4 gives an example of the phase chart of such a patient.

29.3.2.2 Carbamazepine

The first authors who had observations regarding a possible beneficial role of carbamazepine in affective disorders were the Japanese neurologists Takezaki and Hanaoka (1971). Okuma *et al.* (1973) investigated a greater series of patients with affective disorders and observed a complete disappearance of manic and depressive phases in about 35% of the cases, a reduced intensity of the phases in 32% of the cases, and inefficacy in 33%. The findings have been replicated by an NIMH-group (Ballenger and Post, 1978) and in the meantime there are a great number of controlled studies clearly supporting the view that carbamazepine alone and/or in combination with lithium is a very efficacious acute antimanic as well as prophylactic agent in bipolar psychoses (for review see Okuma, 1984).

29.3.3 Considerations Regarding the Mode of Action of Mood Stabilisers

The establishment of the 'psychopharmacological bridge', i.e. the extrapolation from the mechanism of action of a drug to a hypothesis about the biochemical

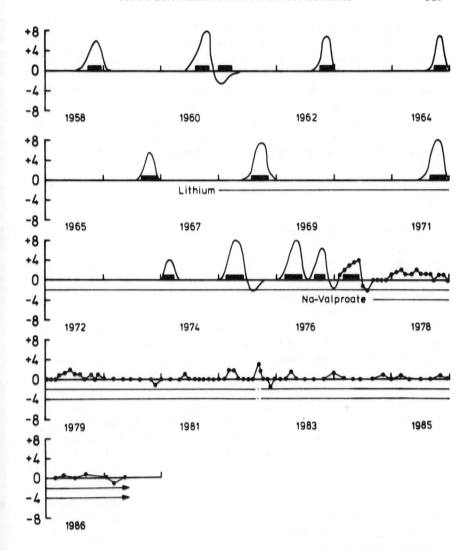

Fig. 29.4 Time-course of the psychopathology of a patient with bipolar affective disorder (ICD-9, No. 296.3), represented by use of the VBS (Verlaufs-Beurteilungs-Skala, i.e. course-assessment-scale; see Emrich *et al.*, 1977) under prophylactic long-term medication with valproate in combination with low doses of lithium. Heavy bars, hospitalisation; +8 = maximal mania; −8 = maximal depression.

bases of the disorder, has provoked attempts to find one common feature of lithium, valproate and carbamazepine, which would explain the observation that these compounds have a similar clinical profile of action, characterised by anti-manic > antidepressant > antischizoaffective antipsychotic efficacy. Attempts in this regard, performed in a fashion similar to that of Dr Post's group (1984), have failed, up to now, to demonstrate such a 'common link'. Valproate can be characterised – in contrast to carbamazepine – in so far as it apparently exerts its anticonvulsive effect via enhancement of GABAergic inhibition (Zeise and Zieglgänsberger, 1987), whereas carbamazepine appears to be an anticonvulsant by non-specific inhibition of excitation, possibly via inhibition of glutaminergic effects at the level of ion channels (Emrich, 1987). Lithium, on the other hand, exerts strong effects on the second messengers cAMP (cGMP) and inositol-3-phosphate (Sherman et al., 1981). As such, up to now, no unifying concept can be demonstrated.

29.4 Bidimensional Model of Affective Disorders

The clinical pharmacology of 'mood stabilisers' having been demonstrated, the question may be readdressed as to how to explain the fact that the mood stabilisers act in two obviously opposite directions, against mania as well as against depression. Two explanations appear possible: one assumes that the mood-stabilisers, pharmacologically, contain two modes of action, antimanic (e.g. antidopaminergic) and antidepressant (e.g. catecholaminergic) ones. However, a pharmacological characterisation of these drugs does not clearly demonstrate such properties. The second view, speculatively hypothesised here, claims that the 'gating zone' of the mood-regulating centre consists of two parts, one relevant for the activation of mania and one for the activation of depression. Such a 'bidimensional' model of regulation of affect would explain the clinical observation that mixed states can occur (often related to the switch process) in which manic- and depression-specific symptoms are present simultaneously. On the other hand, the bidimensional model of affective disorders represents an elegant way to explain why mood-stabilizers are bifunctional, i.e. that they can be therapeutically active simultaneously in obviously opposite conditions, namely mania and depression. It is assumed that mood-stabilisers inhibit the activation of both gating-zones, the depression-specific as well as the mania-specific (from $\emptyset$ to $\oplus$ in Fig. 29.5).

29.5 Conclusions

The anticonvulsant mood stabilisers valproate and carbamazepine, and their derivatives dipropylacetamide and oxcarbazepine, represent a highly challenging new class of compounds, therapeutically useful in affective disorders. If a pharmacological comparison between the modes of action of lithium, carbamazepine and valproate is performed, a lot of dissimilarities, besides some inter-

"GATING ZONE"

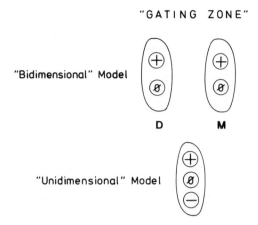

Fig. 29.5 Schematic representation of a 'unidimensional' and a 'bidimensional' model of the regulation of mood. It is assumed that in the 'bidimensional' model two 'gating zones' exist, one depression (D)- and one mania (M)-specific, which, independently, can be activated ($\emptyset \rightarrow \oplus$), whereas in the 'unidimensional' model a simultaneous activation of D and M cannot occur.

esting analogies, are found. Since a unifying concept, explaining the clinical profile of action of mood stabilisers, is presently not supported by neurobiological data, the speculative hypotheses regarding a bidimensionality in the action of mood stabilisers may be legitimate and open a new perspective in future research.

References

Allen, M. J. P., Denney, D., Kendall, J. W., and Blachy, P. H. (1974). Corticotropin release during ECT in man. *Amer. J. Psychiatry*, **131**, 1225-8.

Baastrup, P. C. and Schou, M. (1967). Lithium as a prophylactic agent: its effect against recurrent depressions and manic-depressive psychosis. *Arch. Gen. Psychiatry*, **16**, 162-72.

Ballenger, J. C., and Post, R. M. (1978). Therapeutic effects of carbamazepine in affective illness: a preliminary report. *Commun. Psychopharmacol.*, **2**, 159-75.

Berger, M., Krieg, J. C., Rummler, R., Raptis, C., Morinigo, A., Dose, M., and Benker, B. (1986). The treatment of mania with the cholinomimetic drug RS 86. *Pharmacopsychiat.*, **19**, 326-7.

Bernasconi, R. (1982). In Emrich, H. M., Aldenhoff, J. B., and Lux, H. D. (eds.), *Basic Mechanisms in the Action of Lithium*. Excerpta Medica, Amsterdam, 183-92.

Cade, J. F. J. (1949). Lithium salts in the treatment of psychotic excitement. *Med. J. Aust.*, **2**, 349-52.

Delini-Stula, A., and Meier, M. (1976). Inhibitory effects of propranolol and oxprenolol on excitation induced by a MAO inhibitor and reserpine in the mouse. *Neuropharmacology*, **15**, 383-8.

Emrich, H. M. (1987). In Hopf, H. C. (ed.), *Carbamazepin in der Neurologie*. Thieme, Stuttgart (in press).

Emrich, H. M., Cording, C., Pirée, S., Kölling, A., von Zerssen, D., and Herz, A. (1977). Indication of an antipsychotic action of the opiate antagonist naloxone. *Pharmako-psychiat.*, **10**, 265–70.

Emrich, H. M., Höllt, V., Kissling, W., Fischler, M., Laspe, H., Heinemann, H., von Zerssen, D., and Herz, A. (1979a). β-endorphin-like immunoreactivity in cerebrospinal fluid and plasma of patients with schizophrenia and other neuropsychiatric disorders. *Pharmako-psychiat.*, **12**, 269–76.

Emrich, H. M., von Zerssen, D., Möller, H.-J., Kissling, W., Cording, C., Schietsch, H. J., and Riedel, E. (1979b). Comparison of effects of the d- and the l-stereoisomer. *Pharmako-psychiat.*, **12**, 295–304.

Emrich, H. M., von Zerssen, D., Kissling, W., Möller, H.-J., and Windorfer, A. (1980). Effect of sodium valproate on mania – The GABA hypothesis of affective disorders. *Arch. Psychiat. Nervenkr.*, **229**, 1–16.

Emrich, H. M., Altmann, H., Dose, M., and von Zerssen, D. (1983). Therapeutic effects of GABA-ergic drugs in affective disorders. A preliminary report. *Pharmacol. Biochem. Behav.*, **19**, 369–72.

Emrich, H. M., Okuma, T., and Müller, A. A. (eds.) (1984). *Anticonvulsants in Affective Disorders*. Excerpta Medica, Amsterdam.

Engelken, F. (1851). Die Anwendung des Opiums in Geisteskrankheiten und einigen verwandten Zuständen. *Allgemeine Zeitschrift für Psychiatrie*, **8**, 393–434.

Fink, M. (1979). *Convulsive Therapy*. Raven, New York.

Grahame-Smith, D. G., Green, A. R., and Costain, D. W. (1978). Mechanism of the antidepressant action of electroconvulsive therapy. *Lancet*, i, 254–6.

Green, A. R., and Deakin, J. F. W. (1980). Brain noradrenaline depletion prevents ECS-induced enhancement of serotonine- and dopamine-mediated behaviour. *Nature*, **285**, 232–3.

Guillemin, R., Vargo, T., Rossier, J., Minick, S., Ling, N., Rivier, C., Vale, M., and Bloom, F. (1977). β-endorphin and adrenocorticotropin are secreted concomitantly by the pituitary gland. *Science*, **197**, 1367–9.

Hamilton, M. (1960). A rating scale for depression. *J. Neurol. Neurosur. Psychiat.*, **23**, 56–62.

Harcus, A. H., Ward, A. E., and Smith, D. W. (1980). Buprenorphine in postoperative pain: results in 7500 patients. *Anaesthesia*, **35**, 382–6.

Herz, A., and Emrich, H. M. (1983). In Angst, J. (ed.), *The Origins of Depression: Current Concepts and Approaches*. Springer, Berlin, 221–34.

Holaday, J. W., Tortella, F. C., and Belenky, G. L. (1981). In Emrich, H. M. (ed.), *The role of Endorphins in Neuropsychiatry*. Karger, Basle, 142–57.

Höllt, V., Przewlocki, R., and Herz, A. (1978). Radioimmunoassay of β-endorphin. Basal and stimulated levels in extracted rat plasma. *Naunyn-Schmiedeberg's Arch. Pharmacol.*, **303**, 171–4.

Inturrisi, C. E., Alexopoulos, G., Lipman, R., Foley, K., and Rossier, J. (1982). β-endorphin immunoreactivity in the plasma of psychiatric patients receiving electroconvulsive treatment. *Ann. N.Y. Acad. Sci.*, **398**, 413–23.

Janowsky, D. S., El-Yosef, K. M., Davis, J. M., and Sekerke, H. J. (1973). Parasympathetic suppression of manic symptoms by physostigmine. *Arch. Gen. Psychiatry*, **28**, 542–7.

Jasinski, D. R., Pevnick, J. S., and Griffith, J. D. (1978). Human pharmacology and abuse potential of the analgesic buprenorphine. *Arch. Gen. Psychiatry*, **35**, 501–6.

Judd, L. L., Risch, S. G., Parker, D. C., Janowsky, D. S., Segal, D. S., and Huey, L. Y. (1983). The effect of methadone challenge on the prolactin and growth hormone responses of psychiatric patients and normal controls. *Psychopharmacol. Bull.*, **18**, 204–7.

Lambert, P.-A., Carraz, G., Borselli, S., and Bouchardy, M. (1975). Le dipropylacetamide dans le traitement de la psychose maniaco-depressive. *L'Encephale*, **1**, 25–31.

Lewis, J. W. (1980). In Peck, C., and Wallace, M. (eds.), *Problems in Pain*. Pergamon, Oxford, 87–9.

Lorr, M., Klett, C. J., McNair, D. M., and Lasky, J. J. (1962). *Inpatient Multidimensional Psychiatric Scale*. Consulting Psychologists Press, Palo Alto, CA.

Mello, N. K., and Mendelson, J. H. (1980). Buprenorphine suppresses heroin use by heroin addicts. *Science*, **207**, 657–9.

Mello, N. K., Bree, M. P., and Mendelson, J. H. (1981). Buprenorphine selfadministration by rhesus monkey. *Pharmacol. Biochem. Behav.*, **15**, 215–25.

Okuma, T., Kishimoto, A., Inoue, K., Matsumoto, H., Ogura, A., Matsushita, T., Naklao, T., and Ogura, C. (1973). Antimanic and prophylactic effects of carbamazepine on manic-depressive psychosis. *Folia Psychiatr. Neurol. Jpn*, **27**, 283–97.

Okuma, T. (1984). In Emrich, H. M., Okuma, T., and Müller, A. A. (eds), *Anticonvulsants in Affective Disorders*, Excerpta Medica, Amsterdam, 76–87.

Palmer, R. L. (ed.) (1981). *Electroconvulsive Therapy: An Appraisal.* Oxford University Press, Oxford.

Pandey, G. N., Heinze, W. J., Brown, B. D., and Davis, J. M. (1979). Electroconvulsive shock treatment decreases β-adrenergic receptor sensitivity in rat brain. *Nature*, **280**, 234–5.

Post, R. M., Ballenger, J. C., Uhde, T. W., and Bunney, W. E., Jr (1984). In Post, R. M., and Ballenger, J. C. (eds.), *Neurobiology of Mood Disorders*. Williams and Wilkins, Baltimore, 777–816.

Sherman, W. R., Leavitt, A. L., Honchar, M. P., Hallcher, L. M., and Phillips, B. E. (1981). Evidence that lithium alters phosphoinositide metabolism: chronic administration elevates primarily D-myo-inositol-1-phosphate in cerebral cortex of the rat. *J. Neurochem.*, **36**, 1947–51.

Spitzer, R. L., Endicott, J., and Robins, E. (1978). *Research Diagnostic Criteria (RDC) for a Selected Group of Functional Disorders*, 3rd ed. New York Biometrics Research, New York State Psychiatric Institute, New York.

Takezaki, H., and Hanaoka, M. (1971). The use of carbamazepine (Tegretol) in the control of manic-depressive psychosis and other manic-depressive states. *Clin. Psychiatry*, **13**, 173–83.

Ullrich, A., Adamczyk, J., Zihl, J., and Emrich, H. M. (1985). Lithium effects on ophthalmological-electrophysiological parameters in young healthy volunteers. *Acta psychiatr. scand.*, **72**, 113–19.

Zeise, M. L., and Zieglgänsberger, W. (1987). Valproate augments postsynaptic inhibition and reduces the ability of rat neocortical cells in vitro to discharge repetitively. *Europ. J. Physiol.*, **408**, suppl. 1, R52.

30

Carbohydrate Craving, Obesity, Seasonal Depression and D-Fenfluramine

J. J. Wurtman, D. O'Rourke, H. R. Lieberman and R. J. Wurtman

The excessive amounts of calories ingested by obese individuals has long been thought to be due to their inability to adjust their calorie intake to meet, but not exceed, their energy needs. This over-consumption of calories can be consistent (every time an individual eats he consumes too much) or sporadic (the response to environmental cues such as an overabundance of highly desirable food). Such overeating has been assumed to be the result of some mechanism, as yet unidentified, regulating energy balance. Moreover, this assumption was the basis for the belief that weight loss could be accomplished by teaching overeaters about the caloric value of food and how to select foods to meet but not exceed their nutritional needs. The failure of most behavioural weight-loss programmes to achieve this objective indicates that the problem is more complex than the learning to select calorically correct foods and using 'will-power.'

This relatively simple view of the etiology of obesity may have developed because few studies have actually examined in quantitative ways the patterns of food intake among the obese. Although food records have been used to describe the caloric intake of the obese, they rarely represent actual food intake patterns. Food consumption often 'improves' while records of it are being kept, and snack consumption is usually underestimated. For example, at our Clinical Research Center we have observed that obese subjects under-report their calorie intake by as much as 600 to 800 calories per day if verbal recall is checked against actual consumption.

We have therefore developed a method of monitoring twenty-four-hour patterns of calories, protein and carbohydrate consumption from both meals and snacks. We have found that a subgroup of obese individuals whose weight is stable consume moderate amounts of calories from meals which are similar to those consumed by lean volunteers (unpublished observations). However, their total daily calorie intake is greatly increased by their snack intake; they consume an additional 800 calories or more each day in the form of carbohydrate-rich, protein-poor snack foods. Their snack intake is not random but occurs at a time of day, usually in the afternoon or evening, that is typical for each person. Moreover, the consumption of snack foods is associated not with the desire to relieve hunger but with the desire to produce positive changes in mood (Lieberman *et al.*, 1986; O'Rourke *et al.*, 1986; Wurtman *et al.*, 1981).

We also observed a similar pattern of excessive carbohydrate intake among individuals who undergo an annual period of rapid weight-gain. Their overeating occurs in association with an unusual form of depression that is triggered by the short days and long nights of the fall and early winter and relieved by the longer days of spring and summer (Rosenthal *et al.*, 1984). People with this syndrome, seasonal affective disorder (SAD), not only suffer from changes in mood, sleep, and energy levels but also from an intense desire to consume large amounts of carbohydrate-rich foods (Rosenthal *et al.*, 1984). We have monitored patterns of food intake among such individuals while they were depressed and when they were in remission (Wurtman *et al.*, 1985). These individuals significantly increased their carbohydrate intake both from meals and from snacks during the fall and winter when they were depressed. During the spring, when their mood and energy levels had returned to normal, their food intake decreased. Additionally, these subjects reported positive mood-changes following the consumption of carbohydrate-rich foods.

It is possible that many individuals who are either obese or rapidly gaining weight actually consume excessive amounts of carbohydrate-rich foods as a means of 'self-medication', i.e., to bring about desired changes in mood. For this subgroup of obese individuals, the etiology of their excess weight is not simply an inability to regulate calorie intake but a disorder in the regulation of carbohydrate consumption associated with a possible disorder in the regulation of mood.

Our interest in regulation of carbohydrate consumption and whether it was aberrant in certain types of eating disturbances originated several years ago when we observed that carbohydrate intake is regulated independently of calorie intake (Wurtman and Wurtman, 1977). Also, it was observed in animals that the synthesis and activity of the brain neurotransmitter serotonin was enhanced following the consumption of a carbohydrate-rich, protein-poor meal, owing to the increased uptake into the brain of serotonin's precursor, tryptophan. Conversely, the consumption of protein or a combination of protein and carbohydrate prevented this increase in serotonin synthesis because the amino acids that compete with tryptophan for uptake into the brain were increased following protein consumption. Since carbohydrate consumption could be related to serotonin synthesis, we became interested in whether brain serotonin was involved in regulating the consumption of carbohydrate intake. We therefore carried out a series of animal experiments that demonstrated a separate regulation for energy intake and carbohydrate intake. For example, when animals were treated with drugs that increased serotoninergic neurotransmission, their intake of carbohydrate-rich foods decreased (Wurtman and Wurtman, 1980). Moreover, when animals were given a meal sufficiently high in carbohydrate to increase serotonin synthesis then in a subsequent meal they consumed significantly more protein and less carbohydrate than animals fed a meal containing both protein and carbohydrate (Wurtman et al., 1983).

These studies were followed by a series of clinical investigations to determine whether an appetite for carbohydrate in people could also be observed, and whether it might be regulated, in part, by brain serotonin. Since serotonin's synthesis and release may be increased when carbohydrate-rich, protein-poor, foods are eaten, but not when protein is consumed alone or along with carbohydrate, we monitored the eating patterns among normal and obese individuals to see whether their patterns of food intake might be likely to increase serotonin synthesis and release. That is, did they ever tend to consume carbohydrate-rich foods without protein? Since, in our culture, the opportunity to consume carbohydrates alone occurs most frequently between or after meals, we monitored food intake at these times. In a pilot out-patient study with normal volunteers who claimed to have a tendency to snack, we found that over 60% of their snack choices consisted of carbohydrate-rich foods; in fact, most of the volunteers consumed only carbohydrate-rich foods as snacks (Wurtman and Wurtman, 1981). To determine if serotoninergic mechanisms might be involved in regulating the intake of these largely carbohydrate foods, we treated the subjects with DL-fenfluramine, which increases serotoninergic neurotransmission. The drug significantly reduced the intake of carbohydrate snack foods as compared with the intake of other foods (Wurtman and Wurtman, 1981).

These observations suggested that brain serotonin might be linked with the appetite for carbohydrate-rich foods in people as well as animals; thus, we were interested in whether abnormal regulation of carbohydrate intake by serotonin might be involved in the excessive carbohydrate intake reported by many obese individuals. We therefore carried out a series of in-patient studies designed to monitor patterns of food intake among obese individuals. We initially focused on obese individuals who claimed to have an excessive appetite for carbohydrate-rich snack foods. One of our objectives in this study was to determine whether the appetite for carbohydrate snack foods reported by many obese individuals was related to abnormal regulation of carbohydrate intake by serotonin or, as widely assumed, simply because carbohydrate-rich snack foods are abundant in our culture. To help distinguish between these two possibilities, we developed a method of dispensing snacks that made protein and carbohydrate-rich foods equally accessible any time subjects wished to snack. A refrigerated vending machine, located in a private area of the MIT Clinical Research Centre where the studies were carried out, was stocked with ten snack foods. All contained the same number of calories, an important consideration since many obese people attempt to avoid consuming too many calories when they first give in to the desire to snack. Five of the snack foods were high in carbohydrate and five high in protein. All the snacks contained the same amount of fat; thus, the basis of snack choice was neither calorie nor fat contents. Subjects gained access to the vending machine by typing their personal code onto a keypad attached to the door. The vending machine was interfaced to a microcomputer that recorded the identity of the subject, the time a snack was removed, and the type of snack taken.

In this first study subjects did not have a choice of meal foods but instead consume a standard diet that met their daily nutrient needs and contained about 1000 calories. In subsequent studies, subjects were able to choose the foods they preferred for meals, as well as for snacks. However, the snack foods available in all three studies were similar; thus, choice of foods at meals had no effect on choice of snacks (Rosenthal et al., 1986; O'Rourke et al., 1986). In all three studies, despite the similar accessibility of both protein snacks and carbohydrate snacks, few protein snacks were consumed on a regular basis. Subjects consumed an average five carbohydrate snacks a day in the first study and seven carbohydrate snacks a day in the second and third studies. (This difference was probably due to the slightly lower carbohydrate and calorie contents of the snacks offered in the subsequent studies.) In all of these studies, most subjects tended to eat less than one protein snack a day, and the majority of subjects never consumed any protein snacks (Wurtman et al., 1981; Wurtman, 1984). The pattern of snack intake exhibited was also of interest. The group as a whole tended to snack in the afternoon and evening; however, each individual was most likely to snack at only one of those times.

In the first in-patient study, obese subjects treated with DL-fenfluramine decreased their carbohydrate snack intake by 40% as compared with placebo-treated individuals. In two subsequent studies, D-fenfluramine (which is more specific in its effects than DL-fenfluramine) had similar effects on carbohydrate snack intake; i.e., a reduction by 40 to 41% (O'Rourke et al., 1986; Wurtman et al., 1985). Measurements of calorie and nutrient choice from meals also made in these studies allowed us to determine whether the excessive appetite for carbohydrate-rich foods was confined to snacks or included nutrient intakes from meals. In two separate studies, subjects were allowed to choose their meal foods from a variety of isocaloric items that were either high in carbohydrate (rice, mashed potatoes, muffins) or high in protein (seafood salad; baked chicken, cottage cheese). In both studies calorie intake from meals was moderate (about 2000), as was consumption of both protein and carbohydrate foods from meals. D-fenfluramine treatment had less of an effect on meal intake than it did on snack intake. A drug like fenfluramine may be effective in decreasing snack intake because it mimics the effect of carbohydrate intake itself, i.e. it increases brain serotonin. Thus, subjects respond to treatment with this drug with a reduced appetite for carbohydrate-rich foods.

Anecdotal reports from our subjects on their mood changes before and after carbohydrate snacking led us to investigate whether such snacking behaviour might be associated with mood changes that followed the ingestion of carbohydrates. Serotoninergic neurons have been implicated in the regulation of a variety of mood states, including fatigue, sleepiness and depression, and decrease in pain perception (Wurtman *et al.*, 1981). Since many antidepressant drugs enhance serotoninergic activity, it is possible that carbohydrate cravers consumed large amounts of carbohydrates at specific times of day to bring about specific mood-changes. To test this hypothesis, carbohydrate cravers were given a high-carbohydrate meal (104 g of carbohydrate) and their mood was assessed with standardised mood questionnaires immediately prior to and two hours after the meal. Their responses were compared with those of another sub-group of obese subjects (non-carbohydrate cravers) who also tended to consume an excessive number of their daily calories as snack foods (Wurtman *et al.*, 1981) but whose snack choices almost always included protein as well as carbohydrate foods. (Such snack choices would prevent changes in serotonin synthesis and release and presumably any changes in serotonin-mediated mood states.) We found significant differences in the mood responses of these two groups of obese snackers. The carbohydrate cravers felt more vigorous, alert, less tired and less depressed after the carbohydrate meal than the non-carbohydrate cravers. The considerable difference in mood seen after carbohydrate intake among these two groups of obese snackers suggested that preference for or avoidance of specific snack foods might be associated with subsequent mood-states. These individuals appeared to be overeating carbohydrates to alter their mood.

Some of the most compelling evidence that weight gain might be associated with serotonin-mediated disorders of mood has been provided recently by studies of SAD. We measured patterns of calorie and nutrient intakes among individuals suffering from SAD during the fall and the following spring and treated with D-fenfluramine. Calorie and carbohydrate intake from meals and snacks were significantly lower in the spring when the subjects were in remission than in the fall when they were depressed (Wurtman, 1984). The most marked change in total consumption was seen in snack intake. During the fall measurement period, over 1000 calories a day were consumed as carbohydrate-rich snacks; this decreased to less than 500 calories during the spring measurement period.

To determine whether the excessive intake of carbohydrate that characterised these subjects might involve serotonin, we treated a small number of subjects with D-fenfluramine and measured changes in food intake and mood (Wurtman, 1984). This treatment reduced food intake to levels observed in the spring (when the subjects were eating normally) among 6 out of the 8 subjects treated. 5 of these subjects also experienced almost complete remission of their depression. The next year, in a follow-up study with 18 patients, we observed similar effects of D-fenfluramine. The drug significantly decreased carbohydrate intake and reduced depression as measured by the Hamilton questionnaire. The close association of depression, overeating, and weight gain in the fall and winter, and normal mood, reduced food intake and weight loss in the spring and summer, suggesting a disorder in the regulation of mood, might therefore underlie disorders in the regulation of food intake. It is anticipated that more such studies will eventually result in both dietary and pharmacological therapies that affect both disorders. Moreover, if these disorders of mood and associated overeating recur on a predictable basis, such as in SAD, such treatments may have to be used yearly in order to prevent weight gain and to sustain the weight loss that occurred during remission.

References

Lieberman, H., Wurtman, J., and Chew, B. (1986). Changes in mood after carbohydrate consumption among obese individuals. *Am. J. Clin. Nutr.*, **45**, 772-8.

O'Rourke, D., Wurtman, J., Abou-Nader,T., Brzezinski, A., Chew, B., Marachant, P., and Wurtman, R. (in press). Treatment of seasonal affective disorder with D-fenfluramine. Abstr., *Conf. on Human Obesity, American Academy of Science*, New York.

Rosenthal, N., Sack, D., Gillin, J., Lewy, A., Goodwin, F., Davenport, Y., Mueller, P., Newsom, D., and Wehr, T. (1984). Seasonal affective disorder: a description of the syndrome and preliminary findings with light therapy. *Arch. Gen. Psychiatry*, **41**, 72-80.

Wurtman, J., Wurtman, R., Growdon, J., Henry, P., Liscomb, A., and Zeisel, S. (1981). Carbohydrate craving in obese people: suppression by treatments affecting serotoninergic transmission. *Int. J. Eating Disorders*, **1**, 2-11.

Wurtman, J., Wurtman, R., Mark, S., Tsay, R., Gilbert, W., and Growdon, J. (1985). D-Fenfluramine selectively suppresses carbohydrate snacking by obese subjects. *Int. J. Eating Disorders*, **4**, 89-99.

Wurtman, J. (1984). The involvement of brain serotonin in excessive carbohydrate snacking by obese carbohydrate cravers. *J. Am. Diet Assoc.*, **84**, 1004-7.

Wurtman, J., and Wurtman, R. (1977). Fenfluramine and fluoxetine spare protein consumption while suppressing calorie intake by rats. *Science*, **198**, 1178-80.

Wurtman, J., and Wurtman, R. (1980). Drugs that enhance central serotoninergic transmission diminish elective carbohydrate consumption by rats. *Life Sci.*, **24**, 823-6.

Wurtman, J., Moses, P., and Wurtman, R. (1983). Prior carbohydrate consumption affects the amount of carbohydrate rats choose to eat. *J. Nutr.*, **113**, 70-8.

Wurtman, J., and Wurtman, R. (1981). Suppression of carbohydrate intake from snacks and meals by D-Fenfluramine in tryptophan. In Garrattini, S. (ed.), *Anorectic Drugs: Mechanisms of Action and Tolerance*. Raven, New York, 169-82.

Wurtman, J., Wurtman, R., Reynolds, S., Tsay, R., and Chew, B. (in press). D-Fenfluramine suppresses snack intake among carbohydrate cravers but not among non-carbohydrate cravers, *Int. J. Eating Disorders*.

31

Allosteric Modulation of GABA Receptors and the Symptoms of Affective Disorders

A. Guidotti, M. L. Barbaccia and E. Costa

31.1 Introduction

The benzodiazepines (BZDs) are widely used as therapeutic agents to treat symptoms of numerous neuropsychiatric disorders, particularly when these disorders are associated with anxiety. Recent evidence has shown that BZD binding sites are part of a macromolecular protein complex that includes the GABA recognition sites and the Cl^- ionophore (Casalotti *et al.*, 1986, Haring *et al.*, 1985; Stephenson *et al.*, 1986). Probably, the pharmacological and therapeutic effects of BZDs and their congeners are mediated through a facilitation of GABAergic neurotransmission (Costa and Guidotti, 1985). Indirect evidence suggests that GABAergic function decreases in affective disorders characterised by a high level of anxiety (Bartholini *et al.*, 1986). This inference agrees with the beneficial effects of BZD treatment on anxiety and with the inner tension and panic symptoms elicited in man by derivatives of β-carboline-3-carboxylate esters (BCC) (Dorow and Duka, 1985), which act as negative allosteric modulators of GABA action on Cl^- channels (Costa and Guidotti, 1985).

In their search for endogenous ligands for the BZD receptors, Braestrup and collegues (1980) isolated the β-carboline-3-carboxylate ethyl ester (BCCE) from human urine and showed it to be a potent ligand at the BZD recognition site. Although they immediately showed that this BZD ligand was artificially produced during urine extraction, the BCCs turned out to possess interesting pharmacological properties and in fact they became a tool to elucidate the neuro-chemical processes underlying the pathogenesis of anxiety and panic attacks. For example, FG7142 (N-methyl-β-carboline-3-carboxylate), a metabolically more stable congener of BCCE, was used in clinical pharmacological studies with healthy volunteers. FG7142 (Dorow and Duka, 1985) induced symptoms ranging from inner tension and restlessness to occasional panic attacks lasting thirty minutes and included autonomic effects like sweating, flushes of warmth and increase of blood pressure that were comparable to clinical episodes of acute anxiety and panic attacks. It was also established that FG7142 and other BCC derivatives elicited proconflict responses in animals that might be related to anxiety and panic in man (Corda et al., 1983).

Interestingly, the anticonflict effect of BZD and the proconflict action of BCCE can be antagonised by flumazenil (RO-151788), a specific, high-affinity ligand, for the BZD binding site devoid of intrinsic anti- or proconflict action.

Recently, small peptide fragments of DBI (diazepam binding inhibitor), a polypeptide isolated from human, cow and rat brain (Guidotti et al., 1983), have been identified in human and rat brain (Ferrero et al., 1986a; Ferrero et al., 1986b) and have been measured in human cerebrospinal fluid (Barbaccia et al., 1986). Some of these peptides injected intracerebroventricularly elicit a proconflict activity in rats similar to that of FG7142. This finding suggests that these peptides act as endogenous modulators of the GABA-BZD-Cl⁻ ionophore-receptor complex and might participate in the expression of psychopathological symptoms characterised by high levels of anxiety.

31.2 The GABA$_A$ Receptor Complex as the Focal Point of Action for BZDs or BCCs

The turning point for the elucidation of the molecular mechanisms of BZD and BCC action has been the discovery that a close correlation exists between the pharmacological action of the BZDs and BCCs and their ability to alter GABA-ergic transmission (Costa and Guidotti, 1979). The action of BZDs or BCCs on GABAergic transmission appears to be mediated by a positive (BZD) and nega-tive (BCC) allosteric modulation of the number of the GABA recognition sites that regulate the opening of Cl⁻ channels located in neuronal membranes. At the molecular level, the existence of a close interaction between BZD binding and GABA binding has been demonstrated in preparations of BZD receptors purified to homogeneity by affinity chromatography using BZD derivatives as ligands. These studies indicate that the BZD-BCC recognition sites are located on a large polymeric protein complex whose α- and β-subunits bind GABA, BZD, BCC, picrotoxin and barbiturates. Occupation of one of these sites by GABA induces reversible structural modification of the binding sites for the other ligand, allowing functional characteristics to be modified (Casalotti et al.,

1986; Haring *et al.*, 1985; Stephenson *et al.*, 1986). The subunits of the GABA-BZD-BCC-Cl⁻ ionophore–receptor complex have been identified by fluni-trazepam photoaffinity labelling, affinity purification and monoclonal anti-bodies. With these technologies partial aminoacid sequences of the peptides forming the GABA-regulated Cl⁻ ionophore have been obtained allowing the preparation of oligonucleotide probes for the isolation and sequencing of DNA complementary to the mRNA of the α- and β-subunit (P. H. Seeburg, personal communication). The α-subunit (50 KDa) binds BZDs, while the β-subunit (approximately 55 KDa) binds GABA. On the basis of these findings the GABA-BZD-Cl⁻ ionophore receptor complex is thought to be an heterotetramer of approximately 200 000 mol. wt (Stephenson *et al.*, 1986).

Electrophysiological recording with the whole-cell patch–clamp technique from monolayers of cortical cells in primary culture have shown that GABA application mediates bursts of Cl⁻ channel opening, causing a flux of this ion through the neuronal membrane according to the concentration gradient (Vicini *et al.*, 1986). The addition of BZD or BCC in the absence of GABA fails to modify the Cl⁻ channel. However, when the BZDs are added in the presence of GABA they increase the probability of GABA-Cl⁻ channel opening, whereas the addition of BCC decreases this probability (Vicini *et al.*, 1986).

In an early classification, the BZDs were defined as 'agonists' and BCCs as 'inverse agonists' (Polc *et al.*, 1982). However, since the BZDs and the BCCs do not have a direct action *per se*, but influence the response to GABA through an 'allosteric mechanism', today they should be defined as 'allosteric modulators'. In this chapter, the BZDs are classified as 'positive allosteric modulators' of GABA receptors, while the BCCs are classified as 'negative allosteric modulators' of the GABA$_A$ receptor.

Allosteric modulators of a primary transmitter action are not new to pharma-cologists. For example, the anticholinergic effect of gallamine is supposed to be mediated by an allosteric interaction with the muscarinic receptor. Similarly, the effect of phencyclidine and glycine on glutamate-regulated cationic channels appears to occur through a positive (glycine) or negative (phencyclidine) allo-steric modulation of the action of glutamate on specific cationic channels (Wroblewski *et al.*, 1987).

Drugs that act allosterically to tune up or down ongoing neurotransmission have several advantages over drugs which act directly as agonists or antagonists on the recognition sites for a neurotransmitter. Considering drug therapy for a neuropsychiatric disorder caused by insufficient endogenous neurotransmitter function, a directly acting agonist will replace the endogenous neurotransmitter at its receptor site and produce a generally continuous effect, the magnitude of which depends upon the amount of drug present. This continuous stimulation will disrupt the physiological pattern of neuronal activity and trigger compen-satory interaction via activation of neuronal plasticity. Hence, if too much of a direct agonist is administered then the excessive receptor activation could have potentially adverse consequences. In contrast, an 'allosteric modulator' would only enhance (positive modulator) or decrease (negative modulator) the probability that the endogenous neurotransmitter acts; consequently the normal pattern for the transfer of information through the synapse would be maintained. Also, the maximum effect of the allosteric modulators would have a ceiling dependent upon the amount of positive co-operativity existing between the binding site for the modulator and the binding site for the endogenous neurotransmitter. A drug with positive or negative allosteric modulatory action should only produce an effect determined by the ceiling of the maximal allosteric interaction between the two recognition sites. It could be predicted that a drug that acts as a modulator should produce toxic effects only rarely and the problem of overdose should be minimised. Often, this allosteric modulation may be operative in inducing receptor function desensitisation, hence a problem inherent to the use of drugs acting on allosteric modulatory sites for neurotransmitters may be plagued by drug tolerance. A better understanding of the molecular nature of the allosteric modulation of the GABA-BZD receptor system may bring about progress in our knowledge of the pathoneurobiology of several affective disorders. In particular, with the emerging evidence of the existence of neuromodulatory mechanisms for other major neurotransmitter systems such as serotonin, catecholamines and excitatory aminoacids, the concept of 'allosteric modulation' may provide a powerful means for the characterisation of neurochemical systems regulating emotional responses. Also, a new family of drugs may result, devoid of those unwanted side-effects found with direct agonists and antagonists of the primary putative neurotransmitter receptors.

31.3 Endogenous Ligands for the BZD Recognition Sites

Strictly connected to the concept that the BZD recognition sites function as allosteric modulatory sites coupled to the function of the GABA-Cl$^-$ ionophore complex is the question of the physiological role that those BZD recognition sites may exert and whether there is an endogenous effector for these sites. The understanding of the mechanisms by which the endogenous neurotransmitter GABA and the putative endogenous allosteric modulators interact at the postsynaptic site may be of obvious importance in elucidating polytypic signal transduction, in interpreting the action of drugs and in developing new therapeutic agents effective in neuropsychiatric disorders.

In 1978, at a meeting of the British Society of Psychopharmacology, we reported that brain extracts contain an endacoid (endo=endogenous; akoid= drug) that displaces the BZDs from their binding sites (Costa *et al.*, 1978). This endocoid, later defined as DBI (diazepam binding inhibitor) is an 11-kDa polypeptide which decreases the ability of BZDs to induce a conformational shift of the GABA recognition site from the low- to the high-affinity state (Guidotti *et al.*, 1983).

In a series of pharmacological experiments, it was found that DBI is a putative precursor that is processed in smaller peptide fragments which when injected intracerebroventricularly in rats (Ferrero *et al.*, 1986b), and mice (Kavaliers and Maurice, 1986) mimic the action of the anxiogenic β-carbolines by acting on a site for the negative allosteric control of the GABA$_A$ recognition site. The reversal of their action by the inert BZD receptor antagonist flumazenil supported this contention. Several lines of research suggest that this new family of neuroactive peptides resulting from DBI processing is coded by a specific mRNA whose unique nucleotide sequence has been determined by cDNA cloning analyses (Fig. 31.1). In rat brain, DBI is stored in neurons where it is localised in synaptic vesicles and it is released by veratridine and K$^+$-induced depolarisation (Ferrarese *et al.*, 1987b). DBI is a large polypeptide that can be processed differently in neurons and in glial cells and might function as the precursor of smaller putative neuropeptides acting on various types of BZD recognition sites.

The presence in the DBI structure of typical amino acid signals for tryptic cleavage is compatible with this view. In fact, the tryptic digestion of rat DBI yields an octadecaneuropeptide (ODN) (for the amino acid composition see Fig. 31.1) which shares some of the biological properties of DBI (Ferrero *et al.*, 1986b). Using polyclonal antibodies directed against ODN and DBI, we could demonstrate that DBI coexists in rat brain (Fig. 31.2) or in primary cultures of cortical neurons with at least three different processing products that immunoreact with ODN antibodies. One of the immunoreactive peptides has an HPLC retention time identical to that of synthetic ODN.

Double immunofluorescence staining of primary cultures of cortical neurons with glutamic acid decarboxylase (GAD) and ODN antibodies indicates that ODN and ODN-like peptides are co-localised with GABA in at least 50% of neurons. Moreover, these materials (GABA, ODN, ODN-like peptides and DBI) are co-released following veratridine depolarisation (Ferrarese *et al.*, 1987a).

These experiments suggest that ODN and ODN-like peptides derived from DBI might participate as putative neuromodulators of functional biological significance in changing the probability that a quantum of GABA opens specific Cl$^-$ channels located on postsynaptic cell membranes.

31.4 Dynamic Equilibrium of DBI and DBI-processing Products Following Down-regulation of GABA Receptor Function

31.4.1 Animal Studies

Protracted treatment with BZD yields tolerance to the acute effects of these drugs, induces physical dependence and evokes withdrawal reactions when the BZD treatment is discontinued abruptly. Although the molecular mechanisms of BZD tolerance and withdrawal are not elucidated, it has been shown that the

```
RAT DBI

SQADFDKAAEEVKRLKTQPTDEEMLFIYSHFKQATVGDVNTDRPGLLDLKGKAKWDSWNKLKGTS

KENAMKTYVEKVEELKKKYGI (Mocchetti et al. 1986)



RAT ODN

GATVGDVNTDRPGLLDLK



HUMAN DBI

WGDLWLLPPASANPGTGTEAEFEKAAEEVRHLKTKPSDEEMLFIYGHYKQATVGDINTERPGMLD

FTGKAKWDAWNELKGTSKEDAMKAYINKVEELKKKYGI (Gray et al., 1986)



HUMAN ODN

QATVGDINTERPGLMDFTGK
```

Fig. 31.1   Amino acid sequences of DBI and ODN in rat and human brain. Underlined peptides represent the position of the putative active ODN in the DBI structure.

BZD tolerance and the symptoms of BZD withdrawal might result from GABA receptor down-regulation (Gallager *et al.*, 1984).

To verify whether the content and turnover rate of rat brain DBI changes during chronic BZD-induced tolerance and GABA receptor down-regulation, we studied the content of specific DBI mRNA, DBI and ODN. In this study, we used a cDNA probe complementary to DBI mRNA and specific antibodies for rat DBI and ODN. Diazepam was administered 3 times a day for 10 days by oral gavage as shown in Fig. 31.3. The content of DBI mRNA, DBI and ODN increased in the cerebellum and cerebral cortex (Table 31.1) but failed to change in the hippocampus and striatum of treated rats (Miyata *et al.* 1987). These data suggest that tolerance to BZDs is associated with an increase in the turnover rate of DBI, which in turn may be responsible for, or may be the consequence of, the GABA receptor desensitisation that occurs after protracted benzodiazepine administration.

31.4.2 Human Studies

Since DBI/ODN-like peptides have been found in human brain and cerebrospinal fluid (CSF) (Ferrero *et al.*, 1986a; Barbaccia *et al.*, 1986) it was of interest to investigate whether there was a difference in CSF content of DBI and ODN immunoreactive material in patients suffering from neuropsychiatric disorders

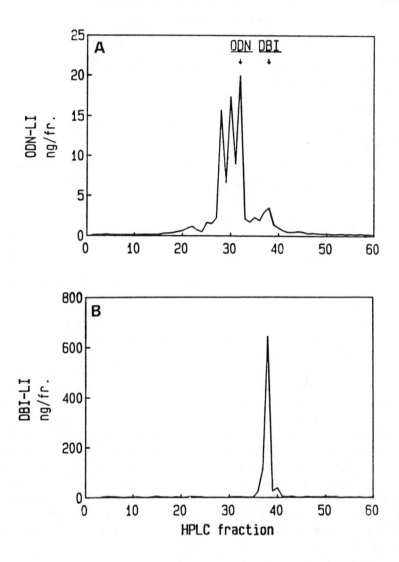

Fig. 31.2 C_{18} HPLC reverse phase of cerebellar acetic acid extract eluted with 0.1% TFA/ acetonitrile. In A, the fractions are assayed with ODN antibodies. In B, the fractions are assayed with DBI antibodies. For details of the method see Miyata *et al.*, 1986.

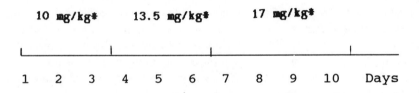

＃ Three doses/day

Fig 31.3 Schedule of chronic diazepam treatment, three doses per day. Diazepam was suspended in water, and administered intragastrically via oral gavage.

Table 31.1 DBI-like immunoreactivity, ODN-like and DBI mRNA in cerebellar extracts after chronic diazepam treatment

Treatment	DBI-like (pmol/mg prot.)	ODN-like (pmol/mg prot.)	DBI mRNA (unit)
Control	99 ± 6.3	15 ± 1.8	1.0 ± 0.08
Chronic diazepam†	130 ± 6.8*	37 ± 4.0*	1.4 ± 0.07*

Experimental details and methods as described by Miyata *et al.* (1986). *$p < 0.05$ when compared with control values. †Diazepam treatment as described in Fig. 31.3.

(depression, schizophrenia, dementia of Alzheimer's type) that also may be associated with an alteration of the GABA receptor function.

As shown in Table 31.2, patients with major depression had significantly higher concentrations of DBI in CSF when compared with age- and sex-matched normal volunteers, while no differences in CSF DBI were found in schizophrenics

Table 31.2 CSF levels of DBI immunoreactivity in depressed patients and control subjects

Subject	Age	Sex	DBI (pmol/ml CSF)
Normal	36.2 ± 2.7	6 female 4 male	1.10 ± 0.09
Depressed	35.8 ± 2.5	6 female 4 male	1.40 ± 0.13*

*$p < 0.05$. Patients were diagnosed according to the DSM III criteria and were free of all medications for at least two weeks prior to study. For details on diagnosis and methods see Barbaccia *et al.*, 1986.

or patients with dementia of the Alzheimer's type when compared with controls. It is difficult at present to know the functional significance of the increased CSF in rats, a reduction of GABA-mediated synaptic inhibition might be expected in association with an increase of DBI turnover rate in brain. There is both direct and indirect evidence for decreased GABAergic function associated with various forms of endogenous depression (Bartholini *et al.*, 1986).

Consistent with these hypotheses, evidence is accumulating supporting the antidepressant efficacy of both direct- and indirect-acting GABA-mimetic drugs. Thus, an increase in DBI immunoreactivity in the CSF of depressed patients might reflect an impairment of central GABAergic neurotransmission. Studies of CSF-DBI immunoreactivity in manic-depressive patients as well as in those treated with antidepressant medication may establish whether the elevated CSF-DBI immunoreactivity is a state or a trait that correlates with depression.

31.5 Summary and Conclusion

In this article we intended to review recent advances in the understanding of the GABA-BSD-BCC recognition site system at CNS synapses. We propose that revealing the molecular organisation of the GABA transmitter system may have immediate relevance to proposed neurochemical correlates of affective states such as anxiety and depression.

Presumably GABAergic synapses, in mammalian CNS, function through a polytypic signalling system including the primary transmitter GABA and one or more endogenous putative allosteric modulators such as DBI and its processing products that function as 'negative allosteric modulators' of GABAergic transmission.

Thus, nature might regulate primary transmitter receptors through modulatory mechanisms rather than through competitive antagonists at primary transmitter recognition sites.

The turnover rate of DBI, measured by establishing the dynamic equilibrium of DBI, ODN and mRNA coding for DBI, is increased during the down-regulation of GABA receptors induced in rats by chronic benzodiazepine treatment.

DBI has been detected by radioimmunoassay (RIA) in human CSF. Spinal fluid DBI content is unchanged in alcoholics, schizophrenics and patients with Alzheimer's disease. Our current working hypothesis is that DBI processing might be increased in the brain of patients with down-regulation of GABA receptor function.

This working hypothesis is undergoing testing. The pharmacology of the allosteric modulation of polytypic signalling at the inhibitory amino acid synapses has brought about the possibility of exploring the neurochemical correlates of anxiety and depressive disorders.

References

Barbaccia, M. L., Costa, E., Ferrero, P., Guidotti, A., Roy, A., Sunderland, T., Pickar, D., Paul, S. M. and Goodwin, F. K. (1986). Diazepam binding inhibitor, a brain neuropeptide present in human spinal fluid: studies in depression, schizophrenia and Alzheimer's disease. *Arch. Gen. Psych.*, 43, 1143-7.

Bartholini, G., Lloyd, K. G., and Morselli, P. L. (eds.) (1986). *GABA and mood disorders: Experimental and Clinical Research*. L.E.R.S., Raven, New York, vol. 6.

Braestrup, C., Nielsen, M., and Olen, C. (1980). Urinary and brain β-carboline-3-carboxylates as potent inhibitors of brain benzodiazepine receptors. *Proc. Natl Acad. Sci. USA*, 77, 2288-92.

Casalotti, S. O., Stephenson, F. A., and Barnard, E. A. (1986). Subunits for agonists and benzodiazepine binding in the γ-aminobutyric acid$_A$ receptor oligomer. *J. Biol. Chem.*, 261, 15013-6.

Corda, M. G., Blaker, W. D., Mendelson, W. B., Guidotti, A., and Costa, E. (1983). Betacarbolines enhance shock-induced suppression of drinking in rats. *Proc. Natl Acad. Sci. USA*, 80, 2072-6.

Costa, E., Guidotti, A., and Toffano, G. (1978). Molecular mechanisms mediating the action of diazepam on GABA receptors. *Br. J. Psychiatry*, 133, 239-48.

Costa, E., and Guidotti, A. (1979). Molecular mechanisms in the receptor action of benzodiazepines. *Ann. Rev. Pharmacol. Toxicol.*, 19, 531-45.

Costa, E., and Guidotti, A. (1985). Commentary: Endogenous ligands for benzodiazepine recognition sites. *Biochem. Pharmacol.*, 34, 3399-403.

Dorow, R., and Duka, T. (1985). Anxiety: Its generation by drugs and by their withdrawal. In Biggio, G., and Costa, E. (eds.), *GABAergic Transmission and Anxiety*. Raven, New York, 211-25.

Ferrarese, C., Alho, H., Guidotti, A., and Costa, E. (1987a). Colocalization and corelease of GABA and putative allosteric modulators of GABA receptor. *Neuropharm.*, in press.

Ferrarese, C., Vaccarino, F., Alho, H., Mellstrom, B., Costa, E., and Guidotti, A. (1987b). Subcellular location and neuronal release of diazepam binding inhibitor. *J. Neurochem.*, 48, 1093-102.

Ferrero, P., Costa, E., Conti-Tronconi, B., and Guidotti, A. (1986a). A diazepam binding inhibitor (DBI)-like neuropeptide is detected in human brain. *Brain Res.*, 399, 136-42.

Ferrero, R., Santi, M. R., Conti-Tronconi, B., Costa, E., and Guidotti, A. (1986b). Study of an octadecaneuropeptide derived from diazepam binding inhibitor (DBI): biological activity and presence in rat brain. *Proc. Natl Acad. Sci. USA*, 83, 827-31.

Gallager, D., Lakoski, J., Gonsalves, S., and Rauch, S. (1984). Chronic benzodiazepine treatment decreases postsynaptic GABA sensitivity. *Nature*, 308, 74-7.

Gray, P. W., Glaister, D., Seeburg, P. H., Guidotti, A., and Costa, E. (1986). Cloning and expression of cDNA for human diazepam binding inhibitor, a natural ligand of an allosteric regulatory site of γ-aminobutyric acid type A receptor. *Proc. Natl Acad. Sci. USA*, 83, 7547-51.

Guidotti, A., Forchetti, C. M., Corda, M. G., Konkel, D., Bennet, C. D., and Costa, E. (1983). Isolation, characterization and purification to homogeniety of an endogenous polypeptide with agonistic action on benzodiazepine receptors. *Proc. Natl Acad. Sci. USA*, 80, 3531-35.

Haring, P., Stahli, C., Schoch, P., Takacs, B., Staehelin, T., and Mohler, H. (1985). Monoclonal antibodies reveal structural homogeniety of GABA$_A$/benzodiazepine receptors in different brain areas. *Proc. Natl Acad. Sci. USA*, 82, 4837-41.

Kavaliers, M., and Maurice, H. (1986). An octadecaneuropeptide derived from diazepam binding inhibitor increases aggressive interactions in mice. *Brain Res.*, 383, 343-9.

Miyata, M., Mocchetti, I., Ferrarese, C., Guidotti, A., and Costa, E. (1987). Protracted treatment with diazepam increases the turnover of putative endogenous ligands for the benzodiazepine/carboline recognition site. *Proc. Natl Acad. Sci. USA*, **84**, 1444–8.

Mocchetti, I., Einstein, R., and Brosius, J. (1986). Putative diazepam binding inhibitor peptide: cDNA clones from rat. *Proc. Natl Acad. Sci. USA*, 7221–5.

Polc, P., Benetti, E. P., Schaffner, R., and Haefely, W. (1982). A three-state model of the benzodiazepine receptor explains the interactions between the benzodiazepine agonist Ro 15-1788, benzodiazepines, tranquilizers, B-carbolines and phenobarbitone. *Naunyn-Schmiederberg's Arch. Pharmacol.*, **821**, 260–4.

Stephenson, F. A., Casalotti, S. O., Mamalaki, C., and Barnard, E. A. (1986). Antibodies recognizing the $GABA_A$/benzodiazepine receptor including its regulator sites. *J. Neurochem.*, **46**, 854–61.

Vicini, S., Alho, H., Costa, E., Mienville, J. M., Santi, M. R., and Vaccarino, F. M. (1986). Modulation of γ-aminobutyric acid-mediated inhibitory synaptic currents in dissociated cortical cell cultures. *Proc. Natl Acad. Sci. USA*, **83**, 9269–73.

Wroblewski, J. I., Nicoletti, F., Fadda, E., and Costa, E. (1987). Phencyclidine is a negative allosteric modulator of signal transduction at two subclasses of excitatory amino acid receptors. *Proc. Natl Acad. Sci.*, **84**, in press.

32

The Benzodiazepine–GABA Receptor Complex in Experimental Stress, Anxiety and Depression

S. I. Deutsch, R. C. Drugan, F. J. Vocci, Jr, A. Weizman, R. Weizman, J. N. Crawley, P. Skolnick and S. M. Paul

32.1 Introduction

Benzodiazepine receptors mediate many of the pharmacological actions of the benzodiazepines and related minor tranquillisers, including their anxiolytic, hypnotic and muscle-relaxant properties (see Tallman *et al.*, 1980; Skolnick and Paul 1982 for review). The benzodiazepine receptor or recognition site is part of an oligomeric glycoprotein receptor complex for the major inhibitory neurotransmitter in brain, γ-aminobutyric acid (GABA). Benzodiazepines and barbiturates augment GABAergic neurotransmission by binding to different allosteric binding sites on this receptor complex, resulting in a potentiation of GABA-receptor-mediated Cl^- ion conductance (Olsen *et al.*, 1984). More recently, a class of compounds referred to as inverse agonists have been discovered and shown to bind to the benzodiazepine receptor to produce 'anxiogenic' and preconvulsant actions (Ninan *et al.*, 1982; Dorow *et al.*, 1983; Insel *et al.*, 1984). The latter finding suggests that the benzodiazepine–GABA receptor complex may participate in the neurochemical events which mediate the physiological (and perhaps psychological) expression of anxiety or fear. One obvious question, therefore, is whether the benzodiazepine–GABA receptor is itself modified by environment stimuli, and whether such modifications are important to the organism's adaptive response to 'stress'. Most studies which have examined for the effects of environmental or experimentally induced 'stress' on the benzodiazepine receptor complex have reported either no, or very modest, changes in the ligand binding characteristics of these receptors (e.g. see Braestrup *et al.*, 1979; Grimm and Hershkowitz, 1981). Recently we have demonstrated rather robust alterations in the benzodiazepine–GABA receptor complex following acute exposure to various environmental stressors in rats. Further, we have also studied the effects of inescapable (as opposed to escapable) 'stress' on the benzodiazepine–GABA receptor complex in rats; since inescapable stress results in a behavioural syndrome (i.e. learned helplessness) which has been proposed as an animal model of depression. Finally, we have recently examined the effects of both acute and chronic 'stress' (electroconvulsive shock) on benzodiazepine receptor binding measured *in vivo*, since the physiological effects of chronic stress are frequently associated with mood disturbances such as depression. This chapter summarises our results which to date suggest a role for central benzodiazepine–GABA receptors in mediating the behaviour response to various types of stressors and perhaps in mediating the neurochemical events underlying some aspect of the 'learned helplessness' syndrome.

32.2 Environmental Stressors Modify the Binding of Radioligands to the Benzodiazepine–GABA Receptor Complex

Although there have been a number of reports on 'stress'-induced changes in the binding of radioligands to the benzodiazepine receptor *in vitro* (Medina *et al.*, 1983; Braestrup *et al.*, 1979; Lippa *et al.*, 1978), these changes have, for the most part, been modest and bidirectional. Recently, we (Havoundjian *et al.*, 1986) have observed rapid changes in the chloride ionophore component of the benzodiazepine–GABA receptor complex in cerebral cortical membranes prepared from rats exposed to brief ambient-temperature swim stress. These changes were manifest as an increase in both the efficacy and potency of chloride ions to enhance agonist binding, as well as an increase in the number and apparent affinity of $[^{35}S]$-t-butylbicyclophosphorothionate (TBPS) binding sites (Fig. 32.1). More recently, Trullas *et al.* (1987) observed similar changes in $[^{35}S]$-TBPS binding to cerebral cortical and hippocampal membranes from rats housed in cohorts in a 'low-stress' environment and then suddenly removed. The increases in both chloride ion-stimulated agonist and $[^{35}S]$-TBPS binding were observed within 15 s following removal of individual animals from a common cage, and prior to any statistically significant changes in circulating α-MSH, β-endorphin, ACTH and corticosterone. These changes, therefore, were rapid enough to subserve some physiologically relevant function, perhaps one related to an adaptive response to stressful or anxiety-producing environmental stimuli. Moreover, simply housing animals in a protected or 'low-stress' environment reduced both the efficacy of Cl^- ions to enhance agonist binding as well as the number of $[^{35}S]$-TBPS binding sites in brain membranes. Thus, the sensitivity of the GABA

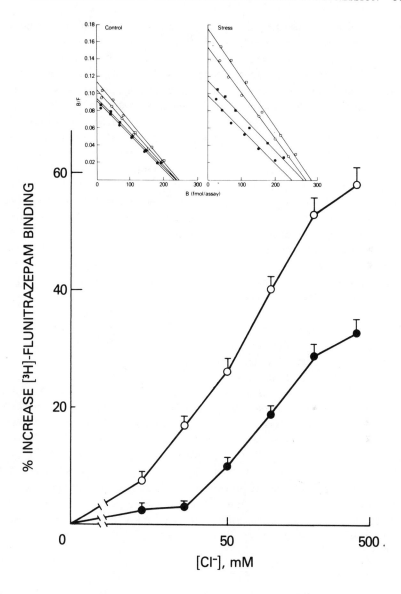

Fig. 32.1 Enhancement of [^{3}H]-flunitrazepam binding by chloride ions: effects of stress. [^{3}H]-Flunitrazepam binding was measured in cerebral cortical membranes from control (•) and swim-stressed animals (○). Animals were swim-stressed under ambient temperature conditions for 10 min. Values represent the $\bar{x}$ ± SEM of 7 to 12 animals. Inset: top: Scatchard analyses of [^{3}H]-flunitrazepam binding in stressed (right panel) and non-stressed (left panel) rats. Binding was measured in the absence (•) and presence of 25 mM (■), 100 mM (○) and 400 mM (□) NaCl. This representative experiment was repeated three times with similar results. Data were obtained by Havoundjian et al. (1986).

receptor gated Cl⁻ ion channel appears to be under both tonic and acute regulation by the environment (Trullas *et al.*, 1987).

The changes in ligand binding characteristics of the benzodiazepine–GABA receptor following swim stress suggests that 'stress' alters the functional sensitivity of the GABA-gated Cl⁻ ion channel. To further examine the consequences of these alterations, we studied the ability of muscimol to stimulate GABA-receptor-mediated ^{36}Cl⁻ uptake in synaptoneurosomes prepared from rats exposed to ambient-temperature swim stress (Schwartz *et al.*, 1987). Previous work from our laboratory has established this technique as a reliable one for measuring the functional properties of the benzodiazepine/GABA receptor complex *in vitro*. As predicted from the ligand binding studies, swim-stress-enhanced muscimol-stimulated ^{36}Cl⁻ uptake in synaptoneurosomes prepared from the cerebral cortex and hippocampus (but not the cerebellum) of stressed compared with non-stressed (or stress-habituated) control rats. Interestingly, the effects of swim stress on muscimol-stimulated ^{36}Cl⁻ uptake were not observed in adrenalectomised rats (Schwartz *et al.*, 1987). These data, coupled with those of other investigators (De Souza *et al.*, 1986), suggest that adrenal hormones (e.g. glucocorticoids) may have an important modulatory action on the benzodiazepine/GABA receptor complex. Recently, we have found that two naturally occurring steroid hormone metabolites, 3α, 5α-tetrahydrodeoxycorticosterone (THDOC, a mineralocorticoid metabolite) and 3α, 5α-dihydroprogesterone (a progesterone metabolite) are relatively potent barbiturate-like ligands of the GABA receptor complex (Majewska *et al.*, 1986). Like pentobarbital, both steroids inhibit [^{35}S]-TBPS binding and enhance [^{3}H]-flunitrazepam binding to the benzodiazepine-GABA receptor *in vitro*. Moreover, both steroids potentiate GABA-mediated Cl⁻ ion conductance in cultured spinal cord and hippocampal neurons at submicromolar concentrations. In behavioural studies, THDOC also has 'anxiolytic' (namely anticonflict) and hypnotic actions in rats and mice (Crawley *et al.*, 1986; Mendelson *et al.*, 1987). These data suggest the possibility that the A-ring-reduced metabolites of progesterone and deoxycorticosterone may serve a physiological role in modulation of central GABAergic inhibitory tone. Interestingly, both steroids have been shown to be released in response to ACTH administration (Schambelan and Biglieri, 1976).

32.3 The Effects of Stress on Benzodiazepine Receptors Labelled *In Vivo*

To further explore alterations in benzodiazepine receptors following 'stress', we employed a recently described method for measuring benzodiazepine receptors *in vivo* (Goeders and Kuhar, 1985). The failure to find consistent and reproducible alterations in the ligand binding properties of agonists to the benzodiazepine receptor *in vitro* following stress may relate to a number of potential artifacts introduced following tissue homogenisation and the subsequent washing of brain membranes.

To label benzodiazepine receptors *in vivo*, a tracer quantity of [³H]-Ro15-1788 (2.5 to 25 μCi) was administered via the lateral tail vein to rats or mice (Goeders and Kuhar, 1985; Miller *et al.*, 1987; Deutsch *et al.*, 1987). After 20 to 30 minutes, the distribution of radioactivity in various brain regions is uneven (Fig. 32.2) and highly correlated with the distribution of benzodiazepine receptors

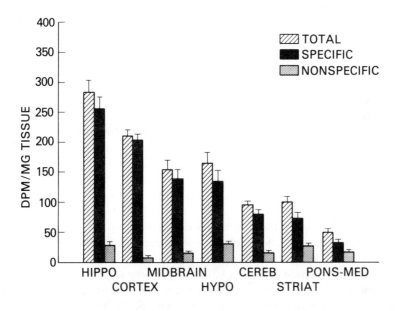

Fig. 32.2   Regional localisation of [³H]-Ro15-1788 bound *in vivo*. Total binding was determined 20 minutes after the intravenous injection of 5 μCi [³H]-Ro15-1788. Non-specific binding was determined by the intraperitoneal administration of clonazepam (5 mg/kg) 30 minutes prior to the intravenous injection of the radioligand. Total binding was determined with 17 to 26 mice and non-specific binding with 7 to 9 animals for each brain region. Values are the mean and SEM.

previously measured *in vitro* (Fig. 32.3). Moreover, pre-injection (or co-injection) of a pharmacologically active benzodiazepine enantiomer (B10 +) results in a dose-dependent inhibition of the *in-vivo* binding of [³H]-Ro15-1788 (Fig. 32.4), whereas the pharmacologically inactive enantiomer [B10 (–)] failed to inhibit specific binding. Specific [³H]-Ro15-1788 binding in most brain regions was 80 to 90% of the total binding, thus yielding high signal-to-noise ratios. The displacement of [³H]-Ro15-1788 binding measured *in vivo* is also correlated with both the brain concentration of drug and its pharmacodynamic actions (Miller *et al.*, 1987).

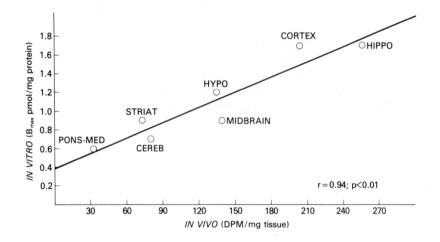

Fig. 32.3   Regional localisation of [³H]-Ro15-1788 binding: correlation of *in vitro* and *in vivo* data.

Using this *in-vivo* method for measuring benzodiazepine receptors we have recently studied the effects of acute ambient-temperature swim stress and intermittent foot-shock stress on benzodiazepine receptor occupancy *in vivo*. Figure 32.5 shows the effects of either 2 or 10 minutes of swim stress on [³H]-Ro15-1788 binding in various brain regions (from Deutsch *et al.*, submitted for publication). Following swim stress, significant increases in the specific binding of [³H]-Ro15-1788 to the benzodiazepine receptor was observed in all brain regions examined. These results are unlikely to be due to elevations in the brain (or intrasynaptic) concentration of GABA, since the binding of [³H]-Ro15-1788 to benzodiazepine receptors *in vitro* (in contrast to agonists) is not influenced by GABA. Moreover, no significant changes in non-specific binding were observed following swim stress, supporting the notion that the stress-induced changes in specific binding were not due to artifacts in the distribution of radioligand.

In contrast to swim stress, which resulted in a rapid increase in benzodiazepine receptor binding *in vivo*, we observed a decrease in specific [³H]-Ro15-1788 binding in animals exposed to 10 minutes of intermittent foot-shock (10 seconds of 2.0 mA scrambled grid-shock every 30 seconds) (Fig. 32.6). Conceivably, the type of 'stress' associated with intermittent foot-shock is qualitatively (or quantitatively) different from that associated with swim stress. These experiments do, however, confirm the rather rapid effects of stress in altering the binding of [³H]-Ro15-1788 to benzodiazepine receptors *in vivo*. Further, the bidirectional changes in [³H]-Ro15-1788 binding observed following swim and intermittent

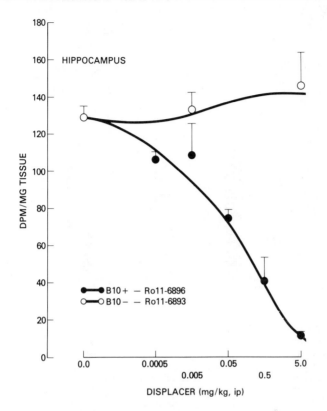

Fig 32.4   The stereospecific displacement of [³H]-Ro15-1788 by the benzodiazepine agonist B10+ (Ro11-6896) in hippocampus. Mice were administered B10+, B10- or saline intraperitoneally immediately prior to an intravenous injection of 2.5 μCi [³H]-Ro15-1788. Animals were sacrificed 20 minutes after the intravenous injection. Values are the mean and SEM of four animals examined at each of the indicated concentrations.

foot-shock stress argue against their being due simply to pharmacokinetic changes in the distrubution of [³H]-Ro15-1788.

More recent experiments have examined the effects of chronic stress on the binding of [³H]-Ro15-1788 to benzodiazepine receptors *in vivo*. In this study mice were subjected to daily swim stress (2 or 10 min) for seven consecutive days and 24 hours following the last swim stress benzodiazepine receptor occupancy was measured *in vivo* as described above. In contrast to the acute effects of swim stress, chronic swim stress (2 and 10 min daily) resulted in a significant decrease in [³H]-Ro15-1788 binding in the cerebral cortex, hippocampus, hypothalamus and striatum, but not in the other brain regions examined (cerebellum, pons medulla and midbrain). In a separate study examining the chronic effects of electroconvulsive shock (ECS) and sham ECS (Weizman *et al.*, submitted), we observed similar decreases in benzodiazepine receptor binding in the

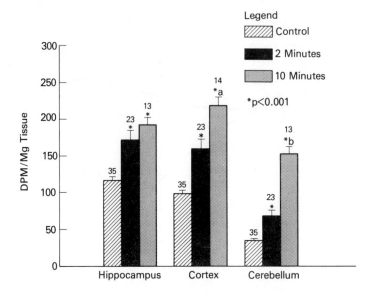

Fig. 32.5 Effect of ambient-temperature swim stress on the specific binding of [³H]-Ro15-1788 *in vivo*. Mice were swim-stressed for 2 and 10 minutes in ambient-temperature water prior to the intravenous injection of 2.5 µCi [³H]-Ro15-1788. Values are the means and SEMs of the number of animals indicated above each bar. Asterisks indicate that values of swim-stressed animals differ significantly from control values. Letters above the bars indicate that 2 and 10 min swim-stressed animals differ significantly from each other: $a (p < 0.005)$ and $b (p < 0.001)$.

hippocampus and hypothalamus of both groups (i.e. ECS and sham ECS). Taken together, it appears that chronic 'stress' may reduce selectively the number of benzodiazepine receptors in specific brain regions (e.g., cerebral cortex, hippocampus, and hypothalamus). Studies are in progress to determine whether such changes result in altered behavioural effects of either benzodiazepine agonists or inverse agonists.

32.4 Benzodiazepine–GABA Receptors Following Inescapable Stress and 'Learned Helplessness'

A body of research on the effects of escapable and inescapable stress in laboratory animals suggests that the lack of control over aversive stimuli results in a syndrome characterised by a variety of behavioural and physiological deficits. This syndrome, called 'learned helplessness' by some, includes deficits in various learning tasks, reductions in aggression and social dominance, opioid-mediated

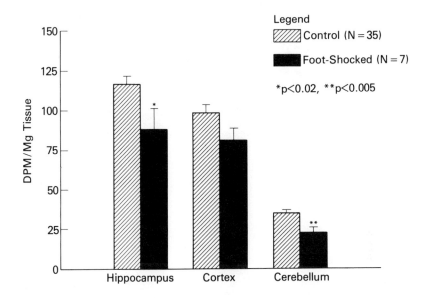

Fig. 32.6 Effect of 10 minutes of intermittent foot-shock on the specific binding of [^{3}H]-Ro15-1788 *in vivo*. Mice received 10 seconds of 2.0 mA scrambled grid shock every 30 s for a 10 min period prior to the intravenous injection of 2.5 μCi [^{3}H]-Ro15-1788. Non-specific binding was determined in three animals receiving clonazepam (5 mg/kg, i.p.) immediately prior to the tail vein injection of radiolabelled ligand and subtracted from total binding. Values are the means and SEMs. Asterisks indicate that values differ significantly from control values.

analgesia, depressed immune function, anorexia, and ulcer formation (see Maier and Seligman 1976 for review). Learned helplessness has been proposed as an animal model of depression and antidepressant drugs have been reported to be effective in attenuating or blocking this syndrome (Sherman *et al.*, 1979). Recently, Drugan and coworkers (1985) have demonstrated that the effects of inescapable tail-shock in producing learned helplessness can be mimicked by administration of the benzodiazepine receptor inverse agonist FG-7142 (Fig. 32.7). Moreover, pretreatment of animals with the benzodiazepine receptor agonist chlordiazepoxide blocks the behavioural deficits observed following inescapable tail-shock (Drugan *et al.*, 1985). Together, these data suggest that central benzodiazepine–GABA receptors may play a role either in the development of learned helplessness or in protecting animals against its development (coping).

In a series of experiments we have examined the *in vivo* occupancy of benzodiazepine receptors in rats who learned and failed to learn a shuttle-escape task 24 hours after they were exposed to a session of inescapable tail-shock. Animals failing to learn the shuttle-escape task in this paradigm are said to exhibit 'learned

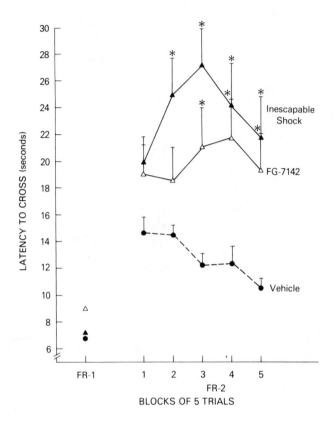

Fig. 32.7 β-Carboline administration mimics inescapable shock in the 'learned helplessness' paradigm. Rats were treated with vehicle, FG-7142 (10 mg/kg, i.p.), or inescapable tail-shock (80 shocks, 1 mA, 5 s), 24 h before testing on an escape task. Rats were placed in a shuttlebox for 5 trials requiring one (FR-1) crossing, and 25 trials requiring two (FR-2) crossings, of the shuttlebox for shock termination. Data were obtained by Drugan *et al.* (1985). Asterisks indicate that values differ significantly from control values.

helplessness'. Immediately following the final learning trial of the shuttle-escape task, [³H]-Ro15-1788 (25 µCi) was injected into the lateral tail vein of the two groups (i.e. learned and failed) and naïve controls. *In vivo* benzodiazepine receptor occupancy was determined 20 minutes after injection. Failure to learn ('helpless' condition) was associated with decreases in specific [³H]-Ro15-1788 binding in cerebral cortex, hippocampus, hypothalamus, cerebellum and striatum, as compared with naïve controls. However, animals that learned the task (coped) also showed decreased specific [³H]-Ro15-1788 binding *in vivo* in the hypothalamus and cerebellum. Thus, some of the observed alterations in the *in vivo* occupancy of benzodiazepine receptors by [³H]-Ro15-1788 may be related to the stress of inescapable shock, rather than related specifically to some aspect of learned helplessness. In any event, these data are consistent with a functional alteration in the GABA-benzodiazepone receptor complex in response to stress. Moreover, these data and the ability of FG-7142 to mimic the learned helplessness syndrome in a Ro15-1788 sensitive manner, suggest that the GABA–benzodiazepine receptor complex may play a pathogenetic role in the development of stress-related behavioural states, including depression.

References

Braestrup, C., Nielsen, M., Nielsen, E., and Lyon, M. (1979). Benzodiazepine receptors in brain as affected by different experimental stresses: the changes are small and not unidirectional. *Psychopharmacology*, 65, 273–7.

Crawley, J. N., Glowa, J. R., Majewska, M. D., and Paul, S. M. (1986). Anxiolytic activity of an endogenous adrenal steroid. *Brain Res.*, 398, 382–5.

De Souza, E., Goeders, N. E., and Kuhar, M. J. (1986). Benzodiazepine receptors in rat brain are altered by adrenalectomy. *Brain Res.*, 381, 176–81.

Deutsch, S. I., Miller, L. G., Weizman, R., Weizman, A., Vocci, F. J., Jr., Greenblatt, D. J., and Paul, S. M. (1987). Characterization of specific [³H]Ro15-1788 binding *in vivo*. *Psychopharm. Bull.* (in press).

Deutsch, S. I., Weizman, R., Weizman, A., Vocci, F. J., Jr., Kook, K., and Paul, S. M. (subm.). The effects of swim stress on the occupancy of brain benzodiazepine receptors measured with [³H]Ro15-1788 in mice.

Dorow, R., Horowski, R., Paschelke, G., Amin, M., and Braestrup, C. (1983). Severe anxiety induced by FG 7142, a β-carboline ligand for benzodiazepine receptors. *Lancet*, 9, 98–9.

Drugan, R. C., Maier, S. F., Skolnick, P., Paul, S. M., and Crawley, J. N. (1985). An anxiogenic benzodiazepine receptor ligand induces learned helplessness. *Eur. J. Pharmacology*, 113, 453–7.

Goeders, N. E., and Kuhar, M. J. (1985). Benzodiazepine receptor binding *in vivo* with [³H]Ro15-1788. *Life Sci.*, 37, 345–55.

Grimm, V., and Hershkowitz, M. (1981). The effect of chronic diazepam treatment on discrimination performance and [³H]-flunitrazepam binding in the brains of shocked and nonshocked rats. *Psychopharmacology*, 74, 132–6.

Havoundjian, H., Paul, S. M., and Skolnick, P. (1986). Rapid, stress-induced modification of the benzodiazepine receptor-coupled chloride ionophore. *Brain Res.*, 375, 401–6.

Insel, T. R., Ninan, P. T., Aloi, J., Jimerson, D. C., Skolnick, P., and Paul, S. M. (1984). A benzodiazepine receptor-mediated model of anxiety: studies in non-human primates and clinical implications. *Arch. Gen. Psychiatry*, 41, 741–50.

Lippa, A. S., Klepner, C. A., Yunger, L., Sano, M. C., Smith, W. V., and Beer, B. (1978). Relationship between benzodiazepine receptors and experimental anxiety in rats. *Pharmacol. Biochem. Behav.*, 9, 853–6.

Maier, S. F., and Seligman, M. E. P. (1976). Learned helplessness: theory and evidence. *J. Exp. Psychol. [Gen.]*, 105, 3–46.

Majewska, M. D., Harrison, N. L., Schwartz, R. D., Barker, J. L., and Paul, S. M. (1986). Steroid hormone metabolites are barbiturate-like modulators of the GABA receptor. *Science*, 232, 1004–7.

Medina, J., Novas, M., Wolfman, C., Levi de Stein, M., and DeRobertis, E. (1983). Benzodiazepine receptors in rat cerebral cortex and hippocampus undergo rapid and reversible changes after acute stress. *Neuroscience*, 9, 331–5.

Mendelson, W. B., Martin, J. V., Perlis, M., Wagner, R., Majewska, M. D., and Paul, S. M. (1987). Sleep induction by an adrenal steroid in the rat. *Psychopharmacology* (in press).

Miller, L. G., Greenblatt, D. J., Paul, S. M., and Shader, R. I. (1987). Benzodiazepine receptor occupancy *in vivo*: correlation with brain concentrations and pharmacodynamic actions. *J. Pharmacol. Exp. Ther.*, 240, 516–22.

Ninan, P. T., Insel, T. R., Cohen, R. M., Cook, J. M., Skolnick, P., and Paul, S. M. (1982).

Benzodiazepine receptor mediated experimental anxiety in primates. *Science*, **218**, 1332-4.

Olsen, R., Wong, E., Stauber, G., and King, R. (1984). Biochemical pharmacology of the γ-aminobutyric acid receptor/ionophore complex. *Fed. Proc.*, **43**, 2773-8.

Schambelan, M., and Biglieri, E. (1976). Deoxycorticosterone production and regulation in man. *J. Clin. Endocrinol.*, **34**, 695-702.

Schwartz, R. D., Wess, M. J., Labarca, R., Skolnick, P., and Paul, S. M. (1987). Acute stress enhances the activity of the GABA-gated chloride ion channel in brain. *Brain Res.* (in press).

Sherman, A. D., Allers, G. L., Petty, F., and Henn, F. A. (1979). A neuropharmacologically-relevant animal model of depression. *Neuropharmacology*, **18**, 891-3.

Skolnick, P., and Paul, S. M. (1982). Molecular pharmacology of the benzodiazepines. In Smythies, J. R., and Bradley, R. (eds.), *International Review of Neurobiology*. Academic, New York, 103-40.

Tallman, J. F., Paul, S. M., Skolnick, P., and Gallager, D. W. (1980). Receptors for the age of anxiety: molecular pharmacology of the benzodiazepines. *Science*, **207**, 274-81.

Trullas, R., Havoundjian, H., Zamir, N., Paul, S. M., and Skolnick, P. (1987). Environ-mentally-induced modification of the benzodiazepine/GABA receptor coupled chloride ionophore. *Psychopharmacology*, **91**, 380-4.

Weizman, A., Weizman, R., Deutsch, S. I., Vocci, F. J., Jr, and Paul, S. M. (subm.). The effects of single and repeated electroconvulsive shock on brain benzodiazepine receptor occupancy *in vivo*.

Index